Property I

Workbook

A Behavioral Approach to Learning

Nelson P. Miller and David Tarrien

Property I
Workbook–

A Behavioral
Approach to Learning

Nelson P. Miller and David Tarrien

Publisher:
Crown Management LLC – November 2018
1527 Pineridge Drive
Grand Haven, MI 49417
USA

ISBN-13: 978-1-64467-364-5

Table of Contents

Introduction

This workbook is for the three-credit course Property I, comprised of thirteen weeks of new studies, identified as Week 1, Week 2, etc., followed by a Review Week and a Final Exam Week.

The exercises in this workbook provide the most benefit when you complete them with other students, in pairs or small groups. The exercises' value is not only in thinking and writing but also talking and listening, getting and giving feedback. The more that you can see, hear, and interact with others, and that others can see and hear you, providing you with feedback, the better these exercises are likely to serve you.

This workbook provides answers to its exercises, questions, and problems, generally on the back of the page from which you work or below the exercises that you complete, on the same page. Immediate feedback enables you to confirm or correct your thought and expression. To use the answers for their best effect, try to complete the exercise first before referring to the answer. The value is in part in striving.

The exercises vary somewhat from week to week to increase your interest and so that you learn in different ways and practice different skills. The exercises help you start with discrete knowledge components that you gradually build into complex sequences involving applying law and solving problems. The exercises generally build from one to another.

Use this workbook to push yourself deeper into grasping, recalling, and applying the fundamental concepts of property law. The more active that your studies are, and the more that you strive at the boundaries of your capabilities, the better you should acquire property-law knowledge and skills for their practical use and benefit, to you, clients, and others. Best wishes for good studies.

Week 1

Acquisition by Discovery or Capture

SHORT OUTLINE:

Most U.S. landowners trace their land's title back to **government grants**.

 The U.S. government traces its title to *discovery* or *conquest,* and *treaty* or *purchase.*

  Discovery meant first right to negotiate with aboriginal populations for ownership.

   Only government had the right to negotiate or to conquer and acquire by treaty.

 Discovery, treaty, and conquest are no longer common local means of acquiring title.

 This origin of title highlights that property rights depend on government power to defend them.

 Related principles of **possession, first in time**, and **labor expended** remain important to ownership.

The law of **capture** requires that the claimant have appropriated the property, not merely pursued it.

 For example, *accession* law involves ownership or compensation claims based on added-value labor.

 Oil and gas, severed from the land, becomes the capturer's property even if reinjected for storage.

 The English rule for water gave the landowner unlimited right to withdraw from a reservoir.

  The American rule limits withdrawal to *reasonable use* so as not to affect neighbors.

  Western states allocate surface waters to the first-in-time user, called *prior appropriation.*

  Eastern states recognize *riparian rights* of landowners to use adjacent waters.

 The claimant must also have been the first in time to capture.

  Taking from a capturer may be the tort of conversion and crime of theft.

  Maliciously interfering with pursuit may also give rise to remedies against the interferer.

  A landowner may have *constructive possession* of wild animals on the land until they leave.

   Trespassers may have to relinquish wild animals to the landowner under that theory.

   But government may confiscate wild animals landowners capture in regulatory violation.

 Custom and usage may influence the decision whether a claimant captured the property.

 Rules of capture can exacerbate the *tragedy of the commons*, promoting destructive over-pursuit.

  Law must account for *externalities*, internalizing costs to the acquiring actor.

 But rules should also not exacerbate the tragedy of the *anti-commons*, where vetos frustrate good.

 Under the *Coase Theorem*, rules do not increase efficiency, just creating winners and losers.

 Courts generally reject equitable divisions (Solomonic compromises), except in rare cases.

LONG OUTLINE:

Acquisition by Discovery or Capture

 Most U.S. landowners trace their land's title back to **government grants**. The U.S. government traces its title to *discovery* or *conquest,* and *treaty* or *purchase.* Discovery does not necessarily mean that one instantly owns what one first possesses before any other possesses. Discovery in the context of the European settlement of the United States meant the first right to negotiate with aboriginal populations for ownership. Importantly, only government had the right to negotiate or to conquer and acquire by treaty. Individuals could not alone do so. Law rejected their claims of title, instead requiring federal acquisition, even if the federal government often transferred its right to states to grant private ownership. With settlement of the continental United States and other territories, discovery, treaty, and conquest are no longer common local means of acquiring title. This origin of title simply highlights that property rights depend on government power to defend them. And related principles of **possession, first in time**, and **labor expended** remain important to ownership.

 The law of **capture** requires that the claimant have *appropriated* the property, not merely pursued it. For example, the law of *accession* involves ownership or compensation claims based on the claimant's value-added labor. Thus, oil and gas becomes the capturer's property once *severed from the land*, even, as many cases hold, if reinjected into the land for storage. The English rule for ownership of water gave the landowner unlimited right to withdraw from a reservoir. Water isn't so scarce in England. The American rule limits withdrawal to *reasonable use* so as not to affect neighbors who also draw from the same reservoir. Western states allocate surface waters to the first-in-time user, called *prior appropriation*, relating to the scarcity of Western waters. By contrast, Eastern states recognize *riparian rights* of landowners to use adjacent waters (passing rivers and streams, or stable lakes) within reasonable limits.

The claimant must also have been the **first in time** to capture to have rightful ownership. Taking from someone who has already captured the thing may be the tort of conversion and crime of theft. Another theory involving *malicious interference* with pursuit may also give rise to remedies against the interferer. A landowner may have *constructive possession* of wild animals on the land until they leave. Thus, trespassers may have to relinquish to the landowner any wild animals that they capture on the trespassed land, under that constructive-possession theory. But government may confiscate wild animals that landowners capture in regulatory violation. Constructive possession and landowner rights do not overcome regulations.

Custom and usage may influence the decision whether a claimant captured the property such as to acquire ownership. Look to what others usually do in that activity. Rules of capture can exacerbate the *tragedy of the commons*, promoting destructive over-pursuit of common resources. Law must in that sense account for *externalities*, internalizing costs to the acquiring actor. Don't let one profit unduly at the expense of others, when harvesting from the commons. But rules should also not exacerbate the tragedy of the *anti-commons*, where veto by anyone may frustrate good by some. Under the *Coase Theorem*, rules do not increase efficiency, just creating winners and losers. Finally, courts generally reject equitable divisions (Solomonic compromises, dividing the discovered or captured resource among equal claimants), except in rare cases.

Fluency Cards

Cover and uncover the response to each prompt until you fluently recall the exact response.

Land-ownership origin

Government grant, not private discovery, purchase, or conquest.

Government acquisition

Discovery and negotiation, or conquest and treaty.

Ownership theories

Possession, first in time, and value-added labor.

Ownership by capture

First to appropriate, not merely first to pursue. Custom may determine.

Accession

Ownership based on value-added labor.

Oil and gas

Must sever from the land but may reinject for storage and still own.

Water

English rule for unlimited use, but American rule only reasonable use.

Capturer rights

Recover in conversion, malicious interference, or constructive possession.

Definitions Worksheet

1. What is the *origin* of land title in the United States, and why?

    _____

    _____

    _____

2. Name three *theories* important to ownership principles.

    _____

    _____

    _____

3. What must claimant prove to establish ownership by *capture*?

    _____

    _____

    _____

4. Name some ways that a claimant may prove *capture*.

    _____

    _____

    _____

5. How does a claimant capture *oil and gas* from beneath land?

    _____

    _____

    _____

6. What limits does law place on capture of *water*? Any regional differences?

    _____

    _____

    _____

7. How does law protect first-in-time capturers as to second-in-time claimants?

    _____

    _____

    _____

8. What is *constructive possession* of wild things? Whom does it help or hurt?

    _____

    _____

    _____

9. What is the *tragedy of the commons*? The tragedy of the *anti-commons*?

    _____

    _____

    _____

Please do not review model answers until you have answered all questions fully and conferred with a seatmate to complete, correct, and supplement your answers.

Answer Key to Definitions Worksheet

1.   Most U.S. landowners trace their land's title back to **government grants**. Only government has the right to negotiate or to conquer and acquire by treaty. Individuals cannot alone do so. Property rights depend on government power to defend them.

2.   Theories of **possession, first in time**, and **value-added labor** can be important to ownership. Who possess, who is first to possess, and who expended labor to possess all influence property law.

3.   The law of **capture** requires that the claimant have *appropriated* the property, suggesting acquisition and control, not merely pursued the property. The claimant must also have been *first in time* to capture.

4.   Evidence of the claimant's *value-added labor, direction* or *control, ability to exclude others*, and *custom* or *usage* in the industry or field may all influence the decision whether the claimant captured for ownership.

5.   **Oil and gas** becomes the capturer's property once *severed from the land*, even, as many cases hold, if reinjected into the land for storage.

6.   An *American rule* limits withdrawal of **water** to *reasonable use* so as not to affect neighbors who draw from the same reservoir. Western states allocate surface waters to the first-in-time user, called *prior appropriation*, while Eastern states recognize *riparian rights* of landowners to use adjacent waters.

7.   Taking from someone who has already captured the thing may be the tort of *conversion* and *crime of theft*. A *malicious-interference* theory may also give rise to remedies against the interferer.

8.   *Constructive possession* involves a landowner's presumed control and ownership of wild animals loose on the land. *Trespassers* may have to relinquish to the landowner wild animals that they capture on the trespassed land.

9.   Rules of capture should avoid worsening the *tragedy of the commons*, which is destructive individual over-pursuit of common resources. Rules should also avoid worsening a tragedy of the *anti-commons*, where veto by anyone may frustrate good by some.

Issue-Spotting Worksheet

State the law that each scenario triggers, rules that you would want to state to address the issue. Do not analyze. Just state the applicable rules that each scenario triggers.

1.   The law partner who hired you calls you into her office saying that she wants your thoughts on a new matter. She explains that a new client with whom she is about to meet gathers ginseng root from local mountainsides to deliver to restaurants and food processors in the city. Apparently, she says, the client is having disputes with other ginseng gatherers and area landowners. She wants to know what property law might apply because she doesn't remember a *thing* about it from law school.

_____

_____

_____

2.   Satisfied with your initial answer, the partner asks you what questions she should ask the new client on the client's first visit, by which she might prove that the client in fact owned the ginseng root that he was collecting.

_____

_____

_____

3.   A few days later, the partner calls you back into her office to discuss the ginseng-root-gatherer client. Apparently, you learn from the law partner, the ginseng-root client may have taken several burlap bags of ginseng that other gatherers had collected but left at various sites because of weather or other interruption. What, the partner asks you, do you make of that?

_____

_____

_____

4.   To make matters worse, the partner tells you that the client intimated that he was also in trouble with area landowners from taking ginseng root from private lands. The partner doesn't seem that concerned about it, but you think you've got something to share with the partner about it anyway.

_____

_____

_____

5.   The partner shares that the client thinks he's doing his customers a service by grabbing every ginseng root he can possibly find because it's not going to be around long at this rate. The partner pauses to see if the client's attitude troubles you.

_____

_____

_____

Suggested answers are on the next page.

Answer Key to Issue-Spotting Worksheet

1.   ***This scenario implicates the law of capture.***   The law of **capture** requires that the claimant have *appropriated* the property, suggesting acquisition and control, not merely pursued the property. The claimant must also have been *first in time* to capture.

2.   ***This scenario implicates factors determining capture.***   Evidence of the claimant's *value-added labor*, *direction* or *control*, *ability to exclude others*, and *custom* or *usage* in the industry or field may all influence the decision whether the claimant captured for ownership.

3.   ***This scenario implicates causes of action that others may pursue against putative capturers.***   Taking from someone who has already captured the thing may be the tort of *conversion* and *crime of theft*. A *malicious-interference* theory may also give rise to remedies against the interferer.

4.   ***This scenario implicates theories that landowners may pursue to dispute claims of capturers.***   *Constructive possession* involves a landowner's presumed control and ownership of wild things on the land, typically applying to animals but perhaps also to plants. *Trespassers* may have to relinquish to the landowner wild things that they collect and capture on the trespassed land.

5.   ***This scenario implicates the tragedy of the commons.***   Rules of capture should avoid worsening the *tragedy of the commons*, which is destructive individual over-pursuit of common resources. Individual interest in capturing dwindling common resources can lead to quicker depletion of the resource. Rules should also avoid worsening a tragedy of the *anti-commons*, where veto by anyone may frustrate good by some.

Application Exercises

Deductive reasoning applies a rule to a fact pattern to determine the outcome. Analogic reasoning (reasoning by analogy) compares a hypothetical scenario to the real scenario to suggest an outcome. A policy argument construes a larger public interest from the advocated outcome of a private dispute. Sort the following fact patterns into deductive (D) or analogic (A) reasoning, or a policy (P) argument. Answers are at the bottom.

1____ Because only government may acquire aboriginal lands through negotiation, conquest, or treaty, the court dismisses the claimant settler's quiet-title action against the respondent tribe.

2____ Allowing the settler a claim against the tribe here would be like accepting theft, conversion, and a land grab as a just means of acquiring ownership, which the court cannot do.

3____ Allowing the settler a claim against the tribe here could promote fraudulent and unfair transactions, undermining relations between the tribe and state.

4____ The court is inclined to recognize plaintiff's claim to the crabs because the labor that plaintiff expended in trapping the crabs is akin to corraling wild beasts or netting wild fowl.

5____ The court recognizes plaintiff's claim to the crabs because a first-in-time rule protects and promotes investment of labor and technology to develop natural resources.

6____ The court grants plaintiff an injunction to restrain defendant from interfering with plaintiff's trapping of the crabs because plaintiff has ownership by capture and appropriation.

7____ The court enters judgment in defendant's favor because recognizing tuna-industry customs as to ownership of double-hooked fish promotes order and peace within the industry.

8____ The court further finds in defendant's favor because case law indicates that clear evidence of an established custom or usage should control, as defendant has shown here.

9____ Claimant should prevail on its oil-and-gas wildcatter's claim that is so similar to the netted-fowl and harpooned-whale cases that the appellate courts of this state previously decided.

10____ Claimant should further prevail on its wildcatter's claim because the well-established rule in this state is that reinjected oil and gas remains the property of the claimant first severing it.

11____ Applying in this case the American rule of limiting water withdrawal to reasonable use will protect the state's natural resources rather than deplete them in a tragedy of the commons.

12____ The court should apply the Eastern *riparian-rights* rule to this case because water in this region is not scarce, and promoting its reasonable use will benefit the state's economy.

13____ The defendant trespasser should pay the plaintiff landowner presumed and actual damages not only for the trespass claim but also for conversion of the stalked and shot deer.

14____ The plaintiff should prevail on her *malicious-interference* claim because defendant's shooting the deer was equivalent to cutting plaintiff's timber, harvesting crops, or outright theft.

15____ The court should hold that plaintiff had constructive possession of the deer because deer that plaintiff feeds daily are substantially the same as tended livestock or farm-raised fish.

16____ The plaintiff should prevail in recovery for the historic baseball because the plaintiff caught, secured, and transported it before conveying it only in a bailment, as law defines it.

1D 2A 3P 4A 5P 6D 7P 8D 9A 10D 11P 12P 13D 14A 15A 16D

Multiple-Choice Questions with Answer Explanations

713.   A woodsman trapped a raccoon by setting traps throughout the woods and monitoring the traps. A motorist removed the trapped raccoon from the woodsman's truck at a rest stop, putting the raccoon in a cage outside the motorist's home. A game warden confiscated the raccoon from the motorist's cage following state regulations against trapping and keeping raccoons. A contractor who was supposed to return the raccoon to the wild instead turned the raccoon into a pen at the contractor's cabin. Who has the strongest claim to the raccoon?

A.   The contractor.
B.   The game warden.
C.   The motorist.
D.   The woodsman.

Answer explanation: Option B is the correct answer because although theories of possession, first in time, and value-added labor influence ownership, private property rights do not defeat law and regulations. The game warden confiscated the raccoon according to regulations and so had the superior right over each of the others. Option A is incorrect because the contractor acquired the raccoon not as an owner but only for release, which the contractor did not do. The warden would have the superior right to retake and release or otherwise dispose of the raccoon. Option C is incorrect because the motorist was only second in time to the first-in-time woodsman and essentially committed a theft, and so would have no superior right, especially following the warden's lawful confiscation. Option D is incorrect because while the woodsman would have had the first-in-time, capture-or-possession, value-added claim, the warden apparently trapped the raccoon illegally and thus had inferior rights to the game warden.

714.   A commercial fisherman hooked a giant tuna from the fisherman's boat miles offshore. After an hour's battle, the fisherman lost the tuna right at the boat when the tuna came unhooked, but not until the fisherman had harpooned the tuna. The tuna was so exhausted from the fight and badly wounded from the harpoon, though, that it swam slowly on the surface past a nearby fisherman's boat, where that second fisherman tail-tied and boated it. The custom for catching giant tuna involves bringing the tuna to the boat on a hook, harpooning the tuna, and boating it with a tail tie. The first and second fishermen disputed who owned the tuna, especially when the fish processor set a $20,000 value on the catch. How would a court be most likely to rule in this dispute between the first and second fishermen over the giant tuna?

A.   For the second fisherman if law treats hooking and harpooning as custom and usage.
B.   For the first fisherman if law treats delivery to processor as custom and usage.
C.   For the first fisherman if custom and usage treat harpooning as appropriation.
D.   For the first fisherman if custom and usage treat tail-tie and boating as appropriation.

Answer explanation: Option C is the correct answer because the law of capture requires that the claimant have *appropriated* the property, suggesting acquisition and control, not merely pursued the property. The claimant must also have been *first in time* to obtain ownership by capture. Evidence of the *custom* or *usage* in the industry or field influences the decision whether the claimant captured for ownership. Here, the first fisherman harpooned, meaning that the first fisherman would likely win if custom and usage treated harpooning as appropriation. Options A and B are incorrect because the question isn't what law would treat as custom and usage but instead what law would treat as appropriation for ownership by capture. Custom and usage may define appropriation. Option D is incorrect because only the second fisherman tail-tied and boated the tuna, not the first fisherman. The second fisherman, not the first fisherman, would win if custom and usage treated tail-tie and boating as appropriation.

9

715.   A landowner learned from published government surveys and private oil-industry reports that a valuable oil-and-gas field extended below the landowner's land. An oil wildcatter leased adjacent land for oil-and-gas exploration of the same field. An oil company went ahead and drilled its own adjacent land to tap the same field, recovered substantial oil and gas, but reinjected much of it for short-term-storage reserve. A speculator drilling on other adjacent land tapped into the oil company's reinjected reserve, withdrawing substantial quantities of it for immediate sale. Who among these four claimants has the strongest claim to the withdrawn oil-and-gas reserves?

A.   The landowner learning of the valuable field below the land.
B.   The oil wildcatter leasing adjacent lands for exploration.
C.   The speculator withdrawing the reserves for immediate sale.
D.   The oil company withdrawing and reinjecting the reserves.

Answer explanation: Option D is the correct answer because oil and gas becomes the capturer's property once severed from the land, even, as many cases hold, if reinjected into the land for storage, consistent with first-in-time, possession, and value-added theories of ownership. Here, the oil company withdrew and reinjected the reserves for short-term storage, satisfying the first-in-time, possession, and value-added theories of ownership. Option A is incorrect because simply learning that a part of an oil-and-gas field is below one's land does not give one ownership to oil and gas withdrawn from adjacent lands. Option B is incorrect because simply leasing land below which lies part of an oil-and-gas field does not give one ownership to oil and gas withdrawn from adjacent lands. Option C is incorrect because once one withdraws oil and gas, that one owns the oil and gas, even if reinjected for short-term storage. Withdrawing another's reinjected reserves does not confer ownership.

716.   A landowner in an Eastern state diverted a stream bordering the landowner's lands so that the stream's water would feed a new system of farm-raised-trout ponds on the landowner's lands. A downstream farmer complained that the landowner's diversion of the entire stream deprived the farmer of the opportunity to use some of the stream to feed long-standing irrigation ditches for the farmer's traditional cash crops. When the landowner and farmer were unable to resolve their dispute over the stream's water, the farmer sued in a court of appropriate jurisdiction. Which one most likely has the greater claim?

A.   The farmer because the landowner exceeded reasonable use of the water.
B.   The farmer because the landowner had no right to water from a bordering stream.
C.   The landowner because Eastern landowners have riparian rights.
D.   The landowner because Eastern landowners have rights of prior appropriation.

Answer explanation: Option A is the correct answer because an *American rule* limits withdrawal of water to *reasonable use* so as not to affect neighbors who draw from the same reservoir. Here, the farmer had a long-established use of irrigating cash crops, whereas the landowner diverted the entire stream to new ponds. The entire diversion under the farmer's pre-existing use is most likely unreasonable. , while. Option B is incorrect because Eastern states recognize *riparian rights* of landowners to use adjacent waters. Option C is incorrect because although Eastern states recognize *riparian rights* of landowners to use adjacent waters, the American rule limits that right to reasonable use. Here, the use was most likely unreasonable given the diversion of the entire stream to a new use to the detriment of a long-established use. Option D is incorrect because Western states, not Eastern states, allocate surface waters to the first-in-time user, called *prior appropriation.*

717.   With a small crew's help, a woodcutter gathered, trimmed, cut into firewood, and stacked several cords of wood out of trees and limbs knocked down in a severe windstorm. The woodcutter had permission of public officials and private landowners to collect, store, and sell the wood as the woodcutter's own. Before the woodcutter could return the next day with his truck, trailer, and crew to load, transport, and store the cut and stacked cords of firewood for sale, an operator came by in the night, loaded, and transported away the firewood to another state for the operator's use in wood-fired kilns. If the woodcutter could identify and locate the operator, then would the woodcutter likely have any right or claim to recover the wood or its value?

A.   No because the woodcutter had not yet appropriated the property.
B.   Yes, under a *theft* theory.
C.   Yes, under a *conversion* theory.
D.   Yes, under a *malicious-interference* theory.

Answer explanation: Option C is the correct answer because taking from someone who has already captured the thing is the tort of *conversion*. Here, the woodcutter clearly appropriated the wood under value-added-labor theory of ownership, if not also under first-in-time and possession theories. The interloping, night-time operator, apparently lacking any equivalent permission from public officials and private landowners, was very likely a converter. Option A is incorrect because gathering, trimming, cutting, and stacking into firewood felled trees and limbs is very likely sufficient value-added labor to constitute appropriation for ownership. Option B is incorrect because although taking another's property under these circumstances may well be the crime of *theft*, a crime is not a private right of action to recover property or its value. A crime is a public charge of wrongdoing. Option D is incorrect because *malicious interference* arises when another keeps an owner from enjoying the benefits of property, not when the other takes the property itself, which is instead the crime of theft and tort of conversion.

718.   A rancher prohibited hunting on his private range lands to protect his cattle. The rancher not only fed and watered the cattle on his private range lands but also put out special feed and dug special watering holes for wild elk and buffalo that shared his private range lands with his cattle. The rancher did so with the intent of protecting the elk and buffalo to increase their health and numbers. The elk and buffalo entered and left the rancher's private range lands at their will but spent substantial time on the range lands and benefited substantially from the rancher's protective actions. Hunters nonetheless shot, killed, gutted, and removed elk and buffalo from the rancher's range lands. On these facts alone, what theories would best support a court's ruling in the rancher's favor, to enjoin such hunting?

A.   Hunting was an unreasonable threat to the rancher's cattle, as to which no one disputed ownership.
B.   The hunters were shooting wild elk and buffalo illegally under federal and state regulations.
C.   The rancher's substantial actions had domesticated the elk and buffalo, giving them the protection of cattle.
D.   The rancher had constructive possession of the elk and buffalo, and the hunters were trespassing.

Answer explanation: Option D is the correct answer because *constructive possession* involves a landowner's presumed control and ownership of wild animals loose on the land, while *trespassers* must relinquish to the landowner wild animals that they capture on the trespassed land. Option A is incorrect because the facts do not indicate any threat to cattle from hunting elk and buffalo, and a threat to other property does not justify enjoining taking wild animals. Option B is incorrect because the facts give no

11

indication of the hunting violating federal or state regulations. The justification must instead rely on private property rights. Option C is incorrect because the facts give no indication of domestication. To the contrary, the elk and buffalo remained free to leave and enter the land.

Week 2

Acquisition by Find

SHORT OUTLINE:

Finders generally hold title to **lost** *personal property* against everyone other than the true owner.

   The finder keeps the personal property in dispute with anyone other than the original owner.

      Owners recover the personal property in *replevin* or its value in *trover*.

   Finders must possess lawfully. Thieves have no right to recover from anyone.

Landowners may generally recover personal property that a trespasser finds on the premises.

   Landowners may or may not recover lost items that a person lawfully on the premises finds.

      May depend if the finder uncovers it by labor unrelated to the reason for being on the land.

Finders generally acquire no right to **mislaid** property left behind, only *lost* property out of place.

Finders have superior title to **abandoned** property, as against everyone *including the true owner*.

   Employees may have to relinquish to their employer property found during employment.

      Depends on factors including the nature of their work and item's relationship to it.

American law rejects *treasure trove* in which the government recovers hidden money.

   States instead apply the *mislaid-lost-abandoned* distinctions, sometimes under complex statute.

Shipwrecks may remain the property of the ship's owner unless abandoned.

   Common law gives abandoned shipwrecks to government with salvage award to finder.

   Federal law grants title to shipwrecks in territorial waters to states making their own rules.

LONG OUTLINE:

Acquisition by find

A finder's *title*, the legal right to possess the property, is good against everyone other than the true owner. The finder may keep the personal property in dispute with anyone other than the original owner. Property is thus not a relationship between the person and thing as much as a relationship between persons relative to the thing. Title is often relative, qualified, rather than absolute. Owners may recover the personal property in an action traditionally called *replevin*. Alternatively, owners may recover the personal property's value in an action traditionally called *trover*. To have superior title over subsequent finders, the one who possesses property must do so lawfully. A thief who steals and then loses an item has no right of action against a finder for the item or its value. Similarly, a landowner or homeowner may generally recover personal property that a trespasser finds on the premises but not necessarily lost items that a person lawfully on the premises finds, especially if the finder uncovers it by labor unrelated to the reason for being on the land. Finders generally acquire no rights in *mislaid* property accidentally left behind. Finders have superior title to *lost* property out of place, as against anyone other than the true owner. Finders have superior title to *abandoned* property, as against everyone including the true owner.

Employees may or may not have to relinquish to their employer property found during employment, depending on factors including the nature of their work and the relationship of the property to it. American law tends to reject the traditional law of *treasure trove* in which the government recovers buried or otherwise hidden money. American states may instead apply the *mislaid-lost-abandoned* distinctions. Many states have complex statutes addressing those distinctions. Shipwrecks may remain the property of the ship's owner unless abandoned. Traditional common law treated abandoned shipwrecks as government property, perhaps with a salvage award up to half for the finder. Federal act grants title to shipwrecks in territorial waters to the state, the states making their own rules.

14

Fluency Cards
Cover and uncover the response to each prompt until you fluently recall the exact response.

Finders	**Actions against finders**
Title to lost property against everyone but owner.	Replevin for item, trover for value.
Trespasser finds	**Landowner claims**
Landowner has superior claim. Must possess lawfully.	Finder may or may not have to relinquish to landowner. May depend on labor to find.
Mislaid property	**Abandoned property**
Finder may have to relinquish to landowner where mislaid.	Finder gets title as to everyone, owner included.
Treasure trove	**Shipwrecks**
Old common law holds hidden money goes to government. States reject for statutes.	Ship owner unless abandoned, then to state under state law if in territorial water.

Definitions Worksheet

1. What is *title*?

    _____

    _____

2. What title does a finder of *lost property* generally acquire?

    _____

    _____

3. What actions may an owner pursue as to lost property found by another?

    _____

    _____

4. What title does a thief acquire relative to a subsequent finder?

    _____

    _____

5. What right does a landowner have to recover property found on the land?

    _____

    _____

6. How does *mislaid* property differ from *lost* property?

    _____

    _____

7. What right does a finder have to *mislaid* property compared to *lost* property?

    _____

    _____

8. What is *abandoned* property?

    _____

    _____

9. What right does a finder have to *abandoned* property?

    _____

    _____

10. Who has superior title, an *employee* who finds or the employee's *employer*?

    _____

    _____

11. When is *treasure trove*? Does its law still apply?

    _____

    _____

12. How does law treat recovery of *shipwrecks*?

    _____

    _____

Please do not review model answers until you have answered all questions fully and conferred with a seatmate to complete, correct, and supplement your answers.

Answer Key to Definitions Worksheet

1.   *Title* is the legal right to possess property as against other claimants to the property—a relationship between persons just as much as between a person and the thing.

2.   A finder's title to *lost property* is generally good against everyone other than the true owner. The finder may keep the personal property in dispute with anyone other than the original owner.

3.   Owners may recover the personal property in an action traditionally called *replevin*. Alternatively, owners may recover the personal property's value in an action traditionally called *trover*.

4.   Thieves acquire no title. To have superior title over subsequent finders, the one who possesses property must do so lawfully. A thief who steals and then loses an item has no right of action against a finder for the item or its value.

5.   A landowner may recover personal property that a *trespasser* finds on the premises but not necessarily lost items that a person lawfully on the premises finds, especially if the finder uncovers it by labor unrelated to the reason for being on the land.

6.   *Mislaid* property is left behind in a location where the owner intentionally placed it. *Lost* property is in a location where the owner did not intend to place it.

7.   Finders generally acquire no rights in *mislaid* property left behind, law generally allowing the landowner to possess it. Finders have superior title to *lost* property, as against anyone other than the true owner.

8.   *Abandoned* property is property as to which the owner intended to relinquish ownership, often construed from its location, condition, or other circumstances.

9.   Finders have superior title to *abandoned* property, as against everyone including the true owner.

10.   Employees may or may not have to relinquish to their employer property found during employment, depending on factors including the nature of their work and the relationship of the property to it.

11.   *Treasure trove* is money buried or otherwise hidden and later discovered by someone other than the original owner. American law tends to reject the traditional law of *treasure trove* in which the government recovers buried or otherwise hidden money. American states may instead apply the *mislaid-lost-abandoned* distinctions. Many states have complex statutes addressing those distinctions.

12.   Shipwrecks remain the property of the ship's owner unless abandoned. Traditional common law treated abandoned shipwrecks as government property, perhaps with a salvage award up to half for the finder. Federal law grants title to shipwrecks in territorial waters to the state, the states making their own rules.

Issue-Spotting Worksheet

State the law that each scenario triggers, rules that you would want to state to address the issue. Do not analyze. Just state the applicable rules that each scenario triggers.

1. Your apartment-complex neighbor asks to see you about an interesting legal question. The neighbor first wants your assurance that the consultation is confidential, of which you assure the neighbor. The neighbor then tells you that she found a fanny pack in the mall containing hundreds of dollars in gift cards. She had taken it to the mall office but only found some teenagers there whom she did not trust, so she said nothing about it and instead brought it home to think about it. She laughs nervously as she says *finders, keepers, right?!*

2. Encouraged by your initial wisdom and thought, your neighbor asks you what would happen if the rightful owner of the fanny pack and gift cards stepped forward.

3. Showing her own good insight, your neighbor wonders aloud what would happen if someone had stolen the fanny back from another but then dropped it in flight or fright, or carelessly. Your neighbor repeats, *finders, keepers, right?!* followed by another nervous laugh.

4. Your neighbor then has another good question having to do with the mall owners. After all, she almost turned the fanny pack and gift cards in to the mall office. Shouldn't, she wonders, the mall get the wallet? But then again, she insists, *she* found it, not the mall.

5. Now you have some questions, like exactly *where* your neighbor found the fanny pack. Your question surprises your neighbor who suddenly looks like she doesn't necessary trust you. But she answers nonetheless: on the vanity in the women's restroom. You raise your eyebrows, causing your neighbor to ask, *So what then?!*

6. Your next question also disconcerts your neighbor: was she working when she found the fanny pack? Turns out that she was working, cleaning the mall's restrooms.

Suggested answers are on the next page.

Answer Key to Issue-Spotting Worksheet

1.   ***This scenario implicates the law of finders.*** A finder's title to *lost property* is generally good against everyone other than the true owner. The finder may keep the personal property in dispute with anyone other than the original owner.

2.   ***This scenario implicates causes of actions that personal-property owners may plead against finders or others holding their property.*** Owners may recover found personal property in an action traditionally called *replevin*. Alternatively, owners may recover the personal property's value in an action traditionally called *trover*.

3.   ***This scenario implicates how to treat title as to stolen property.*** Thieves acquire no title. To have superior title over subsequent finders, the one who possesses property must do so lawfully. A thief who steals and then loses an item has no right of action against a finder for the item or its value, but the original owner has the superior claim against both the thief *and* the subsequent finder. A thief cannot pass good title to a finder or purchaser in good faith for value.

4.   ***This scenario implicates the rights of finders on land of another.*** A landowner may recover personal property that a *trespasser* finds on the premises but not necessarily lost items that a person lawfully on the premises finds, especially if the finder uncovers it by labor unrelated to the reason for being on the land.

5.   ***This scenario implicates the distinction between mislaid, lost, and abandoned property.*** *Mislaid* property is left behind in a location where the owner intentionally placed it. *Lost* property is in a location where the owner did not intend to place it. Finders generally acquire no rights in *mislaid* property left behind, law generally allowing the landowner to possess it. Finders have superior title to *lost* property, as against anyone other than the true owner. *Abandoned* property is property as to which the owner intended to relinquish ownership, often construed from its location, condition, or other circumstances. Finders have superior title to *abandoned* property, as against everyone including the true owner.

6.   ***This scenario implicates the duty of employees to turn over property found in the course of employment.*** Employees may or may not have to relinquish to their employer property found during employment, depending on factors including the nature of their work and the relationship of the property to it.

Rule-Check Exercises

Identify and insert at the ^ mark the omitted law from each statement, following the italicized, parenthetical hints. Some statements are wrong without the omitted detail, while other statements are just incomplete. Suggested answers are on the next page.

1.   A finder's title to lost property is generally good against everyone ^ . *[Everyone? Really, everyone?!]*

2.   A finder may keep the personal property in dispute with anyone ^ . *[Anyone? Really, anyone?!]*

3.   Owners may recover found personal property in a civil action ^ . *[Okay, but what do you call that action?]*

4.   Alternatively, owners may recover the personal property's value in a civil action ^ . *[Okay, but what do you call that action?]*

5.   The original owner has the superior claim against a thief ^ . *[Yes, but not only the thief but also … whom else, someone who might surprise you?]*

6.   A person lawfully on another's land may likely keep an item found on the land ^ . *[Fine, but what makes keeping the item even more likely?]*

7.   *Mislaid* property, as contrasted to *lost* property, is left behind ^ . *[Okay, but what do you mean by "left behind"?]*

8.   Finders generally acquire no rights in *mislaid* property left behind ^ . *[Fine, but then who gets it?]*

9.   *Abandoned* property is property that the owner intended to relinquish, often construed from its ^ condition ^ . *[Just its condition? Anything else?]*

10.   Finders have superior title to *abandoned* property, as against everyone ^ . *[Yes, everyone, but including whom, who might surprise you?]*

11.   Employees may have to relinquish to their employer property found ^ , depending on factors including the nature of their work ^ . *[Property found… whenever, like even on the weekend? And any property, even odd things?]*

20

Suggested Answers to Rule-Check Exercises

These answers are only suggested. You may have added other relevant detail or phrased your additions differently.

1. A finder's title to lost property is generally good against everyone **other than the true owner**.

2. A finder may keep the personal property in dispute with anyone **other than the original owner**.

3. Owners may recover found personal property in a civil action **traditionally called *replevin***.

4. Alternatively, owners may recover the personal property's value in a civil action **traditionally called *trover***.

5. The original owner has the superior claim against a thief **and a subsequent purchaser, even one in good faith for value**.

6. A person lawfully on another's land may likely keep an item found on the land**, especially if in labor unrelated to the reason for being on the land**.

7. *Mislaid* property, as contrasted to *lost* property, is left behind **in a location where the owner intentionally placed it**.

8. Finders generally acquire no rights in *mislaid* property left behind**, law generally allowing the landowner to possess it**.

9. *Abandoned* property is property that the owner intended to relinquish, often construed from its **location**, condition**, or other circumstances**.

10. Finders have superior title to *abandoned* property, as against everyone **including the true owner**.

11. Employees may have to relinquish to their employer property found **during employment**, depending on factors including the nature of their work **and the property's relationship to work**.

Application Exercises

Indicate who probably has the superior title. Answers are at the bottom.

Finder (F) picks up brooch from grass in park:

1____   Public park custodian (C) demands brooch from finder (F).

2____   Brooch owner (O) shows proof of purchase after hearing that finder (F) found brooch.

3____   Thief (T) who lost stolen brooch demands brooch from finder (F).

4____   Finder's employer (E), who paid finder (F) to clean up park, demands brooch from finder.

5____   Finder's employer (E), who paid finder (F) to play banjo in park, demands brooch from finder.

6____   Park was on private land of landowner (L) who demands brooch from trespassing finder (F).

7____   Park was on conference ground of landowner (L) who demands brooch from guest finder (F).

8____   Park was on conference ground of landowner (L) who paid finder (F) to mow park's grass.

9____   Park was on neighbor (N) land that finder (F) gratuitously mowed, discovering brooch.

10____   Park was flea-market land where vendors spread items on grass. Market (M) demands brooch.

11____   Brooch was part of household trash dumped across land of landowner (L) who demands brooch.

12____   Brooch was part of jewelry collection owner (O) left in park for anyone who wanted it.

13____   Government (G) shows brooch was part of ancient treasure trove others unearthed in private park.

Finder (F) picks up unidentified wallet with substantial cash from urban sidewalk alongside street:

14____   Drug dealer (D) demands cash from finder (F) as illicit proceeds of illegal sales.

15____   Nearby shopowner (S) demands cash from finder (F) as possible proceeds of supplier sales.

16____   Wallet's owner (O) demands wallet and cash from finder (F) on reliable evidence of ownership.

17____   Finder (F) demands return from librarian (L) with whom finder left cash while looking for owner.

18____   Employer (E) demands cash from finder (F) on-duty officer assigned to look for missing cash.

19____   Employer (E) demands cash from finder (F) off-duty custodian out for a night on the town.

20____   Local government (G) demands cash from finder (F) to establish fund for the urban homeless.

21____   Radio station (S) demands cash from finder (F) on proof it placed wallet as part of a promotion.

22____   Owner (O) demands cash despite that finder (F) shows owner intended to make self destitute.

1F 2O 3F 4E 5F 6L 7F 8L 9F 10M 11F 12F 13F 14F 15F 16O 17F 18E 19F 20F 21S 22F

22

Multiple-Choice Questions with Answer Explanations

701.   A tourist scouring a beach with a small rake and pail, looking for shells and stones, uncovered an elaborate diamond ring. The beach where the tourist found the ring was in front of a luxury seaside resort that had placed high-quality lounge chairs and other luxury amenities on the beach for its wealthy guests. The tourist was lawfully on the beach but staying at a cheap campground just down the beach that gave the tourist beach access, not staying at the seaside resort. The tourist had a job as a groundskeeper with a municipality in another state. Which party has superior title to the ring?

A.   The seaside resort in trust for its wealthy guests.
B.   The tourist finder of the ring.
C.   The campground giving the tourist beach access.
D.   The municipality for which the tourist worked.

Answer explanation: Option B is the correct answer because a finder's title to lost property is generally good against everyone other than the true owner. The finder may keep the personal property in dispute with anyone other than the original owner. Here, the ring was clearly lost, not mislaid or abandoned. The tourist would have title as against anyone other than the ring's original owner. Option A is incorrect because the resort would only have an argument if the ring's owner had mislaid it rather than lost it, as was the case here. Option C is incorrect because access to lands does not confer any right to recover items found on land. At best, the landowner may have a claim, depending on whether the owner mislaid, lost, or abandoned the item. Option D is incorrect because while an employer may have superior title over an employee who finds an item in the course of and arising out of the work, here, the tourist was not working. An employer has no right to property discovered by an off-duty employee.

702.   A supplier visited a plant to sell cleaning supplies. While using the plant's guest restroom, the supplier noticed an expensive pair of sunglasses placed atop the restroom vanity where a prior guest had clearly left them while washing up. The supplier asked the receptionist to hold the sunglasses while the supplier toured the plant. When finished with the tour and cleaning-supply sale, the supplier asked for the sunglasses back, but the receptionist refused. The plant's reasonable investigation did not locate the sunglasses' owner. Who has superior title to the sunglasses?

A.   The supplier assuming that the facts establish that the owner mislaid the sunglasses.
B.   The receptionist assuming that the supplier intended a bailment of the sunglasses.
C.   The plant assuming that the facts establish that the owner lost the sunglasses.
D.   The plant assuming that the facts establish that the owner mislaid the sunglasses.

Answer explanation: Option D is the correct answer because landowners generally have superior title to mislaid property, as contrasted with lost property, where the finder would have superior title. The plant would hold the sunglasses with superior title as to all but the sunglasses' owner whom law assumes may at some point return for the sunglasses. Option A is incorrect because the supplier would only have superior title if the owner lost or abandoned the sunglasses, not mislaid them, as was apparent here. Option B is incorrect because the receptionist has no claim of title, especially not if the supplier intended only a bailment, which would give the supplier the superior right to have the sunglasses back. Option C is incorrect because finders, not landowners, generally have superior title to lost or abandoned property rather than mislaid property.

703.   A custodian found a brand-new laptop computer in the bottom of a box emptied of several other computers, as the custodian took boxes out to the dumpster behind his employer's office building. The custodian correctly inferred that another of his employer's workers had mistakenly failed to empty the box of all computers. The custodian kept the computer for himself after discretely confirming that no one had reported a missing computer. When the employer learned of the custodian's find and demanded the computer back, the custodian took the dispute to labor arbitration under a union contract. The employer could not determine which department or employee had ordered the computer but mistakenly left it in the box, probably because the unidentified careless employee was concerned over job security for the mistake. Who has superior title to the computer?

A.   The custodian.
B.   The union.
C.   The employer.
D.   The arbitrator to hold in trust for the unidentified careless employee.

Answer explanation: Option C is the correct answer both because the employer was probably the computer's original owner and because an employer generally has superior title over an employee who finds an item in the course of and arising out of the work. Here, the custodian was working and discovered the computer as part of the custodian's cleaning duties. No evidence suggested that the computer belonged to anyone other than the employer, even though the employer could not account for its loss, for good reason. Option A is incorrect because the employer was probably the original owner and because the custodian found the computer in the course of employment-related work. Option B is incorrect because the union was neither the computer's original owner, the custodian's employer, nor the computer's finder. The union has no theory for superior title. Option D is incorrect because the law of finders determines superior title among identified claimants rather than having disinterested parties hold the find in trust.

Week 3
Adverse Possession

SHORT OUTLINE:

Adverse possession is lawful means by which one who occupies land acquires title without dealing with the owner.
   Possessor must use in *exclusive, open and notorious*, and *continuous* manner under *claim of right* for the period.
   Possessor satisfying all conditions may file suit for clear title or defend owner's ejectment action.
      The court issues a recordable judgment granting marketable title to the person adversely possessing.
      The former owner then no longer has any right or title to, or interest in, the land.
   Possessor must be on the property **exclusively** as an owner would exclude, in residence or by exclusive use.
      Possessor need not use all to adversely possess the whole, if limited use excludes others from the whole.
      Possessor who occupies part *without* excluding others from other parts adversely possesses only the part.
      Two or more can adversely possess land, as when a married couple or family continuously use the land.
   Possession must be **open and notorious** in that the owner would likely discover in inspection's ordinary course.
      Open and notorious is *visible* to others, especially the owner. Possessors may need to notify absent owners.
         Owner knowledge of possessor's use establishes that the use was open and notorious.
      Occupier who leave when owner visits, by owner request or to avoid detection, are not open and notorious.
   Possession must be adverse, hostile, or otherwise under a **claim of right**, without owner consent.
      Possession is adverse and under a claim of right when possessor intends and appears to stay permanently.
      Claim of right does *not* mean a *legal* claim but appearing as if to exclude the owner.
      Tenants cannot adversely possess landlord land, and co-tenants cannot possess co-tenants' rights.
      Owner permission destroys claim of right. Conceding owner right fails to satisfy hostility.
      Possessor need *not* have malicious intent or, in most states, even *know* possession is against owner's title.
   Possession must be **continuous**, meaning *uninterrupted* for longer than the statutory period on ejectment.
      Periods vary between five and twenty-one years, with ten or fifteen years being common lengths.
      Continuous does not mean every hour of every day but use typical of one owning the land.
      Abandonment of the property interrupts continuous possession.
      Voluntary transfer from possessor to another supports **tacking** periods of possession.
      Possession runs against all successive owners, no matter how many own the land during statutory period.

LONG OUTLINE:

Adverse possession

   Adverse possession is a lawful means by which one who occupies or uses land can acquire title to the land without dealing with the land's owner. To acquire title by adverse possession, a person must possess the property in an *exclusive, open and notorious*, and *continuous* manner for longer the statutory limitations period for ejectment actions, under a *claim of right*. In this context, **possession** means the satisfaction of each of those conditions. If a person can establish each of those conditions either in an action that the person files to gain clear title to the land, or in defense of the owner's ejectment action, then the court may enter a recordable judgment that has the purpose and effect of granting title to the person adversely possessing. The former owner then no longer has any right or title to, or interest in, the land. The adverse possessor's title will be marketable title if the adverse possessor should wish to sell the land.

   For adverse possession, the person must first be on the property **exclusively** as an owner would be able to exclude. The person may move onto the property as in residence or may simply use the property exclusively, as an owner would. The person need not use the entire land to gain the entire land by adverse possession, if the limited use of the land that the person makes succeeds in excluding others from the entire land. Conversely, an adverse possessor who occupies only part of the land *without* excluding others from other parts adversely possesses only the used part. *Exclusive* use does not necessarily mean *sole* use. Two or more can simultaneously adversely possess land, as when a married couple or family move onto or continuously use the land, the couple or family then taking title together as adverse possessors when they satisfy the conditions.

The person's possession must then **open and notorious**, meaning that the property's true owner would likely discover the person's possession in inspection's ordinary course. Open and notorious means *visible* to others, particularly the owner. If the owner does not ordinarily visit the property or the occupied part of it for inspection, then the occupier's use of the property may not be sufficiently open and notorious, unless the occupier takes special steps to ensure that the owner knows. The owner's knowledge of the use is sufficient to establish that the use was open and notorious. If the occupier leaves the land each time the owner visits, whether by the owner's request or to avoid detection, then the possession is not open and notorious.

The possession must then be adverse, hostile, or otherwise under a **claim of right**, meaning that the possession is without the owner's consent in conflict with owner interests. Possession is adverse and under a claim of right when the possessor remains on the property intending and appearing to remain so permanently. A *claim of right* in this context does *not* mean a legal claim but instead appearing as if having the right to exclude the owner. Thus, tenants cannot adversely possess their landlord's land, and co-tenants cannot adversely possess their co-tenants' rights, because tenants do not occupy with the intent and appearance of ownership rights. The owner's permission destroys the person's claim of right. The person who concedes the owner's right fails to satisfy the hostility condition. Yet to establish adverse possession, the person need *not* have malicious intent or, in most states, even *know* that the possession was unlawful or against the owner's claim of title.

Finally, the possession must be **continuous**, meaning *uninterrupted*, for longer than the statutory limitations period on ejectment actions, varying from state to state between five and twenty-one years, with ten or fifteen years being particularly common lengths. Continuous does not necessarily mean every hour of every day but instead the use typical of one owning the land, depending on its type. Thus, a person would have to remain in a residence more often and consistently than on vacant lands, to adversely possess the residence. By contrast, even occasional use of a guest house or other property that an owner would only use sporadically may suffice. Abandonment of the property, though, interrupts continuous possession.

Claims of adverse possession sometimes raise the question of **tacking** successive periods of possession by different persons, each of whose possession is shorter than the statutory period. Generally, *voluntary transfer* from one possessor to another supports tacking their periods of possession. Claims of adverse possession also might raise the question of whether changes in ownership of the land interrupts the occupier's adverse possession, except that the rule simply holds that once adverse possession begins, it runs against all successive owners, no matter how many own the land during the statutory period.

Fluency Cards

Cover and uncover the response to each prompt until you fluently recall the exact response.

Adverse possession

Acquire title without dealing with owner.

Adverse possession requirements

Exclusive, open, notorious, and continuous, under claim of right for statutory period.

Exclusive use

Must exclude as an owner would. Exclude only part, possess only part.

Open and notorious

Owner would discover on inspection. May have to notify absent owners. Owner knowledge is enough.

Claim of right

Adverse, hostile, without consent, intending and appearing to remain permanently.

Continuous

Uninterrupted, typical of owner. Voluntary transfer tacks periods. Runs against successive owners.

Statutory period

Vary from six to twenty-one years, with ten to fifteen years most common.

Definitions Worksheet

1.   What is *adverse possession*?

_____

_____

2.   What conditions must an adverse posessor satisfy?

_____

_____

3.   What does the *exclusive-use* condition mean?

_____

_____

4.   May two or more adversely posssess land at once?

_____

_____

5.   Must the adverse possessor use the entire land to possess it?

_____

_____

6.   What does *open and notorious* mean?

_____

_____

7.   How does one adversely possess the land of an absentee owner?

_____

_____

8.   What if the possessor leaves the land each time the owner visits?

_____

_____

9.   What does it mean for possession to be under a *claim of right*?

_____

_____

10.   Can tenants adversely possess? Why or why not?

_____

_____

11.   When is adverse possession *continuous*? How can possessors *tack* periods?

_____

_____

12.   How does an adverse possessor turn possession into marketable title?

_____

_____

Please do not review model answers until you have answered all questions fully and conferred with a seatmate to complete, correct, and supplement your answers.

Answer Key to Definitions Worksheet

1.   **Adverse possession** is a lawful means by which one who occupies or uses land can acquire title to the land without dealing with the land's owner.

2.   To acquire title by adverse possession, a person must possess the property in an *exclusive, open and notorious*, and *continuous* manner for longer the statutory limitations period for ejectment actions, under a *claim of right*.

3.   For adverse possession, the person must first be on the property **exclusively** as an owner would be able to exclude. The person may move onto the property as in residence or may simply use the property exclusively, as an owner would.

4.   *Exclusive* use does not necessarily mean *sole* use. Two or more can simultaneously adversely possess land, as when a married couple or family move onto or continuously use the land, the couple or family then taking title together as adverse possessors when they satisfy the other conditions.

5.   The person need not use the entire land to gain the entire land by adverse possession, if the limited use of the land that the person makes succeeds in excluding others from the entire land. Conversely, an adverse possessor who occupies only part of the land *without* excluding others from other parts adversely possesses only the used part.

6.   *Open and notorious* means that the property's owner would discover the person's possession during ordinary inspection. Open and notorious means *visible* to the owner.

7.   If the owner does not ordinarily visit the property or the occupied part of it for inspection, then the possessor's use of the property may not be sufficiently open and notorious, unless the possessor notifies the owner. The owner's knowledge of the use is sufficient to establish that the use was open and notorious.

8.   If the occupier leaves the land each time the owner visits, whether by the owner's request or to avoid detection, then possession is not open and notorious.

9.   Possession is adverse, hostile, without the owner's consent and instead conflicting with owner interests. Possession is adverse and under a claim of right when the possessor remains on the property intending and appearing to remain so permanently.

10.   No, tenants cannot adversely possess their landlord's land because tenants do not occupy with the intent and appearance of ownership rights. The owner's permission destroys the person's claim of right. The person who concedes the owner's right fails to satisfy the hostility condition.

11.   *Continuous* means *uninterrupted*, for longer than the statutory limitations period on ejectment actions, not every minute but instead typical of one owning the land. *Voluntary transfer* from one possessor to another tacks periods of possession, preserving continuity.

12.   If a person can establish each of the conditions for adverse posession either in an action that the person files to gain clear title to the land, or in defense of the owner's ejectment action, then the court may enter a recordable judgment that has the purpose and effect of granting marketable title to the person adversely possessing.

Issue-Spotting Worksheet

State the law that each scenario triggers, rules that you would want to state to address the issue. Do not analyze. Just state the applicable rules that each scenario triggers.

1.   Your new client rants about how a survey that he just got to put an addition on his shop—the bank required a survey, he says—shows that the parking lot that the business next door built some years ago is on *his* property. He says he's ready to take his bulldozer to the business's parking lot.

_____

2.   Your interjection with a little law sure didn't make your client any happier. Just the opposite: now he's hopping mad. He does, though, manage to sputter out a good question having to do with what the business must show to take his property in the way you just inadvertently suggested.

_____

3.   Wait a minute, though, your client says, having heard you say something about *exclusivity*. He points out that parking lots aren't especially exclusive. In fact, he says, the business next door had all kinds of people—customers, suppliers—using the parking lot.

_____

4.   Now you've really got your client worried—not always a good thing for a lawyer-client relationship. When your client asks just *how much* property the business might get out of this adverse-possession thing (as your client refers to it), you have a somewhat reassuring answer.

_____

5.   Your client points out that the business next door never said anything to him. It just built the parking lot on his land. That doesn't sound especially *open, notorious*, or *hostile*, the client insists. You're not sure that the client is going to like what you have to say in response.

_____

6.   *Aha,* your client says, sharing that the business actually changed hands once or twice after building the parking lot. *So there*, the client says. You smirk and answer.

_____

7.   *So now what,* your client asks. You blink senselessly. *No, come on,* the client continues, *what happens next?* You brighten up as you answer, thinking of the fees you're about to earn, even as you try to hide your growing good cheer.

_____

Suggested answers are on the next page.

Answer Key to Issue-Spotting Worksheet

1.   ***This scenario implicates the law of adverse possession.*** *Adverse possession* is a lawful means by which one who occupies or uses land can acquire title to the land without dealing with the land's owner.

2.   ***This scenario implicates the conditions for adverse possession.*** To acquire title by adverse possession, a person must possess the property in an *exclusive, open and notorious*, and *continuous* manner for longer the statutory limitations period for ejectment actions, under a *claim of right*.

3.   ***This scenario implicates the exclusive-use condition for adverse possession.*** For adverse possession, the person must be on the property *exclusively* as an owner would be able to exclude. The person may move onto the property as in residence or may simply use the property exclusively, as an owner would. *Exclusive* use does not necessarily mean *sole* use. Two or more can simultaneously adversely possess land, as when a married couple or family move onto or continuously use the land, the couple or family then taking title together as adverse possessors when they satisfy the other conditions.

4.   ***This scenario implicates the scope of possession.*** The adverse possessor need not use the entire land to gain the entire land by adverse possession, if the limited use of the land that the person makes succeeds in excluding others from the entire land. Conversely, an adverse possessor who occupies only part of the land *without* excluding others from other parts adversely possesses only the used part.

5.   ***This scenario implicates the definitions of open, notorious, and hostile.*** *Open and notorious* means that the property's owner would discover the person's possession during ordinary inspection. Open and notorious means *visible* to the owner. The owner's knowledge of the use is sufficient to establish that the use was open and notorious. Possession is adverse and under a claim of right when the possessor remains on the property intending and appearing to remain so permanently.

6.   ***This scenario implicates the definition of continuous.*** *Continuous* means *uninterrupted*, for longer than the statutory limitations period on ejectment actions, not every minute but instead typical of one owning the land. *Voluntary transfer* from one possessor to another tacks periods of possession, preserving continuity.

7.   ***This scenario implicates a quiet-title action.*** If a person can establish each of the conditions for adverse posession either in an action that the person files to gain clear title to the land, or in defense of the owner's ejectment action, then the court may enter a recordable judgment that has the purpose and effect of granting marketable title to the person adversely possessing.

Rule-Check Exercises

Identify and insert the omitted law detail from each statement, following the italicized, parenthetical hints. Some statements are wrong without the omitted detail, while other statements are just incomplete. Suggested answers are on the next page.

1. *Adverse possession* is a lawful means by which one who occupies ^ land can acquire its title ^ . *[Hints for two additions: Must one occupy the land? And what's so special about acquiring title? Anyone can buy the land.]*

2. To acquire title by adverse possession, a person must possess the property in an *exclusive, open and notorious,* and *continuous manner* under a *claim of right* ^ . *[That's all it takes? Brief possession, and it's yours?]*

3. The adverse possessor must be on the property *exclusively* ^ . *[Okay, but what do you mean by exclusively?]*

4. The adverse possessor may move onto the property as in residence, as an owner would ^ . *[May move onto it? You mean something else will do, too?]*

5. Two or more can simultaneously adversely possess land ^ . *[What does that mean, two possessing at once? An example would sure help.]*

6. The adverse possessor need not use the entire land to gain the entire land by adverse possession ^ . *[So you occupy or use a part but get the whole thing? Wow!]*

7. *Open and notorious* means that the property's owner would discover the person's possession ^ . *[Must an owner hire an investigator to discover the possession?]*

8. Possession is adverse under a claim of right when the possessor remains on the property ^ . *[Temporary squatting, ready to leave at any moment, is enough?]*

9. *Continuous* means *uninterrupted* for longer than the limitations period on ejectment actions ^ . *[You mean every minute of every hour of every day?!]*

10. ^ One possessor to another tacks periods of possession, preserving continuity. *[You mean one can move off and another move on, and you get tacking? What a deal!]*

11. An adverse possessor may ^ defend the owner's ejectment action. *[That's it? The adverse possessor has to wait for an ejectment action? Anything better?]*

32

Suggested Answers to Rule-Check Exercises

These answers are only suggested. You may have added other relevant detail or phrased your additions differently.

1. *Adverse possession* is a lawful means by which one who occupies **or uses** land can acquire its title **without dealing with the land's owner.**

2. To acquire title by adverse possession, a person must possess the property in an *exclusive, open and notorious,* and *continuous manner* **for longer the statutory limitations period for ejectment actions,** under a *claim of right.*

3. The adverse possessor must be on the property *exclusively* **as an owner would be able to exclude.**

4. The adverse possessor may move onto the property as in residence **or may simply use the property exclusively**, as an owner would.

5. Two or more can simultaneously adversely possess land**, as when a married couple or family move onto or continuously use the land.**

6. The adverse possessor need not use the entire land to gain the entire land by adverse possession**, if the limited use of the land excludes others from the entire land.**

7. *Open and notorious* means that the property's owner would discover the person's possession **during ordinary inspection.**

8. Possession is adverse and under a claim of right when the possessor remains on the property **intending and appearing to remain so permanently.**

9. *Continuous* means *uninterrupted* for longer than the limitations period on ejectment actions**, not every minute but instead typical of one owning the land.**

10. **Voluntary transfer from** one possessor to another tacks periods of possession, preserving continuity.

11. A person establishing adverse posession may **file an action to gain clear title to the land or** defend the owner's ejectment action.

Application Exercises

Assuming that the possession satisfies all other conditions for **adverse possession**, indicate whether the stated circumstance satifies (S) an adverse-possession claim or not (N). Answers are at the bottom.

1____   Claimant parks claimant's trailer on owner's land among owner's six parked trailers.

2____   Claimant builds cabin on owner's wild hunting lands and lives in cabin year round.

3____   Claimant plants crops on owner's farmland, harvests crops, and sells crops for claimant's profit.

4____   Claimant occupies and improves abandoned house on owner's land but doesn't mow yard.

5____   Claimant occupies empty bungalow above abandoned garage but not abandoned house.

6____   Claimant plants and tends fruit trees in isolated glade in owner's woods behind owner's house.

7____   Claimant erects fence twenty feet into neighbor's adjacent land and plants flowers inside fence.

8____   Claimant designs, plans, and saves for shop to build in the future on neighbor's adjacent land.

9____   Claimant builds and uses driveway on adjacent undeveloped lands owned by abentee owner.

10____   Claimant notifies objecting absentee owner that claimant installed pool on owner's land.

11____   Neighbor tells objecting absentee owner that claimant extended deck onto owner's land.

12____   Claimant moves secret wood-cutting operation off absentee owner's land when owner visits.

13____   Claimant agrees to move stored hay bales off absentee owner's farmland when owner visits.

14____   Owner consents to claimant planting vegetable garden on owner's land.

15____   Owner builds walkway across land for claimant to access beach.

16____   Claimant builds sundeck on water overlook of owner's lakefront land, over owner's objection.

17____   Claimant erects temporary fall-harvest drying shed on adjacent owner's tobacco lands.

18____   Claimant builds permanent fish-processing hut on adjacent owner's river-mouth lands.

19____   Claimant commercial tenant refuses to relinquish possession to landlord at end of lease term.

20____   Claimant lives continuously on objecting owner's hunting land except when buying supplies.

21____   Claimant leaves owner's empty suburban residence for the South every winter.

22____   Long-time possessor sells on land contract to short-term claimant.

23____   Successive owners sell land several times during claimant's continuous possession.

1N 2S 3S 4S 5N 6N 7S 8N 9N 10S 11S 12N 13N 14N 15N 16S 17N 18S 19N 20S 21N 22S 23S

Multiple-Choice Questions with Answer Explanations

626.   The respective deeds of a farm and a ranch established the boundary between them as "a line drawn along the middle of the river." Over time, the river changed course so that 10 acres of land that was formerly on the farmer's side of the river moved to the rancher's side. Who owns the 10 acres, assuming that the declaratory-judgment action took place in a riparian state?

A.   The owner of the ranch, because accretion belongs to the riparian owner.
B.   The owner of the ranch, if the requirements for adverse possession are satisfied.
C.   The owner of the farm, because accretion does not change property rights.
D.   The owner of the farm, because avulsion does not change property rights.

Answer explanation: Option A is the correct answer because accretion is the increase of riparian land by the slow change of a river over time, in which any resulting deposit of soil belongs to the owner of the abutting land. The owner of the ranch owns the 10 acres because accretion belongs to the riparian owner. Option B is incorrect because adverse possession doesn't apply here. Option C is incorrect because it misstates the law and reaches the wrong result. Option D is incorrect because although avulsion does not change property rights, avulsion is a sudden loss or addition to land, while here we had slow addition.

630.   A statesman owned a country estate in a jurisdiction with a 20-year statute of limitations for ejectment actions. An avid hunter who wanted to make the estate her own moved onto it so as to take it by adverse possession. After 10 years, the hunter left the estate for distant parts. Hearing that the hunter had moved, a naturalist moved onto the estate so as to take it by adverse possession, remaining for the next 15 years. The statesman then sued the naturalist in ejectment, claiming that naturalist was a trespasser. What is the most likely result in the statesman's suit for ejectment?

A.   Naturalist wins by tacking the hunter's 10 years onto her 15 years.
B.   Statesman wins, because hunter and naturalist were not in privity.
C.   Naturalist wins, because statesman should have sued the hunter, too.
D.   Statesman wins, because neither hunter nor naturalist entered under color of title.

Answer explanation: Option B is correct because tacking periods of adverse possession requires privity between successors. The hunter and naturalist were not in privity, meaning that the naturalist cannot tack on the hunter's period. Without privity, the naturalist's statute of limitations began running only 15 years earlier when she entered. She must hold for six more years before the statute of limitations has passed to acquire the property by adverse possession. Option A is incorrect because the naturalist cannot tack without privity. Option C is incorrect because the hunter long ago relinquished possession, and the statesman need only sue the naturalist for ejectment. Option D is incorrect because adverse possession does not require entering under color of title. While color of title can help shorten the statute of limitations in some cases, none are applicable here.

Week 4

Acquisition by Gift

SHORT OUTLINE:

A **gift** is a definite voluntary transfer of a present property interest.

A personal-property **gift** requires *intent* to make present title transfer, *delivery* (possession transfer), and *acceptance*.

For a gift of non-movable personal property, *constructive delivery* of a token of access (key) should suffice.

Symbolic delivery of a writing declaring the gift is traditionally enough only for items *too large to deliver*.

Some state statutes permit symbolic delivery of small items, reversing the common-law delivery rule.

For a gift of land, delivery involves a deed.

Law may *presume acceptance* of a gift of value. Gift acknowledgments are direct acceptance evidence.

Generally, a donee cannot enforce a *promise to make a gift* because the promise lacks consideration.

Traditionally, the donor of an engagement ring recovers it on a breakup only if the donor is without fault.

Gift of a check may require the donee to deposit it and the drawee bank to pay it before the donor dies or revokes.

Gifts *causa mortis* (anticipating death) are effective with intent and delivery. The donor may revoke if recovering.

Gifts causa mortis are *present* gifts anticipating death. *Future* gifts *after* death generally require a will.

The donor may have to redeliver if the donee already had the property before the donor expressed the gift intent.

Courts tend to construe the constructive-delivery and symbolic-delivery limits strictly for gifts causa mortis.

LONG OUTLINE:

A **gift** is a definite voluntary transfer of a present property interest. Completing a gift of *personal property* requires the donor and donee to meet three conditions: (1) donor *intent* to make a present transfer of ownership; (2) *delivery* of the personal property, typically by transferring possession of the personal property, or an equivalent to delivery that law recognizes; and (3) donee *acceptance* of the gift, typically presumed if the gift has value but with acknowledgment as direct evidence.

Donor intent is typically by an oral or written statement of gift. Look closely, though, at the words used to ensure that they communicate a present intent to convey a present interest in the gift property. Delivery typically involves the donor moving the personal property into the donee's possession. Where no one disputes donor intent, and the donor believed the gift complete, *constructive delivery* of a token, such as a key for access or operation, suffices in some courts. By contrast, *symbolic delivery* of a writing declaring the gift is traditionally enough only for items *too large to deliver*, for example, difficult-to-move personal property such as heavy equipment. Symbolic delivery of a writing declaring the gift would not be enough for a movable item, although some state statutes permit symbolic delivery of small items, reversing the common-law delivery rule. A gift of land requires delivery of a deed.

Generally, a donee cannot enforce a *promise to make a gift* because the promise lacks consideration. Traditionally, the donor of an engagement ring recovers it on a breakup only if the donor is without fault. Gift of a check may require the donee to deposit it and the drawee bank to pay it before the donor dies or revokes.

A gift *causa mortis* is one that the donor makes anticipating the donor's death. Gifts causa mortis are *present* gifts anticipating death, not *future* gifts on (after) death. A *future* gift *on* death generally requires a will (a writing satisfying the law of wills). Gifts causa mortis are effective with donor intent and delivery. The donor may revoke a gift causa mortis if the donor recovers rather than dies. Some states require the donor to make an explicit revocation of the gift if and when the donor recovers, otherwise presuming that the donor intends the gift to remain. Also, as to gifts causa mortis, the donor may have to redeliver at the time of the gift if the donee already had the property before the donor expressed the gift intent because the courts tend to construe gift-causa-mortis requirements strictly. Courts also tend to construe strictly the constructive-delivery and symbolic-delivery limits, for gifts causa mortis. The donor would have to make undisputed intent especially clear to allow constructive delivery, and the item would have to be non-movable to accept symbolic delivery through a note.

36

Fluency Cards

Cover and uncover the response to each prompt until you fluently recall the exact response.

Gift	**Gift conditions**
Definite voluntary transfer of present interest.	Intent, delivery, and acceptance.
Gift delivery	**Constructive delivery**
Possession transfer with intent to gift. Land gift requires deed.	Token of access enough if undisputed and donor believes complete.
Symbolic delivery	**Gift promise**
Writing stating delivery enough for non-movable property.	Unenforceable for lack of consideration.
Gift causa mortis	
Transfer of present interest anticipating death. May revoke on health recovery.	

Definitions Worksheet

1. What is a *gift?*

    _____

    _____

2. What *three conditions* must donor and donee satisfy to complete a gift?

    _____

    _____

    _____

3. How does a donor *express intent* to make a gift?

    _____

    _____

4. What does *delivery* typically require?

    _____

    _____

5. What is *constructive delivery*? Give an example.

    _____

    _____

6. What is *symbolic delivery*? When does it apply?

    _____

    _____

7. May a donee enforce a *promise to make a gift*? Why or why not?

    _____

    _____

8. What is a *gift causa mortis*? What does such a gift require for enforcement?

    _____

    _____

9. May a donor *revoke* a gift causa mortis if the donor recovers? If so, how?

    _____

    _____

Please do not review model answers until you have answered all questions fully and conferred with a seatmate to complete, correct, and supplement your answers.

Answer Key to Definitions Worksheet

1.   A gift is a definite voluntary transfer of a present property interest.

2.   (1) Donor *intent* to make a present transfer of ownership; (2) *delivery* of the personal property; and (3) donee *acceptance* of the gift.

3.   Donor intent is typically by an oral or written statement of gift. The donor must communicate the present intent to convey a present interest in the gift property.

4.   Delivery typically involves the donor *moving the personal property into the donee's possession.*

5.   Where no one disputes donor intent, and the donor believed the gift complete, *constructive delivery* of a token, such as a key for access or operation, suffices in some courts.

6.   *Symbolic delivery* is a writing declaring the gift, rather than the donor moving the gift into the donee's possession. Symbolic delivery is traditionally enough only for items *too large to deliver*, for example, difficult-to-move personal property such as heavy equipment. Some state statutes permit symbolic delivery of small items, reversing the common-law delivery rule.

7.   No, generally, a donee cannot enforce a *promise to make a gift* because the promise lacks consideration.

8.   A gift *causa mortis* is one that the donor makes presently, anticipating the donor's death. Gifts causa mortis are effective, like other gifts, with donor intent and delivery.

9.   Yes, the donor may revoke a gift causa mortis if the donor recovers rather than dies. Some states require express communication of revocation rather than presuming it with recovery.

Issue-Spotting Worksheet

State the law that each scenario triggers, rules that you would want to state to address the issue. Do not analyze. Just state the applicable rules that each scenario triggers.

1.   An associate with whom you were hired pokes his head into your office, asking if you remember anything about the law of gifts. He adds with a small that you were the know-it-all who aced the bar exam. You give him only the basic definition, figuring that you'd play along.

_____

2.   *No kidding,* the associate replies with a roll of his eyes and shoulders, clearly dissatisfied with the basic nature of your answer. He whines a little about how hard the bar exam was before begging you to remind him of the conditions (he calls them *elements,* but you properly think of them as being more like conditions) for a gift.

_____

3.   The associate looks puzzled for a moment. Then he spills the beans: he's got a new client—his first!—whose rich aunt promised to give her a new car when she graduated. *That's a gift, isn't it!* the associate almost hollers, gleaming. You're not so sure.

_____

4.   The associate had stormed out after your last answer. A day later, he's back, poking his head in your office doorway. Turns out, he tells you, that the aunt had not just promised the car but already *bought it,* he says, adding *got you!* as if you were opposing counsel rather than the associate's friend. You're still not so sure, though.

_____

5.   The associate had narrowed his eyes in response to your last comment, as if he was deep in thought. He had disappeared for an hour before returning, again with a look of smug confidence. *She got the keys,* he said as if in declarative victory, adding, *symbolic delivery!* You correct the associate. The associate storms out.

_____

6.   Years later, you and the associate both having made partner, the two of you have a good laugh together when a new associate whom the firm just hired brings up a question over lunch of a gift to the associate's first client. After recounting for the associate the prior gift case that you and your friend had shared years earlier, you learn from the new associate that a relative had promised the client a gift if and when the relative died but then had revoked the gift promise.

_____

Suggested answers are on the next page.

Answer Key to Issue-Spotting Worksheet

1. ***This scenario implicates the law of gifts.*** A gift is a definite voluntary transfer of a present property interest.

2. ***This scenario implicates the three conditions for a gift.*** (1) Donor intent to make a present transfer of ownership; (2) delivery of the personal property; and (3) donee acceptance of the gift.

3. ***This scenario implicates donor intent.*** Donor intent is typically by an oral or written statement of gift. The donor must communicate the *present intent* to convey a *present interest* in the gift property. Generally, a donee cannot enforce a promise to make a gift because the promise lacks consideration.

4. ***This scenario implicates delivery.*** Delivery typically involves the donor moving the personal property into the donee's possession. Where no one disputes donor intent, and the donor believed the gift complete, constructive delivery of a token, such as a key for access or operation, suffices in some courts.

5. ***This scenario implicates symbolic delivery.*** Symbolic delivery is a writing declaring the gift, rather than the donor moving the gift into the donee's possession. Symbolic delivery is traditionally enough only for items too large to deliver, for example, difficult-to-move personal property such as heavy equipment. Some state statutes permit symbolic delivery of small items, reversing the common-law delivery rule.

6. ***This scenario implicates*** A gift causa mortis is one that the donor makes presently, anticipating the donor's death. Gifts causa mortis are effective, like other gifts, with donor intent and delivery. The donor may revoke a gift causa mortis if the donor recovers rather than dies. Some states require express communication of revocation rather than presuming it with recovery.

Rule-Check Exercises

Identify and insert the omitted law detail from each statement, following the italicized, parenthetical hints. Some statements are wrong without the omitted detail, while other statements are just incomplete. Suggested answers are on the next page.

1. A gift of personal property requires ^ transfer of ownership along with delivery of the personal property ^ . *[Just transfer of ownership? Missing something there. And missing another condition, too.]*

2. Donor intent may be by ^ written statement of gift. *[May be written, but may it be anything else?]*

3. The donor must communicate the present intent to convey ^ the gift property. *[So, present intent to convey in the future is good?]*

4. A donee cannot generally enforce a promise to make a gift ^ . *[Correct, but any reason why not? Law enforces promises all the time.]*

5. Delivery typically involves the donor moving the personal property ^ . *[Just any movement, anywhere? I don't think so.]*

6. ^ Constructive delivery of a token, such as a key for access or operation, suffices in some courts. *[Constructive delivery is always enough? Don't think so.]*

7. Symbolic delivery by writing declaring the gift is enough ^ . ^ *[Symbolic delivery is always enough? And any statutory rule here?]*

8. A gift causa mortis is one that the donor makes presently ^ . *[So just any present gift is a causa-mortis gift?]*

9. Gifts causa mortis are effective, like other gifts, with donor intent ^ . *[Just intent is enough? It wasn't enough for other gifts.]*

10. A donor may revoke a gift causa mortis ^ . ^ *[May revoke at any time? I don't think so. And any special rules here?]*

Suggested Answers to Rule-Check Exercises

These answers are only suggested. You may have added other relevant detail or phrased your additions differently.

1. A gift of personal property requires **present intent to** transfer of ownership along with delivery of the personal property **and the donee's acceptance**.

2. Donor intent may be by **an oral or** written statement of gift.

3. The donor must communicate the present intent to convey **a present interest in** the gift property.

4. A donee cannot generally enforce a promise to make a gift **because the promise lacks consideration**.

5. Delivery typically involves the donor moving the personal property **into the donee's possession**.

6. **Where no one disputes donor intent, and the donor believed the gift complete,** constructive delivery of a token, such as a key for access or operation, suffices in some courts.

7. Symbolic delivery by writing declaring the gift is enough **only for items too large to deliver. Some state statutes permit symbolic delivery of small items.**

8. A gift causa mortis is one that the donor makes presently, **anticipating the donor's death**.

9. Gifts causa mortis are effective, like other gifts, with donor intent **and delivery**.

10. A donor may revoke a gift causa mortis **if the donor recovers rather than dies. Some states require express communication of revocation rather than presuming it with recovery.**

Application Exercises

Identify whether the donor has completed a gift (G) that the donee may enforce or not (N). As you do so, state the rule that you apply. Answers with explanations are on the next page.

1____ Donor delivers tools to donee saying that the tools will be donee's when donor someday retires.

2____ Donor delivers tools to donee on donee's threat to otherwise falsely accuse donor of assault.

3____ Donor states that she should give her jewelry to donee daughter because she's such a good girl.

4____ Donor hands to donee daughter donor's jewelry, saying it is a gift. Donee says *thank you*.

5____ Donor hands to donee daughter donor's jewelry. Donee says *thank you*.

6____ Donor hands jewelry to donee, saying it is a gift. Donee puts it down, saying *no thank you*.

7____ Donor points to jewelry on bureau, saying it is a gift. Donee says *thank you*.

8____ Donor tells donee that donor has a box of jewelry as a gift for donee. Donee says *thank you*.

9____ Donor hands to donee donor's jewelry, saying it is a gift. Donee says nothing but keeps jewelry.

10____ Donor hands jewelry and card to donee, card saying the jewelry is a gift. Donee says *thank you*.

11____ Donor hands donee car keys, saying car is a gift, believing gift complete. Donee says *thank you*.

12____ Same except donor believes gift requires title transfer not yet completed. Donor later denies gift.

13____ Donor hands donee a card saying donor's jewelry is a gift. Donee says *thank you*.

14____ Donor hands donee a card saying donor's two-ton press is a gift. Donee says *thank you*.

15____ Donor hands donee a card saying donor's timberland is a gift. Donee says *thank you*.

16____ Donor hands donee a card promising to give donee donor's two-ton press. Donee says *thank you*.

17____ Donor hands fiance an engagement ring. Donee says *thank you*. Donor's fling causes breakup.

18____ Donor hands fiance an engagement ring. Donee says *thank you*. Donee's fling causes breakup.

19____ Donor hands donee a check saying it's a gift. Donee deposits, drawee bank pays, then donor dies.

20____ Donor hands donee a check saying it's a gift. Donor dies, then donee deposits.

21____ Donor hands donee a check saying it's a gift. Donor revokes gift, then donee deposits.

22____ Donor hands watch to donee as gift because donor is dying. Donee says *thank you*. Donor dies.

23____ Donor hands watch to donee as gift when donor dies. Donee says *thank you*. Donor dies.

24____ Donor hands watch as gift because donor is dying. Donee says *thank you*. Donor recovers.

25____ Donor says lent watch is now a gift because donor is dying. Donee says *thank you*. Donor dies.

Answers and Explanations for Application Exercises

1 N A gift is a definite voluntary transfer of a *present* interest, not a potential future interest.

2 N A gift is a *voluntary* transfer of a present interest, not an involuntary transfer under duress.

3 N A gift is a *definite* transfer of a present interest, not an indefinite expression of desire to do so.

4 G Completing a gift requires only intent, delivery, and acceptance, all present here.

5 N Completing a gift requires expression of intent to make a gift, absent here.

6 N Completing a gift requires acceptance, absent here given the gift's refusal.

7 N Completing a gift of movable items requires delivery, meaning possession transfer, absent here.

8 N Completing a gift of movable items requires delivery, meaning possession transfer, absent here.

9 G Completing a gift requires acceptance, but law presumes acceptance of retained items of value.

10 G Donor intent may be oral or in writing. The writing suffices here.

11 G Undisputed token constructive delivery may suffice where donor believed the gift complete.

12 N Only *undisputed* token constructive delivery where donor believed gift *complete* may suffice.

13 N *Symbolic delivery* of a writing declaring the gift suffices *only* for items *too large to deliver*.

14 G *Symbolic delivery* of a writing declaring the gift suffices for items too large to deliver.

15 N A gift of land requires delivery of a deed.

16 N Donees cannot enforce a *promise to make a gift* because the promise lacks consideration.

17 G Traditionally, an engagement ring's donor loses the ring if at fault for the breakup.

18 N Traditionally, an engagement ring's donor loses the ring *only* if at fault for the breakup.

19 G Gift of a check is effective once donee deposits it and drawee bank pays it before donor dies.

20 N Gift of a check requires donee deposit before donor dies.

21 N Gift of a check requires donee deposit before donor revokes.

22 G A gift *causa mortis* anticipating donor's death is effective with intent and delivery.

23 N Gifts causa mortis are *present* gifts anticipating death, not *future* gifts after death.

24 N The donor may revoke a gift causa mortis if the donor recovers rather than dies.

25 N Donor may have to redeliver if donee already had property before donor expressed gift intent.

Multiple-Choice Questions with Answer Explanations

704.   An uncle told his nephew that the uncle planned to give the nephew his woodworking tools when the uncle retired someday. The nephew thanked his uncle profusely. The uncle then delivered the tools to a friend, saying that he was giving the tools to the friend out of friendship. The friend kindly declined the gift but took the tools saying that he would store them. The uncle then retired. The uncle then told the friend to deliver the tools to a neighbor as a gift for the neighbor's kindness, which the friend did, the neighbor thanking the uncle. Who has superior title to the tools if all subsequently claim them?

A.   The neighbor.
B.   The friend.
C.   The nephew.
D.   The uncle.

Answer explanation: Option A is correct because acquisition by gift requires intent, delivery, and acceptance. Only the neighbor can satisfy those three conditions. Option B is incorrect because a completed and enforceable gift requires acceptance. Here, the friend refused the gift and only held the tools for storage. Option C is incorrect because a gift requires present intent to transfer a present interest. The uncle only expressed the intent to transfer the tools in the future on his retirement. Option D is incorrect because a gift is incomplete with intent, delivery, and acceptance, all of which the neighbor can satisfy, defeating the uncle's claim.

705.   The board of a newspaper decided to close the business. The board determined to make a gift of a ten-ton printing press to anyone associated with the business who expressed an interest. The board also solicited requests to gift a prestigious trophy award that the newspaper had earned when operating. The newspaper's chief executive and longtime business manager both expressed interest in the printing press and trophy award. After due deliberation, the board conveyed correspondence to the chief executive gifting both the printing press and trophy award, both of which the chief executive gladly accepted. After further deliberation, the board changed its mind, delivering the trophy award to the manager along with correspondence gifting the manager the printing press, the manager accepting both. Who has the enforceable claim and superior title if the chief executive and manager dispute who owns each gift?

A.   The printing press and trophy award to the chief executive.
B.   The printing press to the chief executive and trophy award to the manager.
C.   The trophy award to the chief executive and the printing press to the manager.
D.   The trophy award and printing press to the manager.

Answer explanation: Option B is correct because symbolic delivery is effective only for non-movable property, not for property that the donor could reasonably deliver. Here, the printing press is non-movable, while the trophy award is movable. The manager accepted delivery of the award, while the chief executive accepted symbolic delivery of the printing press in the form of the written correspondence. Option A is incorrect because the board would have had to deliver the movable trophy to the chief executive, which it did not do. Option C is incorrect for the same reason and because the board first made symbolic delivery of the printing press to the chief executive before doing so for the manager. Option D is incorrect because the board first made symbolic delivery of the printing press to the chief executive before doing so for the manager. The chief executive would have the superior claim to the press.

46

706. An elderly widow, learning that she had only a month to live, told her longtime housekeeper that she was thinking that she would give her housekeeper a small but highly valuable painting that the widow had previously let the housekeeper move into the housekeeper's room. The widow later told her beloved granddaughter that her granddaughter could have the same painting when the widow died. The widow later told her admired grandson that the same painting was her gift to him for being such a good grandson and that he should take the painting home, which the grandson did. The widow's will left everything to her son. On the widow's death, who has the strongest claim to the painting?

A. The son.
B. The housekeeper.
C. The granddaughter.
D. The grandson.

Answer explanation: Option D is correct because a gift *causa mortis* is a definite voluntary transfers of a present interest that the donor makes anticipating the donor's death, requiring intent and delivery. The widow clearly expressed her intent and made delivery to the grandson who took possession. Option A is incorrect because the grandson has superior rights over the son, the grandson having received the painting as a gift causa mortis. Option B is incorrect because the widow was not definite in intending a gift, only that she was *thinking* of making a gift. Also, gifts causa mortis require re-delivery of items already in the donee's possession to make the gift sufficiently definite. Option C is incorrect because the widow only expressed an intent to bequeath the painting to her granddaughter at the widow's death, and bequests must satisfy a will, which the widow's oral statement to her granddaughter would not satisfy.

707. A vehicle collector who received a diagnosis that he had a late-stage terminal illness determined to give certain precious vehicles to friends before he died. The collector told a hunter friend to take the collector's roadster when the collector died. The collector told a fisherman friend that the collector's convertible stored in a nearby barn was the fisherman's. The collector told a card-player friend that the collector's muscle car was his and to drive it home, which the card player did. The collector told a co-worker friend that the collector's rally car was his and to take the car's keys, which the card player did. When the collector recovered from his illness, the collector demanded back the convertible and rally car. Which of the donees has the strongest claim to retain which vehicle?

A. The hunter for the roadster.
B. The fisherman for the convertible.
C. The card player for the muscle car.
D. The co-worker for the rally car.

Answer explanation: Option C is correct because a gift causa mortis is complete on intent and delivery. Here, the card player took delivery of the muscle car, driving it home. Option A is incorrect because a gift causa mortis is a transfer of a present interest, not a transfer on future death, which would require a will. The collector only told the hunter that the roadster was the hunter's on death, which would require a will—and the collector did not die. Option B is incorrect because a gift requires delivery, and the facts do not indicate that the fisherman took possession of the convertible or symbolic delivery of keys. Also, a donor may revoke a gift causa mortis if the donor recovers rather than dies. Some states require the donor to make an explicit revocation of the gift if and when the donor recovers. Here, the collector recovered and demanded the convertible back. Option D is incorrect for the same reason that the collector demanded the rally car back. Otherwise, delivery of keys to the rally car may have been sufficient, although states tend to construe strictly the constructive-delivery and symbolic-delivery limits, for gifts causa mortis, and so the co-worker may have had to drive the vehicle away to take possession, which the co-worker did not do.

Week 5
Possessory Estates

SHORT OUTLINE:

Ownership of land involves *duration* of interest and *relative rights* of holding, known as **estates**.
> The deeded language by which an owner transfers land ordinarily determines the estate that the transfer creates.

Present estates mean an owner may take *immediate possession*, the type of present estate depending on duration.
> **Fee simple**, a *freehold estate*, has *infinite* duration but when a **defeasible fee** can terminate earlier.
> **Fee tail**, a *freehold estate*, lasts until the grantee's bloodline terminates.
> **Life estates**, another *freehold estate*, last only for the grantee's life.
> A **term of years**, a *non-freehold estate* or *tenancy*, lasts for a period of any duration, not necessarily in years.

Fee simple, shorthand for **fee simple absolute**, is the theoretical right to hold the property *in perpetuity*.
> An owner of a fee simple *absolute*, rather than *defeasible* fee, holds unaffected by future events.
> Fee-simple estates are **alienable** (owner may transfer to another) and **inheritable** (owner may pass by will).
> A fee simple arises in a transfer *to A and A's heirs*, or in modern law's fee-simple presumption, simply *to A*.
> > Modern law presumes fee-simple transactions unless the parties use other words of limitation.

Defeasible fee-simple estates are fees simple that *end on the stated future condition or event*.
> A grantor creates a defeasible fee to control the property's future use and ownership.
> **Defeasible fees simple** are *determinable, subject to condition subsequent*, or *subject to executory limitation*.
> > Fee simple **determinable** attaches a *condition subsequent* that terminates the land's continued ownership.
> > If the condition occurs, the property automatically reverts by law to the grantor who created the interest.
> > > The grantor's potential future interest is a **possibility of reverter**.
> > A transfer creates a fee-simple determinable with *durational* words like *so long as, unless*, and *until*.
> > Fee simple **subject to condition subsequent** attaches a condition *not* automatically terminating title.
> > Grantor retains a **right of entry** with the *option* to take back the land or ignore the condition's occurrence.
> > Typical **words of limitation** are *but if..., then O may reenter and retake the property*.
> > > The limitation must be expressly conditional *and discretionary*, as in *may* reenter.
> > Fee simple **subject to executory limitation** transfers *to a third party* when the condition subsequent occurs.
> > Typical words of limitation are *to A, but if..., then to C*.
> > The third party holding the **executory interest** receives the land automatically when the condition occurs.

LONG OUTLINE:

Fees simple

The term **fee simple** is shorthand for the **fee simple absolute**. When a person owns property in fee simple absolute, the person has the theoretical right to hold the property in perpetuity. Fee-simple estates are **alienable**, which means that the owner may sell or transfer the land to another, and **inheritable**, which means that the owner may devise the land by will to another, who would then own the property in perpetuity. The vast majority of land sales today transfer fee simple absolute.

The way that the parties write a land transaction determines the estate that they transfer. The language needed to create a fee simple absolute is *to A and A's heirs*, where *A* refers to the buyer's full legal name that would appear in the transfer documents. This language includes **words of purchase** and **words of limitation**. The words of purchase in this transaction are *to A*. The words of limitation in the transaction are *and A's heirs*. Traditionally, the law required the words *and A's heirs* to show that the seller intended to deliver fee-simple estate to the purchaser. Today, however, a transaction *to A* suffices to transfer fee simple. Modern law presumes fee-simple transactions unless the parties use other words of limitation.

Defeasible fees simple

Defeasible fee-simple estates are estates in fee simple that *end on a stated future event*. By *defeasible*, the law means terminable on the occurrence of the stated condition or event. By contrast, the owner of a fee simple *absolute*, rather than a *defeasible* fee, holds the property in perpetuity unaffected by future events. A grantor creates a defeasible fee estate when wanting to control the property's use and ownership. The law recognizes **three types of defeasible fee estates**, a fee simple *determinable*, a fee simple *subject to condition subsequent*, and a fee simple *subject to executory limitation*. The type of defeasible fee depends on the words of limitation used in the transfer that creates the interest.

A fee simple **determinable** is an estate that would be a fee simple absolute but for the language of the conveyance that attaches a condition to the property's ownership. The law calls the **condition subsequent** the event that would terminate the fee-simple interest. For example, a conveyance from grantor *to A so long as A never commits a felony on the property* includes the condition subsequent that A not commit a felony on the property. Thus, A owns the property in fee simple, but if A commits a felony on the property, A's fee simple terminates, and the property automatically reverts to the grantor who created A's interest. When a grantor creates a fee-simple determinable, the law calls the grantor's future interest a **possibility of reverter**. Reverter happens automatically by law when the condition subsequent occurs. To create a fee-simple determinable, the conveyance must include *durational* words of limitation indicating the intent that the possessory estate will end automatically on the happening of the stated condition. Typical words of limitation that suggest a fee-simple determinable include *so long as*, *during*, *while*, *unless*, and *until*. When one of these words addresses a condition subsequent, then the purchaser acquires a present possessory fee-simple determinable, while the grantor retains a possibility of reverter.

A fee simple **subject to condition subsequent** relates closely to the fee-simple determinable. Here, though, with a fee simple subject to condition subsequent, while the owner holds in fee simple, the grantor has attached a condition subsequent that will *not* automatically terminate the owner's fee-simple title. Instead, the grantor retains a future interest called a **right of entry** that gives the grantor the *option* to take the property back *or* let the owner keep the property. The conveyance's **words of limitation** determine whether the fee simple is determinable or, instead, subject to condition subsequent. Typical words of limitation for a fee simple subject to condition subsequent include *but if*, *provided that*, *on condition that*, *if*, *however*, and *provided, however*. For example, a fee simple subject to condition subsequent arises in a conveyance *from O to A, but if A commits a felony on the property, then O may reenter and retake the property*. These words of limitation are expressly conditional *and discretionary*, reflected here in the operative word *may*, rather than purely durational. The grantor may invoke *or ignore* the condition's occurrence.

The final form of fee simple, a fee simple **subject to executory limitation**, is easier to distinguish. Like a fee simple determinable and fee simple subject to condition subsequent, the owner possesses the property in fee simple but subject to a condition subsequent that may terminate the interest. Yet for a fee simple *subject to executory limitation*, the person who takes the property when the condition subsequent occurs is a third party rather than the original grantor or grantor's heirs or assigns. If the interest doesn't revert to the original grantor, then the purchaser has a fee simple subject to executory limitation. For example, a fee simple subject to executory limitation arises in a conveyance from grantor *to A, but if A ever commits a felony on the property, then to C*. The fact that a third party, C in this case, would get the property if A committed a felony on the property indicates the executory limitation. The law calls the third party's interest the **executory interest**, discussed in the future interest section below. If the condition subsequent occurs, then the property automatically goes to the third party.

Fluency Cards
Cover and uncover the response to each prompt until you fluently recall the exact response.

Fee simple absolute	**Fee simple— formation**
Right to hold in perpetuity. Alienable and devisable.	*To A and A's heirs.* Modern law: *to A.*
Defeasible fee	**Defeasible-fee forms**
Ends on stated future condition or event.	Determinable, subject to condition subsequent, or subject to executory limitation.
Fee simple determinable	**Fee simple subject to condition subsequent**
Condition terminates ownership. Grantor has possibility of reverter.	Condition gives grantor option of re-entering (*may* retake).
Fee simple subject to executory limitation	
Executory interest goes to third party on condition occurring (*"but if..., then to C"*).	

Definitions Worksheet

1.   What is a *fee simple* or *fee simple absolute*? What are its primary features (advantages)?

_____

_____

_____

2.   How does a grantor convey fee simple absolute?

_____

_____

_____

3.   What is a *defeasible fee-simple estate*? What three forms may a defeasible fee take?

_____

_____

_____

4.   What is a fee simple *determinable*? How does one create a determinable fee?

_____

_____

_____

5.   What is a fee simple *subject to condition subsequent*? How does one create it?

_____

_____

_____

6.   What is a fee simple *subject to executory limitation*? How does one create it?

_____

_____

_____

Please do not review model answers until you have answered all questions fully and conferred with a seatmate to complete, correct, and supplement your answers.

Answer Key to Definitions Worksheet

1.   What is a *fee simple* or *fee simple absolute*? What are its primary features (advantages)?

A person owning property in fee simple absolute has the theoretical right to hold the property in perpetuity. Fee-simple estates are **alienable**, which means that the owner may sell or transfer the land to another, and **inheritable**, which means that the owner may devise the land by will to another or pass it to heirs under the laws of intestacy. Land sales today usually transfer fee simple absolute.

2.   How does a grantor convey fee simple absolute?

The grant *to A and A's heirs* conveys fee simple absolute. Traditionally, the law required the words *and A's heirs* to show the seller's intent. Today, however, a transaction *to A* suffices to transfer fee simple. Modern law presumes fee-simple transactions unless the parties use other words of limitation.

3.   What is a *defeasible fee-simple estate*? What three forms may a defeasible fee take?

A **defeasible fee-simple estate** *ends on a stated future event*. By *defeasible*, the law means terminable if the stated condition or event occurs. A grantor creates a defeasible fee to control future use and ownership. A defeasible fee may be a fee simple **determinable, subject to condition subsequent,** or **subject to executory limitation**.

4.   What is a fee simple *determinable*? How does one create a determinable fee?

A fee simple **determinable** attaches a *condition subsequent* that terminates the fee simple, giving the grantor a **possibility of reverter**. To create a determinable fee, include durational words like *so long as*, *during*, *while*, *unless*, and *until*. For example, the grant *to A while A continues to the farm the land* would terminate if A or A's heirs stopped farming, the property automatically reverting to the grantor.

5.   What is a fee simple *subject to condition subsequent*? How does one create it?

A fee simple **subject to condition subsequent** attaches a condition that does *not* automatically terminate fee-simple title but instead gives the grantor a **right of entry** choice. To create a fee simple subject to condition subsequent, include conditional words like *but if, provided that, on condition that, if, however,* and *provided, however*. For example, a fee simple subject to condition subsequent arises on grant *to A, but if A stops farming the land, then O may reenter and retake*.

6.   What is a fee simple *subject to executory limitation*? How does one create it?

A fee simple **subject to executory limitation** attaches a condition the occurrence of which transfers the **executory interest** to a *third party* rather than back to the grantor or grantor's heirs or assigns. To create a fee simple subject to executory limitation, include conditional words followed by the third party to whom the executory interest transfers, for example, *to A, but if A stops farming the land, then to C*.

Issue-Spotting Worksheet

State the law that each scenario triggers, rules that you would want to state to address the issue. Do not analyze. Just state the applicable rules that each scenario triggers.

1.   Your law partner is rubbing his head when he walks into your office. You ask what's the matter, and he replies that he hasn't thought about *possessory estates* since law school. You're the property-law expert, he says, asking that you remind him of the basic estate that most everyone owns—and its features.

_____

2.   Reassured, your partner says that he needs to draft a deed conveying that estate you just named, in settlement of a divorce matter. You give him the language. He blinks, asking *that's it?!* Yes, you assure him, that's it.

_____

3.   Your partner returns a day later, rolling his eyes and rubbing his head again while saying, *it's gotten complicated.* You ask what he means. He explains that the client wants the divorcing spouse to lose the house if she cheats on him. You laugh, saying that cheating ends with the divorce. He just says, *you know what I mean.* So you explain what he wants.

_____

4.   Your partner looks pleased, even saying *I knew you'd know this stuff.* So, he asks, how does the client get the house back? You explain.

_____

5.   A day later, your partner returns, once again rolling his eyes and rubbing his head, this time saying, *it's gotten real complicated.* You calmly ask what he means. Your partner explains that the client's not sure that he wants the house back but just wants to have the choice. The client wants to *hold it over her head*, your partner explains. You smile, quipping *all's fair in love and war.* Your partner waves his hand in annoyance, so you explain what he needs.

_____

6.   A day later, your partner returns, once again rolling his eyes and rubbing his head, but this time also with his shirt untucked and eyes glassy, too, saying, *I'm not sure I can handle this anymore.* You smile calmly, knowing the comforting effect that your demeanor has on your law partner. He explains that the client now wants the home to go to his kids by his first marriage if he about-to-be-ex-wife cheats on him after the divorce when she takes the home. You smile at this latest, um, *complication*, before explaining what your partner needs. *Property law!* your partner says to you admiringly, adding, *always was your thing.*

_____

Suggested answers are on the next page.

Answer Key to Issue-Spotting Worksheet

1.   ***This scenario implicates the law of possessory estates.***   A person owning property in *fee simple absolute* has the theoretical right to hold the property in perpetuity. Fee-simple estates are *alienable*, which means that the owner may sell or transfer the land to another, and *inheritable*, which means that the owner may devise the land by will to another or pass it to heirs under the laws of intestacy.

2.   ***This scenario implicates language to create a fee simple.***   The grant *to A and A's heirs* conveys fee simple absolute. Traditionally, the law required the words *and A's heirs* to show the seller's intent. Today, however, a transaction *to A* suffices to transfer fee simple. Modern law presumes fee-simple transactions unless the parties use other words of limitation.

3.   ***This scenario implicates a defeasible fee.***   A **defeasible fee-simple estate** *ends on a stated future event.* By *defeasible*, the law means terminable if the stated condition or event occurs. A grantor creates a defeasible fee to control future use and ownership.

4.   ***This scenario implicates a fee simple determinable.*** A fee simple **determinable** attaches a *condition subsequent* that terminates the fee simple, giving the grantor a **possibility of reverter**. To create a determinable fee, include durational words like *so long as*, *during*, *while*, *unless*, and *until*. For example, the grant *to A while A continues to the farm the land* would terminate if A or A's heirs stopped farming, the property automatically reverting to the grantor.

5.   ***This scenario implicates a fee simple subject to condition subsequent.***   A fee simple **subject to condition subsequent** attaches a condition that does *not* automatically terminate fee-simple title but instead gives the grantor a **right of entry** choice. To create a fee simple subject to condition subsequent, include conditional words like *but if, provided that, on condition that, if, however,* and *provided, however.* For example, a fee simple subject to condition subsequent arises on grant *to A, but if A stops farming the land, then O may reenter and retake*.

6.   ***This scenario implicates a fee simple subject to executory limitation.*** A fee simple **subject to executory limitation** attaches a condition the occurrence of which transfers the **executory interest** to a *third party* rather than back to the grantor or grantor's heirs or assigns. To create a fee simple subject to executory limitation, include conditional words followed by the third party to whom the executory interest transfers, for example, *to A, but if A stops farming the land, then to C.*

Rule-Check Exercises

Identify and insert the omitted law detail from each statement, following the italicized, parenthetical hints. Some statements are wrong without the omitted detail, while other statements are just incomplete. Suggested answers are on the next page.

1. A *fee simple absolute* for ownership in perpetuity is *alienable*, meaning the owner may transfer the land to another ^ . *[Something else, too?]*

2. The grant *to A and A's heirs* conveys fee simple absolute. ^ *[Isn't conveying fee simple absolute even simpler today?]*

3. A *defeasible* fee-simple estate ends on a stated future event, enabling the owner to control future ^ ownership. *[And control something else, too.]*

4. A fee simple *determinable* attaches a condition subsequent that terminates the fee simple ^ . *[So then who gets it (what's left)?]*

5. To create a determinable fee, include durational words like *so long as* ^ . *[Any other examples? There are several.]*

6. For example, the grant *to A while A continues to the farm the land* terminates if A ^ stops farming ^ . *[Only if A stops farming? And then where does the property go?]*

7. A fee simple *subject to condition subsequent* attaches a condition that does *not* automatically terminate fee-simple title ^ . *[Then what does it do instead?]*

8. To create a fee simple subject to condition subsequent, include conditional words like *but if* ^ . *[Any other examples? There are several.]*

9. A fee simple *subject to executory limitation* transfers the conditional interest to a *third party* ^ , as in *to A, but if A stops farming the land, then to C.* *[Instead of who (if it hadn't gone to a third party)?]*

Suggested Answers to Rule-Check Exercises

These answers are only suggested. You may have added other relevant detail or phrased your additions differently.

1. A *fee simple absolute* for ownership in perpetuity is *alienable*, meaning the owner may transfer the land to another, **and *inheritable*, meaning the owner may devise by will or pass to heirs in intestacy.**

2. The grant *to A and A's heirs* conveys fee simple absolute. **A transaction *to A* also suffices, modern law presuming fee-simple transfer.**

3. A *defeasible* fee-simple estate ends on a stated future event, enabling the owner to control future **use and** ownership.

4. A fee simple *determinable* attaches a condition subsequent that terminates the fee simple, **giving the grantor a possibility of reverter.**

5. To create a determinable fee, include durational words like *so long as, during, while, unless,* **and** *until.*

6. For example, the grant *to A while A continues to the farm the land* terminates if A **or A's heirs** stops farming, **the property automatically reverting to the grantor.**

7. A fee simple *subject to condition subsequent* attaches a condition that does *not* automatically terminate fee-simple title **but instead gives the grantor a right of entry choice.**

8. To create a fee simple subject to condition subsequent, include conditional words like *but if,* ***provided that, on condition that, if, however,*** **and** ***provided, however.***

9. A fee simple *subject to executory limitation* transfers the conditional interest to a *third party* **rather than back to the grantor or grantor's heirs or assigns,** as in *to A, but if A stops farming the land, then to C.*

Application Exercises

A person owning real property in **fee simple** (also called **fee simple absolute**) holds in perpetuity and may sell or devise the land. A grantor creates a fee simple by conveying *to A and A's heirs* or simply *to A*. By contrast, **defeasible fee-simple estates** *end on a stated future event*. A grantor creates a defeasible fee to control future use and ownership, using words of limitation like *unless, until, while, during, if, but if, on condition that,* and *provided however*. Working with a seatmate, sort the following fact patterns into **fee simple (FS)** or **defeasible fee (DF)**:

___: *To Cecilia Beadle and her heirs.*

___: *To Cecilia Beadle unless she dies without heirs.*

___: *To Cecilia Beadle.*

___: *To Cecilia Beadle provided that she commits no felonies on the land.*

___: *To Cecilia Beadle while the land remains in natural state.*

___: *To Frank Abbey and his heirs.*

___: *To Frank Abbey.*

___: *To Frank Abbey on condition that he remain single.*

___: *To Frank Abbey provided however that Maria Forte take on her marriage.*

___: *To Frank Abbey but if the land is fallow over a year then to Maria Forte.*

___: *To Medallion Corp. while it remains solvent.*

___: *To Medallion Corp., but if operations stop, then grantor may reenter.*

___: *To Medallion Corp.*

___: *To Medallion Corp. and its successors.*

___: *To Medallion Corp. while it complies with environmental laws on the land.*

___: *To John and Mary Dever, but if they divorce, then to Ron and Jane Butte.*

___: *To John Dever and Mary Dever and their heirs.*

___: *To John and Mary Dever while they continue the canoe livery on the land.*

___: *To John Dever and Mary Dever.*

___: *To John and Mary Dever until January 1, 2030, then to Ron and Jane Butte.*

Answers are on the back, but please do not review model answers until you have answered all questions fully and conferred with a seatmate to complete and correct your answers.

Answer Key to Application Exercises

A person owning real property in **fee simple** (also called **fee simple absolute**) holds in perpetuity and may sell or devise the land. A grantor creates a fee simple by conveying *to A and A's heirs* or simply *to A*. By contrast, a **defeasible fee** or **defeasible fee-simple estate** *ends on a stated future event*. A grantor creates a defeasible fee to control future use and ownership, using words of limitation like *unless, until, while, during, if, but if, on condition that,* and *provided however*. See the following examples of **fee simple (FS)** or **defeasible fee (DF):**

FS: *To Cecilia Beadle and her heirs.*

DF: *To Cecilia Beadle unless she dies without heirs.*

FS: *To Cecilia Beadle.*

DF: *To Cecilia Beadle provided that she commits no felonies on the land.*

DF: *To Cecilia Beadle while the land remains in natural state.*

FS: *To Frank Abbey and his heirs.*

FS: *To Frank Abbey.*

DF: *To Frank Abbey on condition that he remain single.*

DF: *To Frank Abbey provided however that Maria Forte take on her marriage.*

DF: *To Frank Abbey but if the land lies fallow more than a year then to Maria Forte.*

DF: *To Medallion Corp. while it remains solvent.*

DF: *To Medallion Corp., but if it ceases operations, then grantor may reenter.*

FS: *To Medallion Corp.*

FS: *To Medallion Corp. and its successors.*

DF: *To Medallion Corp. while it complies with environmental laws on the land.*

DF: *To John and Mary Dever, but if they divorce, then to Ron and Jane Butte.*

FS: *To John Dever and Mary Dever and their heirs.*

DF: *To John and Mary Dever only while they continue the canoe livery on the land.*

FS: *To John Dever and Mary Dever.*

DF: *To John and Mary Dever until January 1, 2030, then to Ron and Jane Butte.*

More Application Exercises

Defeasible fee-simple estates *end on a stated future event.* A grantor creates a defeasible fee to control future use and ownership. Law recognizes three types of defeasible fees, depending on the words of limitation that create the fee. A fee simple **determinable** attaches a condition the occurrence of which terminates the interest, the grantor retaining that possibility of reverter. With a fee simple **subject to condition subsequent**, the grantor retains right of entry that gives the grantor the *option* to take the property back *or* let the owner keep the property if the condition occurs. With a fee simple **subject to executory limitation**, a third party, rather than the original grantor or grantor's heirs or assigns, holds an executory interest to take the property if the condition subsequent occurs. Working with a seatmate, sort the following fact patterns into **fee simple determinable (D), subject to condition subsequent (SCS)**, or **subject to executory limitation (SEL)**:

___: *To Cecilia Beadle, but if she dies without heirs, then grantor Murphy may retake.*

___: *To Cecilia Beadle unless she marries, then to Ron Harmondale.*

___: *To Cecilia Beadle while the land remains in natural state.*

___: *To Cecilia Beadle while residing on the land, and then grantor Murphy may retake.*

___: *To Cecilia Beadle if she allows Ron Harmondale as tenant, to Harmondale if not.*

___: *To Frank Abbey on condition that he remain single, and if not, then grantor retakes.*

___: *To Frank Abbey provided however that Maria Forte take on her marriage.*

___: *To Frank Abbey but if the land lies fallow more than a year then grantor may retake.*

___: *To Frank Abbey unless he commits a felony then grantor Bill DeMent may retake.*

___: *To Frank Abbey until he no longer needs the land's rents, then to Sue Gibbs.*

___: *To Medallion Corp. while it remains solvent.*

___: *To Medallion Corp., but if it ceases operations, then grantor Buecher may reenter.*

___: *To Medallion Corp. while complying with environmental laws on the land.*

___: *To Medallion Corp. during wartime, then on the war's end, to Conservancy Trust.*

___: *To Medallion Corp. until no longer making boats, then the Trust may retake.*

___: *To John and Mary Dever, but if they divorce, then to Ron and Jane Butte.*

___: *To John and Mary Dever only while they continue the canoe livery on the land.*

___: *To John and Mary Dever until January 1, 2030, after which grantor may retake.*

___: *To John and Mary Dever unless the river floods the land, then the land reverts.*

___: *To John and Mary Dever provided they farm the land, but if not, grantor may retake.*

Answers are on the back, but please do not review model answers until you have answered all questions fully and conferred with a seatmate to complete and correct your answers.

Answer Key to More Application Exercises

Defeasible fee-simple estates *end on a stated future event.* A grantor creates a defeasible fee to control future use and ownership. Law recognizes three types of defeasible fees, depending on the words of limitation that create the fee. A fee simple **determinable** attaches a condition the occurrence of which terminates the interest, the grantor retaining that possibility of reverter. With a fee simple **subject to condition subsequent**, the grantor retains right of entry that gives the grantor the *option* to take the property back *or* let the owner keep the property if the condition occurs. With a fee simple **subject to executory limitation**, a third party, rather than the original grantor or grantor's heirs or assigns, holds an executory interest to take the property if the condition subsequent occurs. See the following examples of **fee simple determinable (D), subject to condition subsequent (SCS),** or **subject to executory limitation (SEL)**:

SCS: *To Cecilia Beadle, but if she dies without heirs, then grantor Murphy may retake.*

SEL: *To Cecilia Beadle unless she marries, then to Ron Harmondale.*

D: *To Cecilia Beadle while the land remains in natural state.*

SCS: *To Cecilia Beadle while residing on the land, and then grantor Murphy may retake.*

SEL: *To Cecilia Beadle if she allows Ron Harmondale as tenant, to Harmondale if not.*

D: *To Frank Abbey on condition that he remain single, and if not, then grantor retakes.*

SEL: *To Frank Abbey provided however that Maria Forte take on her marriage.*

SCS: *To Frank Abbey but if the land lies fallow more than a year then grantor may retake.*

SCS: *To Frank Abbey unless he commits a felony then grantor Bill DeMent may retake.*

SEL: *To Frank Abbey until he no longer needs the land's rents, then to Sue Gibbs.*

D: *To Medallion Corp. while it remains solvent.*

SCS: *To Medallion Corp., but if it ceases operations, then grantor Buecher may reenter.*

D: *To Medallion Corp. while complying with environmental laws on the land.*

SEL: *To Medallion Corp. during wartime, then on the war's end, to Conservancy Trust.*

SCS: *To Medallion Corp. until no longer making boats, then the Trust may retake.*

SEL: *To John and Mary Dever, but if they divorce, then to Ron and Jane Butte.*

D: *To John and Mary Dever only while they continue the canoe livery on the land.*

SEL: *To John and Mary Dever until January 1, 2030, after which grantor may retake.*

D: *To John and Mary Dever unless the river floods the land, then the land reverts.*

SCS: *To John and Mary Dever provided they farm the land, but if not, grantor may retake.*

Multiple-Choice Questions with Answer Explanations

601.   Under a state statute authorizing the action, a city condemned private property adjacent to a city reservoir, planning to expand the reservoir onto the condemned property. The city paid the private property's former owner just compensation for the condemnation. After holding the property for five years, the city's plans for the reservoir changed such that it no longer needed to expand the reservoir onto the condemned property. The city then sold the land to a private corporation for residential development. The private property's former owner objected, arguing that the land should revert to the former owner because the city did not use the property for the purpose for which it condemned. The state statute authorizing condemnation named the estate that the condemning municipality would receive in condemnation. What estate would give the city the greatest opportunity to convey the greatest interest to the developer, free of the former owner's claims?

A.   Fee simple title.
B.   Fee simple determinable.
C.   Vested remainder.
D.   Life estate.

Answer explanation: Option A is correct because fee simple title is the highest estate in land under which the owner may use, exclusively possess, commit waste on, dispose of by deed or will, and take fruits of the land without interference by others. Fee simple represents absolute ownership under which the owner may do what the owner chooses, such as here, to convey to a private developer. Option B is incorrect because a fee simple determinable, a type of defeasible fee that terminates on the designated condition, is a significantly lesser interest than fee simple and would likely not enable the city to convey to another for development, depending on the condition. Option C is incorrect because a vested remainder is the right to receive title after the present interest in the real property terminates. While a vested remainder could give the city strong title to convey to a developer, it would depend on the conditions terminating the existing interest. Option D is incorrect because a life estate, one held only for the life of the designated person, is a significantly lesser interest than fee simple and one that would likely not enable the city to convey to another for development, depending on whose life the title designated.

603.   An avid elderly bird-watcher had to sell her rural homeland to fund her nursing-home stay. The bird-watcher sold the land to a younger but still elderly friend in a recorded deed that recited that the friend would own the land "as long as retained undeveloped as hospitable for wild songbirds." The bird-watcher died, leaving her entire estate to a national wild-bird-lands conservancy. Soon after the elderly friend died, leaving her entire estate to her land-developer son. The son promptly filed a plat with the local register of deeds to divide the land into one-acre lots for residential development and paid an excavation contractor to begin cutting the roads and digging the septic fields. What result if the national conservancy sues the son over the land?

A.   Conservancy gains an injunction but developer son retains the fee simple determinable.
B.   Conservancy prevails taking the bird-watcher's reversion right in fee simple.
C.   Developer son prevails with full rights to develop the property free of conditions.
D.   Developer son prevails only if compensating the conservancy for the lost condition.

Answer explanation: Option B is correct because a landowner creates a defeasible fee simple by conveying the fee simple title with conditions on it. The holder of a fee simple defeasible then holds the property in fee simple subject to that condition. If the holder violates or does not meet the condition, then

62

the property will either revert to the original grantor or pass on to the third party whom the grant specifies as holding that reversion. A fee simple determinable and the grantor's reversion rights each pass on to heirs or successors in interest as conveyed but still subject to the original condition. Option A is incorrect because when the holder of the fee simple determinable violates the condition, as the developer son did here by filing the plat and hiring the excavator, the fee simple reverts to the grantor or grantor's successor or heir, here the conservancy. Option C is incorrect because the developer son acquired the land as heir of the friend, subject to the bird-watcher's condition. The son lost the determinable interest when violating the condition. Option D is incorrect because the bird-watcher's grant allowed no such condition for compensation in lieu of preservation. The son violated the condition, meaning that the land reverts, in this instance on to the conservancy.

660.   A retiring rancher conveyed fee-simple title to his ranch for valuable consideration to an outdoorsman "and his heirs" by warranty deed. The outdoorsman had a single adult son. A few years later, the outdoorsman conveyed fee-simple title to the ranch, for valuable consideration, to a cattleman, by warranty deed that only the outdoorsman, and not his son, signed. The cattleman was an unmarried and childless bachelor. Soon after the outdoorsman's conveyance to the cattleman, the outdoorsman died leaving his adult son as his only heir. Who now holds fee title to the ranch?

A.   The cattleman in fee simple because of the outdoorsman's deed.
B.   The adult son because the cattleman's life estate ended with the outdoorsman's death.
C.   The adult son and cattleman as joint tenants because both survived the outdoorsman.
D.   The adult son and cattleman as tenants in common with equal shares.

Answer explanation: Option A is correct because the law construes a grant to a named person "and his heirs" not as creating any right in the heirs but instead as conveying fee-simple title to only the named grantee. The law construes "and his heirs" as intent to convey fee-simple title rather than as intent to create a current interest on the heirs' part. The outdoorsman took fee simple title clear of any interest on his adult son's part, making his conveyance to the cattleman likewise of fee-simple title. Options B, C, and D are incorrect because the adult son never gained any interest from the "and his heirs" language. Options C and D are incorrect because the law does not support any theory for the adult son and cattleman sharing tenancy interests.

Week 6
Future Interests

SHORT OUTLINE:

Life-estate owners hold the interest for the *duration of the owner's lifetime*, whether one day or fifty years.
    A life estate is *not* inheritable or descendible, the owner having nothing left to give on demise.
    Life estates are *alienable*, meaning that the owner can sell or transfer a life estate.
        The law measures the transferred life estate's term by the original life tenant's life.
    Typical transfers creating a life estate are *to A for life* or *to A for A's natural life*.
    All life estates include a future interest because the property must go somewhere after the life tenant dies.
    A life estate's future interest can either be a *reversion* or *remainder*.
Future interests are *reversions*, vested or contingent *remainders*, *executory interests*, or *possibilities of reverter*.
    Future interests arise when a person must wait to take possession until the present estate ends.
    Future interests belonging to the original grantor include *reversions, possibilities of reverter*, and *rights of entry*.
    Future interests granted a third party include *vested or contingent remainders*, and *executory interests*.
Reversions are future interests that grantors retain when transferring a present interest less than the grantor owns.
    Conveyance from grantor *to A for life* creates a life estate in A with a *reversion in fee simple* in the grantor.
    Grantors who don't convey the entire interest and don't say to whom the land then goes, retain a reversion.
        The land reverts to grantor or grantor's heirs or devisees if grantor has died, when possession ends.
    Possibilities of reverter arise when the possessory estate is determinable, ending automatically on the condition.
    Right of entry arises when the possessory estate is subject to condition subsequent, giving grantor the option.
Remainders, vested and contingent, are future interests in a third party after the possessory estate ends.
    A **vested remainder** is one that an *ascertained person* holds *and* that is not subject to a condition precedent.
        An *ascertained person* is someone then named or identifiable, thus not including unborn children.
        A condition precedent is an event that must occur before the person obtains the future interest.
        A grant *to A for life, then to B*, creates a vest remainder because B takes without condition precedent.
    A **contingent remainder** is one that *either* an *unascertained person* holds *or* is subject to a *condition precedent*.
        A grant *to A for life, then to B if B attains the age of 21*, creates a contingent remainder because B must be 21.
        A grant *to A for life, then to B's children*, when B has no children, creates a contingent remainder.
    Contingent remainders vest when the condition precedent occurs or unascertained person is ascertained.
        When events could vest others, then vested remainders are **subject to open**.
        When nothing can further dilute the future interest, the holders have **indefeasibly vested remainders**.
    Owners of vested remainders have equal interests as tenants in common.
    Grantors form **alternative contingent remainders** when creating two options for what will happen, such as
        grant *to A for life, then to B if B reaches 21, but if B does not reach 21, then to C*.
Executory interests grant to *a third party* taking effect *when a condition subsequent divests the prior interest*.
    Executory interests vest when someone else loses a vested interest *subject to divestment*.
        Grant *to A for life, then to B, but if B does not reach the age of 21, then to C*, gives C an executory interest.
        B's interest is *subject to divestment* if B dies before 21, that possibility creating C's executory interest.
Possibility of reverter is the future interest that remains after a fee-simple determinable.
    A **fee-simple determinable** attaches a **condition subsequent** the occurrence of which terminates ownership.
    Fee simple determinable arises whenever the grantor has a future interest, called a **possibility of reverter**.
    A **right of entry**, a/k/a **power of termination**, arises with a fee simple **subject to condition subsequent**.
        The grantor retains the **right of entry**, or **power of termination**, at the grantor's option.

LONG OUTLINE:

Life estates

    A **life estate** is a third type of freehold estate. As the estate's name implies, the owner of a life estate owns the property for the *duration of the owner's lifetime*, whether that lifetime lasts one day or fifty years. Because of a life estate's limited and uncertain duration, a life estate is *not* inheritable or descendible. A life estate's owner has nothing left to give on demise. On the other hand, life estates are *alienable*, meaning that the owner can sell or transfer a life estate, although the law continues to measure the transferred life estate's term by the original life tenant's life, not the life of the person who received the life estate. The most common way that transfer documents create a life estate are with the language *to A for life* or *to A for A's natural life*. All life estates include a future interest because the property must go somewhere after the life tenant dies. The future interest can either be a reversion or remainder as following sections discuss in more detail.

Future interests

A second ownership area to address after present estates involves **future interests**. Future interests include *reversions*, both vested and contingent *remainders*, *executory interests*, and finally *possibilities of reverter* including powers of termination. A following section also addresses special rules affecting these interests. Generally, a **future interest** arises when a person must wait until some future time in order to take possession of the property. Estates involve the property's timeline of ownership. The present interest owner possesses the property for some duration, then the **future interest holder** may come into possession of the property after the present estate ends. Future interests belong to two categories, those retained by the original grantor and those held by a third party. Interests retained by the grantor include *reversions*, *possibilities of reverter*, and *rights of entry*. Interests granted a third party include *vested remainders*, *contingent remainders*, and *executory interests*, all addressed in the following sections.

Reversions. A **reversion** is a future interest that the grantor retains when transferring a present interest less than the grantor owns. For example, a conveyance from grantor *to A for life* creates a life estate in A with a *reversion in fee simple* in the grantor. When the grantor both doesn't convey the grantor's entire interest in the property and doesn't say to whom the property passes after the lesser estate ends, then the law construes a reversion in the original grantor or grantor's heirs or devisees if the grantor has already died when the present possessory estate ends. Thus, reversion is an interest that returns to the grantor. The law also recognizes a **possibility of reverter** and **right of entry**, each arising only in limited circumstances when the present possessory estate ends. As stated above as to defeasible fees, **possibilities of reverter** arise only when the present possessory estate is a fee simple determinable, that is, when the determinable fee ends automatically on the condition's occurrence. A **right of entry** arises only when the present possessory estate is a fee simple subject to condition subsequent, that is, when the grantor has the option of retaking the land after the condition occurs. A following section addresses these latter interests.

Remainders, vested and contingent. A **remainder** is a future interest granted to a third party after the present possessory estate ends naturally. Two conditions define remainders. First, the future interest must go to a third party, not revert to the grantor or the grantor's heirs or assigns. Second, the remainder holder must wait until the natural end of the prior possessory estate to take possession. This last point is critical to determining whether the future interest left over is an executory interest or some type of remainder, which the next section addresses.

Remainders can be either **vested remainders** or **contingent remainders**. A vested remainder is one that an *ascertained person* holds, meaning someone named, *and* that is not subject to a condition precedent. A condition precedent is an event that must occur before the person obtains the future interest. For example, the transaction from grantor *to A for life, then to B if B attains the age of 21*, includes a condition precedent to B obtaining the estate that B must attain the age of 21. Thus, B's interest is *not* a vested remainder but instead a **contingent remainder** because of the condition precedent. Similarly, a grant *to A for life, then to B's children*, when B has no children, would be a grant to unascertained persons and thus create only a contingent rather than vested remainder. Again, a contingent remainder involves either an unascertained owner or one who receives the interest subject to a condition precedent. A vested remainder cannot be contingent.

Contingent remainders can vest either when the condition precedent occurs or the unascertained person is ascertained. Thus, in the prior example, if the grantor had granted *to A for life, then to B's children*, and B then had a child, that child would take a *vested* rather than contingent remainder as an ascertained person within the grant. Because B could have other children, the child already born would have a vested remainder **subject to open** to account for the interests of any other children subsequently born to B. Thus, if when B died, B had three children, then those three children would have **indefeasibly vested remainders** because no further births could dilute their interests. Each child would have a one-third interest in the property as tenants in common.

Grantors can form **alternative contingent remainders** when the grantor creates two options for what will happen to the property. For example, the grantor creates alternative contingent remainders in the conveyance from grantor *to A for life, then to B if B reaches 21, but if B does not reach 21, then to C*. In this conveyance, B has a contingent remainder conditioned on B's reaching age 21. Here, though, the grant holds that if B doesn't reach age 21, then the property goes to C. The grantor retains no reversion here because of the stated alternatives.

Executory interests. **Executory interests** are a third type of future interest, one that the grantor creates *in a third party*. Executory interests relate closely to vested and contingent remainders. Yet an executory interest is a future interest in a third party that takes effect only *when a condition subsequent divests, or terminates, the interest that precedes the executory interest*. Executory interests vest when someone else loses a vested interest. For example, in the conveyance from grantor *to A for life, then to B, but if B does not reach the age of 21, then to C*, we have already seen that B has a vested remainder that B could lose if B dies before 21. The ability of B to lose the interest means that B's interest is *subject to divestment*. The possibility of divestment creates C's executory interest, which would vest only if B died before reaching age 21. An executory interest also arises in C in the conveyance from grantor *to A for life, then to B, but if B joins a biker gang, then to C*. Here, if B receives the property on A's death but then joins a biker gang, the condition subsequent occurring would divest B's defeasible fee simple, vesting C's executory interest.

Possibilities of reverter, powers of termination. As the defeasible-fee section addresses, a **possibility of reverter** is the future interest that remains after a fee-simple determinable. A **fee-simple determinable** is an estate that would be a fee-simple absolute but for the conveyance's language of the conveyance attaching a **condition subsequent** to ownership. For example, a conveyance from grantor *to A so long as A never commits a felony on the property* means that A takes the property in fee simple, but if the condition subsequent occurs, A committing a felony on the property, A loses the property, which automatically reverts to the grantor. A fee simple determinable arises whenever the grantor has a future interest, called a **possibility of reverter**. Reverter happens automatically by operation of law on the condition's occurrence.

Also as the defeasible-fee section states, a **right of entry**, also known as a **power of termination**, is the future interest that arises from a fee simple **subject to condition subsequent**. Recall that a fee simple subject to condition subsequent relates closely to the **fee simple determinable**. For any defeasible fee, the owner holds in fee simple, but the grantor attached a **condition subsequent** that could cause the person to lose their present possessory interest. Yet unlike the fee simple determinable, the owner does *not* lose the fee-simple interest automatically on the condition's occurrence. Rather, the grantor retains the **right of entry**, or **power of termination**, to take the property back *or not* at the grantor's option. The **words of limitation** in the conveyance determine the interest. A fee simple subject to condition subsequent arises under words of limitation like *but if, provided that, on condition that, if, however*, or *provided, however*. For example, a fee simple subject to condition subsequent arises in a conveyance *from O to A, but if A commits a felony on the property, then O may reenter and retake the property*.

Fluency Cards
Cover and uncover the response to each prompt until you fluently recall the exact response.

Life estate	**Life estate— formation**
Hold for owner's lifetime. Not inheritable/descendible.	*To A for life.* **Reversion to grantor.**
Grantor future interests	**Possibility of reverter**
Reversion, possibility of reverter, right of entry.	**When life estate ends automatically, e.g.,** *unless, until.*
Right of entry	**Vested remainder**
When grantor has option, e.g., *may reenter.*	**Ascertained person holds future interest not subject to condition, e.g.,** *to A for life, then to B.*
Contingent remainder	**Executory interest**
Unascertained person (unborn) holds or subject to condition subsequent, e.g., *unless, until.*	**Condition subsequent divests remainder, directing to third party:** *to A for life, then B unless felony, then C.*

Definitions Worksheet

1.   What is a *life estate*? What are its primary features? How does a grantor create it?

_____

_____

_____

2.   How does a life estate create a future interest? What two types does it create?

_____

_____

_____

3.   What is a *reversion*? What three forms may a reversion take? Briefly define each form.

_____

_____

_____

4.   What is a *remainder*? What two forms may a remainder take? Briefly define each form.

_____

_____

_____

5.   Define an *indefeasibly vested remainder*. Contrast it with a remainder *subject to open*.

_____

_____

_____

6.   What is a vested remainder *subject to divestment*? What interest follows divestment?

_____

_____

_____

Please do not review model answers until you have answered all questions fully and conferred with a seatmate to complete, correct, and supplement your answers.

Answer Key to Definitions Worksheet

1.   What is a *life estate*? What are its primary features? How does a grantor create it?

The owner of a **life estate** holds the property for *the owner's lifetime*. A life estate is *not* inheritable or descendible but *is* alienable, meaning the owner can transfer a life estate measured by the life tenant's life, not the life of the person receiving the interest. A grant *to A for life* or *to A for A's natural life* creates a life estate in A.

2.   How does a life estate create a future interest? What two types does it create?

Life estates include a future interest because the property must go somewhere after the life tenant dies. The future interest can either be a **reversion** or **remainder**.

3.   What is a *reversion*? What three forms may a reversion take? Briefly define each form.

A **reversion** is the future interest that *the grantor retains* when transferring less than what the grantor owns. A common **reversion** arises on grant *to A for life*, leaving the grantor or grantor's heirs holding when A dies. A **possibility of reverter** arises on occurrence of an uncertain condition, such as *to A unless A ceases farming the land*, leaving the grantor with an automatic reverter in that event. A **right of entry** arises at the grantor's discretion after occurrence of an uncertain condition, such as *to A unless A ceases farming, then grantor may reenter and retake*.

4.   What is a *remainder*? What two forms may a remainder take? Briefly define each form.

A **remainder** is a future interest *granted to a third party*. A **vested remainder** is one that an *ascertained person* holds, meaning someone named *and* that is not subject to a condition precedent, for example *to A for life, then to B*. A **contingent remainder** is one that no ascertained person holds, such as *to A for life, then to B's children* when B has no children, or that an ascertained person holds but is subject to a condition precedent, such as *to A for life, then to B if B attains the age of 21*.

5.   Define an *indefeasibly vested remainder*. Contrast it with a remainder *subject to open*.

A grantee holds an **indefeasibly vested remainer** if no one can dilute the future interest, such as *to A for life, then to B's children*, when B has died. By contrast, a remainder is **subject to open** if someone can dilute the interest, such as *to A for life, then to B's children*, when B remains living.

6.   What is a vested remainder *subject to divestment*? What interest follows divestment?

A vested remainder **subject to divestment** is one that an ascertained person holds but will lose on occurrence of a condition subsequent. An **executory interest** follows the remainder subject to divestment. For example, in a grant *to A for life, then to B, but if B joins a biker gang, then to C*, B holds a vested remainder **subject to divestment**, while C holds an **executory interest**.

Issue-Spotting Worksheet
State the law that each scenario triggers, rules that you would want to state to address the issue. Do not analyze. Just state the applicable rules that each scenario triggers.

1.   Your best friend has come to your office for your law services. Your best friend wants to buy a home for her widowed mother but own the home somehow at the same time so that the home belongs to your friend when her mother dies. Can she do that, she asks, and if so, then how?

_____

_____

2.   Your best friend's relief at your straightforward answer also relieves you. You'd wanted to impress your best friend who'd never shown much interest in your law practice. Your confidence grows when your friend asks what the law would call her interest, and you promptly answer.

_____

_____

3.   Your friend then discusses various things that might happen while her mother still lives in the home, like illness, hospitalization, or remarriage. Your friend wants to know if she can get the house back if she wishes, if one of those things should happen.

_____

_____

4.   Your friend then brings up that she might want to pass the home to her preschool-age daughter when her mother passes away or moves to a nursing home, assuming that her daughter remains in the area. You explain how to accomplish that eventuality.

_____

_____

5.   Your friend is overjoyed at your knowledge. Almost as if to test you, though, she asks what would happen if she wanted to pass the home not just to her preschool daughter but to other children she might have in the future.

_____

_____

6.   Your last test: what, your friend asks, if she wishes to pass the home to one of her children after her mother passes away, but then for her other children to take the home if the first child moves away from the area. You've got the answer!

_____

_____

_____

Suggested answers are on the next page.

70

Answer Key to Issue-Spotting Worksheet

1.   ***This scenario implicates the law of life estates.*** The owner of a **life estate** holds the property for *the owner's lifetime*. A life estate is *not* inheritable or descendible but *is* alienable, meaning the owner can transfer a life estate measured by the life tenant's life, not the life of the person receiving the interest. A grant *to A for life* or *to A for A's natural life* creates a life estate in A.

2.   ***This scenario implicates a reversion.*** A **reversion** is the future interest that *the grantor retains* when transferring less than what the grantor owns. A common **reversion** arises on grant *to A for life*, leaving the grantor or grantor's heirs holding when A dies.

3.   ***This scenario implicates a possibility of reverter and right of entry.*** A **possibility of reverter** arises on occurrence of an uncertain condition, such as *to A unless A ceases farming the land*, leaving the grantor with an automatic reverter in that event. A **right of entry** arises at the grantor's discretion after occurrence of an uncertain condition, such as *to A unless A ceases farming, then grantor may reenter and retake*.

4.   ***This scenario implicates a remainder.*** A **remainder** is a future interest *granted to a third party*. A **vested remainder** is one that an *ascertained person* holds, meaning someone named *and* that is not subject to a condition precedent, for example *to A for life, then to B*. A **contingent remainder** is one that no ascertained person holds, such as *to A for life, then to B's children* when B has no children, or that an ascertained person holds but is subject to a condition precedent, such as *to A for life, then to B if B remains in the area*.

5.   ***This scenario implicates a remainder subject to open.*** A grantee holds an **indefeasibly vested remainder** if no one can dilute the future interest, such as *to A for life, then to B's children*, when B has died. By contrast, a remainder is **subject to open** if someone can dilute the interest, such as *to A for life, then to B's children*, when B remains living.

6.   ***This scenario implicates executory interests.*** A vested remainder **subject to divestment** is one that an ascertained person holds but will lose on occurrence of a condition subsequent. An **executory interest** follows the remainder subject to divestment. For example, in a grant *to A for life, then to B, but if B joins a biker gang, then to C*, B holds a vested remainder **subject to divestment**, while C holds an **executory interest**.

Reversions Exercises

Reversions are future interests that a grantor retains when transferring a present interest less than what the grantor owns. A common **reversion** arises on grant *to A for life*, leaving the grantor or grantor's heirs holding the reversion when A's life estate ends when A dies. A **possibility of reverter** arises on occurrence of an uncertain condition, such as *to A unless A ceases farming the land*, leaving the grantor with an automatic reverter in that event. A **right of entry** arises at the grantor's discretion after occurrence of an uncertain condition, such as *to A unless A ceases farming, then grantor may reenter and retake*. Working with a seatmate, sort the following fact patterns into simple **reversion (R), possibility of reverter (PR),** or **right of entry (RE)**:

___: *To Roberto Aguirre for life.*

___: *To Roberto Aguirre as long his family resides on the land.*

___: *To Roberto Aguirre while the land is in crops, or grantor may reenter and retake.*

___: *To Roberto Aguirre if he commits no felonies indicating moral turpitude.*

___: *To Roberto Aguirre while the land remains wild, failing which grantor may retake.*

___: *To Sharon Peters if she remains married and residing on the land.*

___: *To Sharon Peters provided she care on the land for Edith Peters.*

___: *To Sharon Peters on condition she maintain the orchard, or grantor may reenter.*

___: *To Sharon Peters for life, then the lands revert to grantor or his heirs or assigns.*

___: *To Sharon Peters for life.*

___: *To Medallion Corp. while it remains solvent, failing which grantor may retake.*

___: *To Medallion Corp., but if it ceases operations, then grantor or heirs retake.*

___: *To Medallion Corp. provided that it manufacture motor vehicles on the land.*

___: *To Medallion Corp. while it farms the land, or grantor Michaels may reenter.*

___: *To Medallion Corp. while it complies with environmental laws on the land.*

___: *To John and Mary Dever, but if divorced, then grantor Charles Dever may retake.*

___: *To John Dever and Mary Dever as long as either lives.*

___: *To John and Mary Dever only while they continue the canoe livery on the land.*

___: *To John Dever and Mary Dever while the stables remain, then grantor may reenter.*

___: *To John and Mary Dever unless and until the lands flood destroying the manor.*

Answers are on the back, but please do not review model answers until you have answered all questions fully and conferred with a seatmate to complete and correct your answers.

Reversions Exercises Answer Key

Reversions are future interests that a grantor retains when transferring a present interest less than what the grantor owns. A common **reversion** arises on grant *to A for life*, leaving the grantor or grantor's heirs holding the reversion when A's life estate ends when A dies. A **possibility of reverter** arises on occurrence of an uncertain condition, such as *to A ceases farming the land*, leaving the grantor with an automatic reverter in that event. A **right of entry** arises at the grantor's discretion after occurrence of an uncertain condition, such as *to A unless A ceases farming, then grantor may reenter and retake*. See the following examples of a simple **reversion (R), possibility of reverter (PR),** or **right of entry (RE)**:

R: *To Roberto Aguirre for life.*

PR: *To Roberto Aguirre as long his family resides on the land.*

RE: *To Roberto Aguirre while the land is in crops, or grantor may reenter and retake.*

PR: *To Roberto Aguirre if he commits no felonies indicating moral turpitude.*

RE: *To Roberto Aguirre while the land remains wild, failing which grantor may retake.*

PR: *To Sharon Peters if she remains married and residing on the land.*

PR: *To Sharon Peters provided she care on the land for Edith Peters.*

RE: *To Sharon Peters on condition she maintain the orchard, or grantor may reenter.*

R: *To Sharon Peters for life, then the lands revert to grantor or his heirs or assigns.*

R: *To Sharon Peters for life.*

RE: *To Medallion Corp. while it remains solvent, failing which grantor may retake.*

PR: *To Medallion Corp., but if it ceases operations, then grantor or heirs retake.*

PR: *To Medallion Corp. provided that it manufacture motor vehicles on the land.*

RE: *To Medallion Corp. while it farms the land, or grantor Michaels may reenter.*

PR: *To Medallion Corp. while it complies with environmental laws on the land.*

RE: *To John and Mary Dever, but if they divorce, then grantor Charles Dever may retake.*

R: *To John Dever and Mary Dever as long as either lives.*

PR: *To John and Mary Dever only while they continue the canoe livery on the land.*

RE: *To John Dever and Mary Dever while the stables remain, then grantor may reenter.*

PR: *To John and Mary Dever unless and until the lands flood destroying the manor.*

Remainders Exercises

A **remainder** is a future interest granted to a third party. A **vested remainder** is one that an *ascertained person* holds, meaning someone named, *and* that is not subject to a condition precedent, such as *to A for life, then to B*. A **contingent remainder** is one that no ascertained person holds, such as *to A for life, then to B's children* when B has no children, or that an ascertained person holds but is subject to a condition precedent, such as *to A for life, then to B if B attains the age of 21*. Contingent remainders can vest either when the condition precedent occurs or events ascertain the grantee. Working with a seatmate, sort the following fact patterns into **vested remainder (V)** or **contingent remainder (C)**. Answers are at the bottom of the reverse side.

1. __: *To Roberto Aguirre for life, then to Joe Monte.*

2. __: *To Roberto Aguirre for life, then to Joe Monte if he is then living.*

3. __: *To Christine Matson for life, then to Ron David's first child Matilda.*

4. __: *To Christine Matson for life, then to Ron David's children. (Ron has no children yet.)*

5. __: *To Christine Matson for life, then to Ron David's living children.*

6. __: *To Christine Matson for life, then to Ron David's children. (Ron has two children.)*

7. __: *To Billie Sutton for life, then to Billie's oldest living child.*

8. __: *To Billie Sutton for life, then to Billie's neighbor Janice Garrison.*

9. __: *To Billie Sutton for life, then to Billie's neighbor at Billie's decease.*

10. __: *To Sharon Peters for life, then to Edith Peters if at least age 21. (Edith is age 25.)*

11. __: *To Sharon Peters for life, then to Edith Peters if holding a degree. (Edith has no degree.)*

12. __: *To Sharon Peters for life, then to Edith Peters if she has married. (Edith has married.)*

13. __: *To Sharon Peters for life, then to Edith Peters if the lands remain undeveloped.*

14. __: *To Perry Dee for life, then to Medallion Corp. if solvent.*

15. __: *To Perry Dee for life, then to Medallion Corp. but only if then making instruments.*

16. __: *To Perry Dee for life, then to Medallion Corp. if gone public. (Medallion went public.)*

17. __: *To Perry Dee for life, then to Medallion Corp.*

18. __: *To Perry Dee for life, then to Medallion Corp. if complying with environmental laws.*

19. __: *To Mary Dever for life, then to John Dever unless they had divorced.*

20. __: *To Mary Dever for life, then to John Dever if having naturalized. (John is now a citizen.)*

21. __: *To Mary Dever for life, then to John Dever if they have continued the canoe livery.*

22. __: *To Mary Dever for life, then to her living children. (Mary has three children.)*

23. __: *To Mary Dever for life, then to her children. (Mary has three children.)*

Answers: 1V 2C 3V 4C 5C 6V 7C 8V 9C 10V 11C 12V 13C 14C 15C 16V 17V 18C 19C 20V 21C 22C 23V

More Remainders Exercises

A grantee holds an **indefeasibly vested remainer** if no one can dilute the interest, such as *to A for life, then to B's children*, when B has died. By contrast, a remainder is **subject to open** if someone can dilute the interest, such as *to A for life, then to B's children*, when B remains living. When a grantor forms alternative contingent remainders creating two options, such as *to A for life, then to B if B reaches 21, but if B joins a biker gang, then to C*, B holds a vested remainder **subject to divestment**, while C holds an **executory interest**. Working with a seatmate, sort the following fact patterns into **indefeasibly vested remainder (IV), subject to open (SO), subject to divestment (SD),** or **executory interest (EI)**. Answers are at the bottom of the reverse side.

1. __: *To Roberto Aguirre for life, then to Joe Monte and Phoebe Monte.*

2. __: *To Roberto Aguirre for life, then to Joe Monte and his wife if he marries.* (Joe is not married.)

3. __: *To Christine Matson for life, then to her living siblings.* (Christine has siblings but no parents.)

4. __: *To Christine Matson for life, then to her children.* (Christine has one child and is elderly.)

5. __: *To Christine Matson for life, then to her living children, but if none, then to her sister Sue.* (Sue's interest?)

6. __: *To Christine Matson for life, then to her living children, but if none, then to her sister Sue.* (Child interest?)

7. __: *To Billie Sutton for life, then to Billie's oldest child Erma Sutton.*

8. __: *To Billie Sutton for life, then to Erma Sutton if living, then to Janice Garrison.* (Janice's interest?)

9. __: *To Billie Sutton for life, then to Billie's neighbor Janice and any other new neighbor.* (Janice's interest?)

10. __: *To Sharon Peters for life, then to Edith Peters if at least age 21.* (Edith is age 25.)

11. __: *To Sharon Peters for life, then to Edith if holding a degree, but if not, then to the Trust.* (Edith has no degree. Trust interest?)

12. __: *To Sharon Peters for life, then to Edith Peters if then married.* (Edith is married.)

13. __: *To Sharon Peters for life, then to Edith Peters if the lands remain undeveloped.*

14. __: *To Perry Dee for life, then to Medallion Corp. if solvent.*

15. __: *To Perry Dee for life, then to Medallion Corp. and any other occupying corporation.*

16. __: *To Perry Dee for life, then to Medallion Corp. if having gone public.* (Medallion went public.)

17. __: *To Perry Dee for life, then to Medallion Corp., but if dissolved, then to ABC.* (ABC's interest?)

18. __: *To Perry Dee for life, then to Medallion Corp. if complying with environmental laws.*

19. __: *To Mary Dever for life, then to John Dever unless they had divorced.*

20. __: *To Mary Dever for life, then to John Dever if having naturalized.* (John is now a citizen.)

21. __: *To Mary Dever for life, then to John Dever, but to Jill Dever if John predeceases Mary.* (Jill's interest?)

22. __: *To Mary Dever for life, then to her those of her children Bob, Sue, and Joe then living.*

23. __: *To Mary Dever for life, then to her children.* (Mary is unmarried but has three children.)

Answers: 1IV 2SO 3SD 4SO 5EI 6SD 7IV 8EI 9SO 10IV 11EI 12SD 13SD 14SD 15SO 16IV 17EI 18SD 19SD 20IV 21EI 22SD 23SO

Examples/Non-Examples Exercise
Working with a seatmate, identify each fact pattern as an example (E) or non-example (N) of the *highlighted concept*. Answers are at the bottom reverse. Generate your own example and non-example.

1. The common **reversion** is a future interest that the grantor retains when transferring a present interest less than the grantor owns, certain to return to the grantor.
   ___ Andrea Anatole conveys *to Brian Baxter for life, and then to Andrea Anatole.*
   ___ Andrea Anatole conveys *to Brian Baxter for life.*
   ___ Andrea Anatole conveys *to Brian Baxter for life, and then to Cruela Conway.*

   E: _____

   N: _____

2. The **possibility of reverter** form of reversion arises when the present possessory estate is a fee simple determinable, ending automatically on an uncertain-to-occur condition's occurrence.
   ___ David Drew conveys *to Emily Ernst while married, but if she divorces, then to Fern Forest.*
   ___ David Drew conveys *to Emily Ernst provided the land remains undeveloped.*
   ___ David Drew conveys *to Emily Ernst if she farms the land, but if not, then to David Drew.*

   E: _____

   N: _____

3. The **right of entry** form of reversion arises when the present possessory estate is a fee simple subject to condition subsequent, with the grantor having the option of retaking the land.
   ___ Greg Granger conveys *to Harriet Homer while needing housing, then Granger may retake.*
   ___ Greg Granger conveys *to Harriet Homer unless convicted of a felony, then to Granger.*
   ___ Greg Granger conveys *to Harriet Homer if having a degree by 28, or Granger may retake.*

   E: _____

   N: _____

4. A **remainder** is a future interest granted to a third party after the present possessory estate ends.
   ___ Irma Iglesias conveys *to June Jacks for life, then to Ken Krueger and his heirs.*
   ___ Irma Iglesias conveys *to June Jacks for life, then to Irma Iglesias and her heirs.*
   ___ Irma Iglesias conveys *to June Jacks and her present children for life, then to Ken Krueger.*

   E: _____

   N: _____

5. A **vested remainder** is one that an ascertained person holds, meaning someone named, and that is not subject to a condition precedent.
   ___ Lila Luder conveys *to Mac Morton for life, then to Ned Nolan if Ned is then living.*

___ Lila Luder conveys *to Mac Morton for life, then to Ned Nolan.*

___ Lila Luder conveys *to Mac Morton for life, then to Ned Nolan's oldest child.* (No children.)

E: _____

N: _____

6. A **contingent remainder** is one that no ascertained person holds or that is subject to a condition precedent that may still occur.

___ Opal Oz conveys *to Paul Prough for life, then to Paul's children.* (Paul has no children.)

___ Opal Oz conveys *to Paul Prough for life, then to Paul's child Quentin if living.*

___ Opal Oz conveys *to Paul Prough for life, then to Paul's child Quentin.*

E: _____

N: _____

7. A vested remainder **subject to open** is one that other unascertained persons may later dilute.

___ Raoul Rowe conveys *to Sally Steel for life, then to Sally's children.* (Sally has one child.)

___ Raoul Rowe conveys *to Sally Steel for life, then to Sally's siblings.* (Parents are deceased.)

___ Raoul Rowe conveys *to Sally Steel for life, then to owners of contiguous property.*

E: _____

N: _____

8. An **indefeasibly vested remainder** is a remainder that no newly ascertained person can dilute.

___ Tina Troupe conveys *to Ursula Ute for life, then to Ursula's children.*

___ Tina Troupe conveys *to Ursula Ute for life, then to Ursula's siblings.* (Parents have died.)

___ Tina Troupe conveys *to Ursula Ute for life, then to her children with Vern.* (Vern is dead.)

E: _____

N: _____

9. An **executory interest** is a future interest in a third party that takes effect only when a condition subsequent divests (terminates) the interest that precedes the executory interest.

___ Wilma Webster conveys *to Xavier Xyl unless he leaves the country, then to Yul Ylitch.*

___ Wilma Webster conveys *to Xavier Xyl if he continues the hat shop, otherwise to Yul Ylitch.*

___ Wilma Webster conveys *to Xavier Xyl for life, then to Yul Ylitch.*

E: _____

N: _____

Answers: 1 EEN; 2 NEE; 3 ENE; 4 ENE; 5 NEE; 6 EEN; 7 ENE; 8 NEE; 9 EEN

Multiple-Choice Questions with Answer Explanations

606.   A farmer who owned hundreds of acres of land on his homestead deeded a five-acre plot to his newly married daughter. The farmer's deed to his daughter stated that she would have the interest "as long as she lives." After building a home on the plot, the daughter and her new husband separated, the daughter leaving the state while the husband remained in the home. They later divorced, with the husband taking ownership of the home and plot under the terms of the divorce judgment. The farmer did not get along with the husband, his former son-in-law, following the divorce. So the husband moved out, renting the home to a rock-band leader who played loud music late into the night, disturbing the farmer. When did or when will the farmer or his heirs first have the right to recover the plot as owner?

A.   When the daughter moved out.
B.   When the daughter's husband moved out.
C.   On the death of the farmer's daughter.
D.   Never because of the conveyance by divorce judgment.

Answer explanation: Option C is correct because a life estate is an interest in land that lasts the life of the person holding the interest or, in some cases, measured by another person's life, with the property reverting to the grantor after the person's death. A life estate measured by another's life passes to the heirs of the life estate's holder if the holder dies before the person whose life measures the estate's duration. The holder transferring a life estate transfers nothing more than the life-estate interest, which terminates with the measuring life notwithstanding the transfer. Option A is incorrect because the daughter's life estate would persist until her death. Her moving out would not terminate the life estate. Option B is incorrect because the daughter's husband took the life estate by conveyance through the divorce judgment. The husband still owned the home and plot after moving out. Only the daughter's death would terminate the estate, not moving out. Option D is incorrect because a conveyance cannot convey any more than the grantor owns. The daughter could only give her ex-husband her life estate.

608.   The elderly owner of a beachfront home deeded the home to himself in life estate and then to his eldest grandchild provided that the grandchild retain the home during his life to keep its beach access available to other family members, in failure of which the home would pass in trust to a beach-access conservancy. The owner provided a copy of the deed to the conservancy to ensure the condition's likely enforcement. Federal tax laws require the conservancy to classify and report all donations. What interest, if any, does the conservancy presently hold before the elderly owner's death or any other relevant occurrence?

A.   A vested remainder.
B.   A contingent remainder.
C.   A reversion in fee simple.
D.   No interest.

Answer explanation: Option B is correct because a contingent remainder is one that is uncertain to occur, such as an interest dependent on the occurrence of a condition within the control of an interest holder. The condition may never occur, in which case the remainder grantee would never realize the remainder interest, such that the interest is only contingent. Here, while the owner is sure to die, terminating the life estate and leaving the fee simple remainder with the grandchild, the grandson may retain the home throughout his life to keep beach access available to family members. Indeed when the grandson dies holding the home, the deed's language in effect indicates that the home would pass to his heirs without the restriction (it had to do so to avoid the Rule Against Perpetuities), ending the conservancy's interest. The conservancy may never realize its contingent interest. Option A is incorrect because a vested remainder is one that the remainder grantee or grantee's heir is certain to realize, such as the remainder interest that a grantor gives to another after a life estate. The person's life measuring the life-estate interest is sure to end at some point, meaning that the third party or the third party's heir will at some point surely receive the interest. Here, the conservancy does not hold the remainder to the life estate but instead only holds the conditional interest if the grandchild or heirs convey depriving the family of beach access. Option C is incorrect because a reversion is an interest that returns to the grantor after the occurrence of the condition or death of the person whose life was the measuring life. Here, the grantor did not retain a reversion interest but instead granted that interest to another, the grandchild, as a remainder. Option D is incorrect because the conservancy in fact holds a contingent remainder interest, as explained above. The conservancy could realize the home and beach access as soon as the owner dies and the grandchild conveys, costing the family beach access.

615.   A landowner conveyed his lands to his friend for life, then to a farmer and rancher as joint tenants with the right of survivorship. The rancher, farmer, and friend were subsequently in a single motor-vehicle accident in which all three died within the hour. Hospital records confirmed that they died in that order, first the rancher, then the farmer, and then the friend. The jurisdiction does not have a simultaneous-death act in place. Who takes the farm?

A.   The friend's heirs.
B.   The farmer's heirs.
C.   The rancher's heirs.
D.   The landowner or his heirs.

Answer explanation: Option B is correct because a life estate passes to the heirs of the last-surviving joint tenant in the remainder interest even if neither joint tenant in that remainder survive the person holding the life estate. The farmer's heirs take the farm. The farmer and rancher held an indefeasibly vested remainder as joint tenants. The facts neither state nor imply any condition that they survive the friend in order to take. Because the rancher predeceased the farmer, the farmer took the property interest under the right of survivorship that joint tenants have. Upon the farmer's death, the remainder passed to his heirs. In turn, the farmer's heirs took the farm on the death of the friend, the life tenant. Option A is wrong because the friend had only a life estate; he had no interest to pass to his heirs at his death. Option C is wrong because the farmer survived the rancher and thus owned all of the remainder at his death; the rancher owned nothing. Option D is wrong because the landowner, having granted a life estate and an absolutely vested remainder, retained no interest in the farm.

617.   A grandfather conveyed a parcel of land "to my granddaughter and her heirs, but should my granddaughter or her heirs use the property for illegal purposes, then to my grandson and his heirs." In a jurisdiction that applies the common-law rule against perpetuities, what is the grandson's interest in the property?

A.   An executory interest.
B.   A contingent remainder.
C.   A vested remainder.
D.   Right of entry.

Answer explanation: Option A is correct because a third party's interest that arises only on the occurrence of a condition subsequent as to a fee-simple holder is merely an executory interest, not a remainder and not an interest having a right of entry. The grandson has an executory interest. The language of the grant to the granddaughter creates a fee-simple interest in the granddaughter but subject to a condition subsequent as to the granddaughter's interest. Options B and C are incorrect because the grandson and heirs do not take if the granddaughter and heirs comply with the use restriction. The grandson has no remainder interest. Although a right of entry normally follows a fee simple subject to condition subsequent, when the interest goes to a third party rather than the original owner, that third party has an executory interest.

633. An elderly homeowner with a needful, loving, resident, but untrustworthy son deeded her home to her lawyer "as long as my son lives and uses the home as his residence." She then passed away, leaving her entire estate to her professional and independent daughter. The lawyer retired, transferring his interest in the home to his new young law partner. The son later tired of living with old memories in his deceased mother's home and moved to live on the beach, tend bar, and sell seashells at an exotic resort location. The new young law partner moved into the vacant home for both residence and law office. What, if any, interest does the elderly homeowner's professional and independent daughter have in the home?

A. No interest, the interest having passed to the new young law partner on conveyance.
B. A remainder interest that will revert in fee simple only when the son dies.
C. A remainder interest that will revert in fee simple when the lawyer grantee dies.
D. The reversion interest in fee simple, to charge rent or evict the young law partner.

Answer explanation: Option D is correct because a life estate is an interest in land that lasts the life of the person holding the interest or, in some cases, measured by another person's life, with the property reverting to the grantor after the person's death. A life estate measured by another's life passes to the heirs of the life estate's holder if the holder dies before the person whose life measures the estate's duration. The holder transferring a life estate transfers nothing more than the life-estate interest, which terminates with the measuring life notwithstanding the transfer. A grant may also make a life estate conditioned in the same manner as a defeasible fee. The home reverted to the elderly homeowner or her heirs, in this instance the professional daughter, when the son moved out. The daughter may now rent, sell, or reside in the home at her option as fee simple owner. Option A is incorrect because the lawyer held the home only as long as the son used it as the son's residence, meaning that the lawyer's new partner lost the interest as soon as the son moved out. The daughter now owns the home in fee simple. Option B is incorrect because while the grant had a reversion for when the son dies, it also had a condition that the son continues its residential use. As soon as the son moved out, the daughter took the reversion. Option C is incorrect because while the lawyer initially owned a life estate on grant from his elderly homeowner client, the homeowner made the measuring life her son's life, not the lawyer's life. A grant may measure a life estate by the life of someone other than the grantee.

674. The owner of vacant land died. The owner's will devised the lands to her husband for life or until remarriage, and then to the owner's son. Not wanting anything to do with his deceased mother's affairs, the son promptly sold to an acquaintance, by properly drawn and recorded deed, whatever interest the son held in the land. The son soon died, with his father, the deceased owner's husband, as the son's only heir. With his son dead, the father (the deceased owner's husband) decided to remarry. He then executed a deed to the land purporting to convey the land to his new wife to assure her of his steadfast love for her. Who owns what interest in the land?

A. The husband's new wife owns the land in fee simple.
B. The husband's new wife has a life estate with the remainder in the son's acquaintance.
C. The husband owns the land in fee simple.
D. The son's acquaintance owns the land in fee simple.

PROPERTY I WORKBOOK

Answer explanation: Option D is correct because the words "for life" create a determinable life estate and "or until remarriage" create a condition terminating the life estate, while the interest following that life estate is a vested remainder. Thus, the son held that vested remainder. The owner of a future interest in land, such as the son, may convey that interest, which the son did to his acquaintance. When the husband remarried, his life estate terminated, vesting the remainder in the son's acquaintance. Option A is incorrect because the husband's remarriage terminated the life estate by condition not to remarry. Option B is incorrect because the new wife cannot take an interest after its termination by the husband's remarriage to her. The husband no longer had anything to convey. Option C is incorrect because the husband only ever had a life estate, and his remarriage terminated that life estate by express condition. The son successfully conveyed his remainder interest to the acquaintance, who succeeded to it when the husband's remarriage terminated the life estate.

81

Week 7
Special Future-Interest Rules

SHORT OUTLINE:

Rules affecting these interests limit *dead-hand control* of land, seeking reasonable *alienability* and *marketability*.

A few states follow **destructibility of contingent remainders**, eliminating unvested remainders after life estates.

Merger creates one fee simple when a person acquires both vested life estate and future interest.

A few states follow the **rule in Shelley's Case** giving fee simple to a life tenant whose heirs hold the remainder.

A few states follow the **doctrine of worthier title** giving a reversion to a grantor whose heirs hold the remainder.

The common-law rule against perpetuities requires *executory interests* and *contingent remainders* to vest timely.

These future interests must vest, if at all, within 21 years of a *life in being* when the grant creates the interest.

The rule does *not* limit interests that the grantor *keeps*, like reversions or rights of re-entry.

Some states address the rule's absurdities by presuming that women older than 55 will not bear children.

First, determine whether a grant creates either a **contingent remainder** or **executory interest**.

If not, and the grant only creates *vested* remainders, then the rule does not apply, and the conveyance is valid.

If a grant *does* create a contingent remainder or executory interest, then see if a condition *may never occur*.

If so, as grant *to A so long as A does not use for a landfill, then to B*, then the rule voids the grant.

If an interest vests when *living persons* die, see if vesting can occur more than 21 years after the last death.

If so, as grant *to A, then to A's oldest living child at age thirty*, then the rule voids the grant.

The rule against perpetuities as modified has an exception for **class gifts** as *to A's children or grandchildren*.

The common-law rule is *all-or-nothing*, invalidating the grant if invalid for even one class member.

The modified *rule of convenience* closes the class to new members when at least one member's interest vests.

The common-law rule voids grant *to A's children when they reach age 25* even if a child is 25 at grant.

The modified rule vests the over-25 child's interest at grant, closing the class, allowing in after-born children.

The *Uniform Statutory Rule Against Perpetuities* in over 20 states has a 90-year waiting period for vesting.

If no vesting occurs, then the court may modify the interest.

Other states adopt a similar *wait-and-see approach* to see if circumstances resolve the vesting problem.

LONG OUTLINE:

Special rules affecting future interests

The law recognizes several rules that limit *dead-hand control* over real property, meaning how long and how much a person can control what happens to the person's property after the person's death. The rules seek to ensure reasonable *alienability* and *marketability* of property. Some of these rules no longer apply in most jurisdictions. For example, a few states still follow a rule for the **destructibility of contingent remainders**. In those few jurisdictions, the rule eliminates any contingent remainder that has not vested by the time that all preceding life estates have terminated. The rule for destructibility of contingent remainders ensures that the law can ascertain the person who would have the discretion to exercise a possibility of reverter.

The law continues to recognize a **merger rule** holding that when a person who owns a vested life estate acquires the vested future interest behind the life estate, the two vested estates merge into one fee-simple title. For example, in the conveyance *from O to A for life, remainder to B*, if B then sells B's future interest to the life-estate holder A, then A would own both the present vested life estate *and* B's vested remainder, the two interests of which would merge into fee-simple title in A.

The **rule in Shelley's Case**, in the few states that still recognize it, applies where a life tenant's heirs hold the remainder to the life tenant's present interest, to merge the interests into the life tenant in fee simple absolute. Thus, in a conveyance *from O to A for life, remainder to A's heirs*, the rule in Shelly's Case would give A the fee-simple title to the property. Having a grant of a life estate that also gives that person's heirs the remainder merge into fee-simple title in the life estate holder gives the grantee the ability to convey the property in fee-simple absolute, promoting the land's marketability. Buyers need not wait for the life-estate holder to die to ensure that they properly ascertain, and gain conveyance from, the persons who hold the remainder interests. Only one person, the grantee of the life estate, need sign the deed conveying fee-simple title.

The **doctrine of worthier title**, again in the few states that continue to recognize it, works like the rule in Shelley's Case to simplify future interests, except that the rule applies to future-interest conveyances back to the grantor's own heirs. Thus, the doctrine of worthier title would treat a conveyance *from O to A for life, remainder to O's heirs* as simply leaving the grantor a reversion, as if the conveyance were just *from O to A for life*. The doctrine of worthier title destroys remainders to the grantor's own heirs in favor of leaving the grantor a reversion. Again, the rule promotes the land's marketability because otherwise, buyers could not ascertain a grantor's heirs until the grantor died. The doctrine of worthier title allows the grantor and life tenant to convey the property while both are still alive.

The **rule against perpetuities** provides that *executory interests* and *contingent remainders* must vest, if at all, within twenty-one years of a *life in being* at the time that the grant created the future interest. The rule's purpose is to preserve property's alienability and marketability, while preventing the wishes of persons long dead from controlling the disposition of lands. The rule against perpetuities does *not* limit interests that the grantor *keeps*, like reversions to the grantor or rights of re-entry in the grantor, because a grantor should be able to control the grantor's own property. The rule against perpetuities makes sense to promote alienability and marketability but can produce absurd results, for instance by voiding a conveyance on assumption like a ninety-year-old woman having a child. Some jurisdictions address that absurdity by presuming that women will not bear children after age fifty-five.

Policy aside, to apply the rule against perpetuities, simply determine whether a grant creates either a **contingent remainder** or **executory interest**. If not, and instead the grant only creates *vested* remainders, then the rule does not apply, and the conveyance is valid. Thus, a conveyance *to A for life, then to B*, does not violate the rule against perpetuities because the only remainder interest, B's interest, is a *vested* rather than contingent remainder. The interest does not depend on a condition that may not ever occur or that will vest more than twenty-one years after a currently living person dies. For another example, a conveyance *to A as long as A does not use the land for a landfill* also reserves only a *vested* rather than contingent remainder, in the form of a possibility of reverter in the grantor. Thus, the conveyance does not implicate the rule against perpetuities, and the conveyance is valid even if A's grandchild or a later descendant misuses the land as a landfill and the land reverts to the grantor or grantor's heirs.

If instead a conveyance *does* create a contingent remainder or executory interest, then determine whether the grant limits the interest's vesting by a condition that *may not ever occur*, in which case the grant violates the rule. For example, a conveyance *to A as long as A does not use the land for a landfill, and then to B*, creates an executory interest in B that may not ever occur, if A and A's heirs never use the land for a landfill. Thus, the rule against perpetuities applies to void the interest. If instead the interest will vest when *currently living persons* die, then determine whether the grant allows vesting more than twenty-one years after the last such person dies. For example, a conveyance *to A, then to A's oldest living male child*, does not violate the rule, even though the remainder is contingent, because the remainder vests or not immediately on the measuring life A's death, rather than more than twenty-one years later. If, on the other hand, the prior conveyance was *to A, then to A's oldest living male child when that child reaches age thirty*, then the contingent remainder would violate the rule against perpetuities because it could vest more than twenty-one years after the measuring life A's death. A could die leaving an oldest male child who was under age nine and whose interest would therefore not vest for more than twenty-one years after A's death.

As modified. The modern form of the rule against perpetuities recognizes an exception for **class gifts**. Class gifts are to a group as in *to A's children or grandchildren*. The common-law rule against perpetuities operates under an *all-or-nothing* rule that invalidates the entire conveyance if invalid for even one member of the potential class. Courts, though, have created an exception to the all-or-nothing rule called the *rule of convenience*, closing the class to new members (typically, children born after the conveyance) when at least one member of the class takes possession of the property. For example, in the conveyance *O to A's children when they reach age 25*, the rule against perpetuities may invalidate this interest if A is still alive at the time of the conveyance because A could have after-born children. However, if at the time of the conveyance, A has at least one child who is over twenty-five, that child's interest would vest. The *rule of convenience* would then close the class gift, so that after-born children would not share in the gift.

Because of the harshness of the common-law rule against perpetuities, many states have further modified it for results consistent with the grantor's intent. The *Uniform Statutory Rule Against Perpetuities*, adopted in over twenty jurisdictions, provides a waiting period of ninety years to see if the future interest vests. If it does not, then the court may modify the interest. Other states have adopted a similar *wait-and-see approach* that, instead of invalidating all potential future interests that could remain unresolved, waits to see if the circumstances do resolve before invalidating the interest.

Fluency Cards

Cover and uncover the response to each prompt until you fluently recall the exact response.

Merger doctrine	**Destructibility of contingent remainders**
Owner acquires both vested life estate and future interest.	A few states eliminate remainders not vested after life estates.
Rule in Shelley's case	**Doctrine of worthier title**
Gives fee simple to a life tenant whose heirs hold the remainder.	Gives reversion to a grantor whose heirs hold the remainder.
Rule against perpetuities	**All-or-nothing rule**
Executory interests and contingent remainders must vest within 21 years of a life in being at time of grant.	Common law voids grant if invalid for even one class member.
Rule of convenience	**Uniform Statutory Rule**
Modern rule closes class when first interest vests.	Waits 90 years for vesting, then court modifies.

Definitions Worksheet

1. What is the purpose of the rule against perpetuities?

_____

_____

_____

2. State the *rule against perpetuities*. Be accurate, precise, and complete.

_____

_____

_____

3. What does a *life in being* mean within the rule against perpetuities? Give examples.

_____

_____

_____

4. Does the rule against perpetuities apply to *vested remainders*? Give an example.

_____

_____

_____

5. Give examples of the *executory interests* and *contingent remainders* to which the rule applies.

_____

_____

_____

6. How does the *modern form* of the rule against perpetuities differ? Give an example.

_____

_____

_____

Please do not review model answers until you have answered all questions fully and conferred with a seatmate to complete, correct, and supplement your answers.

Answer Key to Definitions Worksheet

1.   What is the purpose of the rule against perpetuities?

The rule's purpose is to preserve property's *alienability* and *marketability*, while preventing the wishes of persons long dead from controlling the disposition of lands.

2.   State the *rule against perpetuities*. Be accurate, precise, and complete.

The **rule against perpetuities** provides that *executory interests* and *contingent remainders* must vest, if at all, within twenty-one years of a *life in being* at the time that the grant created the future interest. If any interest that the grant creates fails that test, then the rule invalidates the entire grant.

3.   What does a *life in being* mean? Give examples.

A **life in being** means a person the grant names who is alive at the grant. For example, the grant *to A for life, then to B if living* identifies two living persons, A and B, against whose lives one may measure the grant's validity. The contingent-remainder grant to B vests within twenty-one years of A's death. So, also, for the grant *to A for life, then to A's children if living*. The contingent-remainder grant to A's born and unborn children vests within twenty-one years of A's life.

4.   Does the rule against perpetuities apply to *vested remainders*? Give an example.

No, the rule against perpetuities does *not* apply to **vested remainders**, only to *executory interests* and *contingent remainders*. For example, the grant *to A as long as used for farming* leaves only a vested remainder in the grantor, to which the rule does not apply. Similarly, the grant *to A for life, then to B* leaves only a vested remainder in B so that the rule does not apply.

5.   Give examples of the *executory interests* and *contingent remainders* to which the rule applies.

The grant *to A as long as used for farming, then to B* leaves an **executory interest** in B that may never occur, such that the rule would apply to void the grant. Similarly, the grant *to A, then to A's oldest living child* leaves a **contingent remainder** in A's children to which the rule applies, although the grant does not violate the rule because the remainder vests immediately on A's death, not more than twenty-one years after a measuring life. A grant *to A, then to A's oldest living child when that child reaches age thirty* would violate the rule for potentially vesting more than twenty-one years after A's death.

6.   How does the *modern* rule against perpetuities differ? Give an example.

The modern form of the rule against perpetuities recognizes an exception for **class gifts** like *to A's children*. The common-law rule is *all or nothing*, invalidating the entire grant if invalid for even one class member. The modern *rule of convenience* closes the class to new members (typically, children born after the grant) when at least one member of the class takes possession of the property. For example, the grant *to A's children when they reach age 25* violates the rule against perpetuities if A is still alive at the grant because A could have after-born children. However, if at the time of the conveyance, A has at least one child who is over twenty-five, that child's interest would vest. The *rule of convenience* would then close the class gift, so that after-born children would not share in the gift.

Issue-Spotting Worksheet
State the law that each scenario triggers, rules that you would want to state to address the issue. Do not analyze. Just state the applicable rules that each scenario triggers.

1.   Now you've done it. Your reputation for property law preceded you. Your developer client brings you a sticky problem: a grantor from decades ago apparently restrained land in a way that if the developer develops it, the land will pass to someone unidentifiable. The title insurer won't insure over it, and so the bank won't lend for development. *What's going on?* the developer wants to know.

_____

_____

_____

_____

2.   So what, exactly, is this rule about which you are speaking, the developer wants to know, because the developer has the title insurer's analysis with him. Always the game-player, he won't show it to you until you tell him the rule.

_____

3.   No dummy, the developer wants to figure this thing out with you. What, exactly, is a *life in being*, he wants to know?

_____

_____

_____

4.   What, though, if the grantor had just restricted the land against development, your client wants to know, letting it revert to his estate if so? Or what if the grantor had left it to a relative who left it to a relative—and so on?

_____

_____

_____

_____

5.   Finally, your client shows you the title insurer's documents. Sure enough, the grantor's old deed had the form of *to my child Hal as long as he farms the land, but then to the conservancy if the land lies fallow or faces development.*

_____

_____

_____

_____

_____

Suggested answers are on the next page.

Answer Key to Issue-Spotting Worksheet

1. ***This scenario implicates the rule against perpetuities.*** The rule's purpose is to preserve property's *alienability* and *marketability*, while preventing the wishes of persons long dead from controlling the disposition of lands.

2. ***This scenario implicates the contours of the rule against perpetuities.*** The **rule against perpetuities** provides that *executory interests* and *contingent remainders* must vest, if at all, within twenty-one years of a *life in being* at the time that the grant created the future interest. If any interest that the grant creates fails that test, then the rule invalidates the entire grant.

3. ***This scenario implicates the definition of a life in being.*** A **life in being** means a person the grant names who is alive at the grant. For example, the grant *to A for life, then to B if living* identifies two living persons, A and B, against whose lives one may measure the grant's validity. The contingent-remainder grant to B vests within twenty-one years of A's death. So, also, for the grant *to A for life, then to A's children if living.* The contingent-remainder grant to A's born and unborn children vests within twenty-one years of A's life.

4. ***This scenario implicates a vested remainder.*** No, the rule against perpetuities does *not* apply to **vested remainders**, only to *executory interests* and *contingent remainders.* For example, the grant *to A as long as used for farming* leaves only a vested remainder in the grantor, to which the rule does not apply. Similarly, the grant *to A for life, then to B* leaves only a vested remainder in B so that the rule does not apply.

5. ***This scenario implicates an executory interest to which the rule against perpetuities applies.*** The grant *to A as long as used for farming, then to B* leaves an **executory interest** in B that may never occur, such that the rule would apply to void the grant. Similarly, the grant *to A, then to A's oldest living child* leaves a **contingent remainder** in A's children to which the rule applies, although the grant does not violate the rule because the remainder vests immediately on A's death, not more than twenty-one years after a measuring life. A grant *to A, then to A's oldest living child when that child reaches age thirty* would violate the rule for potentially vesting more than twenty-one years after A's death.

Rule-Check Exercises

Identify and insert the omitted law detail from each statement, following the italicized, parenthetical hints. (Yes, this exercise tests the rule against perpetuities more than once.) Some statements are wrong without the omitted detail, while other statements are just incomplete. Suggested answers are on the next page.

1.　The rule against perpetuities provides that ^ contingent remainders must vest, if at all, within twenty-one years of a life in being at the time that the grant created the future interest. *[Only contingent remainders?]*

2.　The rule against perpetuities provides that executory interests and contingent remainders must vest, if at all, ^ at the time that the grant created the future interest. *[Must vest immediately? I don't think so.]*

3.　The rule against perpetuities provides that executory interests and contingent remainders must vest, if at all, within twenty-one years of a life in being ^ . *[In being when?]*

4.　The rule against perpetuities provides that executory interests ^ must vest, if at all, within twenty-one years of a life in being at the time that the grant created the future interest. *[Only executory interests?]*

5.　If any interest that a grant creates fails the rule against perpetuities, then the rule invalidates the ^ grant ^ . *[Only the interest that fails?]*

6.　The rule's purpose is to preserve land's alienability and marketability ^ . *[Preserve against whose wishes?]*

7.　A life in being means persons the grant names who are alive at the grant. The grant *to A for life, then to B if living* identifies A ^ against whom to measure the grant's validity. *[Measure only against A's life?]*

8.　The rule against perpetuities does *not* apply to vested remainders, only to executory interests ^ . *[Only to executory interests?]*

Suggested Answers to Rule-Check Exercises

These answers are only suggested. You may have added other relevant detail or phrased your additions differently.

1.   The rule against perpetuities provides that **executory interests and** contingent remainders must vest, if at all, within twenty-one years of a life in being at the time that the grant created the future interest.

2.   The rule against perpetuities provides that executory interests and contingent remainders must vest, if at all, **within twenty-one years of a life in being** at the time that the grant created the future interest.

3.   The rule against perpetuities provides that executory interests and contingent remainders must vest, if at all, within twenty-one years of a life in being **at the time that the grant created the future interest**.

4.   The rule against perpetuities provides that executory interests **and contingent remainders** must vest, if at all, within twenty-one years of a life in being at the time that the grant created the future interest.

5.   If any interest that a grant creates fails the rule against perpetuities, then the rule invalidates the **entire** grant **for all interests**.

6.   The rule's purpose is to preserve land's alienability and marketability**, while preventing the wishes of persons long dead from controlling lands.**

7.   A life in being means persons the grant names who are alive at the grant. The grant *to A for life, then to B if living* identifies A **and B** against whom to measure the grant's validity.

8.   The rule against perpetuities does *not* apply to vested remainders, only to executory interests **and contingent remainders**.

Application Exercises

The **rule against perpetuities** provides that *executory interests* and *contingent remainders* must vest, if at all, within twenty-one years of a *life in being* at the time that the grant created the future interest. Apply the rule against perpetuities following two steps. (1) First determine whether a grant creates either a **contingent remainder** or **executory interest**. If not, and instead the grant only creates *vested* remainders, then the rule does not apply, and the conveyance is valid. (2) If instead a conveyance *does* create a contingent remainder or executory interest, then determine whether the interest's vesting either *may never occur* or *may occur more than twenty-one years after the last currently living person dies*, in which case the grant violates the rule. Work with a seatmate through the following exercises on each step.

STEP ONE: Place a check mark next to the grants that create a **contingent remainder** or **executory interest** to which the rule against perpetuities applies, even if the grant may still be valid (the next section has the answers):

1____: *To Alvin as long as Alvin does not use the land for a landfill.*

2____: *To Barbara, then to Barbara's oldest living child.*

3____: *To Carlos, then to Carlos's children.*

4____: *To Darla as long as Darla does not cut the land's timber, then to Emily.*

5____: *To Fred, then to Fred's children when reaching age 18.*

6____: *To Greta, then to the Herman trust.*

7____: *To Irma, then to Irma's children when reaching age 25.*

8____: *To Jane unless the city rezones the land commercial, then to Ken.*

9____: *To Lou, then to Lou's grandchildren.*

10____: *To Mark, then to Neil's living children.*

11____: *To Opal's children when reaching age 30.* (Opal is dead. Her youngest child is age ten.)

12____: *To Peter's children when reaching age 30.* (Peter is alive, youngest child age ten.)

13____: *To Quentin's children when reaching age 30.* (Quentin is dead, youngest child five.)

14____: *To Rand's children when reaching age 30.* (Rand is dead, youngest child age 35.)

STEP TWO: Place a check mark next to the grants where vesting either *may never occur* or *may occur more than twenty-one years after the last currently living person dies*, violating the rule against perpetuities:

2____: *To Barbara, then to Barbara's oldest living child.*

4____: *To Darla if Darla does not use the land for a landfill, then to Emily.*

5____: *To Fred, then to Fred's children when reaching age 18.*

7____: *To Irma, then to Irma's children when reaching age 25.*

8____: *To Jane unless the city rezones the land commercial, then to Ken.*

10___: *To Mark, then to Neil's living children.*

11___: *To Opal's children when reaching age 30.* (Opal is dead. Her youngest child is age ten.)

12___: *To Peter's children when reaching age 30.* (Peter is alive, youngest child age ten.)

13___: *To Quentin's children when age 30.* (Quentin is dead, youngest child age five.)

Answers: 4 7 8 12

The rule against perpetuities' modern form recognizes an exception for **class gifts**. A class gift is to a group, like *to A's children and grandchildren*. The traditional rule against perpetuities follows an *all-or-nothing* rule invalidating the entire grant if invalid for any member of the potential class. A modern *rule of convenience* instead closes the class to new members (typically, children born after the conveyance) when at least one member of the class takes possession of the property. For example, in the grant *to A's children when they reach age 25*, the rule against perpetuities invalidates the grant if A is still alive at the conveyance because A could have after-born children whose interests would vest more than twenty-one years after the grant. However, if adopted in the jurisdiction, the *rule of convenience* would instead close the class gift when A's oldest child reached age 25, so that children born after that date would not share in the gift. Which of the following grants violating the rule against perpetuities would the *rule of convenience* save?

4____: *To Darla if Darla does not use the land for a landfill, then to Emily.*

7____: *To Irma, then to Irma's children when reaching age 25.*

8____: *To Jane unless the city rezones the land commercial, then to Ken.*

12___: *To Peter's children when age 30.* (Peter is alive. His youngest child is age ten.)

Answer: 12

Law recognizes a **merger rule** holding that when a person who owns a vested life estate acquires the vested future interest behind the life estate, the two vested estates merge into one fee-simple title. In which of the following grants would the **merger rule** apply to create one fee-simple title?

14___: *To Rand for life, then to Shirley.*

15___: *To Tina for life, then to Tina and Ursula if living.* (Tina is alive. Ursula is dead.)

16___: *To Venn for life, then to Wanda.* (Venn has purchased Wanda's remainder interest.)

17___: *To Xander for life, then to Yvette if living.* (Xander has purchased Yvette's interest.)

Answers: 15 16

The **rule in Shelley's Case**, in the few states that still recognize it, applies where a life tenant's heirs hold the remainder to the life tenant's present interest, to merge the interests into the life tenant in fee simple absolute. In which of the following grants would the **rule in Shelley's Case** apply to create one fee-simple title?

18___: *To Zeus for life, then to Zeus's children when reaching age 18.*

19___: *To Alma for life, then to Alma's heirs.*

20___: *To Baker for life, then to Baker's heirs having no felony convictions.*

Answer: 19

93

Multiple-Choice Questions with Answer Explanations

611.   The owner of a historic but declining horse racetrack deeded the property to her granddaughter "as long as used for horse racing and then to the historic preservation trust," a national organization established to reclaim declining historic properties of abandoned uses. The jurisdiction's Rule Against Perpetuities treats future interests just as it does other interests. Is the owner's conveyance valid?

A.   Yes because the granddaughter maintains control over the horse-racing condition.
B.   Yes because the trust's interest cannot vest more than 21 years after a life in being.
C.   No because the trust's interest may vest more than 21 years after a life in being.
D.   No because the racetrack is declining, and the granddaughter cannot sustain it.

Answer explanation: Option C is correct because a third party's interest that arises only on the occurrence of a condition subsequent as to a fee-simple holder is merely an executory interest to which the Rule Against Perpetuities applies, not a remainder interest or an interest having a right of entry, which would avoid the Rule. The Rule Against Perpetuities requires that an interest vest or fail within a life in being plus 21 years. The facts provide that the jurisdiction's Rule Against Perpetuities treats future interests just as it does other interests, which would be more like the common law Rule rather than the Rule as modified by the doctrine of cy pres or even abolished, in a modern trend. A future interest cannot follow a defeasible fee because the executory interest may never vest or fail, thus violating the Rule Against Perpetuities. Option A is incorrect because whether the grantee retains control over the condition is not really the law issue. Rather, the issue is whether the conveyance can meet the Rule Against Perpetuities, which it cannot for the reason just given. Option B is incorrect because the granddaughter may leave the property to her heirs who could use the property as a racetrack for decades before stopping that use, when the trust's interest would then vest, well beyond 21 years after a life in being. Option D is incorrect because whether the granddaughter can sustain the racetrack is of no legal bearing. Maybe she can, and maybe she cannot. If she could, then she'd keep it, but if she couldn't, then under the conveyance it would go to the trust. The issue is instead whether the conveyance is valid, which it is not because of the Rule Against Perpetuities.

620.   A matriarch devised her parcel of land to her daughter and her daughter's heirs "so long as the property is used for residential purposes, then to my niece and her heirs." The rest of the matriarch's property passed through the residuary clause of her will to her grandson. The daughter lived on the land until her death, when ownership passed to her husband who resided on the land only a short time before vacating and leasing to a developer to build a shopping center. The matriarch's grandson and the niece both filed quiet title and ejectment actions. Applying common law, how should the court rule as to ownership of the land?

A.   For the daughter's husband.
B.   For the niece.
C.   For the developer.
D.   For the grandson.

Answer explanation: Option D is correct because the common law Rule Against Perpetuities voids an interest that could vest in possession more than 21 years after a life in being. While the matriarch attempted to give her daughter and heirs a fee simple subject to executory interest, the attempted gift to the niece and her successors fails because the niece's interest could vest in possession more than 21 years after the daughter's life. The court will rule for the matriarch's grandson who received a possibility of reverter through the matriarch's residuary clause. Option A is incorrect because when the daughter's husband ceased using the property for residential purposes, the possibility of reverter automatically enacted, taking the interest back to the grandson. Option B is incorrect because after the niece's interest voids, the daughter and her heirs have a fee simple determinable and the landowner a possibility of reverter, which passed to the grandson through the residuary clause. Option C is incorrect because the developer lost the interest when the daughter's husband vacated for the developer to build a shopping center.

672.   A landowner executed and delivered a deed to his niece granting her and her heirs and assigns the land as long as used solely for residential purposes. The deed further provided that if occupants used the land for other than residential purposes, then title to the land would pass to a conservation charity. The landowner soon died, leaving all his real estate interests to his son and remaining assets to his daughter. The jurisdiction's Rule Against Perpetuities treats future estates as it does possessory estates and interests. The landowner's niece and daughter then made a signed and delivered contract to convey fee-simple title to the land to a purchaser. The purchaser subsequently refused to close believing after investigation that the niece and daughter could not convey good title to the land. What result if the niece and daughter sue the purchaser for specific performance?

A.   Purchaser wins because the charity has a valid interest in the land.
B.   Purchaser wins because the son has a valid interest in the land.
C.   Niece and daughter win because the niece alone owns fee-simple interest.
D.   Niece and daughter win because niece and daughter together hold fee-simple interest.

Answer explanation: Option B is correct because the Rule Against Perpetuities requires that an interest vest or fail within a life in being plus 21 years. The facts provide that the jurisdiction's Rule Against Perpetuities treats future interests just as it does other interests, which would be more like the common law Rule rather than the Rule as modified by the doctrine of cy pres or even abolished, in a modern trend. A future interest cannot follow a defeasible fee because the executory interest may never vest or fail, thus violating the Rule Against Perpetuities. Here, the landowner's conveyance violated the Rule Against Perpetuities because the land might at any time outside a life in being plus 21 years revert to the charity because of a non-residential use. Thus, the landowner held a possibility of reverter until he died, after which his son held that interest under the will. Thus, a person holding a possibility of reverter under the Rule must join in any conveyance to ensure marketable title. The son would have to sign the deed to the purchaser for the purchaser to have good title, which the niece and daughter had not assured, making their title not marketable. Option A is incorrect because the Rule Against Perpetuities invalidates the charity's interest as just explained. Option C is incorrect because the niece does not hold the full title but is instead lacking the son's interest in the possibility of reverter. She thus holds only a fee simple determinable, a type of defeasible fee that in this case terminates on use of the land for charity. Option D is incorrect for the same reason and because the daughter holds no interest.

Week 8

Co-Ownership

Short Outline:

Co-tenancies divide ownership interests among two or more persons, *tenant* here *not* referring to leaseholds.
Types of co-tenancies include **tenancies in common** and **joint tenancies**, *grantor language* determining type.
Tenancy in common is a shared fee-simple title that does *not* grant *survivorship rights* in the co-tenants.
  Each of two or more tenants in common owns an *alienable* and *inheritable* share of the property.
  Tenants in common may own *unequal shares* that they may transfer to other owners during life or at death.
    A co-tenant's interest passes at death as the tenant directs in a will or law directs by intestacy.
  Tenants in common, equal or unequal in share, hold **undivided** interests, using all or any part of the property.
  Tenants in common may sell their share so that the remaining co-tenant shares with a new co-tenant.
  Grant *to A and B* creates a tenancy in common, as does *to A and B as tenants in common*.
  Tenants in common may receive interests separately, an owner conveying to a tenant in common with the owner.
Joint tenancy is a co-tenancy of *equal* undivided interests with *rights of survivorship*. Joint tenants own equally.
  If a joint tenant dies, the other joint tenant or joint tenants receive the decedent's interest automatically by law.
  Grant *to A and B as joint tenants* or *to A and B with full rights of survivorship* creates a joint tenancy.
    Grant not indicating intent to create a joint tenancy or survivorship right creates a tenancy in common.
    Joint tenants must have *unity of time, title, interest*, and *possession*, taking at once under the same document.
  A joint tenant may alienate the interest, but doing so severs the joint tenancy, creating a tenancy in common.
A **tenancy by the entireties** is a joint tenancy between married individuals.
  Grant *to A and B as tenants by the entireties* or *to A and B as husband and wife* creates an entireties tenancy.
  Most states presume tenancy by the entireties from grant *to A and B as joint tenants* if A and B are married.
  Divorcing tenants by entireties become tenants in common.
  A creditor of only one spouse cannot reach the spouse's tenancy-by-the-entirety interest.
    Married owners hold entireties property free of claims of creditors of either spouse, but not both spouses.
  Tenants by the entireties cannot transfer their individual interests.
Severance refers to the process, intentional or inadvertent, of converting a joint tenancy into a tenancy in common.
  Severance *destroys the right of survivorship* that accompanies a joint tenancy.
  Joint tenants may agree to sever their joint tenancy, for instance by selling the land and dividing proceeds.
  A conveying joint tenant severs the joint tenancy, the grantee then a tenant in common with the other co-tenants.
  Lease of a joint tenancy does *not*, in most states, sever the joint tenancy in favor of a tenancy in common.
  Conveying to a trustee for one's own benefit, or in some states to one's self, severs the joint tenancy.
Partition involves equitable division of the land to represent each co-tenant's individual interest.
  A court may at the request of any co-tenant impose and enforce partition, if the co-tenants cannot agree.
  Partition may be **in-kind**, physical division, or **by sale** if division is impossible, impractical, or not best interest.
    Co-tenants must divide sale proceeds equitably to represent their individual interests.
Relations among cotenants, whether in-common or joint tenants, involve sharing possession, rent, and duty.
  One co-tenant may not **oust** another, pays rent if the tenant does, but need not o/w pay rent for sole possession.
  Co-tenants share in **rents** received from the premises and may enforce their right to a fair share.
  Co-tenants generally *share expenses*, each having a right to make the other contribute as necessary.
Alienability, descendibility, devisability differ among types of co-tenancy.
  Tenants in common and joint tenants may **alienate** their co-tenancy interest, meaning *transfer* it away.
    Tenants by the entireties cannot transfer their co-tenant interest.
    Tenants in common convey whatever fractional interest they own. Joint tenants convey their equal interest.
  A tenant in common's interest is **descendible**, heirs inheriting, and **devisable**, passed by will.
    A joint tenancy is *not* descendible or devisable because of the right of survivorship in the other co-tenants.
      When a joint tenant dies, the tenancy interest passes by law to the surviving joint tenant or joint tenants.

Long Outline:

Co-tenancy

Another area to address on ownership, after treating present estates and future interests above, involves **co-tenancies** between or among owners. Grantors may divide ownership interests among two or more persons, creating co-tenancies. Co-tenancies come in two different *types*, treated in the following sections. Co-tenancies also involve the *severance* of co-tenancies or their *partition*, each addressed in following sections. Another following section addresses the *relations* of co-tenants in their common use of the property. This part on co-tenancies then ends with rules on *alienability*, *descendibility*, and *devisability*.

Types. The following two sections address **tenancies in common** and **joint tenancies**, as the two types of co-tenancy. As the sections illustrate, one significant distinction between the two types of co-tenancy has to do with *rights of survivorship*, addressing the question of whether a co-tenant's heirs or devisees receive the co-tenant's interest on the co-tenant's death or, instead, the other co-tenant or co-tenants receive the interest. Tenancies in common differ from joint tenancies in other ways, too, such as the ability to form and hold unequal shares, and rights of use and conveyance. As to each type of co-tenancy, the *grantor's language* determines the type of co-tenancy formed. Ensure that you recognize the language that forms each type, while being able to distinguish the survivorship, use, and other rights afforded as to each type.

Tenancy in common. A **tenancy in common** is a type of co-tenancy that does *not* grant *survivorship rights* in the co-tenants. *Tenant*, in this context, does *not* mean one taking under a lease but instead means a co-owner in fee-simple title. Each of two or more tenants in common owns an alienable and inheritable share of the property. In contrast to a joint tenancy, tenants in common may own *unequal shares* that they can freely transfer to other owners either during life or at death by inheritance or will. Because death does not terminate the tenant in common's interest, the interest passes as the tenant directs in a will or law directs by intestacy. Whether tenants in common own equal or unequal shares, all tenants in common have the right to occupy and use all or any part of the property. A tenant in common's ownership interest is an **undivided** interest. Thus, if tenants in common own a home, then each may use any part of the home, even if one tenant owns a one-quarter share and the other tenant owns three quarters.

Either tenant in common may sell their share so that the remaining co-tenant would share with a new tenant in common. Language *from grantor to A and B* creates a tenancy in common, as would more-specific language *to A and B as tenants in common*. Tenants in common may also receive their interests from separate conveyance documents. Thus, a grantor may convey fee-simple title to an owner who then conveys a tenancy in common to a co-tenant with the owner. Either co-tenant may then convey to other co-tenants whose interests arise out of those other conveyance documents. A tenancy in common differs from a joint tenancy in this additional respect, insofar as only a single conveyance document can create a joint tenancy.

Joint tenancy. A **joint tenancy** is a co-tenancy in which two or more co-tenants have equal undivided interests in the property with *rights of survivorship*. Thus, if a joint tenant dies, the other joint tenant or joint tenants receive the deceased joint tenant's interest automatically by operation of law. Joint tenants all have equal rights of the property's use. Unlike in a tenancy in common, joint tenants cannot own unequal shares. Language *from grantor to A and B as joint tenants* or *to A and B with full rights of survivorship* creates a joint tenancy, if the co-tenants have *unity of time*, *title*, *interest*, and *possession*, meaning that they take at precisely the same time, under the same document, with the same interest, and the same right of possession. The conveyance language must indicate the grantor's intent to create rights of survivorship either by saying so or by indicating that the grantees take as joint tenants. A conveyance that does not indicate the intent to create a joint tenancy or rights of survivorship instead creates a tenancy in common. As indicated in the prior section, only a single conveyance document can create a joint tenancy. A joint tenant may alienate, meaning transfer, the joint tenant's interest, but in doing so the joint tenant severs the joint tenancy and creates a tenancy in common.

A **tenancy by the entireties** is a joint tenancy between married individuals. Language *from grantor to A and B as tenants by the entireties*, or *to A and B as husband and wife*, creates a tenancy by the entireties, if A and B are in fact married. Most states also presume a tenancy by the entirety from a grant *to A and B as joint tenants* if A and B are then married. If grantees are not married but receive property in a grant indicating rights of survivorship, then they can be at most joint tenants. If they divorce, then they become tenants in common. An advantage of a tenancy by the entireties over a joint tenancy or tenancy in common is that a creditor of only one spouse cannot in execution reach the spouse's tenancy-by-the-entirety interest. Married couples hold entireties property free from the claims of creditors of either spouse, if the creditor has a claim only against one of the spouses. Creditors whose claims are against both spouses can reach entireties property. Unlike both tenancies in common and joint tenancies, tenants by the entireties cannot convey away their individual interests.

Severance. **Severance** refers to the process, whether intentional or inadvertent, of converting a joint tenancy into a tenancy in common. Severance is significant because it *destroys the right of survivorship* that accompanies a joint tenancy. Joint tenants may agree to sever their joint tenancy, as for instance by agreeing to sell the land and divide the proceeds. Also, one joint tenant may convey away the interest, in doing so severing the joint tenancy and leaving the grantee in a tenancy in common with the other co-tenants who remain joint tenants as to one another. Lease of a joint tenancy does not, in most states, sever the joint tenancy in favor of a tenancy in common. Yet a joint tenant can by other action indicate the intent to sever and in doing so accomplish it, for instance by conveying to a trustee for the co-tenant's own benefit, or in some states, to the co-tenant's self, thus destroying the unity of time and title. Indeed, a conveyance to a trust, trustee, conservator, or other individual would inadvertently destroy the unity of time and title, and sever the joint tenancy, even if the co-tenant had not so intended.

Partition. Tenants in common and joint tenants may at any time seek **partition** of the land. Partition involves equitable division of the land to represent each co-tenant's individual interest. A court may at the request of any co-tenant impose and enforce partition, if the co-tenants cannot agree. Some real property co-tenants can easily divide, while other real property they cannot. Partition may thus be **in-kind**, accomplishing a physical division of the property, or partition may be **by sale** if the court cannot divide the property, division is impractical, or division is not in the co-tenants' best interests. Co-tenants must divide sale proceeds equitably to represent their individual interests.

Relations among cotenants. Co-tenants, whether tenants in common or joint tenants, share the rights of possession and rent, and share in responsibility. One co-tenant may not **oust** another co-tenant from possession. Most jurisdictions do *not* require one co-tenant to pay another co-tenant rent even if the co-tenant has the property's only use *unless* the co-tenant ousts the other co-tenant, in which case the tenant in possession may owe for the other's lost use. Co-tenants share in **rents** received from the premises. Thus, if one co-tenant collects rents but refuses to share, other co-tenants may enforce their right to a fair share. Co-tenants generally *share expenses*, each having a right to make the other contribute as necessary. Thus, if one co-tenant pays real-property taxes, mortgage payments, and reasonably necessary insurance, upkeep, or repair expenses to which other co-tenants refuse to contribute, then the paying co-tenant may enforce a right of contribution.

Alienability, descendibility, devisability. Both tenants in common and joint tenants may **alienate** their co-tenancy interest, meaning sell or otherwise *transfer* it away. By contrast, tenants by the entireties cannot transfer their co-tenant interest. Tenants in common convey whatever fractional interest they hold, whereas joint tenants convey their equal interest. The interest of a tenant in common is also **descendible**, meaning that an heir can inherit the interest, and **devisable**, meaning that the tenant in common can pass the interest to another by will, on the co-tenant's death. By contrast, a joint tenancy is *not* descendible or devisable because of the right of survivorship attendant on a joint tenancy. When a joint tenant dies, the tenancy interest passes by operation of law to the surviving joint tenant or joint tenants.

Fluency Cards
Cover and uncover the response to each prompt until you fluently recall the exact response.

Co-ownership forms

Tenancy in common, joint tenancy, tenancy by the entireties.

Tenancy in common

To A and B. Alienable and inheritable. May own unequal interests, but co-owners share in occupying whole.

Joint tenancy

Must have unity of time, title, interest and possession, with survivorship.

Joint tenancy— formation

To A & B as joint tenants or *to A & B with rights of survivorship* plus unity of time, title, interest, & possession.

Joint tenancy— restrictions

No inheriting possible. Alienating interest severs joint tenancy into tenancy in common.

Tenancy by the entireties

Joint tenancy between married individuals. Most states presume if joint tenancy and married.

Tenancy by the entireties—protections

No alienating interests. Creditor of just one spouse cannot reach any part of the interest.

Co-owner rights

Co-owners share income and expenses. Court may on request partion physically or by sale.

Definitions Worksheet

1. Name the three forms of co-ownership.

    _____

    _____

    _____

2. State grant language creating each of the three forms of co-ownership.

    _____

    _____

    _____

3. What rights distinguish a *tenancy in common* from a *joint tenancy*?

    _____

    _____

    _____

4. What does the law mean by *rights of survivorship*?

    _____

    _____

    _____

5. What else must be present to create a **joint tenancy**, beyond survivorship language?

    _____

    _____

    _____

6. How does a **tenancy by the entireties** differ from a **joint tenancy**?

    _____

    _____

    _____

Please do not review model answers until you have answered all questions fully and conferred with a seatmate to complete, correct, and supplement your answers.

Answer Key to Definitions Worksheet

1.   Name the three forms of co-ownership.

Tenancy in common, joint tenancy, and **tenancy by the entireties**.

2.   State grant language creating each of the three forms of co-ownership.

Any grant creating co-ownership rights can establish a **tenancy in common**, although the simplest form would be *to A and B*. A grant indicating survivorship can create a **joint tenancy**, like *to A and B as joint tenants* or *to A and B with rights of survivorship*. A grant to a married couple indicating survivorship rights creates a **tenancy by the entireties**, like *to A and B as tenants by the entireties, to A and B as joint tenants,* or *to A and B with rights of survivorship*, if A and B are then married.

3.   What rights distinguish a *tenancy in common* from a *joint tenancy*?

While both tenancies provide rights of survivorship, a **tenancy in common** does *not* grant *survivorship rights* in the co-tenants, while a **joint tenancy** *does* grant survivorship rights. Also, tenants in common may own different percentage interests, while joint tenants must hold equal undivided interests.

4.   What does the law mean by *rights of survivorship*?

Right of survivorship means that on the death of one co-tenant, the other co-tenant or co-tenants retain the full co-tenancy interest of the deceased co-tenant. The co-tenancy interest of the deceased co-tenant does not pass by will to devisees or by intestacy to heirs.

5.   What else must be present to create a **joint tenancy**, beyond survivorship language?

A **joint tenancy** must have *unity of time*, *title*, *interest*, and *possession*, meaning that co-tenants take at the same time, under the same document, with the same interest and right of possession. Grant langugage purporting to create a joint tenancy instead creates only a tenancy in common if any of the four unities are absent. Transfers that destroy any of the four unities convert the joint tenancy into a tenancy in common.

6.   How does a **tenancy by the entireties** differ from a **joint tenancy**?

A **tenancy by the entireties** is only between two co-owners who are presently married to one another. Joint tenants need not be married to one another. Also, entireties tenants (the married co-owners) have no right to convey away their separate interests. Joint tenants may convey, although conveyance converts the joint tenancy into a tenancy in common. Also, sole creditors of either entireties tenant cannot reach any part of the entireties property. Creditors may reach joint-tenancy interests.

Co-Ownership Exercises

A **tenancy in common** is co-ownership that does *not* grant *survivorship rights* in the co-tenants. A **joint tenancy** is co-ownership in which two or more co-tenants have equal undivided interests in the property *with rights of survivorship*, if the co-tenants have *unity of time*, *title*, *interest*, and *possession*. A **tenancy by the entireties** is a joint tenancy between married individuals, most states presuming such a tenancy from joint-tenancy language if the co-tenants are married. Working with a seatmate, identify the following grants as **tenancy in common (TIC), joint tenancy (JT),** or **tenancy by the entireties (TBE).**

1_____: *To Arn and Barbara.* (Arn and Barbara are not married to one another.)

2_____: *To Carly and Don with rights of survivorship.* (Carly and Don are not married to one another.)

3_____: *To Emilio and Freda as husband and wife.* (Emilio and Freda are married to one another.)

4_____: *To Gary and Henrietta as joint tenants.* (Henrietta has conveyed her interest to Ingrid.)

5_____: *To Iglesias and June as joint tenants.* (Iglesias and June are married to one another.)

6_____: *To Kirk and Louise with rights of survivorship.* (Kirk and Louise divorced before the grant.)

7_____: *To Mel and Nita as joint tenants, two thirds to Mel and one third to Nita.*

8_____: *To Oliver and Petra with survivorship rights.* (Petra has conveyed her interest to Quincy.)

9_____: *From Raoul to Raoul and Susan as joint tenants.* (Raoul and Susan are not married.)

10_____: *To Tom and Urmine as tenants by the entireties.* (Tom and Urmine are engaged to marry.)

11_____: *To Val, Wendell, and Xavier with full survivorship rights.*

12_____: *To Yul and Zed, 40% each, and 20% to Anna, as joint tenants.*

13_____: *To Bill and Carol with full rights of survivorship.* (Carol has conveyed to her kids.)

Answers: 1TIC 2JT 3TBE 4TIC 5TBE 6JT 7TIC 8TIC 9TIC 10TIC 11JT 12TIC 13TIC

Survivorship Exercises

Survivorship rights mean that the survivor after a joint tenant or tenant by the entireties dies takes the deceased tenant's interest. A joint tenant or tenant by the entireties cannot devise the interest by will or pass the interest to heirs by intestacy. A joint tenant may, however, convey the interest, turning the joint tenancy into a tenancy by the entireties and destroying the survivorship right. A tenant by the entireties cannot convey the interest and so cannot destroy the survivorship right. Tenants in common have no survivorship rights and so can convey, will, or pass interests by intestacy. Identify the party or parties owning what interests.

1. Dan and Earl are joint tenants. Earl dies intestate.

Ownership interests: _____

2. Dan and Earl are joint tenants. Earl conveys to Freda. Earl dies intestate.

Ownership interests: _____

3. Dan and Earl are joint tenants. Earl conveys to Freda. Freda dies intestate.

Ownership interests: _____

4. Dan and Earl are joint tenants. Earl conveys to Freda. Dan dies intestate.

Ownership interests: _____

5. Dan and Erma are tenants by the entireties. Dan dies intestate.

Ownership interests: _____

6. Dan and Erma are tenants by the entireties. Dan conveys to Freda.

Ownership interests: _____

7. Dan and Erma are tenants by the entireties. Dan conveys to Freda. Erma dies intestate.

Ownership interests: _____

8. Dan and Erma are tenants by the entireties. Dan wills to Freda. Dan dies.

Ownership interests: _____

9. Dan and Earl are tenants in common. Dan dies intestate.

Ownership interests: _____

10. Dan and Earl are tenants in common. Dan wills to Freda. Dan dies.

Ownership interests: _____

11. Dan and Earl are tenants in common. Earl conveys to Freda.

Ownership interests: _____

12. Dan and Earl are tenants in common. Earl conveys to Freda. Dan dies intestate.

Ownership interests: _____

Answers: 1Dan 2Dan with Freda as TIC 3Dan with Freda's heirs as TIC 4Dan's heirs with Freda as TIC 5Erma 6Dan with Erma as TBE 7Dan 8Erma 9Dan's heirs with Earl as TIC 10Dan's heirs with Freda as TIC 11Earl with Freda as TIC 12Dan's heirs with Freda as TIC

Examples/Non-Examples Exercises

Working with a seatmate, identify each fact pattern as an example (E) or non-example (N) of the *italicized rule or concept*. Answers are at the end. Generate your own example and non-example.

1.   **Tenants in common**, whether owning equal or unequal shares, have the right to occupy and use all or any part of the property. Tenants in common hold *undivided interests*.

____   Gary, tenant in common with Harriet in an urban walkup, wanted its sunroom to himself but shared.

____   Gary and Harriet, tenants in common in a commercial kitchen, coordinated hours when they each cooked.

____   Gary, subtenant to Harriet in a rented apartment, wanted its sunroom, but Harriet refused to sublease it.

E: _____

N: _____

2.   Married couples hold **entireties property** *free from the claims of creditors of one spouse*, if the creditor holds the claim against only one spouse rather than both of the spouses.

____   Ingrid and Jack, tenants by the entireties in their home, together face the home's mortgage foreclosure.

____   Keith seeks to enforce his tort judgment against Ingrid by execution on Ingrid and Jack's marital home.

____   Midwest Bank seeks to collect Jack's credit-card debt by execution on Ingrid and Jack's marital home.

E: _____

N: _____

3.   *Severance*, whether intentional or inadvertent, converts a **joint tenancy** into a **tenancy in common**, destroying the survivorship right that accompanies a joint tenancy.

____   Norma conveyed her joint tenancy interest in the cabin with Oliver to her daughter Paula.

____   Norma leased her joint tenancy interest in the cabin with Oliver to her daughter Paula.

____   Norma and Oliver agreed to sell the cabin in which they had a joint tenancy, dividing the proceeds.

E: _____

N: _____

4.   **Tenants in common** and **joint tenants** may at any time seek *partition*, equitably dividing interests, with a court imposing and enforcing partition on request if co-tenants cannot agree.

____ Quentin and Rupert agreed Quentin would buy Rupert's interest in their cabin but couldn't agree on price.

____ Quentin wanted Rupert to sell Quentin Rupert's adjacent lot so that Quentin could expand operations.

____ Quentin didn't care whether he bought out Rupert or vice versa but just wanted out of their joint cabin.

E: _____

N: _____

5.   **Partition** may be *in-kind*, physically dividing the property, or partition may be *by sale* if the court cannot divide the property, division is impractical, or division is not in the co-tenants' best interests.

____ Shay and Tina each wanted the other out of their bungalow permanently without relinquishing it.

____ Shay and Tina wished to divide their ranch so that each could own and develop their own portion.

____ Shay and Tina no longer wanted to share their studio flat and just wanted to get their money out of it.

E: _____

N: _____

6.   Co-tenants in a **tenancy in common** or **joint tenancy** *share rights* of possession and rent, *share in responsibility* for expenses, and *may enforce those rights* in court against one another.

____ Unger and Val own a home together in which neither no longer live. Val rents it out for $1,000 a month.

____ Unger and Val own a home together in which Unger no longer lives. Val paid for a needed new roof.

____ Unger and Val each own one half of a duplex. Unger wants to improve his half with wood flooring.

E: _____

N: _____

Answers: 1 EEN; 2 NEE; 3 ENE; 4 ENE; 5 NEE; 6 EEN

Drafting Exercise

Review the **partition-fence agreement** on the next page to answer the following questions:

1. What do you think: do good fences make good neighbors? Or do you find it a little sad or ridiculous that neighbors would have to retain counsel to draft this partition-fence agreement? _____

2. It's just speculation, but what do you think might have caused the necessity for or advisability of this partition-fence agreement? _____

3. The agreement's recitals state that it is to help maintain good relations between the parties. Do you think that they have good relations, or is the agreement an indication that they do not have good relations? _____

4. The agreement recites that it runs with the land, binding future owners. Is that term wise? Why or why not? How could that term affect either property's sale or value? _____

5. Read the paragraph of the agreement on *construction*. This agreement seems mostly to be an agreement to agree. Do you think that the agreement is really that helpful? _____

6. How do you think that these parties will proceed? Will one build the fence, or will they agree and build the fence together? _____

7. The agreement anticipates witnesses and notarization. Is that degree of circumspection overkill for a neighbor agreement? Why or why not? _____

8. If you were the lawyer drafting this agreement, then how would you avoid a conflict of interest in its drafting and execution? _____

9. What if one party builds the fence on the other party's land? How does the agreement address the risk of adverse possession? _____

10. The agreement states that either party may record it. What are the advantages and disadvantages of recording it? _____

PARTITION-FENCE AGREEMENT

This partition-fence agreement is made on January ____, 2018, by _____ whose address is _____ and her adjoining landowner _____ whose address is _____.

RECITALS

The parties to this agreement recite and declare that:

A. This agreement is over a partition fence to be erected on or near the common boundary of the two adjoining properties at the above addresses. Legal descriptions of each property are attached as Exhibit A to this agreement and incorporated here.

B. The maintenance of partition fences is not regulated by statute in the State of Michigan, such former regulations appearing at MCL 43.1 et seq. having been repealed effective October 1, 1978, and such state or local regulation, if any, does not provide a procedure for the construction and maintenance of partition fences sufficient for the parties' needs and does not, by its terms, prohibit a private agreement at variance from it. In the event of the enactment of such a provision, the parties intend that this agreement shall survive it to the extent permitted by such enactment.

C. The parties further desire to bind themselves, their heirs, and their assigns to this agreement for the construction and maintenance of a partition fence so that their properties may be separated by a good and sufficient fence, and they and future owners of their properties will have clearly defined rights and duties with respect to the maintenance of that fence, all to the end that good relations between owners and tenants of the respective properties may be maintained. It is the intention and agreement of the parties that this partition fence agreement shall run with the land and be binding on successors in interest to the adjoining properties.

AGREEMENT

For the reasons set forth above, and in consideration of the mutual covenants contained in this agreement, the parties agree as follows:

Construction. A partition fence shall be constructed along the boundary of the two adjoining properties or along such portion of it to which the two parties agree. The construction of the fence shall be as agreed upon by the parties in writing in a graphic design and to written specifications expressly approved and initialed by the parties, and not to any other design or specifications. The parties shall further agree in a writing, bid, or estimate expressly approved and initialed by the parties, on the cost and manner of construction, following which the parties shall divide equally the cost of such construction so approved. This agreement shall not require either party to advance expenses of construction on the part of the other party, the agreement instead being that each party shall pay its share of the cost of construction directly, but in the event that one party does advance costs or expense in connection with the construction, the other party shall reimburse to that party an equal share of the costs or expenses so advanced. Any party performing such construction or contracting that it be performed shall obtain all necessary building permits and licenses, and shall see that the work is performed by licensed and insured contractors where such licenses and insurance are available to the trades for the work to be performed. Neither party shall be entitled to charge or be reimbursed for their personal time or labor in connection with construction, construction management, or planning or preparation for construction, unless expressly so agreed in writing by the other party.

Maintenance. Once constructed, the partition fence shall be maintained by the parties to its original specifications or as near to those original specifications as law or ordinance and conditions reasonably permit, unless the parties agree to a change in the specifications. Expenses of maintenance shall be shared equally by the parties, provided that neither party shall charge the other for any labor performed by that party with respect to such maintenance, such cost sharing instead being restricted to the sharing of actual out-of-pocket expense for materials and the like. Maintenance may be performed by either party with or without the express permission of the other party, provided that such maintenance shall be performed only by such party and not by contracted service, the intent of this provision being to limit the liability of the other party for the sharing of maintenance expense to actual out-of-pocket expense for materials and the like and not to the cost of contracted service which may include labor costs. Notwithstanding this provision, the parties may agree to have maintenance performed by such contracted service provided that such agreement be in writing and include an agreement with respect to the cost or expense to be shared. In the event that either party shall breach this provision by contracting for and incurring maintenance expense without the agreement of the other party, such first party shall bear the full expense for such contracted service.

PROPERTY I WORKBOOK

Encroachments. Any fence erected pursuant to this agreement shall be erected on the surveyed boundary between the two properties or as close to that boundary as the topography permits. In the latter case that the fence or any portion of it is erected off of the surveyed boundary of the two properties, then there must first be agreement between the parties as to the placement and location of such fence or portion of fence. Further, in the event that the fence or any portion of it is erected off of the surveyed boundary between the two properties, then the erection and maintenance of such fence shall be construed only as a permissive use of the property on which it is located and not as a adverse use or hostile taking of such property. Thus the boundary between the two properties shall remain as surveyed and shall not be changed by the erection or maintenance of any partition fence under this agreement, notwithstanding the erection and maintenance of any partition fence under this agreement for any period of time including that period beyond which actions respecting the taking of lands may be filed in the courts of this state. Each party agrees to permit encroachment by the other party where necessary to the construction or maintenance of the fence, provided that such encroachment shall not exceed that reasonably necessary to the work to be performed and shall not damage the other's property beyond ready repair or interfere with the other's use of the property for any period of time other than that brief period of time incidental to the work to be performed. If such damage shall occur as the result of negligence, the cost of repair shall be borne by the negligent party, but if not by negligence, then the cost of repair after application of any insurance coverage shall be borne equally between the parties.

Miscellaneous. This agreement may, though need not, be recorded by either party. This agreement shall be governed by and construed and enforced in accordance with the laws of the State of Michigan and any local ordinances which may apply. This agreement contains the entire agreement between the parties and is not modified or supplemented by any oral agreement of the parties.

IN WITNESS WHEREOF, each party to this agreement has caused it to be executed under oath at Chelsea, Michigan, on the date(s) indicated below.

WITNESSED: LAND OWNER:

Printed name:

Printed name:

                                                    LAND OWNER:

Printed name:

_____
Printed name:

STATE OF MICHIGAN   )
) ss
COUNTY OF WASHTENAW   )

On this _____ day of January, 2018, before me, a Notary Public in and for said County personally appeared _____ known to me as the same person described in the foregoing Partition Fence Agreement, and acknowledged that she executed this document as her free and voluntary act and deed.

                    Notary Public, Washtenaw County, MI
                    Commission expires:

STATE OF MICHIGAN   )
) ss
COUNTY OF WASHTENAW   )

On this _____ day of January, 2018, before me, a Notary Public in and for said County personally appeared _____, known to me as the same person described in the foregoing Partition Fence Agreement, and acknowledged the execution of this document as a free and voluntary act and deed.

                    Notary Public, Washtenaw County, MI
                    Commission expires:

110

Multiple-Choice Questions with Answer Explanations

613.   A fisherman and hunter bought a cabin on a stream together, accepting and recording a deed that identified them as "tenants in common." Their shared use worked well because the fishing and hunting seasons differed. They fell into disagreement, though, when after several years the cabin's roof began to leak and needed not just repair but replacement. The fisherman refused either to contribute to the work or pay for the roof's replacement. When the hunter paid several thousand dollars for the roof replacement and demanded that the fisherman contribute, the fisherman refused and instead sold his interest on land contract to a writer. The fisherman passed away shortly later, leaving his entire estate to his children who, like the fisherman, demanded the writer's land-contract payments while refusing to pay for the roof's replacement. What interest does the hunter now hold?

A.   Tenant in common with the children who owe contribution for the roof.
B.   Tenant in common with the writer who owes contribution for the roof.
C.   The sole interest subject to a one-half life estate in the writer.
D.   The sole interest free and clear of any interest of the children or writer.

Answer explanation: Option B is correct because a tenancy in common is a tenancy held by two or more persons in equal or unequal shares, each having equal right of possession over the entire property but no right of survivorship. A tenant in common has only concurrent right of possession and can lease that right, but the lessee obtains what the lessor tenant in common conveys, which is a transferable and inheritable right of concurrent possession. Tenants in common owe one another fiduciary duties and duties of contribution. The fisherman's conveyance to the writer was of a transferable and inheritable tenancy-in-common interest. The fisherman's death was of no consequence. Option A is incorrect because the fisherman conveyed his full interest to the writer, not simply a life estate. Options C and D are incorrect because a tenancy in common has no right of survivorship. The fisherman conveyed a transferable and inheritable interest to the writer.

616.   Three unrelated women owned purchased a building together with the grantor deeding the building to them "as joint tenants." For many years, the women treated the building as a literary guild for meetings and events related to books, authors, and publications. One woman sold her interest to a publisher who for several more years worked well with the other two women. Then one of the women passed away, leaving her entire estate to her son who had no interest in literature. What interests do the remaining woman, the publisher, and the son now hold in the building?

A.   The remaining woman owns two thirds as tenant in common with the publisher who owns one third, while the son owns nothing.
B.   The remaining woman owns one half as joint tenant, with the publisher who owns the other half, while the son owns nothing.
C.   The remaining woman owns one third as joint tenant with the publisher who owns one third and the son who owns one third.
D.   The remaining woman owns one third as tenant in common with the publisher who owns one third and the son who owns one third.

Answer explanation: Option A is correct because to create a joint tenancy, which is an interest in which each owner has a right of survivorship, the grantor must satisfy the four unities of time (creating the interest at once), title (all acquiring under one deed), interest (all having equal interest), and possession (all having equal right of possession). The three women held a valid joint tenancy. When one woman conveyed to the publisher, the publisher did not have unity of time and title, so the publisher had a one-third tenancy in common while the other two women each had a one-third joint tenancy. When one woman died, her one-third joint-tenant interest passed to the remaining joint tenant, the other woman, who then had two thirds of the property as tenant in common with the publisher who still had only one third. The son took nothing because his mother joint tenant lost to the other woman who had right of survivorship. Option B is incorrect because the woman who survived took the other woman's interest, thus gaining two thirds, while the publisher had only one third, not one half. Option C is incorrect because the son took nothing, and the publisher was a tenant in common, not a joint tenant, because the publisher did not have unity of time and title. Option D is incorrect because the son took nothing.

618.   A painter and a sculptor together owned a studio apartment in a major metropolitan city. They had purchased the apartment together, accepting and recording a deed identifying them "as joint tenants." While the apartment barely provided room for them both, the substantial amount of time that each spent at galleries, workshops, and studios made the tiny apartment sufficient for their common use. The painter, however, began to sculpt, while the sculptor began to paint, bringing them into competition for galleries, customers, and clients. They found themselves unable any longer to share their tiny studio apartment. If they are unable to reach any agreement, then how could a court action help them proceed to end their apartment ownership-and-use relationship?

A.   Partition by division.
B.   Partition by sale.
C.   Severance by conversion.
D.   Severance by sale.

Answer explanation: Option B is correct because partition occurs by court action, either dividing the real property if possible or ordering its sale if not. Partition by sale appears to be the only viable option because the court could not divide a tiny studio apartment between them. Option A is incorrect because a court could not divide a tiny studio apartment between two owners who are already unable to live together without the court's intervention. Partition by division would not help. Option C is incorrect because severance of a joint tenancy occurs by the owners' agreement to convert to a tenancy in common or by one owner's transfer of the interest to another, or even to one's self (often through straw man). Severing the joint tenancy by conversion simply turns the interests into a tenancy in common, leaving the painter and sculptor still together in the apartment, which solves nothing. Option D is incorrect because while they could sever by one of them selling to others, the challenge would be to find a buyer willing to move into a studio apartment with the remaining owner. Moreover, the question asks how court action could help them. Partition by sale is the appropriate court action.

640.   A real-estate mogul died leaving an office-building property to his only child and a stepchild as joint tenants with right of survivorship. The child and stepchild agreed that the stepchild, who had worked in the mogul's business, would manage the office building. Several years later, the stepchild incurred a $100,000 personal debt on which the creditor recorded a judgment lien against the office building as a state statute permitted. The stepchild died before paying any part of the judgment and before the creditor had attempted to enforce the judgment lien against the office-building property. May the creditor enforce the judgment lien against the office-building property now that the stepchild debtor has died?

A.   Yes because the stepchild debtor had not paid any part of the judgment.
B.   Yes because the devise could only create a tenancy in common, not joint tenancy.
C.   No because the creditor's recording of the judgment lien severed the child's interest.

D.   No because the child became the sole owner of the building at the stepchild's death.

Answer explanation: Option D is correct because joint tenants with rights of survivorship have only a joint interest in the property, a judgment lien or recording of judgment lien would not alone sever that interest, the death of a joint tenant leaves the property with the surviving joint tenant, and one joint tenant does not owe another joint tenant's debts, before or after the death of the debtor joint tenant. The stepchild's death extinguished the creditor's rights, whether by judgment or judgment lien. Option A is incorrect because one joint tenant does not owe another joint tenant's separate debts, whether before or after the debtor joint tenant's death. Option B is incorrect because devises may create joint tenancy if the devise so states and intends. Option C is incorrect because recording of a judgment lien does not sever a joint tenant's interest. The joint tenants continue to share the property interest, although only the debtor tenant remains obligated for the judgment debt. Recording the judgment lien simply secures the creditor's right against the judgment debtor.

643.   An accountant, a psychologist, and a therapist purchased a small office building, taking a deed as tenants in common. The three professionals each took an office suite within the building, while they shared the building's restroom, kitchen, supply room, and lavatory. After four years, the therapist decided to take a year off to travel and so rented out her office suite and access to the restroom, kitchen, supply room, and lavatory, to a masseuse tenant for that one year. Neither the accountant nor psychologist consented to the lease. Both didn't want to share an office building with a masseuse. What result if they sue to evict?

A.   Masseuse evicted because a tenant in common cannot lease without consent.
B.   Masseuse remains in the therapist's office suite while evicted from the other rooms.
C.   Masseuse retains the lease but shares all possession with the accountant and psychologist.
D.   Masseuse retains exclusive possession of the office suite and shares the other rooms.

Answer explanation: Option C is correct because a tenant in common has only concurrent right of possession and can lease that right, but the lessee obtains only what the lessor tenant in common conveys, which at most is a right of concurrent possession. The therapist could lease up to all of her tenancy in common, which would be concurrent use of the whole building, but could not grant exclusive possession of any part of it. Option A is incorrect because a tenant in common can form a lease for a tenant to share all or any part of the tenant in common's concurrent rights of possession. Option B is incorrect because the other tenants in common could not evict the masseuse from the common rooms if as here the therapist had leased that access to the masseuse. Option D is incorrect because while the lease purported to convey use of the office suite to the masseuse, the therapist only had concurrent use of the whole possession and so could not lease exclusive possession to the masseuse.

669.   Two women owned a retail shop as tenants in common, each with an undivided one-half interest. One woman ran the shop, while the other woman conducted her unrelated profession in a distant city. The professional woman sold her interest to a property speculator. The woman who ran the shop soon passed away, leaving to her daughter her entire estate including any interest in the shop. The daughter also ran the shop but over the years so poorly as to fall into arrears on the real-property taxes. Taxing authorities duly arranged for the real property's sale at auction. Seeking to preserve the interest in the property's value, the speculator purchased the shop at auction for an amount sufficient to pay the back taxes. What result if the speculator then filed suit against the daughter to quiet title in the speculator's own name as sole owner of the real property in fee simple?

A.   The speculator wins because he survived his co-tenant, the woman who ran the shop.

B.   The speculator wins because the daughter defaulted in running the shop.
C.   The daughter wins because the professional woman's interest was inalienable.
D.   The daughter wins but only if she pays one-half the amount of the sale at auction.

Answer explanation: Option D is correct because tenants in common have no rights of survivorship. The other woman's interest would pass to her daughter rather than expire. Option A is incorrect because tenants in common have no rights of survivorship and while living would owe one another fiduciary duties and duties of contribution. The daughter took her mother's interest in the shop but would have failed in her fiduciary duty as to taxes and would preserve her half interest as tenant in common only if fulfilling her duty of contribution as to her co-tenant's tax sale payment. Option B is incorrect because default on taxes and breach of fiduciary duty alone would be insufficient to extinguish the interest if the daughter made good on her duty of contribution. Option C is incorrect because the interest of a tenant in common is alienable. The professional woman did not extinguish her interest when selling it to the speculator. The daughter would only have to pay half of the tax-sale amount to preserve the interest.

670.   Brothers owned a cottage in fee-simple title, as equal tenants in common, on inheritance from their parents. One brother lived in the cottage for 25 years, paying the taxes and utilities, collecting occasional rents when renting the cottage out for especially desirable times in the summer, and performing all maintenance and repairs. The other brother, who lived across the country, never visited, contributed to costs, or received rent or other benefit from the cottage. Needing money to pay substantial medical expenses, the distant brother demanded that the brothers sell the cottage. What result if the resident brother refuses, and the distant brother files an action for partition and accounting for the net benefit that the resident brother obtained from 25 years of using the cottage?

A.   Grant partition but provide no accounting or any adjustment for net benefit.
B.   Grant partition and provide an accounting, ordering adjustment for net benefit.
C.   Deny partition but provide an accounting, ordering adjustment for net benefit.
D.   Deny partition, vesting title in the resident brother by adverse possession.

Answer explanation: Option B is correct because tenants in common have rights of both partition and accounting at any time. The court would order adjustment for any net benefit based on the accounting and would attempt to divide the property, or if not feasible, then order sale and equal division of proceeds. Option A is incorrect because tenants in common have the right to both partition and accounting. Options C and D are incorrect because tenants in common have a right to partition at any time. Option D is also incorrect because the resident brother's possession was not adverse but by the knowledge and consent of the distant brother. Adverse possession must be hostile in order for the statute to apply. Tenants in common who consent to equitable use are not hostile.

673.   A brother and sister owned a suburban bungalow together as joint tenants with full rights of survivorship, which they had inherited from their uncle. They sometimes lived alone in it, sometimes lived in it together, and occasionally rented it out, always by agreement. Later in life, though, their lifestyles and family arrangements changed, and they fell into sharp disagreement over its use. The brother wanted his adult daughter to have the bungalow's use, while the sister wanted to use it as a getaway for her recreational drug use. The brother even wrote out an agreement with his adult daughter that she would have free use of the bungalow at any time she wished. The sister, though, would visit and disrupt the daughter's enjoyment of the bungalow anytime that the sister learned that the daughter was there. The brother died suddenly. What action, if any, must the sister take to improve and perfect her position with respect to the bungalow's ownership and control, to be able to exclude the daughter?

A.   No action because the brother is no longer around to protect the daughter.
B.   No action because ownership passed by operation of law at the brother's death.
C.   File suit to quiet title in the sister, confirming her right of survivorship.
D.   Negotiate a conveyance by quitclaim from the brother's estate or the daughter.

Answer explanation: Option B is correct because a transfer of real property can occur by operation of law rather than only by agreement or court order. A joint tenant obtains full title to real property when the other joint tenant dies, without the necessity of court action. Option A is incorrect because whether the brother is around to protect isn't the question. The daughter could presumably protect herself by taking legal action if she had the right, but the daughter has no rights because the brother died, leaving ownership in the sister by operation of law. Option C is incorrect because the daughter has not raised and cannot raise a genuine dispute over title. The sister has no need to quiet title. The sister has sole title free and clear of any claim by the brother's estate or the daughter. If the estate or daughter made such a claim, then a counterclaim to quiet title would be appropriate. Option D is incorrect because negotiations are unnecessary. The title passed by operation of law at the brother's death. Voluntary agreement to convey is unnecessary and, in any case, unlikely under these circumstances.

Week 9
Marital Estates

Short Outline:

Most states have common-law marital property, but ten states have community property systems.
  In theory, common-law marital property means separate marital estates, while community means one estate.
  The difference is much less significant today. Most states treat property acquired during the marriage as marital.
    Before-marriage property commingled during marriage can also become marital property.
    Degrees earned or licenses obtained during marriage are likely not marital property but may warrant support.
    Property received as gift or by inheritance during the marriage remains separate property.
Common-law marital property distinguishes rights during marriage, on divorce, and at death.
  Sole creditors of one spouse cannot reach property two spouses hold together as tenants by the entireties.
    Most states recognize tenancies by the entirety as to personal property, too, not just real property.
    Divorce converts a tenancy by the entirety into a tenancy in common.
    Federal tax liens attach to one spouse's interest in entireties property.
    Federal forfeiture law permits attachment only as to the criminally responsible spouse's survivorship interest.
      The criminally responsible spouse may have had to use the property for the criminal activity.
Nearly all states have abolished dower rights of a wife and curtesy for a husband after death of the other spouse.
  Where dower survives, the wife obtains a life estate of a portion of the deceased husband's lands.
    The key, though, is to simply have both husband and wife sign deeds no matter who holds formal title.
  States also have elective-share or forced-share statutes.
    A surviving spouse may take a statutory portion of the deceased spouse's estate no matter what the will said.
Community marital property treats property acquired and accumulated during marriage as owned equally.
  Neither spouse may sell community property without the other's consent, like entireties property.
    But either spouse *may* dispose of their half of community property by will at death, *unlike* entireties property.
    Either spouse may manage community marital property but only to benefit both spouses.
      Creditors of only one spouse may reach only the portion that spouse manages and controls.
For spouses moving between common-law/community-property states, property remains as initially characterized.
Unmarried couples depend on contract rights, not community-property theories.

Long Outline:

  How law treats the personal and real property of married couples depends on whether the state is a **common-law marital property** state or a **community marital property** state. Forty states including Michigan and New York have common-law marital property, but ten states including California and Texas have community property. In grand theory, common-law marital property means separate marital estates, husband and wife each owning that which they earn or acquire and hold in their own name. In grand theory, community property means one estate, husband and wife owning together everything that either earns or acquires during the marriage, no matter how they title the property. The difference, though, is much less significant today, at least in the event of divorce, which is one of the main events where the forms once made a bigger difference.

  Common-law marital property distinguishes rights during marriage, on divorce, and at death. During marriage, sole creditors of one spouse cannot reach real property that two spouses hold together as tenants by the entireties. Most states recognize tenancies by the entirety as to personal property, too, not just real property. During marriage, federal tax liens do attach to one spouse's interest in entireties property but not to the interest of the other spouse who did not owe the tax obligation. The IRS typically waits until the property's sale or until divorce to foreclose the lien on the owing spouse's interest. Federal forfeiture law permits attachment only as to the criminally responsible spouse's survivorship interest. Indeed, the criminally responsible spouse may have had to use the property for the criminal activity for the attachment to work at all.

Divorce, though, severs the tenancy by the entireties, which can only exist between spouses. Divorce converts a tenancy by the entirety into a tenancy in common. Today, in divorce cases, most common-law states treat property acquired during the marriage as *marital property*—in effect, like a community-property state would treat the property. Law in most states presumes that *each spouse gets half* of property earned or acquired during marriage. Indeed, property that either spouse brings into the marriage may also become marital property if *commingled* with other marital property rather than held separately. Degrees earned or licenses obtained during marriage are not marital property in most states but may warrant additional spousal support for the other spouse lacking equal earning power. Property received as gift or by inheritance during the marriage remains separate property.

Nearly all states have abolished dower rights of a wife and curtesy rights of a husband after death of the other spouse. Where they exist, dower and curtesy rights protect the surviving spouse's interest on the other spouse's death. Where dower survives, the wife obtains a life estate of a portion of the deceased husband's lands. Dower and curtesy rights can also protect a spouse from the other spouse conveying away property on which the non-conveying spouse may depend. Spouses may, though, relinquish their dower and curtesy rights. The key, then, to avoiding dower and curtesy problems in the chain of title is to have both husband and wife sign deeds as either of them conveys away property, no matter who holds formal title to the property.

States also have elective-share or forced-share statutes that protect a surviving spouse when the deceased spouse has willed away to others, property that the surviving spouse deems necessary for that spouse's continuing support. Under an elective-share statute, the surviving spouse may take a statutory portion of the deceased spouse's estate, often one third or one half, no matter what the decedent's will provided. Some states require the electing spouse to relinquish anything that the will would otherwise have provided to them, but other states let the spouse keep willed property and add to it the elective share.

Community marital property treats property acquired and accumulated during marriage as owned equally in undivided shares. Property that either spouse owned separately before the marriage remains separate property. During the marriage, neither spouse may sell community property without the other's consent, like entireties property. But either spouse *may* dispose of their half of community property by will at death, *unlike* entireties property. Either spouse may manage and control community marital property but only to benefit both spouses, in effect acting as a fiduciary for the other spouse. Creditors of only one spouse may reach only the portion of community property that spouse manages and controls. For spouses moving between common-law and community-property states, property remains as initially characterized when either spouse acquired it. If it was originally separate property under that state's law, then it remains separate property even if the state to which the spouses move would have characterized it as marital property. Unmarried couples depend on contract rights, not community-property theories.

Fluency Cards
Cover and uncover the response to each prompt until you fluently recall the exact response.

Marital property	**Separate property**
Earned or acquired during marriage.	Before marriage or by gift or inheritance during marriage.
Common-law marital property	**Community marital property**
Separate estates in most states but often treated as one marital estate in divorce.	Single estate in ten states for all property earned or acquired during marriage.
Tenancy by the entirety issues	**Dower and curtesy**
Federal tax liens and forfeiture attach only to owing spouse's interest.	Nearly all states abolish rights of surviving spouse to life estate in part of property.
Elective share	**Community property**
Statutes permit surviving spouse to take third or half share against will.	Can't sell without other spouse's consent but can dispose half interest by will.

Definitions Worksheet

(Answers are on the next page.)

1. Distinguish *common-law marital property* from *community property*.

    _____

    _____

2. How do most common-law property states treat property on divorce?

    _____

3. How does law treat property brought into the marriage or gifted or inherited?

    _____

4. How does law treat degrees earned or licenses obtained during marriage?

    _____

5. How does law treat federal tax liens against one spouse?

    _____

6. How does law treat federal civil forfeiture against one spouse?

    _____

7. What are *dower* and *curtesy*? Does either right survive today in law?

    _____

8. How does an *elective-share* statute operate?

    _____

9. What happens to a surviving spouse's bequest when electing a forced share?

    _____

10. What interest does each spouse own or hold in *community marital property*?

    _____

11. What happens to community marital property at a spouse's death?

    _____

12. What use may either spouse make of community marital property?

    _____

13. What rights do unmarried couples have to the other's property?

    _____

Please do not review model answers until you have answered all questions fully and conferred with a seatmate to complete, correct, and supplement your answers.

Answers to Definitions Worksheet

1. **Common-law marital property** means separate marital estates, husband and wife each owning that which they earn or acquire and hold in their own name. **Community property** means one estate, husband and wife owning together everything that either earns or acquires during the marriage, no matter how they title the property.

2. In divorce, most common-law states treat property acquired during the marriage *as marital property*—in effect, like a community-property state would treat the property. Law in most states presumes that *each spouse gets half* of property earned or acquired during marriage.

3. Property that either spouse brings into the marriage remains separate property unless *commingled* with other marital property. Property received as **gift** or by **inheritance** during marriage remains separate property.

4. Most states do *not* treat degrees earned or licenses obtained during marriage as marital property. On divorce, though, degrees and licenses may warrant additional spousal support for the other spouse lacking equal earning power.

5. **Federal tax liens** attach to one spouse's interest in entireties property but not to the interest of the other spouse who did not owe the tax obligation. The IRS typically waits until the property's sale or for divorce to foreclose the lien on the owing spouse's interest.

6. Federal **forfeiture** law permits attachment only as to the criminally responsible spouse's survivorship interest. The criminally responsible spouse may have had to use the property for the criminal activity for attachment to work.

7. Nearly all states have *abolished* dower rights of a wife and curtesy rights of a husband after death of the other spouse. Where they exist, dower and curtesy rights protect the surviving spouse's interest on the other spouse's death, typically preserving a life estate of a portion of the deceased spouse's lands.

8. States have **elective-share** or forced-share statutes to protect a surviving spouse when the deceased spouse has willed away to others property that the surviving spouse deems necessary for that spouse's continuing support. The surviving spouse may take a statutory portion of the deceased spouse's estate, often one third or one half, no matter what the decedent's will provided.

9. Some states require the electing spouse to relinquish anything that the will would otherwise have provided to them. Other states let the spouse keep willed property and add to it the elective share.

10. **Community marital property** treats property acquired and accumulated during marriage as owned equally in undivided shares. During the marriage, neither spouse may sell community property without the other's consent, like entireties property.

11. Either spouse *may* dispose of their half of community property by will at death, *unlike* entireties property.

12. Either spouse may manage and control community marital property but only to benefit both spouses, in effect acting as a fiduciary for the other spouse. Creditors of only one spouse may reach only the portion of community property that spouse manages and controls.

13. Unmarried couples depend on contract rights, not community-property theories. They must prove an express, or in some states an implied, contract if they wish to claim any interest in property that the other person earned or acquired during their relationship.

Application Exercises
(Answers and explanations are on the next page.)

Distinguish whether husband (H) or wife (W) receives the property, they divide it (D), or creditor (C) receives the property:

1____ Husband brings home to the marriage. Husband and wife divorce five years later.

2____ Wife brings motor vehicle to the marriage. Husband and wife divorce one year later.

3____ Husband in common-law state earns $100,000 bonus. Wife claims half during marriage.

4____ Wife in community-property state buys cottage with her earnings. Husband claims half.

5____ Husband earns $100,000 bonus during marriage. Husband and wife divorce year later.

6____ Wife buys furniture with earnings during marriage. Husband and wife divorce year later.

7____ Husband buys sports vehicle with earnings during marriage. Husband and wife divorce.

8____ Wife inherits lake cottage during marriage. Husband and wife divorce ten years later.

9____ Husband inherits $1 million in securities during marriage. Husband and wife divorce.

10____ Wife receives $13,000 cash gift during marriage. Husband and wife divorce.

11____ Husband earns law degree during marriage. Wife claims half of degree in divorce.

12____ Wife obtains medical license during marriage. Husband claims half of license in divorce.

13____ IRS records lien on home for husband's unpaid income tax. Husband claims half on sale.

14____ IRS records lien on home for husband's unpaid income tax. Wife claims half on sale.

15____ FBI seeks forfeiture on land where husband grew pot. Husband dies, willing all to wife.

16____ FBI seeks forfeiture on land where husband grew pot. Wife dies, willing all to husband. C: civil forfeiture attaches to criminally responsible spouse's survivorship interest.

17____ In dower state, husband dies, leaving his home to girlfriend. Wife claims life estate.

18____ In curtesy state, wife dies, leaving her cottage to boyfriend. Husband claims life estate.

19____ Husband conveys marital home to creditor, in community-property state. Wife objects.

20____ Wife conveys stock account to creditor, in community-property state. Husband objects.

21____ Husband wills half of home to creditor, in community-property state. Wife claims whole home on husband's death.

22____ Wife wills whole home to creditor, in community-property state. Husband claims half of home on wife's death.

23____ Unmarried partner conveys partner's property to creditor, in community-property state. Other partner claims half of property.

Answers and Explanations to Application Exercises

1 H   Property acquired before marriage remains separate property.

2 W   Property acquired before marriage remains separate property.

3 H   Common law states treat property earned or acquired during marriage as separate.

4 W   Common law states treat property earned or acquired during marriage as separate.

5 D   Most states treat property acquired in marriage as marital property to divide in divorce.

6 D   Most states treat property acquired in marriage as marital property to divide in divorce.

7 H   Most states treat property acquired in marriage as marital property to divide in divorce.

8 W   Gifts and inheritances during marriage remain separate property.

9 H   Gifts and inheritances during marriage remain separate property.

10 W   Gifts and inheritances during marriage remain separate property.

11 H   Most states treat degrees as separate property but may adjust support on earning disparity.

12 W   Most states treat degrees as separate property but may adjust support on earning disparity.

13 C   Tax liens attach only to the owing spouse's half.

14 W   Tax liens attach only to the owing spouse's half.

15 W   Civil forfeiture attaches only to the criminally responsible spouse's survivorship interest.

16 C   Civil forfeiture attaches to the criminally responsible spouse's survivorship interest.

17 W   Dower rights protect a life-estate interest in the surviving wife.

18 H   Curtesy rights protect a life-estate interest in the surviving husband.

19 W   A spouse may not convey community property without the other spouse's consent.

20 H   A spouse may not convey community property without the other spouse's consent.

21 C   A spouse may convey that spouse's half of community property by will.

22 H   A spouse may only convey that spouse's half of community property by will.

23 C   Unmarried couples have no interest in the other partner's property other than by contract.

Drafting Exercise

Review the **antenuptial agreement** on the next page to answer the following questions:

1. Why do prospective spouses *with* substantial property propose antenuptial agreements? _____

2. Why do prospective spouses *without* substantial property entertain entering into antenuptial agreements with spouses who do have substantial property? _____
_____

3. Would you advise any client *without* property to enter into an antenuptial agreement with a spouse who *has* substantial property? Why or why not? _____
_____

4. If you advised a property-less client against entering into an antenuptial agreement with a propertied spouse, but your client intended to proceed with the agreement anyway, then would you document your advice? Why or why not? _____
_____

5. Articulate reasons why two prospective spouses, each with substantial property having approximate value of the other spouse's property, might still enter into an antenuptial agreement. _____
_____

6. Which party, the propertied spouse or property-less spouse, does the antenuptial agreement on the next page favor? Why? _____
_____

7. Why does the antenuptial agreement on the next page recite that the parties have made a full disclosure of their property? _____
_____

8. The agreement does not recite that the parties made a full disclosure of their debts? Should it require that disclosure, too? Why or why not? _____
_____

9. How should each party make its disclosure of property? _____
_____

10. If you were this agreement's drafter, then would you have the parties each attach a schedule of their assets and debts, instead of just saying that they each disclosed? Why or why not? _____
_____

ANTENUPTIAL AGREEMENT

This agreement is made on [fill in date of signing] _____. This agreement is between the prospective wife Cheryl Hamm, 116 Grandmont Avenue, St. Croix, MI 49227, and prospective husband Gary Cartel, of the same address.

The prospective husband and wife agree that: 1) they intend to marry; 2) they each own property and owe debts the full nature and approximate value of which they have disclosed to each other; 3) they desire to retain their respective property rights in property currently owned and debts currently owed by each; 4) they desire to jointly share property acquired after marriage; 5) they each desire to release certain marital property rights in property owned by the other and for contribution as to debts owed by the other. For these and other good reasons, and in consideration of the mutual covenants made in this agreement, the prospective husband and wife agree one with the other as follows:

SECTION ONE: GRANT OF LIFE ESTATES: Prospective husband and wife each grant to the other a life estate in all property, real and personal, that each now owns or will acquire before marriage as separate property. The life estate entitles the surviving spouse to hold, use, and receive the income from the property until the death of the survivor. The property then passes to the estate of the granting spouse for distribution to his or her heirs or distributees, as directed by the granting spouse.

SECTION TWO: RELEASE OF MARITAL PROPERTY RIGHTS: The parties each waive and release all right, title, and interest that each may acquire by operation of law upon the solemnization of the marriage, to that property which is the separate property of the other spouse before the date of the marriage. The parties recognize that property as the separate property of the other spouse.

SECTION THREE: RELEASE OF MARITAL RIGHTS TO CONTRIBUTIONS: The parties each waive and release all rights that each may acquire by operation of law upon the solemnization of the marriage, to have the other contribute to the payment of the separate debts of the other accrued before the date of the marriage. The parties recognize those debts as the separate obligation of the other spouse.

SECTION FOUR: AFTER-ACQUIRED PROPERTY: All property acquired by either prospective husband or wife or both of them after the solemnization of the marriage, whether real or personal, is jointly owned property of the parties as tenants by the entireties, including all rents, issues, profits, and proceeds of the property.

SECTION FIVE: EFFECTIVE DATE OF AGREEMENT: This agreement becomes effective upon the solemnization of the marriage between the parties and is null and void if the marriage fails to occur for any reason.

SECTION SIX: SUBSEQUENT DOCUMENTS: Prospective husband and wife will execute and deliver any other instruments or documents necessary or convenient to give effect to the provisions of this agreement.

SECTION SEVEN: AMENDMENT, MODIFICATION, OR RESCISSION: This agreement may be modified, amended, or rescinded at any time after the solemnization of the marriage between the parties by a written agreement between them.

SECTION EIGHT: FULL DISCLOSURE BY PARTIES: Each of the parties has made a full disclosure to the other party of all property owned or otherwise held by each of them.

SECTION NINE: REPRESENTATION BY COUNSEL: The parties acknowledge that they have been represented by separate counsel of their choice or that they were advised of the right to be represented by such separate counsel of their choice, in the preparation, consideration, and execution of this agreement, that their rights in the property and debts affected by this agreement have been fully explained to them to their satisfaction, that the legal effect of this agreement has been explained to them to their satisfaction, and that they understand the terms, provisions, and legal effect of this agreement.

IN WITNESS WHEREOF, the parties have executed and delivered this agreement on the date indicated above.

_____   _____
Gary Cartel, Prospective husband   Cheryl Hamm, Prospective wife

_____   _____
Witness   Witness

_____   _____
Witness   Witness

There came before me on this date, Gary Lee Heslet, the above prospective husband, and Cheryl Lynn Humbarger, the above prospective wife, known or proven to me to be those persons, who were both sworn, and then who voluntarily executed and delivered this agreement.

_____
Petra Czyczk, Notary Public
Isabella County, Michigan.
My commission expires: 06/09/19

Multiple-Choice Questions with Answer Explanations

708.   Husband and wife remained married for twenty years before determing to divorce. Husband owned a cottage before and throughout the marriage. Husband also received a $100,000 work bonus during the marriage that he placed in his own brokerage account. Wife bought shares in a technology company during the marriage with her own earnings. Wife also owned a collector vehicle before and throughout the marriage. How is a court most likely to treat these properties in a division in the divorce?

A.   Husband keeps cottage and bonus, while wife keeps shares and vehicle.
B.   Husband keeps cottage, husband and wife split bonus and shares, and wife keeps vehicle.
C.   Husband keeps bonus, husband and wife split cottage and vehicle, and wife keeps shares.
D.   Husband and wife split cottage, bonus, shares, and vehicle.

Answer explanation: Option B is correct because in divorce, each spouse keeps separate property owned before the marriage and brought into the marriage, while spouses share property earned or acquired during the marriage. Option A is incorrect because the husband must share the bonus earned during the marriage, and the wife must share the shares she bought from earnings during the marriage. Option C is incorrect because husband would not split the cottage he owned before the marriage, and wife would not share the vehicle she owned before the marriage, while both would split the bonus and shares that they earned and acquired during the marriage. Option D is incorrect because husband would not split the cottage he owned before the marriage, and wife would not share the vehicle she owned before the marriage.

709.   A husband received a gift of an expensive watch from his college roommate. The husband also received a bequest of a valuable firearms collection when his brother passed away. The husband's wife received a gift of valuable heirloom jewelry from her mother. The wife also received a devise of family ranchlands when her father passed away. The husband and wife each titled and held these properties separately during the rest of their marriage.   When they subsequently divorced, how would the court most likely divide these properties?

A.   Husband and wife spit equally the value of the watch, firearms, jewelry, and ranchlands.
B.   Husband and wife split the value of the watch and jewely, while husband keeps firearms and wife keeps ranchlands.
C.   Husband and wife split the value of the firearms and ranchlands, while husband keeps watch and wife keeps jewelry.
D.   Husband keeps watch and firearms, while wife keeps jewelry and ranchlands.

Answer explanation: Option D is correct because gifts, bequests, and devises received during marriage remain separate property rather than becoming marital property like earnings or things acquired from earnings. Husband keeps his gifted watch and bequested firearms, while wife keeps her gifted jewelry and devised ranchlands. Options A, B, and C are incorrect because each keeps separate their gifts, bequests, and devises received during the marriage.

710.   Husband purchased a rental property with earnings during the marriage. Husband and wife used the rental property's earnings to help supplement their incomes and sustain their modest lifestyle. Husband then fell into gambling debt at a casino. To satisfy his debt, husband conveyed the rental property to the casino. When the wife learned of the conveyance, she

promptly challenged it with a quiet-title action against the casino in a proper court. What would the outcome be if husband and wife were domiciled throughout in a community-property state?

A.   Wife wins because husband could not convey without wife's consent.
B.   Wife wins because gambling debt is unenforceable by assignment.
C.   Casino wins because husband bought and owned the rental property.
D.   Casino wins because wife lacks the legal capacity to sue.

Answer explanation: Option A is correct because in community-property states, one spouse may not convey community property without the other's consent. Community property includes anything that either spouse earns or acquires from earnings during the marriage. Option B is incorrect because gambling debts owed to lawfully operated entities like an established casino are enforceable by ordinary means including assignments of assets. Wife would win but for the above reason that the rental was community property. Option C is incorrect because the wife, not the casino, would win for the above reason. Community property includes anything earned or purchased with earnings during the marriage. Option D is incorrect because a wife has capacity to sue just like a husband would have capacity. The wife also here has standing because of her community-property interest.

711.   Wife acquired a business out of earnings during her marriage and then employed her siblings in the business. After operating the business for many years without her husband's assistance, the wife willed the business to her employee siblings. The husband learned of the devise shortly later when his wife died. If the husband challenges the devise in the proper probate proceeding, then what interest will he likely establish, if any?

A.   A joint-tenancy interest with the siblings.
B.   No interest in the business.
C.   A half interest in the business.
D.   The whole interest in the business.

Answer explanation: Option C is correct because community property includes anything earned or acquired from earnings during the marriage, and spouses holding community property may will only their half of the community-property interest, not the other half owned by their spouse. The wife could will only half of the business, leaving the other half as the husband's community-property interest. Option A is incorrect because the will and death converts the decedent spouse's community-property interest into a one-half interest subject to passing by will, rather than a joint-tenancy interest. The wife and siblings would not have unity of time, title, possession, or interest required to form a joint tenancy. Option B is incorrect because a spouse owning a community-property interest retains that interest when the other spouse dies. The decedent spouse may have willed only that spouse's half interest. Option D is incorrect because a spouse owning community property may pass by will that spouse's one-half interest.

712.   A man moved in with a woman who owned a luxurious mansion that she had long prior purchased and continued to maintain with dividends paid to her from her family's large business. The man and woman cohabited as if married, although they were not married. For a decade, the man provided substantial household and personal services to the woman. The woman did not reciprocate in services but did allow the man to enjoy the full benefit of the mansion and her love, society, and companionship. At one point, the man and woman agreed that the woman would buy the man a sharp-looking sportster if he would use it to run household errands, which he did, although the woman kept the sportster titled in her own name. Years later, the woman kicked the man out for excessive drinking. What is the likely result if the man sues for the sportster and half the mansion?

A.   The man gets only half the mansion, not the sportster.
B.   The man gets only the sportster, not half the mansion.
C.   The man gets both the sportster and half the mansion.
D.   The man gets nothing.

Answer explanation: Option B is correct because unmarried couples generally have no interest in the other partner's property other than by contract. Community-property protections apply only to married couples, not cohabiting partners. Here, the facts suggest no agreement between the man and woman relative to the woman's mansion. On the other hand, the facts clearly state that the man and woman agreed that the woman would buy the man the sportster if he would use it to run errands, which he did. The man may enforce that agreement despite the woman's title. Option A is incorrect because the man and woman had no agreement for the manion but did have an agreement for the sportster. Option C is incorrect because the man and woman had no agreement for the mansion. Option D is incorrect because the man and woman agreed as to the sportster, and the man completed his part of the bargain.

Week 10
Land-Sale Contracts

Short Outline:

Contracts for the sale of land follow contract law but also address unique or unusual issues.

Real estate brokerage involves a **broker** or *agent* representing seller, buyer, or both, under **listing agreement**.

The listing agent assumes the duty to list, show, and sell the land, the seller paying a percentage *commission*.

Listing agents earn the commission if sale occurs during the agreement's term, split with buyer's agent.

Seller and buyer may consult lawyers for a land sale contract or use a standard form broker prepares.

Some listing agreements require commission if a contract forms, others only when the sale closes.

If seller refuses to perform the sale contract with a willing buyer, then the seller owes the commission.

Creation and construction: seller & buyer form a *purchase contract, purchase agreement,* or *land sale contract.*

Statute of frauds requires that contracts transferring interests in land be *in a writing signed* by the charged party.

A *purchase agreement* anticipates a later closing weeks or months following the agreement's execution.

Buyer prepares and presents a signed purchase agreement, constituting the buyer's offer.

If seller accepts, then seller countersigns the offer and delivers the completed agreement to the buyer.

Seller countersigning but not delivering, and not notifying buyer, would not complete the agreement.

If seller counteroffers presenting countersigned but modified agreement, then buyer must sign and deliver.

Part performance can take a contract out of the statute of frauds: possession with part payment acknowledged.

Where buyer makes no payment, some states may accept buyer *improving* the land as *detrimental reliance.*

Possession alone is not enough to take the transaction out of the statute of frauds.

Essential terms must be in the land sale contract or it will ordinarily be unenforceable.

Essential terms *identify seller and buyer.* Identifying buyer's agent for *unidentified principal* is sufficient.

Essential terms provide *description*, ordinarily metes and bounds, but address is enough if no ambiguity.

Metes-and-bounds description controls over reference to different number of acres.

Essential terms include **price** or objective means of calculating price, agreement to agree *not* sufficient.

Other essential terms arise only if intended, like *financing, inspection,* and *attorney-review contingency.*

Parties benefitting from contingencies must exercise them in **good faith**, not to alter or avoid the agreement.

Time for performance involves setting a *closing date* when seller exchanges deed for payment.

Buyer needs time to complete contingencies, while seller needs to pack and move.

When contingencies reveal defects, the parties may adjust the sale price.

The **closing date** requires both sides to perform as *time of the essence*, failure voiding the contract at election.

Remedies for breach of land sale contracts follow remedies for breach of other contracts.

Parties may *rescind* and seek *damages* when the other party fails to close or may seek *specific performance.*

Specific performance requires seller to convey deed and possession or buyer to pay the purchase price.

Specific performance may require seller to vacate, provide keys or other access, and remove equipment.

If seller refuses to execute a deed, then buyer may obtain the court's recordable order conveying title.

When a party breaches some other term or condition of transfer, the non-breaching party may sue for damages.

Damages include additional expense or consequential and foreseeable losses.

Land sale contracts may provide for liquidated damages, such as seller overstaying, charged at $100 per day.

Closing agreements, releases, and merger may not prevent the buyer from later claiming the seller's fraud.

Marketability of title: land sale contracts routinely require that the seller convey **marketable title**.

Law *implies* a *promise* or *warranty* of marketable title in the absence of an express term.

Marketable title is title that reasonable persons would not doubt validity and third parties would not challenge.

Sellers conveying title that reasonable persons would reject due to impending challenges breach the warranty.

Buyers may pursue one of the above remedies including rescission and damages, or specific performance.

Specific performance may include that the seller act to clear title, including paying just claims.

Sellers convey marketable title showing good **chain of title** reflecting seller's clear ownership.

Real-property records enable seller, buyer, lawyer, or title company to complete a **title search**.

A seller may instead prove good title by adverse possession, requiring *court judgment* as recordable order.

Common law does not require sellers to disclose other defects and conditions beyond marketable title.

The rule of *buyer beware* requires buyers to exercise the inspection contingency with *due diligence.*

Many states today require residential sellers to disclose certain defects, using *statutory disclosure forms.*

Law today may also require seller to disclose defects seller knew but not apparent to buyer on inspection.

Law also prohibits seller from *actively concealing* defects to frustrate the buyer's discovery.

Breaches of these duties may give rise to fraud remedies including rescission and damages for lost bargain.

Equitable conversion holds equitable interest to transfer to buyer *on land-sale-contract execution.*

The traditional doctrine passes the risk of interim loss or gain *to the buyer* who holds equitable ownership.

Equitable conversion enables court to adjust rights and duties to reflect changes between contract and close.

Some states alter equitable conversions' *risk-of-loss* rule so that the seller retains the risk until the closing date.

If either party is *responsible* through deliberate act or carelessness for the loss, then that party bears the loss.

Fire, flood, or other loss insurance adjusts rights and responsibilities for the best and fairest outcome.

Options: seller and buyer may form an **option contract** for the sale of land to keep an offer open for a period.

An *option contract* must ordinarily have consideration, although nominal consideration is traditionally enough.

An option contract must be in a writing signed by the charged party, to satisfy the *statute of frauds.*

Buyer may exercise the option at any time during the period, while seller *cannot revoke the offer* until expiration.

Option contracts must state the *sale price* or a reliable way of calculating a certain price, as an essential term.

Option-contract breach gives the buyer alternative remedies of specific performance or damages.

Rights of first refusal, instead of stating an option sale price, require seller to present to buyer third-party offers.

The buyer may match the offer, requiring seller to sell under the right of first refusal.

When seller presents third party's good-faith offer, buyer must buy or lose the property and right of first refusal.

One typically finds rights of first refusal in leases or other relationships closer than an arm's length.

Fitness and suitability: law implies a **fitness** warranty for residential sales / **suitability** warranty for commercial.

The warranties arise for *new construction* on lands, breach of which creates damages or rescission remedy.

Law generally rejects implied warranties of fitness and suitability in the purchase of *established* construction.

Parties then treat conditions through any statutory disclosure requirements and inspection rights.

Most states allow initial *and* subsequent buyers to enforce implied warranties but a minority only initial buyers.

Claimants must trace the defect to the construction rather than subsequent conditions and events.

Buyers must enforce within a reasonable time from discovery of the defect.

Merger doctrine holds that guarantees either party makes in the land sale contract *merge* into the deed at closing.

Merger eliminates buyer's right to rely on sale-contract terms once the buyer accepts seller's deed at closing.

Merger bars post-closing claims over quality of title, as the deed reflects, and defects in the premises.

Merger also bars disputes over unpaid taxes and other charges against the property.

Some states treat merger more like a rebuttable presumption against claims than an absolute bar.

States are more likely to apply the doctrine and bar the claim when having to do with the property's *title.*

Courts also look to the parties' intent as to what rights and claims they meant to merge into the deed.

Claims for misrepresentation fall outside the doctrine's bar.

Long Outline:

The law treats **contracts** for the sale of land as it treats other contracts. However, unique practices having to do with the sale of land, such as **real estate brokerage**, implicate other principles, rules, and concerns outside of the ordinary concerns surrounding contracts. Real-estate transactions also follow certain *customs* in the **creation** and **construction** of contracts. Also, unique questions over the **marketability of title** to land arise, given land's permanence and significant value, and the complex relationships and transactions of persons taking interests in the land. The following sections also treat **equitable conversion**, **options** and **rights of first refusal**, **fitness** and **suitability**, and the doctrine of **merger**, all unique issues relating to contracts for the sale of land.

Real estate brokerage. Because of land's high value and the complexity of a real-estate transaction, land sales often occur through a **broker**. A broker is the agent who either represents the seller in preparing, listing, and selling the land, or the agent who represents the buyer in locating, evaluating, and buying the land. Agents sometimes act as both the *listing agent* or *seller's agent* and *buyer's agent*. The seller of land forms a **listing agreement** with the listing agent under which the agent assumes the duty to list, show, and sell the land. The seller promises to pay a *commission* reflecting a sale-price percentage, often around six percent, whether the listing agent finds the buyer or not, if the sale occurs during the listing agreement's term. Listing agreements typically have a term of around three months to give the buyer the opportunity to list with a more-effective agent if the land doesn't sell. When a seller and buyer agree to terms, the seller and buyer may consult lawyers to prepare, review, and negotiate the land sale contract, although often the broker prepares a standard contract form that includes an attorney-review contingency.

When the land sells, the listing agent typically *divides* the commission with the buyer's agent, unless of course the listing agent has also attracted the buyer. States and listing agreements may follow different rules as to when a commission is due. A traditional rule required the seller to pay the broker a commission if the broker brought a buyer who signed a contract to purchase the land, even if the buyer subsequently refused to perform the contract. While some states and listing agreements still follow this rule, many other states and listing agreements now provide instead that the seller owes the commission only when the sale closes with the buyer's payment of the purchase price. Uniformly, though, if the seller fails or refuses to perform the land sale contract with a willing buyer, then the seller owes the commission for which the listing agreement calls.

Creation and construction. Because of their complexity and unique issues around financing and inspections, real-estate transactions follow two steps. The first step involves the seller and buyer forming a contract for the sale of the land, variously called a *purchase contract*, *purchase agreement*, or *land sale contract*, as just mentioned above. A signed purchase contract is necessary to complete or compel the sale of land, which is subject to the **statute of frauds**, as the next section addresses. As is true for other contracts, land sale contracts must include the **essential terms**, treated in a following section. Another following section addresses the **time for performance** of land sale contracts. The second step in the two-step procedure involves a *closing* at which the seller conveys the *deed* and the buyer conveys the sale price. The seller may also execute a *bill of sale* for any personal property transferred in the transaction such as appliances or furnishings. Closings in which the buyer finances the purchase through a mortgage lender involve executing many other documents including the mortgage, promissory note, and statutory disclosure forms. A last following section addresses **remedies for breach** of land sale contracts.

Statute of frauds and exceptions. The **statute of frauds** requires that contracts transferring an interest in real estate be *in a writing* and *signed* by the party against whom another seeks to enforce the contract. As indicated in the prior section, the enforceable writing that seller and buyer typically prepare is the *purchase agreement* anticipating a later closing, usually thirty, sixty, or ninety days following the purchase agreement's execution. Usually, the buyer will prepare and present a signed purchase agreement, constituting the buyer's offer. If the seller accepts, then the seller countersigns the offer and delivers the completed agreement to the buyer so that the agreement is formed and enforceable. The seller's simply countersigning but not delivering the completed agreement and not notifying the buyer of its countersigning with the intent to deliver would not ordinarily complete the agreement. Delivery completes the agreement. If the seller counteroffers by presenting the countersigned but modified agreement, then the buyer must sign and deliver the seller's counteroffer.

As is true for other contracts, parties may in certain circumstances enforce an agreement for the sale of real estate without a writing signed by the charged party. **Part performance** can take a land sale contract out of the statute of frauds, just as part performance can in other statute-of-frauds restricted transactions. Part performance in land sales typically involves the buyer taking possession of the land while also making part payment that the seller accepts in acknowledgment of the transfer. Where the buyer has not yet made any payment, jurisdictions may instead accept that the buyer *improve* the land, such as by commencing renovations, or otherwise change position in *detrimental reliance* on the sale. Possession alone is not enough to take the transaction out of the statute of frauds.

Essential terms. As is true for other contracts, a land sale contract must include the **essential terms** for either party to enforce the contract. A contract missing one or more essential terms is ordinarily unenforceable. Because land sale contracts fall within the statute of frauds, their essential terms must be in a *writing* that the charged party has signed. The essential terms in a land sale contract begin with *identifying the seller and buyer*. A contract may identify a buyer's agent acting for an *unidentified principal*, even a principal unknown to the seller, if the contract adequately identifies the agent and agency role. The next essential term involves a *property description*. Ordinarily, land sale contracts will include the land's metes-and-bounds description, often by reference to an attachment already stating that description. A metes-and-bounds description, though, is not always necessary if identifying the street address, city, and state, or other manner in which others commonly know the property, adequately remove ambiguity as to the parties' intent. If the contract refers to the number of acres sold but includes a metes-and-bounds description that contradicts the acres number, then the metes-and-bounds description controls.

Other essential terms include land's **price**. If the contract does *not* include the price, then it *must* include an objective means of calculating the certain price. Agreements to negotiate a price are *not* sufficient to satisfy the essential price term but are instead merely unenforceable commitments to continue negotiating, sometimes called *agreements to agree*. Again, because of the statute of frauds, a land sale contract must include any other terms and conditions on which either party intends to rely in completing the transaction. Common terms, none of which would necessarily be essential to a complete agreement but any of which may be essential to the party's interests, include a *financing contingency* that the contract is not enforceable unless the buyer qualifies for financing, *inspection contingency* that the buildings pass inspection to the buyer's satisfaction including as to environmental contamination, and *attorney-review contingency* that the seller and buyer may consult counsel about the agreement's legal sufficiency. Parties benefitting from contingencies must exercise them in **good faith** rather than manipulate them to change contract terms or avoid the agreement.

Time for performance. As briefly indicated above, land sale contracts typically include **time for performance** by setting a *closing date* when the seller will exchange a deed for the buyer's payment of the purchase price. The closing date, constituting time for performance, is ordinarily long enough after the land sale contract's execution, typically thirty, sixty, or even ninety days, for the buyer to accomplish several important tasks. One of those tasks is to confirm that the buyer has the necessary *financing* to complete the purchase. An appraisal satisfactory to the mortgage lender is routinely part of the financing process. The buyer may thus need some weeks to have the buyer's mortgage lender approve the purchase agreement and appraisal, and even confirm or re-confirm the buyer's creditworthiness. Another common buyer task between the land sale contract and time of performance at closing involves exercising the common *inspection* contingency in which the buyer reserves the right to retain a builder or other expert to examine the premises for defects. Scheduling, completing, and reviewing the results of inspections requires some time before closing. Commercial lands in particular may also require *environmental* testing before the closing date.

When contingencies reveal defects, the parties may require additional time to negotiate and accept adjustments to the land sale contract, including adjustments to the sale price. The seller may also require time for performance between the land sale contract and closing date, particularly if the seller must pack and move either residential furnishings and personal property, or business equipment. The **closing date**, though, sets a time limit within which both sides must be ready to perform. Land sale contracts often make the closing date *time of the essence*, where a party's failure to close by the required date voids the contract at the other party's election. In a hot market with land values increasing, the seller may have other buyers ready to perform and thus may hold the buyer to the closing date. In a soft market, the seller may accept extensions of the closing date to ensure a sale to a buyer who may have overpaid. The time for performance, in the form of a hard closing date, gives the parties grounds on which to enforce, modify, renegotiate, or void the contract. A party who fails to perform within the time for performance may also owe the other party contract-breach damages.

Remedies for breach. Remedies for **breach** of land sale contracts follow remedies for breach of other contracts. Buyers may *rescind* and seek *damages*. For example, a buyer whose contract calls for the seller to convey title to a commercial premises for $500,000, when the buyer can prove that the premises have a $750,000 value, may obtain the $250,000 difference in damages on rescission. A buyer may alternatively seek *specific performance*, disfavored in other contracts unless involving a unique subject but common as a remedy in land sales because land is routinely unique. **Specific performance**, the equitable remedy requiring the parties to perform their contract obligations, involves the reluctant seller conveying a deed to the land and possession of the land, or the reluctant buyer to pay the purchase price. Orders for specific performance may require that the seller vacate, unlock locks or provide keys or other access, and remove equipment. If the seller fails or refuses to execute a deed as ordered, then a buyer due specific performance may obtain the court's recordable order conveying title.

Occasions also arise where seller and buyer are willing to transfer the land for the agreed sale price but one party breaches some other term or condition of the transfer. In those cases, the non-breaching party may sue for damages that the other party's breach caused, notwithstanding that the parties followed through with the land transfer. For example, a buyer may not close by the required date, causing the seller to incur additional expense or consequential and foreseeable losses, in which case the buyer could recover those damages in a breach-of-contract action. Likewise, a seller may convey the premises in an unclean or unsafe condition that the sale contract prohibited. Parties often use a closing agreement to attempt to address, resolve, and require release of contract-breach claims, so that litigation does not follow the closing. The land sale contract itself may provide for liquidated damages, particularly as to the seller overstaying, often treated at a charge of $100 per day or a like figure approximating damages. A concluding section below also addresses the doctrine of **merger**, barring certain claims over defects in the transaction predating deed transfer at closing. Closing agreements, releases, and the doctrine of merger may not prevent the buyer from later claiming the seller's fraud in inducing the sale, when the seller has actively concealed and misrepresented the premise's true condition.

Marketability of title. Land sale contracts routinely require that the seller convey **marketable title**. Indeed, in the absence of a contrary term, the law *implies* a *promise* or *warranty* of marketable title. *Marketable* title is title that reasonable persons would not doubt as to validity and that third parties would not likely challenge with claims or ownership or encumbrances like mortgages or easements limiting the buyer's rights in the property. When a seller fails to convey marketable title, and instead conveys title that reasonable persons would reject due to impending or actual third-party challenges, then the seller breaches the contract, and the buyer may pursue one of the above remedies including rescission and damages, or specific performance. Specific performance may include that the seller act to clear the title, including by paying the just claims of competitors to the marketable title or otherwise obtaining their release.

Sellers typically convey marketable title by showing the property's good **chain of title** reflecting a history of the property's sale that shows the seller's clear ownership. Real-property records enable either seller or buyer, or a lawyer or title company employed by either seller or buyer, to complete a **title search** revealing and confirming the condition of title. A seller may alternatively prove good title by adverse possession, although doing so would likely require a *court judgment* including a recordable order of title, to constitute marketable title. Buyers are otherwise understandably reluctant to accept the seller's proof of adverse possession, which would not be recordable. Unmarketable title reflects a defect likely to cause a buyer to reject the purchase or to suffer injury in the future from accepting purchase. The buyer having to defend a third party's lawsuit over title may constitute injury due to unmarketable title, even if the proceeding proves that the seller had good title. A later section addresses a land sale contract's common contingency for **title insurance** and the title insurer's obligation to defend and indemnify as to title challenges, and cure title defects.

While sellers have a duty to convey *marketable title*, traditional common law does not require sellers to disclose other defects and conditions. The rule of *buyer beware* would instead require the buyer to exercise the inspection contingency with *due diligence* to discover those conditions. Yet many states today require that the seller disclose certain defects, using *statutory disclosure forms*, particularly in residential sales. Even absent a statutory disclosure requirement, the law today would tend to require that the seller disclose defects about which the seller knew but that would not be apparent to the buyer on reasonable inspection. The law also prohibits the seller from *actively concealing* defects to frustrate the buyer's discovery. Breaches of these duties may give rise to fraud remedies in the buyer's favor, including rescission and damages for lost benefit of the bargain.

Equitable conversion (including risk of loss). Issues can arise when events occur changing the property's condition between the time that the seller and buyer execute the land sale contract and the closing date. In that interim period, the buyer has the right to own the land, but the seller still has possession and legal title. The doctrine of **equitable conversion** holds in its majority form that equitable interest in the property transfers to the buyer *on land-sale-contract execution* rather than later at the closing date. The traditional form of the doctrine passes the risk of interim loss or gain *to the buyer* who, after all, has the equitable ownership. Equity does what is fair and just. Equitable-conversion doctrine enables the court to adjust the rights and responsibilities of the parties to reflect changes occurring between contract execution and closing. For example, if the buyer dies after contract execution but before closing, then the buyer's estate remains the equitable owner. Likewise, if fire or flood destroys buildings on the property in interim, then the buyer must still go through with the closing. On the other hand, if the parties discover oil, gas, or minerals on the property in the interim, the seller must still go through with the closing.

Some states alter equitable conversions' *risk-of-loss* rule so that the seller retains the risk until the closing date. In those states, if natural disaster destroys or diminishes the property's value, then the law reduces the land's sale price to reflect the loss, forcing the loss on the seller. If, though, either party was *responsible* through deliberate act or carelessness for the loss, then the law in all jurisdictions places the loss on that party rather than the other. Fire, flood, or other loss insurance may also affect the rights and responsibilities of the parties. If, for instance, the buyer bears the loss risk under the traditional rule, but the seller has insurance that would pay for a structure's damage or other reduction in land value, then the court acting in equity would adjust the parties' rights and responsibilities accordingly for the fairest outcome.

Options. A seller and buyer may form an **option contract** for the sale of land, just as parties may form option contracts for personal property or other goods or services, the same rules applying. An *option contract* is a contract promise, ordinarily supported by consideration, to keep an offer open for a specific period. In land-sale option contracts, the buyer may exercise the option at any time during the option period, while the seller *cannot revoke the offer* during the option period. Land option contracts can be especially beneficial to buyers who need time to obtain financing, sell other property, or, if already a tenant on the land, investigate and confirm the land's suitability for business or other purposes. For example, a tenant intending to lease, improve the premises, and operate a business for the five-year lease term may also negotiate a *purchase option* at the end of the five years or any other time during the lease, at a specific purchase price.

Option contracts relating to land sales must be in a writing signed by the charged party, to satisfy the *statute of frauds*. Like option contracts addressing other subjects, land-sale option contracts also require *consideration*, although the law traditionally accepts nominal consideration to support an option contract. Option contracts must state the *sale price*, or a certain way of establishing the sale price, as an essential term to make the option complete and enforceable. The seller's option-contract breach gives the buyer alternative remedies of specific performance or damages.

Rights of first refusal. Option contracts within a land *lease* often take the alternative form of a **right of first refusal**. Instead of stating an option sale price, a right-of-first-refusal clause in a lease requires the landlord to present to the tenant any third-party offers to buy the land during the term of the lease. If the tenant chooses to match the offer, then the landlord must sell the premises to the tenant rather than to the third-party offeror. Rights of first refusal solve the option-contract problem of setting a sale price for the land in advance of the date on which the tenant decides to exercise the option. Rights of first refusal also solve the landlord's option-contract problem that an option contract prevents sale of the land. Whenever a landlord presents a third party's good-faith offer under the right of first refusal, the tenant must either buy the land or give up the option. Seller and buyer may contract for a right of first refusal outside of a lease, too, although one typically finds them in leases or other relationships closer than an arm's length sale between unrelated seller and buyer.

Fitness and suitability. The law implies a warranty of **fitness** in favor of residential buyers, and warranty of **suitability** in favor of commercial buyers, in the purchase of *new construction* on lands. Thus, if a buyer of a new residence finds defects in the home that make the home unfit for habitation, then the buyer may have warranty-breach remedies including damages or rescission. Settling soil, foundation cracks, significant materials defects exposing occupants to hazards, and defects in the home's plumbing, electrical, and heating/cooling systems are examples of possible warranty breaches. Similarly, if a buyer of a commercial premises finds roof leaks, nonworking electrical, plumbing, or heating/cooling systems, and structural defects that make the premises unsuitable for commercial use, then the buyer will warranty-breach remedies. In most jurisdictions, both the initial purchaser and subsequent purchasers may enforce the implied warranties relating to new construction, if they can trace the defect to the construction rather than subsequent conditions and events, while a minority of jurisdiction limit the rights to the initial purchaser. Buyers, though, must act to enforce the right within a reasonable time from discovery of the defect. The law is generally unwilling to imply warranties of fitness and suitability in the purchase of *established* construction. The parties instead treat the condition of the premises through any statutory disclosure requirements and through inspection contingencies.

Merger. The doctrine of **merger** holds that guarantees that either party make, although particularly the seller, in the land sale contract *merge* into the deed at closing. The effect of merger is to eliminate or limit the buyer's right to rely on sale-contract terms once the buyer accepts the seller's deed at closing. In effect, the merger doctrine encourages or requires that all negotiations to resolve disputes over the condition of the premises, the condition of title, and other terms and conditions of the sale, take place before or at the closing, so that the parties can leave the closing without any continuing dispute or subsequent litigation over pre-closing rights. If the deed does not reflect the right that the buyer wishes to claim based on the sale contract, then the buyer has no such right.

Where recognized and enforced, the merger doctrine can bar post-closing claims not only over the quality of the title that the seller conveys to the buyer, as the deed reflects, and defects in the condition of the premises, but also disputes over unpaid taxes and other charges against the property. The doctrine, though, has fallen into some disfavor so that it many jurisdictions it operate more like a rebuttable presumption against claims than an absolute bar. Decisions are more likely to apply the doctrine and bar the claim when it has to do with the property's *title*, which is at the core of what the deed conveys, but less likely to apply the doctrine when the claims are only incidental to the title that the deed reflects. Courts will also look to the parties' intent as to what rights and claims they may have meant to merge into the deed versus which claims they did not intend to merge. Claims for misrepresentation, in particular, tend to fall outside the doctrine's bar. Indeed, exceptions to the merger doctrine may today be as numerous as applications of its rule.

Fluency Cards
Cover and uncover the response to each prompt until you fluently recall the exact response.

Brokerage

Agent represents seller, buyer, or both under listing agreement.

Commission

On sale or close according to listing agreement's terms.

Statute of frauds

Contract must be in a writing the charged party signs.

Statute of frauds exceptions

Possession *with part payment*. Some states also property improvement as detrimental reliance.

Formation

Buyer signs/delivers offer, seller signs/delivers acceptance. Counter requires buyer to resign/redeliver.

Essential terms

Seller, buyer or agent, description, and price or calculation means.

Description

Metes and bounds over number of acres. Address enough if no ambiguity.

Contingencies

Commonly financing, inspection, attorney-review. Must exercise in good faith.

Performance time

Closing date after contingencies. Closing time is of the essence.

Breach remedies

Damages or specific performance with liquidated per-day damages.

Marketable title

Must convey good chain, usually title search, reflecting seller ownership.

Seller disclosures

Inspection contingency usually handles, but statutes may require residential-sale disclosures.

Fraud

Affirmative misrepresentation or active concealment. Rescission or benefit-of-bargain remedies.

Equitable conversion

Buyer takes risk on contract execution of change in property's condition.

Option contract

Only in signed contract with at least nominal consideration, stating price or calculation means.

First refusal

Seller must present third-party offers for buyer to choose whether to match.

Warranties

Implied fitness (residential) and suitability (commercial) for new construction only. Damages or rescission for breach.

Merger

Contract promises merge into deed. No claims other than on deed, except for fraud.

Definitions Worksheet
(Answers are on the next page.)

1. Under what terms do *brokers* sell land? How and when do they earn a fee?

2. What does the *statute of frauds* require for land sale? Any exceptions?

3. How do seller and buyer form an enforceable sale contract?

4. What are an enforceable contract's essential terms?

5. What are common contingencies? How must a buyer exercise them?

6. What remedies do parties have for breach of a land sale contract?

7. What is *marketable title*? What role does it play in a land sale?

8. What must a seller disclose about the land's condition?

9. What does the *equitable-conversion doctrine* accomplish?

10. What is an *option contract*? When is an option enforceable?

11. What is a *right of first refusal*? How does it differ from an option contract?

12. What are the warranties of *fitness* and *suitability*? When do they apply?

13. What does the *merger doctrine* accomplish? Any exceptions to it?

Please do not review model answers until you have answered all questions fully and conferred with a seatmate to complete, correct, and supplement your answers.

Answers to Definitions Worksheet

1. A **broker** or *agent* represents seller, buyer, or both, under a **listing agreement**. The agent lists, shows, and sells the land for a percentage *commission*. Agents earn the commission if sale occurs during the agreement's term, split with buyer's agent. Some listing agreements require commission if a contract forms, others only when the sale closes. If seller refuses to perform the sale contract with a willing buyer, then the seller owes the commission.

2. The **statute of frauds** requires that contracts transferring interests in land be *in a writing the charged party signs*. **Part performance** of possession plus acknowledged partial payment satisfies the statute of frauds. Some states also accept the buyer *improving* the land as *detrimental reliance*. Possession alone is not enough to take the transaction out of the statute of frauds.

3. Buyer prepares and presents a signed offer. An accepting seller countersigns the offer and delivers the completed contract to the buyer. Seller countersigning but not delivering, and not notifying buyer, does not complete the contract. If seller counteroffers, signing a modified document, then buyer must re-sign and re-deliver.

4. Terms must *identify seller and buyer or an agent for an unidentified buyer*. Terms must *describe the land*, usually by metes and bounds (controlling over a different number of acres), but an address is enough if unambiguous. Terms must include *price or objective means of calculating price*.

5. Contingencies for *financing, inspection,* and *attorney review* are common but not required. Parties benefitting from contingencies must exercise them in **good faith**, not to alter or avoid the agreement.

6. Parties may *rescind* and seek *damages* when the other party fails to close or may seek *specific performance*. **Specific performance** requires seller to convey deed and possession or buyer to pay the purchase price. Specific performance may require seller to vacate, provide keys or other access, and remove equipment. If seller refuses to execute a deed, then buyer may obtain the court's recordable order conveying title. Land sale contracts may provide for liquidated damages, such as seller overstaying, charged at $100 per day.

7. Land sale contracts routinely require that the seller convey **marketable title**. Law implies a *warranty* of marketable title absent an express term. *Marketable* title means reasonable persons would not doubt, and third parties would not challenge, validity—good *chain of title* as title search or adverse possession reveal. Buyers may require sellers to clear title, paying just claims.

8. Common law does not require sellers to disclose defects. *Buyer beware* cautions buyers to exercise the sale contract's inspection contingency with *due diligence*. But many states today require *residential sellers* to disclose defects using *statutory disclosure forms*. Sellers must also not *actively conceal* defects to frustrate buyer discovery. Fraud remedies for breaches of these duties include rescission and damages for lost bargain benefit.

9. **Equitable conversion** holds that the buyer holds the risk of a change in the property's condition after *land-sale-contract execution*. The doctrine adjusts rights and duties as to changes between contract and close, although any party *responsible* for deliberate or careless loss still bears that loss. Some states alter equitable conversions' *risk-of-loss rule* so that the seller retains the risk until the closing date.

10. Seller and buyer may form an **option contract** in which an interested buyer holds a right to buy at specific price or means of calculating the price within specific period. An option contract must be in a writing that the seller signs and must ordinarily have consideration, although nominal consideration is traditionally enough.

11. **Rights of first refusal**, instead of stating an option sale price, require seller to present to buyer any other offers. The buyer may match the offer, requiring seller to sell under the right of first refusal.

12. Law implies a **fitness** warranty for residential sales and **suitability** warranty for commercial sales, but most states allow initial *and* subsequent buyers to enforce implied warranties, if able to trace the defect to construction rather than subsequent events. The warranties arise for *new construction* on lands, not resale of established structures. Breach creates damages or rescission remedies, but buyers must enforce within a reasonable time of discovery.

13. Guarantees in the land-sale contract *merge* into the deed at closing. Merger eliminates sale-contract terms once the buyer accepts seller's deed at closing. Buyer gets what the deed, not the sale contract, reflects. Merger also bars disputes over unpaid taxes and other charges against the property, although some states treat merger more like a rebuttable presumption than an absolute bar, with courts most likely to apply the doctrine and bar the claim over *title*. Fraud claims fall outside the doctrine's bar.

Land-Sale Contracts Exercises
(Answers are at the bottom reverse.)

1. Distinguish whether the agent earns a commission (C) or not (N) under the above **brokerage rules**:

____ Land without a listing agreement sells to a buyer whom the agent referred.

____ Buyer signs sales contract after agent's listing agreement expires.

____ Land under listing agreement sells to buyer whom the listing agent referred.

____ Land under listing agreement sells to buyer whom buyer's agent referred.

____ Land under agent's listing agreement sells to buyer whom no agent referred.

____ Seller decides not to sell land under agent's listing agreement signing a sale contract.

2. Distinguish whether the party may enforce (E) the land-sale contract or not (N), under the **statute of frauds**:

____ Buyer refuses to close after counter-signing and delivering contract with essential terms.

____ Seller refuses to convey title on oral agreement after buyer takes possession.

____ Seller refuses to sell on oral agreement after buyer possesses and seller takes a payment.

____ In state recognizing detrimental reliance, seller refuses sale after buyer improves land.

____ In state *not* recognizing reliance, seller refuses sale after buyer improves land.

3. Distinguish whether the party may enforce (E) the land-sale contract or not (N), under this **formation**:

____ Buyer presents signed offer. Seller countersigns and delivers.

____ Buyer presents signed offer. Seller secretly countersigns and holds.

____ Buyer presents signed offer. Seller countersigns, notifies buyer, and holds.

____ Buyer presents signed offer. Seller alters, signs, and delivers.

____ Buyer presents signed offer. Seller alters, signs, and delivers. Buyer signs and holds.

____ Buyer presents signed offer. Seller alters, signs, and delivers. Buyer signs and delivers.

4. Distinguish whether the land-sale contract includes all **essential terms** (Y) or not (N):

____ Identifies seller and buyer, and describes land by metes and bounds.

____ Identifies buyer, describes land by metes and bounds, and states price.

____ Identifies seller and buyer, describes land by clear address, and states price.

____ Identifies seller and buyer, states price, and describes land by metes and bounds.

____ Identifies seller and buyer, describes land by ambiguous address, and states price.

____ Identifies seller & buyer, describes land by metes/bounds, and states price calculation.

____ Identifies seller and buyer, describes land by metes and bounds but with conflicting acreage, and states price.

5. Distinguish whether the seller has conveyed **marketable title** (M) or not (N):

____ Seller shows that seller adversely possessed the land rather than purchased good title.

____ Title search shows that seller has good title other than pending foreclosure litigation.

____ Title search shows that seller has good title despite rumors to the contrary.

____ Title search shows that seller has good title other than divorced spouse's claim.

_____ Title search shows that seller has good title other than neighbor's boundary dispute.

_____ Title search shows that seller has good title other than construction contractor's lien.

6.   Distinguish whether the buyer has a **fraud** claim (F) or not (N):

_____ Seller failed to disclose missing shingles on roof of industrial structure.

_____ Seller refused to disclose age of roof, siding, and decks of restaurant structure.

_____ Seller failed to disclose basement flooding, on residential statutory disclosure form.

_____ Seller refused to disclose foundation cracks, on residential statutory disclosure form.

_____ Seller painted over water stains on ceiling from leaks around residence's skylight.

_____ Seller rolled decorative bolder in front of cracks in residence's exterior masonry.

_____ Seller failed to disclose weathered and warped cedar shakes on residence's exterior.

7.   Identify if seller (S) or buyer (B) bears the loss under the **equitable-conversion** doctrine:

_____ A windstorm fells a tree limb on a residence's roof before parties form sale contract.

_____ A basement flood destroys flooring and wall finishes between contract and closing.

_____ Seller leaves window open in downpour, damaging floor between contract and closing.

_____ A backed-up drain causes washer drain tub to flood, damaging floor after sale closes.

_____ Seller uproots decorative shrubbery in retaliation for buyer's insult at closing.

_____ Buyer breaks stained-glass window during inspection between contract and closing.

8.   Distinguish whether the buyer has an enforceable **option contract** (O) or not (N):

_____ Seller gives signed writing to buyer paying $5,000 to buy for $100,000 within one month.

_____ Seller gives oral promise to buyer paying $2,500 to buy for $250,000 within two months.

_____ Seller gives signed writing to buyer paying $100 to buy for $150,000 within 120 days.

_____ Seller gives signed writing to buyer paying $1,000 to buy at no price within one month.

_____ Seller gives signed writing to buyer paying nothing to buy for $200,000 within 90 days.

_____ Seller gives signed writing to buyer paying $900 to buy at calculable price w/i 60 days.

9.   Identify if the **merger doctrine** bars (B) or does not bar (N) the buyer's claim:

_____ Buyer claims sale contract for a warranty deed, after closing for quit-claim deed.

_____ Buyer claims sale contract for two parcels, after closing for deed on one parcel.

_____ Buyer claims warranty to clear disputed title, after closing for warranty deed.

_____ Buyer claims for two parcels, after closing for warranty deed on the two parcels.

_____ Buyer claims for additional unpaid property taxes, after closing with tax proration.

_____ Buyer claims for road assessment against property, after closing without assessment.

_____ Buyer claims for fraud concealing construction defects, after closing before discovery.

_____ Buyer claims sale-contract liquidated damages for closing delay, after closing.

10.   Identify whether a **warranty of fitness** or **suitability** applies (Y) or not (N):

_____ Buyer buys a new home with a defective foundation, from the construction contractor.

_____ Buyer buys an old home with a cracked foundation, from the fifth owner.

_____ Buyer buys a home from a seller who bought the home new on subsiding fill dirt.

_____ Buyer buys a new industrial plant with defective HVAC, from the developer.

Answers: 1NNCCCC 2ENEEN 3ENENNE 4NNYYNYY 5MNMNNN 6NNFFFFN 7SBSBSB 8ONONNO 9BBNNBBNB 10YNYY

Contingencies Exercises

(Answers are at the bottom.)

Distinguish whether the frustrated buyer or sell may enforce (E) the land-sale contract or not (N) relating to **contingencies**. Conjecture why the party may have refused to close:

1____ Buyer timely waives the financing contingency but seller refuses to close.

2____ Buyer waives the financing contingency but refuses to close, claiming no financing.

3____ Buyer reasonably relies on inspection results, invoking contingency to refuse to close.

4____ Buyer invokes inspection contingency to refuse to close. Buyer didn't inspect.

5____ Buyer reasonably relies on attorney review, invoking contingency to refuse to close.

6____ Buyer invokes inspection contingency to refuse to close. Inspection showed no defect.

7____ Buyer invokes attorney-review contingency to refuse to close. Attorney didn't review.

8____ Buyer fails to timely waive financing contingency. Seller refuses to close.

9____ Buyer timely waives inspection continency without inspecting. Seller refuses to close.

10___ Buyer invokes inspection contingency, demanding needed repair. Seller refuses.

11___ Inspection reveals needed repair. Buyer waives contingency. Seller refuses to close.

12___ Inspection reveals needed repair. Buyer timely invokes contingency, refusing to close.

13___ Buyer timely invokes financing contingency, refusing close, but did not seek financing.

14___ Buyer timely invokes attorney-review contingency due to market crash, refusing to close.

15___ Buyer timely invokes title-search continency based on title defect, refusing to close.

16___ Buyer timely invokes title-insurance contingency over standard exception, refusing close.

17___ Buyer demands price reduction for title defect under search contingency. Seller refuses.

18___ Buyer timely invokes title-insurance contingency over lawsuit exception, refusing close.

19___ Buyer timely invokes title-search contingency over unpaid assessment, refusing close.

20___ Buyer discovers foundation crack, refusing close, despite no inspection contingency.

21___ Buyer refuses to close after realizing contract promised quit-claim, not warranty, deed.

22___ Seller refuses close after getting much higher offer. Buyer waives all contingencies.

23___ Seller refuses close after getting contingency-free offer. Buyer waives all contingencies.

24___ Buyer timely invokes home-sale contingency, refusing close, because home has not sold.

25___ Buyer timely invokes home-sale contingency, refusing close, after refusing to sell home.

26___ Buyer waives home-sale contingency despite not selling home. Seller refuses to close.

1E 2E 3N 4E 5N 6E 7E 8N 9E 10N 11E 12N 13E 14E 15N 16E 17N 18N 19N 20E 21E 22E 23E 24N 25E 26E

Drafting Exercise

Review the **land-sale agreement** on the next pages to answer the following questions:

1. What is the agreement's title? What other names might you see for an agreement that parties make to sell and buy land? _____
_____

2. Does the agreement include a financing contingency? If so, then how soon must the buyer waive or rely on it? _____

3. Does the agreement include an inspection contingency? If so, then how soon must the buyer waive or rely on it? _____

4. Does the agreement include the buyer's right to inspect and approve a title-insurance commitment? _____ What is the purpose of that right? _____
_____

5. How soon must the parties close? _____

6. What remedy does the agreement offer the seller if the buyer fails to close? _____
_____

7. How much earnest money would you advise your seller client to require from a buyer? Do you have any recommended figures or percentage amounts? On what might your advice depend? _____
_____

8. Do any of the general provisions at the agreement's end appear to you to be non-standard? If so, then which ones? _____

9. Would you include any other general provisions? _____
_____

10. This agreement simply has the seller and buyer sign without witnesses or notarization. Is that sufficient? Wise? Practical? Why or why not? _____
_____

11. How might one include at the agreement's end a way of showing that the seller had delivered the signed agreement to the buyer? _____
_____ Why do so? _____
_____

PURCHASE AND SALE AGREEMENT

DATED: _____

BETWEEN: _____ SELLER

AND: _____ PURCHASER

Seller desires to sell to Purchaser, and Purchaser desires to purchase from Seller, all of Seller's right title and interest in and to, including improvements on, the real property commonly known as _____ on the terms and conditions set forth in this Purchase and Sale Agreement (the "Agreement").

1. **PURCHASE AND SALE OF LAND AND IMPROVEMENTS.** Seller agrees to sell Seller's interest in and to the Land and Improvements to Purchaser and Purchaser agrees to buy Seller's interest in and to the Land and Improvements from Seller for the price and on the terms and conditions set forth below.

2. **PURCHASE PRICE.** Purchaser promises to pay Seller as the total purchase price for the Land and Improvements the sum of $_____. Upon the execution of this Agreement by Seller and Purchaser, Purchaser shall pay Seller $_____as earnest money deposit ("Earnest Money").

3. **PRECONDITION TO PARTIES OBLIGATION. Purchaser's Contingency Period.** Purchaser shall have ninety days from this agreement's execution to satisfy itself concerning the availability of financing for the acquisition of the Land and Improvements. **Purchaser's Inspection.** At Purchaser's expense, Purchaser may have the Property and all elements and systems inspected by one or more professionals of Purchaser's choice. Purchaser shall specifically identify in this Agreement any desired inspections which may include testing or removal of any portion of the Property due to the possible presence of any environmentally hazardous substance or condition. If an inspection shows a material defective condition in the Property, Purchaser may terminate the transaction by delivery to Seller of a written notice of Purchaser's disapproval of the inspection report within ninety days of this agreement's execution. Purchaser understands that if Purchaser does not disapprove of an inspection report in writing within the time provided, that constitutes acceptance of the condition of the Property. **Termination.** In the event Purchaser determines that satisfactory financing is unavailable or the inspection report is not satisfactory, Purchaser may, at any time on or before ninety days from execution of this agreement, rescind this Agreement by giving written notice to Seller. This Agreement thereafter shall be null and void and neither party shall have any obligation to the other.

4. **SELLER'S TITLE TO THE PROPERTY.** As soon as practicable after the execution of this Agreement, Seller at its expense shall furnish to Purchaser a preliminary title report from American Title Insurance Company of Oregon ("Title Company") showing its willingness to issue title insurance on the Land and Improvements, together with full copies of all exceptions. Purchaser shall have ten days after receipt of the preliminary title report and exceptions within which to notify Seller in writing of Purchaser's disapproval of any exceptions shown in the report, other than exceptions for any liens to be satisfied by Seller at Closing. In the event of such disapproval, Seller shall have until the Closing to eliminate any disapproved exception. Failure of Purchaser to disapprove any exception within the 10-day period shall be deemed an approval of the exceptions shown in the title report. If Seller is unable to eliminate any disapproved exception, the Purchaser may either elect to rescind the Agreement by notice to Seller or elect to waive its prior disapproval and proceed to close the sale.

5. **SELLER'S REPRESENTATIONS AND WARRANTIES.** Seller makes the following representations and warranties, which representations and warranties will survive Closing and the conveyance of the Land and Improvements to Purchaser: (a) Seller is the owner of the Land and Improvements and has the right and power to sell both to Purchaser. (b) Seller has received no written notice from any governmental agency of any violation of any statute, law, ordinance, or deed restriction, rule, or regulation with respect to the Land and Improvements. (c) If the Improvements were constructed before 1978, Purchaser may conduct a risk assessment or inspection to determine the presence of lead-based paint or lead-based paint hazards on the Improvements. Purchaser may terminate this transaction by delivery to Seller written notice of Purchaser's disapproval of the risk assessment or inspection within ten (10) days after the date of this Agreement, in which case, this transaction shall be null and void. The parties shall complete and execute a Disclosure of Information and Acknowledgment and Seller shall furnish to Buyer a Lead-Based Paint brochure. (d) Except as provided above, Seller has made no representations, warranties, or other agreements concerning matters relating to the Property. Seller has made no agreement or promise to alter, repair, or improve the Property. Purchaser represents that Purchaser has made their own examination of the Property and is buying the Land and Improvements based on Purchaser's own examination and personal knowledge of the Property and that Purchaser takes the Property in the condition, known or unknown, existing at the time of this Agreement "AS IS." Seller has provided Purchaser with a Seller's Property Disclaimer Statement.

6. **CLOSING.** This transaction will be closed on a date to be selected by the parties but no later than one-hundred-twenty days from this agreement's execution. This transaction will be closed in the offices of American Title Insurance Company at 4500 Kings Way, Suite 100, in Portland, Oregon ("Escrow"), or at such other place as the parties may mutually select. Closing is in the manner and in accordance with the provisions set forth in this Agreement. Real property taxes and assessments shall be prorated as of Closing. Seller shall be responsible for any

and all deferred or abated taxes and related interest and charges, any past due taxes and assessments through Closing and shall cause such to be paid and removed at or before Closing. The current year's taxes shall be prorated between the parties as of Closing. In addition, insurance, interest, water and other utilities constituting liens shall be prorated as of Closing. Provided the Title Company is in a position to cause the title insurance policy to be issued as described below, sale of the Land and Improvements will be closed on the Closing as follows: (a) The Escrow officer will perform the prorations described in **Section 6.3,** and the parties shall be charged and credited accordingly. (b) The total purchase price less the Earnest Money shall be payable to Seller at Closing by check or Federal Reserve bank wire to an account designated by the Seller. (c) Any liens required by this Agreement to be paid by Seller at closing and title exceptions and defects to be removed or cured by Seller at or before Closing shall be removed, cured, paid and satisfied of record at Seller's expense. (d) Seller shall convey the Land and Improvements to Purchaser by Statutuory Warranty Deed. (e) Title Company will deliver its Commitment letter committing to issue the policy described in Section 6.6 insuring title to the Improvements upon recordation of the closing documents. The title insurance premium will be charged to Purchaser. (f) The Escrow officer will record the Deed. (g) The parties will split the escrow fee of the Title Company for closing this transaction. Each party shall pay its own attorney's fees and other items customarily required to be paid by the party. **Title Insurance.** As soon as possible after Closing, Seller shall furnish Purchaser with owner's policy of the title insurance to Purchaser in the amount of the total purchase price for the Land and Improvements, subject only to the standard printed exceptions of the title company and exceptions of the title company and exceptions for the matters accepted by Purchaser. **Possession.** Seller shall deliver possession of the Property to Purchaser on the Closing date.

7. **FAILURE TO CLOSE.** In the event that this transaction fails to close on account of Purchaser's fault or inability to close, the amount previously deposited or paid as earnest money shall be forfeited by Purchaser and retained by Seller as liquidated damages. Such amount has been agreed by the parties to be reasonable compensation and the exclusive remedy for Purchaser's default, since the precise amount of such compensation would be difficult to determine.

8. **GENERAL PROVISIONS. Time of Essence.** A material consideration to Seller entering into this transaction is that Purchaser will close the purchase of the Property by the Closing described above. Except as otherwise specifically provided in this Agreement, time is of the essence of each and every provision of this Agreement. **Binding Effect.** This Agreement shall be binding upon and inure to the benefit of the parties, and their respective heirs, personal representatives, successors, and assigns. Either party may transfer such party's interest under this Agreement, provided that the transferee assumes such party's obligations hereunder. **Notices.** Notices under this Agreement shall be in writing and shall be effective when actually delivered. If mailed, a notice shall be deemed effective on the second day after deposited as registered or certified mail, postage prepaid, directed to the other party at the address shown above. Either party may change its address for notices by written notice to the other. **Waiver.** Failure of either party at any time to require performance of any provision of this Agreement shall not limit the party's right to enforce the provision. Waiver of any breach of any provision shall not be a waiver of any succeeding breach of the provision or a waiver of the provision itself or any other provision. **Attorneys' Fees.** In the event suit or action is instituted to interpret or enforce the terms of this Agreement or to rescind this Agreement, the prevailing party shall be entitled to recover from the other party such sum as the court may adjudge reasonable as attorneys' fees at trial, on any appeal, and on any petition for review, in addition to all other sums provided by law. **Prior Agreements.** This Agreement supersedes and replaces all written and oral agreements previously made or existing between the parties. **Applicable Law.** This Agreement shall be construed, applied and enforced in accordance with the laws of the State of Oregon. **Brokers.** Each party will defend, indemnify, and hold the other party harmless from any claim, loss, or liability made or imposed by any other party claiming a commission or fee in connection with this transaction and arising out of its own conduct. **Changes in Writing.** This Agreement and any of its terms may only be changed, waived, discharged or terminated by a written instrument signed by the party against whom enforcement of the change, waiver, discharge or termination is sought. **Survival of Covenants.** Any covenants and agreements which this Agreement does not require to be fully performed prior to Closing shall survive Closing and shall be fully enforceable thereafter in accordance with their terms. **Counterparts.** This Agreement may be executed simultaneously or in counterparts, each of which shall be deemed an original, but all of which together shall constitute one and the same Agreement. **Invalidity of Provisions.** In the event any provision of this Agreement, or any instrument to be delivered by Purchaser at Closing pursuant to this Agreement, is declared invalid or is unenforceable for any reason, such provision shall be deleted from such document and shall not invalidate any other provision contained in the document.

IN WITNESS WHEREOF, the parties have caused this Agreement to be executed in duplicate as of the day and year first above written.

SELLER: **PURCHASER:**

_____   _____

Multiple-Choice Questions with Answer Explanations

610.	A property developer rented a rehabbed house to a young couple who could not qualify for a housing loan. After one year, the young couple decided to accept the developer's oral offer to sell the house to the couple for twenty percent over the amount of the developer's outstanding loan on the house. Although neither side put anything in writing, the couple paid the twenty percent and also took over the loan payments, real estate taxes, and home insurance. Two years later, after the young couple accepted an offer to sell the home to a buyer for a substantial profit, the developer refused to convey title. What are the relative rights of the developer and young couple?

A.	The developer has no enforceable obligation to convey title because of the statute of frauds.
B.	The developer must convey title, the young couple having partially performed.
C.	The developer need not convey title but must reimburse the young couple if not.
D.	The developer and young couple will split the sale profits equally in quantum meruit.

Answer explanation: Option B is correct because while the statute of frauds requires a writing signed by the party to be charged relating to the conveyance of real property, part performance removes a case from the reach of the statute of frauds. Here, the young couple gave substantial performance in paying twenty percent and taking over the payments, taxes, and insurance, all of which the developer accepted, confirming the oral agreement. Option A is incorrect because the statute of frauds permits an exception for part performance. Option C is incorrect because the developer must convey title rather than keep title, earn the sale profit, but reimburse the young couple. Option D is incorrect because quantum meruit is a quasi-contract theory rather than a real-property concept, and the young couple partially performed such that they have an enforceable oral agreement.

624.	A decedent had executed a will devising a parcel of land "to my sister for life, then to my brother for life, and then to my nieces and nephews." The sister and brother contracted to sell the land to a buyer for $225,000. At the closing, the sister and brother tendered a quitclaim deed to the buyer, who refused to complete the sale. The sister and brother brought suit against the buyer for specific performance. Will the court award specific performance in a jurisdiction that does not follow the Doctrine of Worthier Title?

A.	Yes, because the quitclaim deed conveyed the sellers' entire interest.
B.	Yes, because the sellers' interest is freely alienable.
C.	No, because the jurisdiction does not follow the Doctrine of Worthier Title.
D.	No, because the title is unmarketable.

Answer explanation: Option D is correct because title is unmarketable where owners of present and future estates attempt to convey in fee simple absolute interests of the unborn or unascertainable. The title is unmarketable. The sister has a life estate, while the brother has a vested remainder subject to open because there may be other nieces and nephews born during the sister's life, who then become entitled to share in the remainder. The sister and brother can transfer their title to others, but the interest of after-born nieces and nephews could cloud title to the property, making it unmarketable. Option A is incorrect because while a quitclaim deed transfers whatever interest the grantor has, transfer does not assure marketability of title. Option B is incorrect because a title unmarketable due to remainder interest subject to open is not freely alienable. Option C is incorrect because that doctrine does not apply here, the

148

question having to do with the buyer refusing the purchase of unmarketable title, not whether the conveyance or the descent is the stronger interest.

628. The owner of a mechanic's facility decided to retire but to keep the facility in case he needed or wanted to resume work. He leased the mechanic's shop to a young man who had just graduated from a vocational program. He separately leased a bungalow on the back of the property to a young woman who had just quit college to find herself. A city inspector tagged and closed the shop because it lacked the fire-suppression equipment mandated for commercial rentals. The inspector simultaneously tagged the bungalow as uninhabitable for not having a second means of egress in the event of fire. If the leases did not address such events, then what if any would be the owner's obligations to the young man running the shop and young woman living in the bungalow, and the tenants' remedies?

A.   Warranty of suitability owed the young man and warranty of habitability owed the young woman, requiring renovation and repair, or reduction in rent or lease termination.
B.   Duty of commercial care owed the young man and duty of ordinary care owed the young woman, requiring compensation for damages caused by unreasonable conditions.
C.   Obligation to hold harmless both the young man and young woman in the event of injury, property damage, or other loss, to the tenants and visiting third parties.
D.   No duties owed to either tenant because the leases did not address these eventualities, and the tenants have possession, leaving the tenants with no remedies.

Answer explanation: Option A is correct because a landlord owes a residential tenant a warranty that the apartment is habitable and owes a commercial tenant a warranty that the property is suitable for the anticipated business. If the breach is substantial, then a tenant may leave without lease liability, repair the breach and withhold rent in the cost of repairs, withhold rent representing the breach's reduction in the leasehold value, or sue for damages. Option B is incorrect because while tort law imposes duty of care, real-property law imposes warranties of suitability and habitability. Option C is incorrect because hold-harmless clauses might be appropriate if the tenants became liable to a non-party to the lease because of the owner's breach, but the concern as to the tenants is not their future loss but their present inability to use their premises. Option D is incorrect because the law imposes warranties of suitability for commercial use and habitability for residential use. Commercial leases may shift those obligations, but residential leases by law cannot.

637. An investor signed an agreement with a farmer to purchase development lands, with the closing and conveyance within two months. The investor promptly located a big-box retailer to purchase the development lands from the investor for a new store. The investor and retailer entered into a signed purchase agreement with closing to take place two weeks after the investor would receive the farmer's title to the lands. A delay occurred in the farmer's closing with the investor, requiring the investor to notify the retailer that the investor could not close in time. If the farmer did convey title to the investor a month later than promised, but the investor refused to convey to the retailer because another buyer was willing to pay more, then may the retailer promptly compel specific performance of the investor's sale to the retailer?

A.   No because the farmer never signed an agreement to convey to the retailer.
B.   No because the investor unreasonably delayed after notice of the closing's delay.
C.   Yes because the retailer still acted within a reasonable time after the scheduled close.
D.   Yes because the retailer's contract merged into the investor's deed from the farmer.

Answer explanation: Option C is correct because a sale contract purporting to sell an interest that the seller does not yet have is still enforceable, and the retailer appears to have promptly sought specific performance of that promise as soon as the investor obtained the title from the farmer. Option A is incorrect because a buyer need not have an agreement directly with the owner of land, when as here the owner agrees to sell to an intermediary who promises to sell to the buyer. The buyer may still enforce the agreement. Option B is incorrect because the retailer need not have sued the investor when the investor notified the retailer that the investor's closing with the farmer was delayed. The retailer need only have sued reasonably promptly when the investor had the title to convey. Option D is incorrect because a sale contract does not merge into a deed. The actual doctrine of estoppel by deed applies when a seller purports to convey title that the seller does not actually have but later receives. Here, the retailer had no deed yet from the investor, and so the retailer had nothing into which the investor's deed from the farmer later could merge.

647.   An executive owned two lots overlooking the ocean, one slightly higher and behind the other. The executive built a retirement home on the higher back lot. To fund the construction, he agreed orally to sell the lower ocean-side lot to a friend who wanted beach access provided that the friend never build on the lot so as to preserve the executive's view. The executive's deed to the friend, which only the executive signed, included the grantee's covenant that neither the grantee nor successors, heirs, or assigns would build on the lot, specifically to preserve the ocean view for the higher back lot's owner and successors, heirs, and assigns. The friend accepted and recorded the deed. Years later, the executive decided to retire somewhere else and so sold the back lot and its home to a sports agent. The friend then promptly sold the vacant lot to a developer who began construction of a fabulous ocean-front home. What result if the sports agent sues to enjoin the developer's construction?

A.   Developer wins because the grantee friend never signed the executive's deed.
B.   Developer wins because equitable servitudes do not survive promisor conveyance.
C.   Sports agent wins because equitable servitudes run with the land binding on notice.
D.   Sports agent wins because the executive built before the developer bought and began.

Answer explanation: Option C is correct because a valid equitable servitude arises when touching and concerning both the benefitted and burdened properties, the parties intend that it bind others, the servitude satisfies the statute of frauds such as here by poll deed, and owners of the burdened land take with notice such as here by recorded deed. The outcome makes no difference that the initial sale agreement was oral. Once the executive reduced the agreement to a poll deed and the friend accepted that deed, all terms of the oral agreement that the written deed later recorded, whether contrary or inconsistent to the deed, would have merged into the deed so that only the deed terms were enforceable by either party. Option A is incorrect because a poll deed, one signed only by the grantor, binds the grantee and successors if the grantee accepts and especially, as here, the grantee records the deed. Even though not signed by the grantee, a poll deed satisfies the statute of frauds under these conditions. Option B is incorrect because servitudes meeting the above conditions including that they indicate the intent to bind successors in interest run with the land. Option D is incorrect because who builds first would not matter unless the deed so indicated, which it clearly did not do so here.

648.   An out-of-town couple needed a local real-estate agent to help purchase a residence into which the couple planned to move. They retained an agent under the standard buyer's representation agreement that the agent would receive half of the listing commission. The couple then chose several listings that the agent shared with them online, flew in for weekend showings, and instructed their agent to tender their written offer at the list price on their favorite home. In doing so, their agent told the seller's agent that he thought that the couple would pay more for the home than the list price, offering to split anything over the list price equally with the

seller's agent. The seller's agent then tendered the list-price offer to the seller to sign while giving the couple's agent a counter at $20,000 over the list price for the couple to sign, which the couple did. The agents then secretly split the extra $20,000 equally, with the sellers paying the higher price to which they had agreed and the buyer receiving the list price to which the buyer had agreed. What duties owed to the couple, if any, did the couple's agent violate?

A.   Fiduciary duties of loyalty, obedience, disclosure, confidentiality, and accounting.
B.   Fiduciary duties of reasonable care and diligence, competence, and compliance.
C.   Contract duties to represent the couple so as to accomplish their stated objective.
D.   No duties because the seller and buyers all received exactly that to which they agreed.

Answer explanation: Option A is correct because a real-estate broker owes fiduciary duties to the broker's principal (the person whom they represent), in addition to the representation contract's duties. Fiduciary duties include loyalty, obedience, disclosure, confidentiality, reasonable care and diligence, and accounting. Here, the couple's agent was disloyal to the couple, disobeyed the couple's instruction, didn't disclose that the seller was willing to sell at the list price, violated confidences that the couple was willing to pay more, and failed to account for the extra $20,000. Option B is incorrect because the violations were of the intentional, disloyal type rather than of the negligent, incompetence type. Option C is incorrect because although the standard representation agreement would require the agent to proceed with the representation to accomplish the couple's objectives, the agent did so, obtaining for the couple the home that they desired at a price they willingly paid. The breach wasn't as to objectives but instead as to fiduciary duties of loyalty, obedience, disclosure, confidentiality, and accounting. Option D is incorrect because although true that each side agreed to the transaction, they did so under false pretenses and the fraud that the two agents perpetrated on them. The couple's agent owed the buyer couple the duties of loyalty, obedience, disclosure, confidentiality, and accounting that the agent breached.

649.   A developer befriended an heiress who by inheritance owned a thousand-acre parcel of prime residential-development lands with a river bisecting it. On a helicopter flight over the parcel on their way to a lavish meal, the heiress agreed to sell the developer 200 contiguous acres out of the 1,000 acres, at a price of $5,000 per acre. At the meal, the developer wrote out that agreement, which the heiress promptly signed. The agreement did not further specify the location of the 200 acres other than that the creek must cross the parcel. The heiress and developer visited the lands several more times but were unable to agree on and stake out the parcel's final location. What result if the developer sues the heiress for specific performance?

A.   Developer wins because the court's equitable powers enable it to fashion relief.
B.   Developer wins because the agreement required good faith in executing its terms.
C.   Heiress wins because the agreement did not adequately state the purchase price.
D.   Heiress wins because the agreement did not adequately describe the lands.

Answer explanation: Option D is correct because the statute of frauds requires agreements for the sale of lands to be in a writing signed by the charged party, and thus a party cannot compel specific performance of an agreement missing an essential term. While the courts are generous in finding agreements sufficiently complete, the agreement must adequately describe the conveyed lands. Option A is incorrect because equitable powers cannot satisfy the statute of frauds, if as here the parties have not agreed in a signed writing to an essential term. Option B is incorrect because even assuming an obligation of good faith and fair dealing relating to the contract, that obligation cannot satisfy the statute of frauds, if as here the parties have not agreed in a signed writing to an essential term. Option C is incorrect because while price is an essential term of a contract for the sale of land subject to the statute of frauds, a reasonably certain method of calculating the price satisfies the price term, as here providing for a price per acre and the number of acres.

651.   An increasingly popular recording artist located a suburban mansion he wanted to buy. He knocked on the mansion's door and, when the owner answered, handed the owner a suitcase containing $2 million in cash (roughly twice the mansion's value), offering it to the owner for the mansion with immediate occupancy, with paperwork to follow. The owner accepted on the spot, immediately moving into his sister's residence while arranging to remove his belongings. The artist promptly called in his painter buddy to paint the mansion purple that weekend and a contractor buddy to excavate for a recording-studio addition. What result if two weeks later, after the artist's further work on the studio and interior and exterior renovations, the owner sued the artist for return of the mansion?

A.   Owner loses and artist wins because the artist paid approximately twice the value.
B.   Owner loses and artist wins because the artist's payment and work estop the owner.
C.   Artist loses and owner wins because the statute of frauds requires a signed writing.
D.   Artist loses and owner wins because the owner hasn't yet conveyed the deed of transfer.

Answer explanation: Option B is correct because while the statute of frauds requires a contract to buy real estate to be in a writing signed by the charged party, part performance can be an exception to the statute of frauds authorizing specific performance (not money damages), where the buyer has paid and either occupied or improved or otherwise relied in a way that refusal to enforce would work an injustice such as fraud on the buyer. Option A is incorrect because the courts will not look to the amount of consideration to confirm or reject a sale as long as consideration exists. Option C is incorrect because while the statute of frauds would require a signed writing, the owner's accepting payment, relinquishing occupancy, and allowing the work to proceed would very probably estop the owner from preventing the sale. Option D is incorrect because while a deed would be necessary to complete the transaction, a party may enforce a purchase contract including obtaining a deed by court order if necessary. Given that the artist has an enforceable oral contract by part performance and estoppel, the court would order a deed if the owner refused one.

653.   An adult son remained in his parents' home after each parent died. The parents had owned the home without any interest in the son. The parents left everything to their son in their will. The home had a mortgage on it, and the parents at death owed substantial debts to others well in excess of the little equity that they held in the home. The son made a written contract for the home's sale to a buyer who agreed to pay the son $25,000 cash and to assume the mortgage. The contract recited that the son owned the home free and clear of any other interest other than the mortgage. The son took the cash, gave a quitclaim deed to the buyer, and left town, while the buyer took occupancy and began to pay the mortgage. The parents' creditors sued the buyer in a probate proceeding adjudicating the parents' estates, to recover the home to sell for payment of just debts. Assuming that the court has jurisdiction over the matter and parties, who prevails as between the buyer and creditors?

A.   The creditors because the buyer's right merged into the quitclaim deed that conveyed nothing more than what the son held subject to the parents' creditors.
B.   The creditors unless the son returns to provide the buyer with a general warranty deed that the son has the interest to convey that the contract promised.
C.   The buyer because the son promised in the sale contract that the son owned the home free and clear of any interest other than that of the mortgage holder.
D.   The buyer because the buyer took possession and began to pay the mortgage, and so partly performed the contract as written.

Answer explanation: Option A is correct because while a sale contract typically provides that a seller's deed must deliver marketable title, in the failure of which the buyer may refuse the deed for a deed conveying good title or refuse the deed and sue for breach of contract, accepting the deed merges contract claims into the accepted title, although the buyer may sue on warranties of title if made. A quitclaim deed makes no warranties. Only a general warranty deed covenants that the seller has the interest and right to convey free of encumbrances, while a special warranty deed covenants only that no breach of warranty arose during the grantor's ownership without warranting as to prior owners. Here, the son's only interest was the willed estate after the probate court saw to the payment of the creditors' debts. The son had no interest to pass, given that the debts exceeded the home's equity value. The son's promise that the home was free and clear of those debts merged into the quitclaim deed when the buyer accepted it. Option B is incorrect because the son granting a warranty deed, while creating a claim on the buyer's part against the son for breach of warranty, cannot create an interest in the home that the son never held. Option C is incorrect because a seller cannot in a contract create an interest to sell that the seller does not hold. Just because the son's contract said that he had a home to sell doesn't mean that the son did have such a home. The son had only an interest in the estate subject to the claims of the estate's creditors. Because those claims exceed the home's value, the son has nothing to convey. Option D is incorrect because taking possession and paying a mortgage would not create an interest that the son was unable to convey. The problem is not performance of the contract but instead that the son had no interest to convey.

654. A seller and buyer entered into a written, signed, contingency-free, and otherwise valid contract for the sale of a farmhouse and its farmlands. The agreement provided for a closing date within three months. The seller died suddenly and unexpectedly one month later, two months before the due date for closing. The personal representative for the seller's estate nevertheless executed a deed in the buyer's favor, placing the sale proceeds in the estate for distribution. The seller's will left all real property to a farmer daughter while leaving the estate's residue to a businessman son. If no other will provision affects the treatment of the sale proceeds, then what determines whether the farmer daughter or businessman son receives the sale proceeds?

A. Whether the probate court approved and ordered the closing of the sale.
B. Whether the applicable law follows the doctrine of equitable conversion.
C. Whether the closing date in the sale contract was before or after the seller's death.
D. Whether the will describes the farmland specifically or just all real property.

Answer explanation: Option B is correct because at the seller's death, the doctrine of equitable conversion converts the seller's interest into personal property (the cash sale proceeds) and the buyer's interest into real property. The seller's death means that the seller no longer holds the real property but instead the interest in the coming sale proceeds, while the buyer gains a right to the real property. Option A is incorrect because a court order makes no difference. The law determines the rights, and the court would need to follow the law. Option C is incorrect because the doctrine of equitable conversion, not the anticipated sale date, determines the outcome, as here where the scheduled sale date was for after the date of death, but the buyer still received the real property. Option D is incorrect because the doctrine of equitable conversion determines the outcome as to all real property whether the will specifically describes it or not.

656. A mining company worked its land for gravel to sell for road repairs. Expecting to run low on gravel in the next decade, the mining company paid a neighboring landowner $10,000 for a written and signed right of first refusal under which the company agreed to match the price and terms of any good-faith offer that the landowner received if the landowner should ever decide to sell the landowner's property. A few years later, the landowner listed the land for sale and received a $250,000 offer approximating the land's appraised value. By then, the landowner had

153

decided that gravel mining was bad for the environment. Must the landowner sell to the mining company if the landowner wishes to accept the $250,000 offer?

A.   Yes unless the landowner returns the $10,000 with interest to the mining company.
B.   Yes because the landowner granted an enforceable right of first refusal to the company.
C.   No because rights of first refusal in land violate rules against restraint on alienation.
D.   No because the landowner had a change in circumstances as to environmental causes.

Answer explanation: Option B is correct because a right of first refusal is a written agreement between a person wishing to buy property not currently for sale and the owner who currently is not ready to sell it. The owner grants the prospective buyer an option to buy in the future after the owner receives and tenders to the prospective buyer a good-faith offer from a third party. The right does not grant the prospective buyer any immediate ownership. The owner simply agrees not to sell the property without giving the holder an opportunity to purchase the property based on the third party's offer. Option A is incorrect because returning the consideration with interest does not undo a right of first refusal. The mining company paid for the right. If a seller could defeat such rights by returning the consideration, then such rights would be virtually meaningless. Option C is incorrect because rules against restraints on alienation do not apply to first-refusal rights, which generally do not frustrate sale, instead only directing sale to one rather than another party. Option D is incorrect because the facts do not indicate a change in circumstances, rather only a change in heart, which would not relieve the landowner of performing the contract. If changes of heart could frustrate contracts, then we would have no contracts.

676.   An older woman who had never married deeded to a nephew with whom she was close the right to purchase for $1,000 per acre specific farmland that she owned. The deed further provided, though, the nephew would only have that right either at any time that woman should decide during her life to sell, or if she did not decide to sell, then within sixty days of her death. The nephew recorded the instrument, which did not constitute a will. What interest if any does the nephew now possess?

A.   No interest because the nephew gave no valuable consideration for the instrument.
B.   No interest because the first-refusal rights restrain the owner's alienation on death.
C.   A valid option in the form of a right of first refusal on either of the two conditions.
D.   A valid option in the form of a right of first refusal because the nephew recorded it.

Answer explanation: Option C is correct because a landowner creates a valid option in the form of a right of first refusal when conveying the interest in an executed deed. Option A is incorrect because while an option holder must ordinarily give consideration to secure the option against the grantor's termination, a deeded interest requires no consideration. Option B is incorrect because the rule against unreasonable restraints on alienation does not apply to a grantor offering rights of first refusal but instead only to grantor restraints on further conveyances of the property after the grantor conveys. Unreasonable restraints on alienation of fee-simple title are void, while disabling restraints on life estates may be void depending on the type of restraint, but restraints on leaseholds are generally permissible. The rules against restraints on alienation have nothing to do with preserving rights to alienate on death. Option D is incorrect because recording does not validate an otherwise invalid instrument. Recording simply ensures the priority of the recorded interest under certain circumstances.

679.   The owner of a small-town sandwich-shop business and the building housing the shop decided to rent the shop along with the apartment upstairs. The owner entered into a five-year written lease calling for the tenant, a youthful entrepreneur, to take possession in three months. Two months before the tenant took occupancy, the sandwich shop had a small fire the modest damage from which the owner took pains to clean up. At about the same time, the

entrepreneur's inspection revealed some mold in the apartment upstairs. Thus, one month before the tenant was to take occupancy, the entrepreneur notified the owner that the entrepreneur was refusing to take occupancy but that he had a buddy who was interested in taking over the lease. The owner simultaneously discovered that the entrepreneur had joined the military and already left for training. If the owner sues the entrepreneur accelerating damages for the entire lease term, then what legal arguments should each side raise?

A.   The entrepreneur the servicemembers' civil relief act, and the owner breach of the duty of occupancy and specific performance.
B.   The entrepreneur the protection of the recording statute, and the owner breach of the warranty of habitability.
C.   The owner breach of the duty of good faith and fair dealing, and the entrepreneur impossibility and impracticality, and the absence of any damage.
D.   The owner anticipatory breach, and the entrepreneur breach of the warranties of habitability and suitability, and the obligation to mitigate damages.

Answer explanation: Option D is correct because a landlord may sue for anticipatory breach whenever a tenant refuses to perform a lease before the lease term begins or it reasonably appears that the tenant has made it impossible to perform the lease. On the other hand, a landlord owes a residential tenant a warranty that the apartment is habitable, a commercial tenant a warranty that the premises is suitable for the anticipated business, and owes a tenant a duty to mitigate damages. The facts implicate each of these legal theories. Option A is incorrect because although the servicemembers' civil relief act ordinarily holds immune from civil suit a servicemember whom authorities call up for active duty, here the entrepreneur apparently just voluntarily joined rather than received a call up. Even if the relief act applies, the law doesn't recognize a duty of occupancy or give the landlord a right of specific performance to force the tenant to occupy. Option B is incorrect because the recording act does not in any way apply, and the landlord doesn't have a claim against a tenant for breach of the warranty of habitability. It would be the other way around that the landlord owes the residential tenant that duty. Option C is incorrect because the landlord would sue for anticipatory breach, not breach of the duty of good faith and fair dealing. The entrepreneur would not defend on impossibility (the premises could with appropriate repair or cleaning still be occupied) or impracticality (the facts give no indication of occupancy being impractical other than the need to complete any clean up after the fire and remediate any dangerous mold). And the landlord hasn't found another tenant yet, even if the entrepreneur had an interested friend, so the landlord may well suffer damage.

680.   A property manager who owned fifty old rental homes in an urban district decided to reduce his holdings in anticipation of retirement. The manager knew a house flipper with whom he had competed over the years to buy some of his rental homes. The manager and house flipper signed an agreement that an unnamed limited-liability company that the flipper would form would buy five of the manager's rental homes over the next ninety days for fair prices. The agreement required the manager to disclose all fifty homes for the flipper to inspect from which the flipper would make his five choices. Halfway into the ninety days, the manager decided that the whole idea was bad from the start. Does the flipper have any legal recourse to compel the agreement's performance?

A.   Yes because course of dealing and usage of trade supply any missing terms.
B.   Yes because the law implies a duty of good faith and fair dealing in contracts.
C.   No for not identifying the real properties, contract price, or contract performer.
D.   No because the manager likely made a reasonable judgment that the deal was bad.

Answer explanation: Option C is correct because the statute of frauds requires agreements for the sale of lands to be in a writing signed by the charged party, and thus a party cannot compel specific performance of an agreement missing essential terms. While the courts are generous in finding agreements sufficiently complete, the agreement must adequately identify the parties, name a stated or calculable price, and describe the conveyed lands. Here, the agreement did none of those things, especially as to the homes sold and the prices, but possibly also as to the identity of the unnamed and unformed limit-liability company making the promise and purchase. Option A is incorrect because course of performance, course of dealing, and usage of trade are UCC concepts applying to contracts for the sale of goods, not real property. Option B is incorrect because while law may impose duties of good faith and fair dealing, law does so with respect to contracts already formed, not to complete contracts that lack essential terms. Law does not require parties to contract but instead enforces contracts that include all terms necessary to make the contract complete. Option D is incorrect because courts will not decide which party is exercising the better judgment. The problem here is that the writing was incomplete, missing such material terms as not to make the writing an enforceable contract.

681. A real estate agent contracted with a military veteran to sell the veteran's home. The selling agent's listing of the home caught the attention of a buyer's agent whose clients then made an offer on the home through their agent. The veteran accepted the offer through his agent. At the closing, the veteran took aside the selling agent complaining confidentially that he had just learned that the buyers had the same ethnicity as that of the combat opposition that had imprisoned and tortured the veteran. Also at the closing, the agents disagreed on how to treat the standard commission on sale of the home. How should both issues ordinarily resolve?

A. The veteran sells the home because now bound, and the agents increase the commission.
B. The veteran sells the home disregarding ethnicity, while the agents split the commission.
C. The veteran rescinds for unilateral mistake, while the selling agent gets the commission.
D. The veteran rescinds for misrepresentation, while the buying agent gets the commission.

Answer explanation: Option B is correct because fair-housing laws prohibit discrimination based on race, ethnicity, and other protected classes. Also, selling agents and buying agents ordinarily split the commission equally, the selling agent for having marketed the home and the buying agent for having brought the buyers to it. Option A is incorrect because the veteran would under fair-housing laws have to sell the home disregarding ethnicity even if not yet bound under sale contract. Also, agents owe fiduciary duties to their own clients and would not ordinarily be able to increase a commission beyond the contract amount to resolve their own dispute. Option C is incorrect because unilateral mistake is ordinarily not grounds to set aside a contract, and the buyer's ethnicity is not one of those grounds that would warrant such relief because sellers must not in any case discriminate based on race or ethnicity. Also, the agents usually split the commission. Option D is incorrect because the facts give no indication that the buyers deliberately concealed their ethnicity, which would not be a material fact and instead would be a fact on which the veteran must not discriminate. Also the agents usually split the commission.

Week 11

Deeds

Short Outline:

Transfer by deed: land transfers usually involve seller executing a **deed** in buyer's favor, meeting requirements.

Sellers offer and buyers accept *warranty* or *non-warranty* deed, including *covenants for title*.

Warranty: the land sale contract specifies the *type* of deed that the seller promises to convey at the closing.

Deed type determines **warranties** that the transferor makes in the transfer, not the actual title buyer receives.

Seller has whatever title seller has, notwithstanding warranties, which only create breach causes of action.

General warranty deed is a standard term in the common form of land sale contract.

Sellers covenant *owning* with *right to convey* without *encumbering* mortgages, liens, or easements.

Sellers must also *defend* buyer's *superior title* and *right to enjoy* the land, *curing title defects*.

Special warranty deed assures only that no defects or encumbrances arose *during the seller's ownership*.

Special warranty deed makes no assurances about title of prior owners.

Non-warranty deeds, common form **quit-claim deed**, make *no* warrants, even what seller knows.

Quit-claim deeds transfer only what the seller in fact owns without assurances or rights of action to enforce.

Covenants for title involve assurances limited to whatever deed recitals expressly state.

Buyer only has recourse if seller's title does not match the special covenants seller's deed makes.

Necessity for a grantee and other deed requirements: a deed must meet two precise requirements.

A deed must include a **granting clause** identifying grantor and grantee while indicating transfer of title.

Deed usually *name* grantor and grantee but need not do so if identification leaves no ambiguity.

A deed must also **describe the property** in a way that clearly and precisely identifies what the deed conveys.

Metes-and-bounds description is custom, but references to survey, features, markers, or monuments does.

Street address, city, and state will also do if description leaves no ambiguity as to property contours.

Courts allow external evidence to resolve ambiguities.

A deed need *not* mention consideration, although some do to show *bona fide purchaser* taking for value.

Deeds should state what warrants of title, but if not, then law presumes a *general warranty deed*.

State law determines requirements for deed execution, beginning with grantor signature intending execution.

Two adult and competent witnesses may need to sign acknowledging grantor identity and signature.

Most grantees record with the county register of deeds, recording acts adding other deed requirements.

Notary public signature indicating that the grantor signed under oath creates presumed validity.

Recording acts may also require name and address of deed preparer.

Delivery with intent to complete transfer must ordinarily take place after grantor executes the deed.

Execution without delivery and delivery without intent to transfer do not create enforceable right of title.

Escrow involves execution and delivery of deed to an *agent* awaiting conditions to satisfy escrow terms.

Escrow agreements determine conditions on which the agent may release deed, payment, and other items.

Escrow facilitates transactions by eliminating the need for contemporaneous exchange.

Escrow agents bear liability for breaching escrow terms, insuring exchange against mistake or wrongdoing.

Long Outline:

Transfer by deed

The usual way of transferring land involves the seller executing a **deed** in the buyer's favor. The first section below on *transfers by deed* shows that sellers may offer, and buyers may accept, either *warranty* deed or *non-warranty* deed, including *covenants for title*. The quality of the deed thus varies, some transferors warranting, in the deed itself, more than others. The next section summarizes *deed requirements*, referring to what a transferor must include in a deed for the deed to accomplish the transfer in the manner that transferor and transferee intend, followed by a section on the necessary *delivery* of deeds including the treatment of deeds *in escrow*.

Warranty. The land sale contract usually refers to the *type* of deed that the seller promises to convey at the coming closing. The type of deed determines the **warranties** that the transferor makes in the transfer. Just because the seller or other transferor executes and delivers a certain type of deed, with greater or fewer warranties, does *not* mean that the transferee in fact receives that quality of title that the deed warrants. The transferor has whatever title the transferor has, whether the deed is accurate in its warrants or not. Thus, the effect of transferring a certain type of deed is to give the transferee a breach-of-warranty cause of action if the transferor's title does not match the deed's warrants. Even though deeds in general *merge* the land sale contract's obligations into the deed's warrants, deeds thus serve in their own way, somewhat like the land sale contract, of creating or continuing assurances on which the transferee may rely and that the transferee may enforce.

The standard form of land sale contract provides for a **general warranty deed**. When sellers convey under general warranty deed, they covenant that they *own the land* with the *right to convey*, that the land has no *encumbrances* such as mortgages, liens, easements, of covenants, that the seller will *defend* the buyer's *superior title* and *right to enjoy* the land, and that the seller will *cure title defects*. So, if a seller transfers the property to a buyer by executing and delivering a general warranty deed, but the seller instead has defects in the title including mortgages, liens, or easements, then the buyer may look to the seller to cure those defects when the buyer discovers them. If the seller does not cure, then the buyer may sue to enforce those warrants, often joining the title insurer in the suit to have the insurer's resources to cure the defect and indemnity in the event of its failure. Title defects can include the seller's co-tenant, including a spouse or ex-spouse, who failed to sign the deed transferring the co-tenant's interest, predecessor co-tenants who failed to sign a deed transferring to the seller, a lien for unpaid improvements to the property, or other undisclosed defects or encumbrances.

While the general warranty deed offers the transferee the greatest assurance, other deeds offer less. A **special warranty deed** is one in which the transferor warrants and assures only that no defects or encumbrances arose *during the transferor's ownership*. The special warranty deed makes no assurances about the knowledge, experience, or title of prior owners. The only enforcement action that the transferee can thus take is as to defects that arose during the transferor's ownership, a limited remedy that leaves the transferee with the risk that the transferor held that the transferor's own title had defects or was subject to mortgages, liens, easements, covenants, or other encumbrances.

Non-warranty deeds. If a transferor wishes to make *no* warrants at all, not even as to what the transferor knows or doesn't know, then the transferor executes and delivers only a **quit-claim deed**, transferring only what the transferor in fact owns without making any assurances. If the transferor owns nothing, then the transferee gets nothing. Quit-claim deeds purport to give no right of recourse to the transferee at all. In theory, the transferee must accept whatever defects the title includes, although given trends away from the *merger doctrine*, especially around misrepresentations inducing the transaction or defects not going to the core of title, quit-claim deeds do not effectively bar all litigation. Yet in an arm's length sale on an open market in which the seller seeks full market value, the seller would typically need to offer a general warranty deed because offering anything less transfers to the buyer greater risk of owning land having title defects and unmarketable title.

Covenants for title. A similar type of deed to a special warranty deed, in that it provides only limited assurances, is one that makes specific **covenants for title**. Covenants for title warrant only what the deed's recitals state, rather than making the general warrant of fee-simple title against all challengers or special warrant of no defects arising during the transferor's ownership. The specific assurances may include that the transferor has *no knowledge* of title defects, owns the property without *known* co-tenants, or *knows of* no easements or covenants, leaving open whether the title has defects, the owners include co-tenants, or the property has easements and covenants *about which the transferor does not know*. Specific covenants may also include affirmative assurances such as that the transferor received, holds, and transfers the full former rights of a certain co-tenant or predecessor in title. If the transferor's title does not match the special covenants, then the transferee has special recourse as to those defects.

Necessity for a grantee and other deed requirements. The transferor's deed must meet two precise **requirements**. The deed must include a **granting clause** that identifies the transferor and transferee together with a statement that the transferor is transferring title to the transferee. The deed usually identifies the transferor and transferee *by name* but need not do so if the deed's identification leaves no ambiguity as to the parties, such as that the transferor is a named person's eldest son or only daughter. The other requirement beyond the granting clause is that the deed must **describe the property** in a way that clearly and precisely identifies what the transferor conveys. The usual means will be by *metes-and-bounds* description, although references to survey maps, natural features, artificial markers or monuments, common name, or a street address, city, and state can do if that description leaves no ambiguity as to the property's contours. Courts will allow external evidence to resolve ambiguities.

A deed need not mention consideration, although some deeds do so to promote that the transferee is a *bona fide purchaser*, having taken for value. Deeds should state what warrants of title the transferor makes. Indeed, deeds typically bear a title *General Warranty Deed*, *Special Warranty Deed*, or *Quit Claim Deed*, indicating the warrants that they include. Yet the text of the deed itself should then refer specifically to the warrants that the transferor makes, such as that *grantor warrants generally that grantor has and transfers fee-simple title free of all defects and encumbrances*, or, conversely for a quit-claim deed, that *grantor transfers in quit claim only that title that grantor holds, making no warrants*. If the deed does not state its type, then the law presumes that the deed is a general warranty deed.

State law determines the requirements for a deed's execution. The transferor must sign the deed, not mistakenly but with the intent of its execution. State law typically requires two adult and competent witnesses to sign, acknowledging the transferor's identity and signature. Most transferees record the deeds that they receive, with the county register of deeds. Recording acts may add other requirements as to the deed's form and execution for recording, such as that a notary public also sign indicating that the transferor signed under oath. The addition of a notary's attestation and signature creates a presumption of the execution's validity. Recording acts may also require the name and address of the deed's preparer, often a lawyer for the transferor, transferee, or title company.

Delivery. As is true to make other contracts and commitments enforceable, when the transferor has executed the deed, the transferor must **deliver** the deed to the transferee with the intent of completing the transaction. Execution alone, without delivery, does not create an enforceable right of title. Nor does delivery without the intent of transferring title. For example, if a seller executes a deed at the office of the seller's lawyer but instructs the lawyer to hold the deed awaiting the buyer's payment or other action, then the deed's execution does not transfer title. Likewise, if the seller executes the deed and then delivers it to the buyer instructing the buyer to hold it until the buyer supplies the payment or satisfies some other condition, then the seller will also not yet have transferred title. The action would still lack the seller's intent to transfer title. But if the seller executes the deed and delivers it to the buyer with acknowledgment of transfer, or in silence without condition, then the actions would complete delivery and effect transfer.

Escrows. As just mentioned, some transfers involve the transferor's execution of a deed and delivery of the deed to a person acting as an **escrow** agent. *Escrow* involves an agent holding an instrument, funds, or other items anticipating exchange, while awaiting satisfaction of the conditions of escrow. Escrow agreements, often in writing but also oral, determine the conditions on which the agent may release the items. An agent, often a title company or one of the parties' lawyers, typically holds the seller's deed awaiting the buyer's funds from the lender financing the transaction. The agent only releases the items out of escrow, directing them to the appropriate party, when the agent can meet all conditions of the escrow. The agent would direct the deed to the buyer for the buyer's recording, the funds to the seller for the seller's deposit, the buyer's executed promissory note and mortgage to the lender, among other items. Escrow facilitates transactions by eliminating the need for contemporaneous exchange. An escrow agent can also bear liability for breaching the escrow agreement, thus insuring the exchange against mistake or wrongdoing.

Fluency Cards
Cover and uncover the response to each prompt until you fluently recall the exact response.

Deed

Transfers title. Sale contract specifies type.

Warranties

General warrants no encumbrances, special none during seller's ownership, quit-claim no warranties.

Deed essential terms

Grantor, grantee, intent to transfer, description (usually metes/bounds but other is enough if clear).

Execution

Sign intending conveyance. Two adult competent witnesses in many states.

Delivery

Necessary, with intent to transfer. Escrow agent may hold for exchange.

Recording

With register of deeds. Notarization may presume validity. Many states require deed preparer.

Definitions Worksheet
(Answers are on the next page.)

1. What is a *deed*?

_____

2. What are deed *requirements*?

_____

_____

3. Must a deed mention *consideration*? Does doing so provide any advantage?

_____

4. What are usual deed execution requirements?

_____

5. What role does *delivery* play in completing transfer of title?

_____

_____

6. What is *recording*? What does recording require? Why record?

_____

_____

7. What is *escrow* and what role can it play in completing title transfer?

_____

8. What is a deed *warranty* and how does it arise?

_____

9. What is the standard form of warranty, and what does it assure?

_____

10. What is a *special warranty deed,* and what does it assure?

_____

11. What is a *quit-claim deed,* and what does it assure?

_____

12. What are *covenants for title*?

_____

_____

**Please do not review the answers until you have answered all questions fully and conferred
with a seatmate to complete, correct, and supplement your answers.**

Answers to Definitions Worksheet

1. A **deed** is the legal document that conveys an interest in land.

2. A deed must include identify grantor and grantee while expressing grantor's intent to transfer title, and **describe the property**. *Metes-and-bounds* description is customary, but references to surveys, natural features, artificial markers or monuments, common name, or a street address, city, and state can do. Courts may allow external evidence to resolve ambiguities.

3. A deed need not mention consideration, although some deeds do so to promote that the transferee is a *bona fide purchaser*, having taken for value.

4. The grantor must sign the deed, not mistakenly but with intent to execute. State law typically requires two adult and competent witnesses to sign, acknowledging the transferor's identity and signature.

5. A grantor must **deliver** the deed to the grantee with the intent of completing the transaction. Execution alone, without delivery, does not create enforceable title. Nor does delivery without intent.

6. Recording involves supplying the deed to the county register of deeds so that an indexed copy remains on public file. Recording acts may require that a notary public sign indicating that the grantor signed under oath, creating a presumption of valid execution. Recording acts may also require the name and address of the deed's preparer.

7. **Escrow** involves an agent holding an instrument, funds, or other items anticipating exchange, until persons or events satisfy escrow conditions. Escrow agreements determine conditions on which the agent may release the items. Escrow facilitates transactions by eliminating the need for contemporaneous exchange and insuring against mistake.

8. A **warranty** is the grantor's promise or guarantee as to the quality of title, reflected in the deed. The land-sale contract usually specifies the warranty that the grantor must make in the deed. The effect of a warranty is to give the grantee a breach-of-warranty cause of action if the title does not match the deed's warrants.

9. The standard land-sale contract provides for a **general warranty deed**. When sellers convey under general warranty deed, they covenant that they *own the land* with the *right to convey*, that the land has no *encumbrances* such as mortgages, liens, easements, of covenants, that the seller will *defend* the buyer's *superior title* and *right to enjoy* the land, and that the seller will *cure title defects*.

10. A **special warranty deed** is one in which the transferor warrants and assures only that no defects or encumbrances arose *during the transferor's ownership*.

11. A **quit-claim deed** makes *no* warrants at all, not even as to what the grantor knows or doesn't know, transferring only what the grantor in fact owns without making any assurances.

12. **Covenants for title** warrant only what the deed's recitals state. Examples include that the grantor has *no knowledge* of title defects, owns the property without *known* co-tenants, or *knows of* no easements or covenants. If the grantor's title does not match the covenants, then the grantee has special recourse as to those defects.

Deeds Exercises

(Answers are at the bottom.)

1.   Assuming the document satisfies all other **deed requirements**, state whether the deed includes *essential terms* (Y) or instead omits an essential term (N):

_____   Granting clause states *first party is Abe Awad and second party is Ben Bull.*

_____   Granting clause states *grantor Abe Awad conveys title to the described land to Ben Bull.*

_____   Granting clause states *grantor conveys to grantee* without identifying either.

_____   Property description is by metes and bounds but conflicts with stated acreage.

_____   Property description refers only to recognized markers and monuments on land.

_____   Property description refers only to street address, city, and state, for an established parcel.

_____   Property description refers only to street address when nearby lands bear the same address.

_____   Deed omits any mention of consideration grantee gave for deed.

2.   Identify whether the deed's **execution** satisfies typical requirements (Y) or does not (N):

_____   Grantor signs, attorney preparer signs, and grantor leaves deed in grantor's vault.

_____   Grantor signs, attorney preparer signs, and grantor mails deed to grantee's business.

_____   Grantor signs with two minor witnesses and mails deed to grantee's residence.

_____   Grantor signs with two adult competent witnesses and drops deed off at grantee's house.

_____   Grantor signs with two adult competent witnesses and grantee sneaks deed off grantor's desk.

_____   Grantor signs with one adult competent witness and delivers deed to grantor at closing.

3.   Distinguish if the **escrow agent** has likely satisfied escrow conditions (Y) or not (N):

_____   Agent releases bank check to grantor simultaneous with release of executed deed to grantee.

_____   Agent releases grantee's money order to grantor for deposit while waiting for executed deed.

_____   Agent releases executed deed to grantee for recording while waiting for grantee's funds.

_____   Agent accepts grantee's personal check in exchange for release of grantor's executed deed.

_____   Agent releases executed deed to grantee after grantee's deposited funds clear to grantor's bank.

4.   Distinguish the deeds likely to meet **recording requirements** from those not (N):

_____   Copy of deed with preparer name and address supplied to county clerk of court.

_____   Copy of notarized deed with preparer name and address supplied to county register of deeds.

_____   Notarized original deed with preparer name and address supplied to county register of deeds.

_____   Notarized original deed with attorney signature supplied to county clerk of court.

_____   Notarized original deed with attorney signature supplied to county register of deeds.

5.   Distinguish whether the grantee has a **general warranty** (G), **special warranty** (S), or **quit-claim** (Q) deed:

_____   Warrant that grantor conveys title free of encumbrances arising under grantor's ownership.

_____   Warrant that grantor conveys only such interest as grantor in fact holds and no other.

_____   Warrant that grantor conveys title free of all encumbrances of any origin, age, or kind.

_____   Grantor relinquishes to grantee such interest as grantor may presently own.

_____   Warrant that conveyed title has no liens, mortgages, other burdens, or competing interests.

_____   Warrant that no lien, mortgage, or other burden accrued as a result of grantor's actions.

Answers: 1NYNYYYNY 2NNNYNN 3YNNNY 4NNYNN 5SQGQGS

Warranty Exercises
(Answers are at the bottom.)

Identify whether the grantor has **breached** (B) the stated warranty deed such that grantor owes a duty to clear title or provide other remedy or not (N):

1____ Under general warranty, grantee discovers unpaid street assessment from two owners prior.

2____ Under general warranty, grantee finds new mortgage fraudulently recorded in grantee's term.

3____ Under general warranty, grantee receives compensation demand from grantor's ex spouse.

4____ Under general warranty, grantee learns of utility easement claim from three owners prior.

5____ Under general warranty, grantee served with adverse-possession suit commenced under grantor.

6____ Under general warranty, city serves stop-work order in lieu of variance.

7____ Under general warranty, grantor's excavator asserts tradesman's lien rights.

8____ Under special warranty, grantee discovers unpaid street assessment from two owners prior.

9____ Under special warranty, grantee finds new mortgage fraudulently recorded in grantee's term.

10___ Under special warranty, grantee receives compensation demand from grantor's ex spouse.

11___ Under special warranty, grantee learns of utility easement claim from three owners prior.

12___ Under special warranty, grantee served with adverse-possession suit commenced under grantor.

13___ Under special warranty, city serves stop-work order in lieu of variance.

14___ Under special warranty, grantor's excavator asserts tradesman's lien rights.

15___ Under quit claim, grantee discovers unpaid street assessment from two owners prior.

16___ Under quit claim, grantee finds new mortgage fraudulently recorded in grantee's term.

17___ Under quit claim, grantee receives compensation demand from grantor's ex spouse.

18___ Under quit claim, grantee learns of utility easement claim from three owners prior.

19___ Under quit claim, grantee served with adverse-possession suit commenced under grantor.

20___ Under quit claim, grantor's excavator asserts tradesman's lien rights.

21___ Under quit claim, city serves stop-work order in lieu of variance.

22___ Under special covenant for title only, grantee learns of undisclosed mortgage.

23___ Under special covenant for title only, grantee notified of grantor ex-spouse dower-rights claim.

24___ Under special covenant for title only, deceased grantor's devisee asserts probate claim.

25___ Under special covenant for no contractor liens, grantor's mortgage holder forecloses.

26___ Under special covenant for no contractor liens, grantor's excavator asserts tradesman's rights.

27___ Under special covenant for zoning compliance, grantee learns of prior neighborhood protests.

28___ Under special covenant for zoning compliance, city serves stop-work order in lieu of variance.

Answers: 1B 2N 3B 4B 5B 6N 7B 8N 9N 10B 11N 12B 13N 14B 15N 16N 17N 18N 19N 20B 21N 22B 23N 24B 25N 26B 27N 28B

Drafting Exercise

Review the example deed on the next page to complete the following exercises:

1. Place an "A" on lines 1 through 4 where the drafter has left space for the Register of Deeds to place stamps or other notations required for recording. Statute will require that the drafter leave such space. Did this drafter leave the required two inches? _____

2. Place a "B" on line 5 where the drafter has left blanks after "Liber" and "Page." The Register of Deeds will place the volume and page numbers here once having recorded the deed.

3. Place a "C" on lines 6, 8, and 10 where the drafter indicates that the deed is a *warranty* deed rather than a quit-claim deed. The drafter hasn't indicated whether the deed is a general or special warranty deed. Which is it? _____

4. Circle the grantors on lines 8 and 9. Then circle the grantees on line 11.

5. What title does the deed convey, shown on line 9? _____

6. In what form of tenancy, in common, joint, or by the entireties, does the deed suggest at line 11 that the grantees will hold the property? _____

7. What does the deed indicate at line 19 about how this transfer came about, by listing and broker sale, private sale by owner, or land contract? _____

8. How many witnesses will sign for each grantor's signature? _____ Place a "D" on each witness signature line.

9. Place an "E" next to the jurat at lines 33, 34, and 35. Some states require a jurat with notarization.

10. Place an "F" next to the notary's recital at lines 36 and 37 that the notary knew the grantors or saw proof that they were who they said they were. Which do you think it was, knew them or saw proof from them? _____ If proof, then what proof? _____

11. Place a "G" next to the preparer's name and address at lines 45, 46, and 47. Why do you think that statute requires a preparer's name on each recorded instrument?

_____

12. Place an "H" next to the "return to" designation at line 44. One leaves the original instrument with the Register of Deeds for recording but then retrieves it (typically by mail), the Register keeping only a copy or electronic image on file. Do you see why the recording party might want the original instrument back?

Liber   Page

WARRANTY DEED

Warranty deed made this _____ day of October, 2018. Grantors William Marks and Sue Marks, of mailing address 123 Lovers Lane, Riverside, CA 92123, convey fee-simple title to the following described real property, warranting that they have good and clear title to such real property, to their grantees John Wesley and Karen Wesley, as husband and wife, of mailing address 321 Peak Avenue, Manistee, MI 49444, that real property commonly known as 321 Peak Avenue, Manistee, MI 49444, and having the following legal description, in the City of Manistee, Manistee County, State of Michigan:

Revised plat of 1910, north 71 ½ feet of the east 60 feet, lot 2 block 389, subject
to easements and restrictions of record.

This conveyance is in consideration of the satisfaction of land contract dated July 3, 2015. In witness of which, we have set our hands on the date first written above.

Witnessed: Grantor:
X_____   X_____
Printed name: William Marks
X_____
Printed name:

Witnessed: Grantor:
X_____   X_____
Printed name: Sue Marks
X_____
Printed name:

County of Riverside   )
) ss.
State of California   )
William Marks and Sue Marks both came before me, known to me personally or shown by proof to be those persons, who as competent persons I then swore and subscribed under oath to the above, by their signatures immediately above, on this date October ___, 2018.

_____
Raoul Portagio, Notary Public
Riverside County, California.
My commission expires: 10/18/2021.

Prepared by: Return to:
Nelson P. Miller (P40513)   John and Karen Wesley
41 Washington Street, Suite 280   321 Peak Avenue
Grand Haven, MI 49417   Manistee, MI 49444

Multiple-Choice Questions with Answer Explanations

622.   A grower owned a large parcel of land. The western half was undeveloped, and the eastern half contained a grove of apple trees. The grower gave to a buyer a deed conveying "the western half of the parcel from the western boundary to the grove of apple trees, comprising 220 acres." Survey later determined that the land conveyed to the buyer was 229 acres. Which of the following accurately describes the deeded interest?

A.   The deed is invalid because of mutual mistake.
B.   The deed is invalid because parole evidence cannot determine intent.
C.   The deed is valid, and the buyer owns 220 acres.
D.   The deed is valid, and the buyer owns 229 acres.

Answer explanation: Option D is correct because on mistake in a deed, physical description supersedes and corrects quantity description unless mutual mistake establishes a right of reformation, while reformation under mutual mistake requires that both parties have intended something other than the deeded description. Here, the parties intended to convey the parcel's western half to the apple grove, which the controlling physical description did actually convey notwithstanding the quantity error. Option A is incorrect because the parties were not mutually mistaken as to the deed's controlling physical description, which the parties actually intended. Option B is incorrect because the deed is valid and parole evidence could if necessary establish intent. Option C is incorrect because the buyer receives the intended physically described land, which was 229 acres, not 220 acres.

645.   A woman determined to honor and favor her sweet adult daughter over the woman's rebel son. The woman instructed her lawyer to prepare a deed to the woman's home in her daughter's favor. The woman then executed the deed and left it with her lawyer with the oral instruction that the lawyer return the deed to the woman undelivered if the woman ever asked but otherwise to convey the deed to her daughter when the woman died. Learning of the escrowed deed from the lawyer, the daughter secretly conveyed the home to a glamorous boyfriend. The daughter died a few years later in a motor-vehicle accident, leaving her entire estate to her new husband. The woman died of grief a short while later without having further instructed the lawyer as to the return or delivery of the deed. The woman's rebel son would have received the woman's entire estate if she had died intestate, but she instead willed her entire estate to a charity. Who gets the woman's home?

A.   The glamorous boyfriend through the daughter's conveyance.
B.   The daughter's husband through the daughter's estate.
C.   The rebel son as if the woman had died intestate.
D.   The charity through the woman's will and estate.

Answer explanation: Option D is correct because while a gratuitous death escrow (placing an executed deed in escrow for delivery on death) ordinarily effects delivery on escrow, delivery only occurs on death if the grantor has not reserved a right of return. Here, the woman reserved a right of return, and so escrow did not deliver the deed. When the daughter died before the woman died, the escrow terminated. The woman retained title to the home, which then passed to the charity on the woman's death. Option A is incorrect because the daughter did not receive the home to convey to the boyfriend. The woman reserved a right of return, so that only the woman's death would have effected delivery, and instead the escrow terminated on the daughter's death. Option B is incorrect because the daughter's estate did not receive the home on the woman's death to convey to the daughter's husband, because the daughter predeceased the woman, terminating the escrow before delivery of the deed. Option C is incorrect because the woman willed her entire estate to the charity, and the son has no theory to obtain the home.

650.   A conservationist borrowed money under mortgage to buy undeveloped lands to preserve before others could develop them. The lender required the conservationist to purchase standard title insurance covering both the lender and conservationist. The title insurer's search disclosed no liens, and its policy contained no exceptions. The conservationist soon paid the loan, extinguishing the mortgage. The conservationist then sold the land by full covenant and warranty deed to a nature conservancy. The nature conservancy later quitclaimed the lands by donation to a public trust. Following that conveyance, the public trust's manager discovered an unsatisfied old mortgage recorded against the lands, predating the conservationist's conveyance to the nature conservancy. The title insurer would have discovered the old mortgage if it had exercised reasonable care in its title search. On the public trust's demand, the conservationist paid the old mortgage. What result if the conservationist sues the title insurer for reimbursement?

A.   Conservationist wins because the title insurer's obligation persists after sale.
B.   Title insurer wins because the public trust took by quitclaim rather than warranty.
C.   Title insurer wins because the conservationist conveyed away the insured title.
D.   Title insurer wins because the conservationist repaid the insured lender.

Answer explanation: Option A is correct because standard title insurance policies cover an insured landowner's warranties when conveying away the lands. The title insurance persists after sale to protect the insured seller. Option B is incorrect because the conservationist properly met the public trust's demand to pay off the old mortgage. The conservationist gave a warranty deed to the nature conservancy and so owed the conservancy the obligation to remove the undisclosed old mortgage. The public trust took the conservancy's rights by quitclaim deed, which only conveys the grantor's interest without making any warranties. Option C is incorrect because an owner insured under a standard title policy remains insured after conveying away the title. Option D is incorrect because although the lender no longer retained an insurable interest after the conservationist paid the mortgage, the conservationist still had an insurable interest in holding title and in then conveying the title under warranty deed.

671.   The dying owner of a secluded cabin decided to sell it to his longtime friend with whom he had spent many fine days at the cabin. The owner prepared and executed a deed for the cabin to share and discuss with the friend. After agreeing on a modest price, the owner left the deed with the friend, telling his friend that he would review a copy with his lawyer before letting the friend know whether he could have and record the deed. When the owner's wife found out that the owner was thinking of conveying the cabin, the wife objected, saying that their children had expected to receive and enjoy it. The owner died the next day before seeing his lawyer to review the deed and before communicating anything further to the friend. Did the owner complete delivery of the deed to the friend?

A.   Yes because the owner executed the deed intending to favor his friend.
B.   Yes because the owner physically delivered the executed deed to the friend.
C.   No because the owner's wife gave the owner second thoughts about conveying.
D.   No because the owner did not intend delivery even though conveying the deed.

Answer explanation: Option D is correct because delivery of the deed is necessary to convey title. A deed is ineffective in conveying title until delivered. Delivery requires physical conveyance plus the intent to convey. The grantee's receipt without the grantor's intent to convey is ineffective to complete delivery. Recording by a third party of the grantor's notarized deed creates a presumption of delivery that the grantor must rebut if challenging delivery. Both grantor and grantee must be living for delivery to take place. Option A is incorrect because execution of the deed with intent to convey isn't enough. For delivery, the grantor must physical convey with simultaneous intent to deliver, which didn't occur here. The owner physically delivered while reserving consult with his lawyer, which did not occur. Option B is incorrect because physical delivery is not enough unless intent to deliver is then present, which it wasn't here. The owner intended first to consult with his lawyer about the deed. Option C is incorrect because second thoughts are not the deciding factor in whether delivery took place. Delivery instead depends on the action of conveying, present here, and the intent of conveying, not yet present here until after the owner consulted the lawyer.

693.   The seller of a beautiful, undeveloped five-acre seaside overlook sold the property to a buyer who, based on the seller's oral and written assurances of suitability, planned to build a spectacular home. At the closing, the seller executed and delivered a general-warranty deed that the buyer duly recorded. The buyer then discovered that the seller owned only a one-half interest in the property with an investor who had not participated in the sale and who had a claim to the property. The buyer further discovered that the seller and investor held the property in a limited-liability company that had not granted the seller the authority to convey the property. The buyer further discovered a public right-of-way easement across the property that would frustrate the buyer's ability to build a home. What obligation, if any, has the seller to address these matters?

A.   None because the seller's obligations merged into the deed, extinguishing the buyer's rights against the seller.
B.   Only to obtain the limited-liability company's authority to convey so that the seller's deed will stand as written.
C.   Only to obtain the investor's approval and signature so that the seller will have conveyed controlling interest.
D.   Full obligation to cure, remedy, and redress including pursuing and defending legal action, and providing indemnity.

Answer explanation: Option D is correct because a general-warranty deed assures that the seller passes valid title free of claims. The seller warrants ownership, right to convey, absence of easements and other encumbrances, defense and indemnity against title claims (quiet enjoyment), and to correct title. Option A is incorrect because merger does not prevent enforcement of the general-warranty deed's covenants, which instead take the place of those prior obligations and assurances. Option B is incorrect because while the seller would need to confirm the seller's authority to convey, the seller would also have all those other general-warranty obligations to cure. Option C is incorrect because while the seller would need to get the approval of the investor to convey, and if not available, then to pay the buyer for all associated losses and damages, the seller would also owe those other obligations to get the limited-liability company's authorization and to address the easement in whatever way possible including rescission or to pay damages.

695.   A mature couple each of whom had held influential political office had a friend who wished to favor them by conveying an investment property to the couple's only child, an adult son. In an informal gathering at the couple's home, the friend drafted and duly executed a handwritten deed stating in grand language only that the couple's son "would enjoy" the investment property. The deed identified the son not by name but as the "only child" of the couple, whom the deed did name. The deed described the property by its street address and township but misidentified the state in which the property was located. If the couple subsequently lost political influence, and the friend attempted to avoid the conveyance, would the son have a valid claim that the deed was sufficient to convey the property?

A.	No because the deed did not adequately identify the property or communicate a fee grant.

B.	No because the deed did not adequately communicate a fee grant or identify the son.

C.	No because the deed did not adequately identify the property or identify the son.

D.	Yes because the deed adequately communicated a grant and identified property and son.

Answer explanation: Option A is correct because a valid deed requires both a granting clause stating that a certain transferor is transferring to a reasonably identifiable transferee and a property description clearly identifying the property conveyed. Here, a statement that the son "would enjoy" the property does not communicate an intent to convey fee title because it instead sounds like a use easement. By listing the wrong state, the deed also inadequately described the property. Although a street address with correct city and no state might have been adequate because circumstances might prove the intended state, one cannot go outside of a complete description to prove that the grantor intended a different property than the one that the deed describes. Option B is incorrect because although the deed did not adequately communicate the intent to transfer fee title ("would enjoy" is not enough), the deed did adequately identify the son by naming the parents and stating their only son. Option C is incorrect because although the deed did not adequately identify the property, the deed did adequately identify the son by naming the parents and indicating their only son. Option D is incorrect because the deed did not adequately identify the property or communicate a fee grant for the reasons given above.

Week 12

Mortgages

Short Outline:

Mortgages/security devices: parties use *mortgages*, *deeds of trust*, and *land contracts*, as forms of security.

Mortgages: a **mortgage** is a security interest in land that secures the mortgage *loan*, written for statute of frauds.

    In general: mortgage transactions involve borrower signing a *note* and *mortgage* instrument lender records.

    The note is borrower's contract with lender including amount, term, schedule, interest, and default terms.

    The mortgage is the lender's security interest including grantor, property description, and rights and duties.

        Rights include to assign or foreclose, and obligations to discharge on payment.

    Absent writing, courts may find an **equitable mortgage** if borrower conveys a **deed in trust** to lender.

        Some states expressly recognize a **deed of trust** as a mortgage alternative.

        Borrower executes a deed purporting to convey to lender, which lender or escrow agent hold.

        Lender destroys or returns the deed if borrower pays the full loan, but records deed if borrower defaults.

        Lender can then readily execute on the real property, typically without judicial foreclosure.

        Lenders may record a deed-of-trust instrument just as lenders do with mortgages, to show superior rights.

Purchase-money mortgages are security interests that buyers grant to purchase the real property.

    Purchase-money mortgage can also mean one that the buyer grants *back to the seller* to meet financing shortfall.

    Purchase-money mortgages have priority over other encumbrances such as mechanics' liens and judgment liens.

    Property owners also grant mortgages for *construction loans* and *home-equity loans* as a general line of credit.

        The associated mortgages are often second or subsequent mortgages behind purchase-money mortgages.

    Mortgage priority is critical in sale of *underwater* properties secure against debt greater than land value.

Future-advance mortgages secure loans not yet made, enabling the owner to draw future advances on need.

    Future-advance lenders have priority as of recording date even if only later advancing funds.

    Some states only give retroactive priority to *obligatory* future advances rather than optional future advances.

    Other states permit borrowers to give lenders *cut-off notice* so that borrower can give priority to new lenders.

Land contracts are means of purchasing *and* financing real-property purchase without lenders.

    A contract conveying land creates a security device in the seller because only deeds convey title.

        A land contract specifies the terms on which the buyer will receive a deed.

        Land contracts are also known as *installment sales contracts*, *contracts for deed*, or *contracts for sale*.

        Distinguish a land contract from the *purchase contract* that seller and buyer execute anticipating closing.

    Even though buyer does not receive a deed, buyer holds **equitable title**, while **legal title** remains with seller.

    Buyers under land contract often record a **memorandum of land contract** to show their interest in title chain.

        They then have priority of equitable title over later interests, memorandum acting in place of deed.

Absolute deeds as security: lenders may take an **absolute deed** from borrowers, granting lender fee-simple title.

    Absolute deed appears as if lender owns, which is the legal effect, but lender holds awaiting borrower default.

    On default, lender records the absolute deed to sell the property as defaulted-loan security.

    In disputes, borrowers may prove by parol evidence that absolute deed was instead an *equitable mortgage*.

    Absolute deeds as security may violate truth-in-lending and other laws, exposing lender to fines and penalties.

Security relationships arise around mortgages, land contracts, deeds in trust, and absolute deeds.

    Necessity and nature of obligation: borrower and lender must agree in writing satisfying **statute of frauds**.

    Theories of security include **title**, **lien**, and **intermediate**, rights and duties varying accordingly.

    In a *lien-theory* state, a mortgage is simply a lien against the property, *not* conveyance of title in the property.

        Joint tenants granting a mortgage do *not* destroy unity of title for joint tenancy, retaining survivorship.

    In a *title-theory* state, a mortgage conveys title to the property, joint tenants destroying unity of title.

        The mortgage severs the joint tenancy, creating a tenancy in common and ending rights of survivorship.

    In an *intermediate-theory* state, a mortgage is a lien until borrower defaults when the mortgage conveys title.

Rights and duties prior to foreclosure: standard mortgage forms require borrowers to maintain the property.

    Borrowers must also pay taxes, maintain insurance, and not conduct illegal activity on the premises.

        Lenders may sue for breach of these contract promises, obtaining specific performance and damages.

        Lenders may pay taxes, insurance, and other charges to preserve land value and get reimbursement.

        The law of **waste** also permits lenders to get court help to ensure borrowers do not destroy property value.

        Mortgage default may include a significant change in the use of the premises including its abandonment.

    Lenders must grant borrowers free use of the mortgaged property if borrower is not in default.

Lenders may **enter for inspection** against waste, but borrowers retain full owner rights to use and enjoy.

Lenders interfering with borrower rights may be liable in trespass or contract breach, or by statute.

Borrowers have rights that lenders not place clouds on borrower's title such as by refusing due discharge.

Right to redeem: borrowers may have statutory rights to **redeem** mortgaged residential property out of foreclosure.

Redemption requires paying the mortgage obligation within a statutory period, before or after foreclosure sale.

Lenders may not demand that borrowers waive redemption rights.

Clogging the equity of redemption: law prohibits alternative arrangements skirting redemption rights.

Law holds invalid *clogs on the equity of redemption*, protecting owners' critical housing or home equity.

Transfers by mortgagor: mortgages do not bar borrowers from conveying mortgaged property.

Lenders *record* mortgages to ensure borrower conveyance does not affect lender security, protecting lenders.

Lenders *discharge* mortgages when borrowers pay off the mortgage using sale proceeds.

Distinguishing "subject to" and "assuming" becomes important when transfer does *not* pay off the mortgage.

Buyers taking *subject to* mortgages do *not* become directly liable to the lender on the mortgage note.

Seller remains liable on the note, while buyer's property remains subject to the mortgage.

Buyer expressly agreeing to **assume** an existing mortgage obligation is *directly liable* to lender on the note.

Rights and obligations of transferor: borrowers *remain obligated* on the note when conveying the property.

The note remains a contract between borrower and lender even after borrower sells the land.

If buyer does not make mortgage payments, then lender may look to seller/borrower to make note payments.

Lenders may agree to accept buyer *assuming* the note debt and to relieve seller/borrower from obligations.

Law calls a **novation** this rare action of lender relieving the original borrower.

If buyer defaults on mortgage payments, seller's agreement with buyer likely grants seller buyer recourse.

Recourse may include damages from buyer to pay note or seller recovery of land under right of re-entry.

Unless lender granted seller a novation, seller owes lender, but seller looks to buyer for help in paying.

Subrogation: sellers may pay taxes, insurance, or other charges buyer owes, and **subrogate** to recover from buyer.

To *subrogate* is to take the place or *stand in the shoes* of another to exercise that other's rights.

Seller's contract with buyer provides for subrogation, absent which law implies **equitable subrogation**.

Lender may also subrogate to pay taxes and charges and then obtain reimbursement from seller or buyer.

The mortgage provides contractually for subrogation, absent which law implies *equitable subrogation*.

Suretyship principles involve a *surety* guaranteeing borrower's mortgage obligation to borrower and lender.

A **surety** signs the original contract along with the borrower, while a **guarantor** signs a separate guarantee.

A surety or guarantor owes what the contract or guarantee states, typically to pay when borrower fails to pay.

Suretyships and guarantees require a *signed writing* satisfying the **statute of frauds**.

A surety or guarantor may compel borrower to perform, called **exoneration** or to *reimburse* for performance.

A surety may obtain *contribution* from other sureties and has the primary obligor's defenses against the lender.

Due-on-sale clauses: many mortgages include a **due-on-sale** clause permitting lender to *accelerate* on sale.

Under a typical clause, lender have the *option* to call the entire principal balance due if the buyer sells the land.

Due-on-sale clauses often include a trigger for *land-contract* sales, which are efforts at private financing.

Federal law limits the ability of states to frustrate due-on-sale clauses.

Transfers by mortgagee: lenders may transfer notes and mortgages to assignees such as investors.

Rights on assignment depend on whether assignee is a **holder in due course**.

A holder in due course is one who receive in good faith, without knowing defects, and having paid value.

Assignees who are *not* holders in due course take *subject to borrower defenses* against the lender.

Assignees who *are* holders in due course take *free of borrower personal defenses*.

Personal defenses address loan formation and include *fraud, lack of consideration*, and *unconscionability*.

Holders in due course or not take *subject to real defenses* on loan *illegality* like *forgery, incapacity*, or *coercion*.

Payment: borrowers owe lenders **payment** on mortgage-note obligations, the note stating the obligation.

Note terms include amount, interest rate, payment schedule, payment amount, and note term.

Notes may amortize principal and interest over the full term or lower payments and require balloon payment.

Payment is borrower's primary obligation but also to maintain the property and not cause destruction or waste.

Mortgage and note require borrower to pay property taxes and assessments, and keep buildings insured.

Mortgage permits lender to make borrower payments and subrogate to recover payments from borrower.

Discharge: lender has contractual obligation to *discharge* the mortgage when borrower pays the note.

Note cancellation relieves borrower of further obligation. Mortgage discharge ends lender's security interest.

Discharge occurs at end of note term when borrower pays final installment or earlier when borrower sells.

Notes also typically permit borrower to prepay the note without sale including in a refinancing.

Discharge is a signed instrument borrower records in chain of title to reflect title clear of mortgage.

Lender who fail to promptly discharge may be liable for **slander of title** when borrower loses a sale.

Defenses: borrowers may have *defenses* to mortgage and note obligations in a judicial foreclosure.

If the state permits foreclosure outside of a judicial proceeding, then borrower raise defenses in a civil action.

Lender may have *misapplied payments* or made other *mistakes* in calculating amounts due.

Lender may not have followed default *notice procedures* in the mortgage or mandated by state or federal law.

Lender may have *misrepresented* terms, inducing borrower to deal, or imposed *unconscionable* terms.

Lender may not have complied with federal and state truth-in-lending *disclosure requirements*.

Federal law grants a *servicemember on active duty* a stay against foreclosure.

Defenses may lead to rescission of mortgage and note obligations, reform, damages, and correcting credit.

Foreclosure is the process through which the lender executes on the land as security.

Lenders must follow state-mandated procedures and mortgage terms, to *accelerate* debt and foreclose on land.

Foreclosure results in the mortgaged property's sale in satisfaction of the debt.

Sale proceeds first go to sale expenses including costs and attorney's fees as statute or mortgage provide.

Proceeds then pay the foreclosed debt, then subordinate mortgage holders, and only then debtor equity.

Any mortgagee may foreclose, naming subordinate mortgagees whose interests foreclosure extinguishes.

Foreclosure does *not* extinguish *superior* mortgages, whose holders need not participate.

Types: most states require **judicial foreclosure**, but some **non-judicial foreclosure** if mortgage so provides.

Non-judicial states require *public auction* rather than private sale and strict mortgagor and owner notice.

Law discourages self-help and closely regulates foreclosure to avoid overreach and breach of the peace.

Law may require or seller desire judicial rather than private **land-contract forfeiture**.

Land contracts typically provide that on forfeiture, buyer loses or *forfeits* payments already made to seller.

A recordable forfeiture judgment confirms seller has extinguished buyer's equitable and legal title.

Rights of omitted parties: a **first mortgagee** has priority over subsequent mortgagees, using *recording* dates.

Purchase-money mortgages are an exception, giving priority to lenders or sellers financing purchase.

Purchase-money mortgages also have priority over mechanics' liens, judgment liens, and other encumbrances.

Subordinate mortgage holders are *necessary parties* to foreclosure, which *extinguishes* their subordinate rights.

If foreclosure proceeds without a subordinate mortgage holder, the action does *not* extinguish the right.

Winning bidders take subject to superior mortgages and un-foreclosed subordinate mortgages.

Winning bidders may *re-foreclose* in a second proceeding naming the subordinate mortgagee.

Deficiency and surplus: *judgment of foreclosure* provides for debt acceleration, sale, and proceeds application.

Judgment includes *deficiency* award for total indebtedness less sale amount net of costs if sale does not satisfy.

Lender may enforce deficiency by other means such as wage or account garnishment.

If sale produces **surplus** over lender's costs, fees, and loan, surplus pays subordinate debt and then to borrower.

Redemption after foreclosure: states allow borrowers to **redeem** property by paying mortgage indebtedness.

Common law treats the right as **equity of redemption**, but many states provide for greater *statutory* rights.

Redemption gives the mortgagor additional time, often six months, to pay the foreclosed debt.

Foreclosure triggers the redemption period in some states, ending with auction sale.

In other states, sale triggers the redemption period, during which buyer waits to see if mortgagor redeems.

Deed in lieu of foreclosure: lenders may try to take a **deed in lieu of foreclosure** from the borrower.

If borrower voluntarily grants lender a deed in lieu of foreclosure, lender may avoid foreclosure.

Borrowers typically demand lender *waive* deficiency, lender then executing an *estoppel affidavit*.

Some states and federally backed mortgages require deficiency waivers for deeds in lieu of foreclosure.

Lenders may instead agree to a **short sale** in which the borrower sells to a third party for less than the debt.

Lender gets proceeds, borrower gives deed to buyer, and lender discharges mortgage, waiving deficiency.

Long Outline:

Mortgages

Buyers and owners of land use several forms of security, including *mortgages*, *deeds of trust*, and *land contracts*, to draw on and benefit from the value of the secured land. While lenders make unsecured loans, lenders gain advantages when securing the loan against the borrower's assets. Real property makes peculiarly valuable security because of its permanence, immobility, and value. Thus, mortgages and other forms of security in real property are critical not only to the sale, purchase, and improvement of real property but also to personal and business economics in general. The following sections address the above *types* of security devices in land, security *relationships*, *transfers* by either the mortgagor or mortgagee, the effect of *payment* of the loan, and *foreclosure* of the security interest.

Types of security devices. As just indicated, landowners and lenders to landowners use several types of security device both for the purchase and development of the land, and for other economic interests of the borrower. **Mortgages**, as the next section addresses, are the primary real-property security device, enabling the lender to record a document against the property reflecting the lender's security interest. States also recognize, and convention sometimes prefers, a **deed of trust** operating much like a mortgage but in which the borrower grants the lender a deed to the real property to hold in trust contingent on payment. Sellers of land also sometimes offer a **land contract** as an alternative, particularly when the buyer cannot qualify for a mortgage but also for other purposes. Less common is the **absolute deed**, as the last section on types of security device addresses.

Mortgages (including deeds of trust). A **mortgage** is a security interest in land that secures the mortgage *loan*. The word *mortgage* at times refers to the entire transaction involving borrower and lender but also has a strict meaning as to the *specific document* that the lender records against the real property. While the lender's purpose in obtaining a mortgage is to have a security interest to protect the loan, the lender's purpose in *recording* the mortgage is ensure that the lender's security interest has *priority* over the interests of others who may obtain second or subsequent mortgages on the land or record liens arising out of other obligations. A later section on foreclosure addresses the relative priority of mortgages. Borrowers use mortgages for different purposes, and mortgages come in different types, as the next sections address.

In general. A mortgage transaction typically involves the borrower signing both a *note*, also referred to as a *promissory note*, reflecting the loan *and* signing a *mortgage* instrument that the lender records to show the world that the lender has perfected a priority security interest. The note is the borrower's contract obligation to the lender, including amount, term, payment schedule, interest, and default terms. The mortgage is the lender's security interest against the land, typically referring to the note but not including the note's detailed terms. The mortgage instead includes the grantor's identity, the property description, and the rights to assign, foreclose, or otherwise treat the mortgage, and obligations to discharge it on payment. Recording statutes may require other mortgage terms. Because mortgages are interests in real property, they must ordinarily be in writing signed by the mortgagor (the borrower) to satisfy the **statute of frauds**.

Where the borrower signs no written mortgage, courts may recognize an **equitable mortgage** if, for instance, the borrower conveys a **deed** in trust to the lender. Some jurisdictions expressly recognize a **deed of trust** as a mortgage alternative. With a deed of trust, the borrower executes a deed to the property purporting to convey the land to the lender. The lender, or a trustee agent, then holds the deed according to the terms of the trust, which provide for destroying or returning the deed if the borrower pays the full loan, or releasing and recording the deed if the borrower defaults, so that the lender can then readily execute on the real property, typically without judicial foreclosure. Lenders can typically record a deed-of-trust instrument in the real-property records and transfer a deed of trust by assignment, just as lenders can do with mortgages.

Purchase-money mortgages. A **purchase-money** mortgage can mean one of two things. In the conventional sense, a purchase-money mortgage is a security interest that the buyer grants to the lender whose loan pays the purchase price of the property. Yet in the special sense, a purchase-money mortgage can also mean one that the buyer grants *back to the seller*, usually to make up a shortfall in the financing that the buyer can get from other sources. Purchase-money mortgages are generally treated with priority over other encumbrances such as mechanics' liens and judgment liens, even when the holders of those liens recorded them before the seller recorded the purchase-money mortgage. The rationale is that a purchase-money mortgage does not further encumber the property in the way that mortgages taken out of the land's equity for other purposes would encumber the property. Yet no matter the rationale, purchase-money mortgages gain higher priority than other mortgages.

Beyond a purchase-money mortgage, a property owner may also grant a mortgage for a *construction loan* for improvement of the real property or *home-equity loan* or other line of credit for any other purpose. In such cases, particularly as to home-equity loans, the associated mortgages are often second, third, or subsequent mortgages behind the purchase-money mortgage. Mortgage priority can become critical in attempted sales of an *underwater* property, referring to property mortgaged to secure greater debt than the land's value. Mortgage priority can become even more critical in foreclosure, as a later section addresses.

Future-advance mortgages. A property owner may alternatively grant a lender a **future-advance mortgage**. An owner grants a future-advance mortgage without yet receiving a loan in return or when receiving only part of the funds that the loan anticipates. A future-advance mortgage enables the owner to draw future advances against the mortgage as the owner's needs arise, operating in effect like a line of credit. The owner's advantages can include to arrange for funds before the owner needs them, for greater speed and flexibility in financing, and to secure interest rates and other mortgage terms when advantageous. The lender's advantage can include to have priority for the security interest as of the date of the mortgage's recording, even if the lender only later advances funds, as law typically provides. State laws vary, though, on the treatment of future advances, some giving retroactive priority only to *obligatory* future advances rather than optional future advances, while others give retroactive priority to *all* future advances but permit the borrower to give the lender a *cut-off notice* so that the borrower can give other new mortgages priority over subsequent advances.

Land contracts. A **land contract** is both a means of purchasing real property *and* a means of financing the real-property purchase. Deeds formally convey title to real property, not contracts. By declining to grant a deed to a buyer, and simply signing a contract conveying the land instead, a seller in effect creates a security device. The contract specifies the terms on which the buyer will receive a deed, typically either payment of the full contract price after a long period or, more often, payments for a period of months or a few years until the buyer qualifies for a conventional mortgage, at which time the mortgage proceeds will pay off the land contract. Sellers who offer a land contract expand the market for the property to buyers who cannot obtain mortgage financing. Land contracts are also known as *installment sales contracts*, *contracts for deed*, or *contracts for sale*.

Distinguish a land contract from the *purchase contract* that seller and buyer execute in anticipation of a closing where they would exchange the deed. Even though the buyer does not receive a deed until paying off the land contract, the law considers the buyer to hold **equitable title**, while the **legal title** remains with the seller. Buyers under land contract often record a **memorandum of land contract** to show their land-contract interest in the chain of title, ensure the priority of their equitable title over later-recorded interests, and prevent a devious seller from selling the property again to an unwitting buyer. The memorandum acts in the place of recording a deed, which of course the land-contract buyer does not yet have.

Absolute deeds as security. Lenders desire the most-efficient manner of executing on their security. Mortgages are not especially efficient, particularly when the state's law requires judicial foreclosure of mortgage and a lengthy redemption period in the mortgagor delaying the finality of sale for as much as up to a year. Lenders thus sometimes demand an **absolute deed** from the borrower, granting fee-simple title to the lender, as an attempt to avoid restrictions on foreclosure, particularly the right of redemption. The absolute deed appears as if the lender owns the real property, which is the deed's legal effect, although in practice the lender will hold it escrow awaiting the borrower's default. On default, the lender may record the absolute deed to list and sell the real property as security for the defaulted loan. Disputes, though, sometimes arise when the lender records the absolute deed without default or under terms with which the borrower does not agree. The borrower may then prove by parol evidence that the absolute deed was instead an *equitable mortgage*, invalidating the deed so that the court can treat it as a mortgage. The law disfavors absolute deeds as security, which may violate truth-in-lending laws and other restrictions and expose the lender to fines or other penalties.

Some security relationships. While the above sections describe *types* of security used in real-property transactions, the following sections address certain **security relationships**. The first section addresses the *necessity* and *nature* of a security obligation. The next section addresses three alternate *theories* of security in land, used in different jurisdictions. Other following sections address rights and duties *before* foreclosure (later sections addressing foreclosure), and the right to *redeem* along with efforts at *clogging the equity of redemption*.

Necessity and nature of obligation. Security interests in land do not arise by implication. Borrower and lender must instead express their agreement, as previously indicated, in a signed writing satisfying the **statute of frauds**. On the other hand, also as previously indicated, mortgages are frankly necessary to transactions in real property, including not only land purchasers but also construction and improvement of buildings, because of the high relative cost of real property. A home is the most-expensive asset that most individuals buy, just as a business premises is the most-expensive business asset that most businesses buy. The value of a home or business real property also serves as capital on which to draw for other personal or commercial economic activity. Thus, mortgages are ubiquitous. Without mortgages or equivalent security devices for land, the economy would not function as it does. Debt financing through real-estate mortgages is critical to many individuals and businesses.

Theories: title, lien, and intermediate. States vary in whether they treat a mortgage as a **lien** against the land or instead as passing a special form of **title** to the land. The distinction matters primarily when a *joint tenant* grants a mortgage. In a lien-theory state, the joint tenant granting a mortgage does *not* destroy the unity of title on which a joint tenancy depends. By contrast, in a title-theory state, a joint tenant who conveys a mortgage destroys the unity of title with other joint tenants, thus severing the joint tenancy as to the mortgaging co-tenant, and creating a tenancy in common between that mortgaging co-tenant and other joint tenants. Some states, though, follow an **intermediate** theory that applies the lien theory unless the borrower defaults, giving the parties the relative convenience of dealing only with a lien rather than transfer of title. On default, though, the law applies the title theory, giving the lender greater enforcement rights as a title-holder in the land.

Rights and duties prior to foreclosure. Standard forms of mortgages require the borrower to maintain the mortgaged property in good repair, pay taxes, maintain insurance, not conduct illegal activities on the premises such as would forfeit the land, and otherwise protect the mortgagee's security interest. These obligations are contractual, and the mortgagee who identifies their breach can sue for specific performance. The mortgage will also likely grant the mortgagee the right to pay taxes, insurance, and other charges or costs to preserve the value of the land, and then have the borrower's reimbursement, as further described in a section below on subrogation. While contract terms impose the borrower's primary obligations, the law of **waste** may permit a mortgagee to obtain court assistance in ensuring that the borrower does not destroy the property's value. A building without heat in the winter or with a leaky roof can quickly depreciate because of natural conditions, as can a building with inadequate lighting, locks, and other security against vandalism.

The borrower's principal right, on the other hand, and the corollary mortgagee restriction, is for the borrower's free use of the mortgaged property if the borrower is not in default. A mortgage may grant the mortgagee a right to **enter for inspection** against waste, but generally, the borrower retains full rights of an owner to use and enjoy the premises, including to exclude others. Mortgagees interfere with those borrower rights at their peril of trespass, breach of contract, or statutory actions for breach of the peace with respect to security interests. A mortgage may, on the other hand, define the terms of default to include a significant change in the use of the premises including its abandonment. Once again, these terms are contract obligations, enforceable in specific performance or damages, like other contracts. While mortgagees properly record a mortgage, borrowers would also have rights not to have a mortgagee place other clouds on the borrower's title.

Right to redeem and clogging equity of redemption. The law of mortgages and other security interests in land grants the borrower rights to **redeem** the mortgaged property out of a foreclosure proceeding, meaning to pay off the mortgage obligation either before or a certain statutory period, such as six months, after foreclosure sale. A section below summarizes those redemption rights after foreclosure. Here, though, recognize that the law generally prohibits borrowers from waiving redemption rights in advance and prohibits lenders from demanding or contracting for that waiver. The law also prohibits borrower and lender from fashioning alternative loan arrangements, such as a deed in escrow or an option to purchase on default, treating default in ways intended to skirt redemption rights. The law holds that *clogs on equity are invalid*. Redemption rights can protect homeowners from losing critical housing or losing home equity, if the homeowner is able to redeem, although prospects for doing so are usually poor because the mortgagor could not even meet the original mortgage. Alternatively, the statutory period of redemption simply allows the foreclosed homeowner to accumulate savings and locate other housing, often while living in the premises without making mortgage payments. Public policy judges these redemption rights and their advantages sufficiently important to deny parties the opportunity to alter them in advance.

Transfers by mortgagor. Mortgages do not prohibit the borrower from selling or otherwise conveying away the mortgaged land, although seller and buyer must deal with the mortgage. Lenders taking mortgages as security for their loans routinely *record* those mortgages to ensure that the borrower's conveyance of the mortgaged land does not adversely affect the lender's security

177

interest. A recorded mortgage protects the mortgagee's interest on transfer. If, as happens in the typical case, the borrower sells the mortgaged land while realizing sufficient funds to pay off the mortgage lender, then the lender *discharges* the mortgage. A mortgage securing indebtedness greater than the property's value, though, can make transfer difficult as a practical matter. If a sale does not bring sufficient funds to satisfy the mortgage, then the mortgagee will not discharge the mortgage, and the buyer will not buy, unless the buyer is willing to take **subject to** the mortgage or even to **assume** the mortgage as the following section addresses. Other following sections address related issues of the seller's rights and obligations on transfer, and application of **subrogation** and **suretyship** principles, and **due-on-sale** clauses.

Distinguishing "subject to" and "assuming." In some situations, the seller and buyer of land find it either necessary or advantageous *not* to pay and discharge a mortgage on the land. For example, the buyer may not be able to obtain financing or locate financing on the same advantageous terms as the existing mortgage. In such instances, and if the mortgage permits it, the buyer may agree to take the property's title **subject to** the mortgage. The buyer pays a reduced sale price that reflects the mortgage obligation and then makes the mortgage payments to the lender. When a buyer takes *subject to* a mortgage, the buyer does *not* become directly liable to the mortgage lender on the promissory note. Rather, the *seller* remains liable on the note, while the buyer's property remains subject to the mortgage, giving the buyer incentive to make the seller's note payments.

In other instances, a buyer may expressly agree to **assume** an existing mortgage obligation. To *assume* an obligation here means for the buyer to become *directly liable* to the mortgage lender for the indebtedness that the mortgage secures. Direct liability means that the buyer then has personal liability on the seller's promissory note with the mortgage lender, rather than merely having the buyer's property at risk as mortgage security. Ordinarily, buyers would prefer not to accept such direct, personal liability. On the other hand, sellers *would* prefer that buyers assume mortgage indebtedness rather than merely take subject to the mortgage, for the increased incentive that assumption of debt creates. In other words, a seller may in negotiations require a buyer to assume. If, as a following section on *due-on-sale* clauses addresses, the mortgage lender also has a say in the transaction, then the lender may also require the buyer to assume.

Rights and obligations of transferor. Just because a borrower manages to sell the mortgaged land subject to the mortgage, or even with the borrower assuming the mortgage obligation, does not mean that the borrower has no further obligations. To the contrary, the borrower *remains obligated* on the promissory note that accompanied the mortgage. The note remains a contract between borrower and lender even after the borrower sells the land. The terms of that contract determine the borrower's obligation, which is routinely that the borrower remains liable notwithstanding the borrower's conveyance of the note's security. If the buyer does not make the mortgage payments reflecting the note obligation, then the lender may look to the borrower to make those payments. In some cases, the mortgage lender may expressly agree to accept the buyer's new commitment to pay the mortgage, including the buyer's *assuming* the note debt, to relieve the borrower from the note's contractual liability. The law calls this action of lender relief of the original borrower a **novation**.

The seller does not necessarily lose all rights when selling to a buyer who takes subject to the mortgage or agrees to assume the mortgage note. If the buyer defaults on payments, leaving the seller exposed to the unpaid mortgage note, then the seller's agreement with the buyer will likely provide the seller with recourse against the buyer. That recourse may include money from the buyer so that the seller can pay the note, in the nature of specific performance, or the seller may recover the property under a right of re-entry on default, extinguishing the buyer's interest. Unless the mortgage lender granted the seller a novation releasing the seller from liability, the seller owes the lender, but the seller has the buyer to whom to look for help in meeting the mortgage-note obligation.

Application of subrogation. The prior section shows that a borrower/mortgagor who sells the real property subject to the mortgage, or with the buyer even assuming the mortgage, retains the risk that the buyer does not pay make the mortgage payments, unless in the unlikely instance the mortgage lender grants the borrower a novation and release from the mortgage-note obligation. The prior section also shows that when the buyer fails to make a mortgage payment, the seller has contract rights against the buyer to make the buyer perform. Yet in those instances, the buyer may also have failed to pay real estate taxes, insurance, or other charges associated with maintaining the property. Because the seller retains an interest, the seller may make those payments for the buyer and then **subrogate** to the rights of the assessor, insurer, or other creditor to recover the payments from the buyer.

To *subrogate* is to take the place or, proverbially, *stand in the shoes* of another to exercise that other's rights. A seller has sound economic reasons to preserve the property's title and value against the destruction or the claims of others. The seller's sale contract with the buyer may provide for subrogation rights, or the law may imply *equitable subrogation*. Even more commonly, the mortgage lender, the financial resources of which are seldom in question and whose economic interest is often greatest, will exercise similar rights to pay taxes and charges related to the property to preserve its value and then *subrogate* to those creditors' rights to obtain reimbursement from the seller or buyer. The mortgage instrument will ordinarily provide contractually for those subrogation rights, while in their absence, the law would likely imply them through *equitable subrogation*.

Suretyship principles. Mortgages can also involve the law of **suretyships**, referring generally to the relationship of a *surety* or *guarantor* for the borrower's mortgage obligation to both the borrower and the lender. A surety signs the original contract along with the obligor, while a guarantor signs a separate guarantee, although the distinction is unimportant here. Lenders do sometimes require a surety or guarantor, also loosely referred to as a *co-signer*, for a mortgage note when the borrower's credit is insufficient. The surety or guarantor owes the obligation that the contract or guarantee states, which is typically to pay when the primary obligor fails to do so. Suretyships and guarantees require a *signed writing* satisfying the **statute of frauds**. The surety or guarantor has rights, too, though, including to compel the primary obligor to perform, called *exoneration*, or to *reimburse* the surety or guarantor for performing, in the nature of *subrogation* as the prior section discussed. If the suretyship involves more than one surety, then the paying surety may also obtain *contribution* from other sureties. A surety also has the primary obligor's defenses, if any, when the lender pursues the surety.

Due-on-sale clauses. The above sections treat the lender as acquiescing in the borrower's transfer of the land subject to the lender's mortgage, or with the buyer assuming the mortgage. Yet many mortgages include a **due-on-sale** clause. The clauses typically permit the mortgage lender to accelerate the mortgage note and call its entire principal balance due if the buyer sells the land. Due-on-sale clauses typically give the lender the *option* of declaring the note due, enabling the lender to determine which action to choose, whether approval of the sale subject to the mortgage, approval of the sale only with the buyer assuming the debt, or simply acceleration of the debt. Federal law limits the ability of states to frustrate due-on-sale clauses. Due-on-sale clauses typically include a trigger for *land-contract* sales, in other words for efforts at private financing, giving the lender the greatest leverage.

Transfers by mortgagee. For their part, lenders may either hold the note and mortgage pending the borrower's payments or, as is commonly the case with residential mortgages, transfer the note and mortgage to an assignee such as an investor or mortgage-servicing company representing investors. Issues can arise, though, when the borrower defaults but raises defenses, such as fraud, against the lender about which the assignee may not have been aware. The rights of a person taking a note and mortgage on assignment can depend on whether the person is a **holder in due course**, meaning one who received the instrument in good faith, without knowing of defects, and having paid value. If the assignee is *not* a holder in due course, then the borrower can raise any defenses against the assignee that the borrower could have raised against the lender.

If the assignee is a holder in due course, then the assignee takes the borrower's obligation *free of personal defenses*. Personal defenses, addressing conduct surrounding the obligation's formation, include *fraud in the inducement*, *failure of consideration*, and *unconscionability*. Thus, if the lender misrepresented the loan's terms in order to induce the note and mortgage, but the assignee took the assignment as a holder in due course, in good faith for consideration without knowing of the misrepresentation, then the borrower owes the assignee the full obligation. Holders in due course, though, take *subject to real defenses*. Real defenses, addressing the *legality* of the obligation's formation rather than surrounding conduct, include *forgery*, *infancy* or other *incapacity*, *illegality*, and *duress* or *coercion*. Thus, if the lender forged the instruments, or the transaction violated state or federal statutes regulating mortgage loans, then the borrower could raise those defenses to defeat an assignee, even one who was a holder in due course.

Payment. The borrower owes the lender **payment** on the mortgage-note obligation. The note states the total obligation, interest rate, periodic payment amount, and note term over which the borrower pays. A note may amortize the full amount of principal and interest over the full term, or the note may lower payments and require a balloon payment at the end of the note's term. Mortgage notes are often for ten, fifteen, twenty, or even thirty years, although notes with balloon payments may be for terms as short as five, three, or two years, or even one year. Payment is the borrower's primary obligation, although the borrower will have other duties to maintain the property and not to cause its destruction or waste. The mortgage and note will also require the borrower to pay property taxes and assessments, and keep buildings insured, often through an escrow that the lender maintains out of the payments. As indicated in another section, the mortgage instruments will permit the lender to make those payments for the borrower if the borrower fails to do so and to recover the payments from the borrower on foreclosure.

Discharges. The lender has the contractual and legal obligation to **discharge** the mortgage when the borrower satisfies the note's payment obligations. Cancellation of the note relieves the borrower of further note obligation, while discharge of the mortgage ends the lender's security interest in the land. Discharge may occur at the end of the note's term when the borrower makes the final payment or at an earlier date when the borrower sells the property and pays off the note out of the sale proceeds at close. Notes also typically permit the borrower to prepay the note without sale. Borrowers may do so out of other funds or may do so in a refinancing of the mortgage. The lender's discharge is a signed instrument that the borrower records in the property's chain of title to reflect that the title is clear of the prior mortgage. The lender who fails to promptly discharge a mortgage when payment of the note requires the lender to do so may be liable not only for breach of contract but also for **slander of title**, particularly when the borrower loses an opportunity to sell, mortgage, or otherwise benefit from clear title to the land.

Defenses. The borrower may have **defenses** to a mortgage and its note obligation. In a judicial foreclosure, the borrower will plead and argue defenses in response to the lender's foreclosure action. If the state permits foreclosure outside of a judicial proceeding, then the borrower may have to bring a civil action to raise mortgage and note defenses. For example, the lender may have *misapplied payments* or made other *mistakes* in calculating amounts due. Alternatively, a lender may not have followed default *notice procedures* in the mortgage or mandated by state or federal law. The lender may have *misrepresented* mortgage terms, fraudulently inducing the borrower into the mortgage transaction without disclosing such things as adjustable interest rates or balloon payments. The lender may not have complied with federal and state truth-in-lending *disclosure requirements* on terms like the annual percentage rate, finance charges, and total interest over the loan term. Also, federal law grants a *servicemember on active duty* a stay against foreclosure. A borrower may also object to *unconscionable* mortgage terms. Defenses may lead to rescission of the mortgage and note obligation, reform of terms, damages, and equitable remedies such as specific performance of terms or correcting credit records.

Foreclosure. **Foreclosure** is the process through which the lender or other mortgage holder executes on the land as security. For a lender to *foreclose* a mortgage requires following the state's mandated procedures and procedures spelled out in the mortgage, to *accelerate* the total mortgage debt beyond overdue payments and then to secure and sell the mortgaged property in satisfaction of the debt. Sale proceeds first go to sale expenses including costs and attorney's fees as provided by statute or mortgage, then to pay the foreclosed debt, then to subordinate mortgage holders, and only then to the debtor if proceeds are sufficient. Any mortgagee may bring a foreclosure action, although who brings the action is of no consequence to priority. A foreclosing mortgagee names subordinate mortgagees whose interests the foreclosure would extinguish. Because the foreclosure does *not* extinguish *superior* mortgages, superior mortgage holders need not participate, although in practice many would simultaneously foreclose, treating the subordinate foreclosure and sale as an event of default.

Types. Most states require a court proceeding, known as **judicial foreclosure**, to foreclose on a mortgage in most instances, particularly with residential mortgages where concerns for overreaching are greater than in commercial mortgages. Some jurisdictions alternatively allow for **non-judicial foreclosure** in some circumstances, *if* the mortgage or deed of trust expressly permits non-judicial foreclosure. Because of concerns about lender overreach, particularly as to residential mortgages, and to protect the borrower's equity, those states tend to require *public auction* of the foreclosed property rather than private sale through a broker and strict advance personal notice to the mortgagor and other recorded owners. As indicated above, a few jurisdictions also allow borrower to grant and lender or trustee to hold a *deed of trust* as a mortgage substitute, although the law will likely regulate that alternative form closely and may require specific foreclosure procedures as just indicated. The law strongly discourages lender self-help and closely regulates foreclosures to avoid lender overreaching including breaches of the peace.

When seller and buyer form a land contract instead of the buyer obtaining lender financing and granting the lender a mortgage, and the buyer defaults on the land contract, the law may require or seller may desire to pursue a judicial **land-contract forfeiture**. Land contracts typically provide that the buyer *forfeits* payments made to the seller in the forfeiture proceeding. The forfeiture proceeding confirms that the seller has extinguished the buyer's equitable title. After the forfeiture judgment enters, the seller will once again have legal title, which the seller never relinquished under the land contract, and equitable title, restored to the seller from the buyer. The seller can also record the judgment of forfeiture so that the chain of title reflects the extinguishment of the land-contract interest reflected by the recorded memorandum of land contract.

Rights of omitted parties. As a prior section suggests, the **first mortgagee** generally has priority over subsequent and thus subordinate mortgagees as to sale proceeds, using *recording* dates and times to establish that priority. The law ordinarily grants an exception for *purchase-money* mortgages, meaning a mortgage that the buyer grants to the lender who finances the purchase *or* back to the seller as seller financing, usually to make up a shortfall in the financing that the buyer can get from other sources. Purchase-money mortgages generally take priority over prior encumbrances. States are especially likely to recognize the exception when the competing security interests are mechanics' liens, judgment liens, and other similar interests. Also as indicated above, a foreclosing mortgage holder need not add superior mortgage holders because the foreclosure would not extinguish those superior mortgages, only *subordinate* mortgages. Superior mortgage holders may, on the other hand, join in a subordinate mortgage holder's action, treating the subordinate foreclosure as a default if the mortgage so permits.

A problem arises when a foreclosing mortgage holder fails to join a subordinate mortgage holder. Subordinate mortgage holders are *necessary parties* to the action because the action affects, indeed *extinguishes*, their subordinate rights. A court will require that subordinate parties join when learning about their non-joinder. Yet if the foreclosure proceeds without a subordinate mortgage holder participating, the law does *not* extinguish the subordinate mortgage. The winning bidder at foreclosure auction takes subject not only to any superior mortgages who did not seek foreclosure but also as to the subordinate mortgages that the foreclosing mortgagee did not name. The winning bidder, though, may *re-foreclose* the foreclosed mortgage in a second proceeding that names the subordinate mortgagee, either extinguishing the subordinate mortgage by bidding in the superior mortgage's value or, if the sale realizes more, then paying off the subordinate mortgage.

Deficiency and surplus. Foreclosure of the mortgage, execution on the real property, and the real property's sale are not the lender's only rights. The borrower will also have executed the promissory note, constituting a contract for the breach of which the lender may also sue. Thus, judicial foreclosure proceedings typically include a contract-breach count in addition to the foreclosure count. The *judgment of foreclosure* will provide for acceleration of indebtedness, execution on and sale of the real property, and application of proceeds to reduce the debt. Yet the judgment may also include a money judgment against the debtor for the total indebtedness, reduced by the sale amount net of costs. If the sale does not satisfy the judgment debt, then the lender may treat the remaining money obligation as a **deficiency** enforceable by other means such as wage or account garnishment, depending on the borrower's collectability.

If, on the other hand, the sale proceeds produce a **surplus** above the foreclosing mortgagee's costs, attorney's fees, and loan indebtedness, then as previously indicated, the law provides that the proceeds go first to extinguish debt owed to subordinate mortgagees. If the land has no subordinate mortgages, or if any proceeds remain after their payment, then the borrower landowner receives the remaining surplus representing the borrower's equity. Borrowers rarely receive any equity because if the land had any equity value, then the borrower would have sold the land to avoid foreclosure or would have refinanced either with the lender threatening foreclosure or with another lender.

Redemption after foreclosure. As introduced well above, foreclosure does not entirely terminate the mortgagor's rights. All states allow the borrower to **redeem** the mortgaged property before foreclosure sale, by paying the mortgage indebtedness. The common law treats the right as the **equity of redemption**, although many states provide for greater *statutory* rights of redemption, especially for residential mortgages. A right of redemption gives the mortgagor additional time, defined differently from state to state but often six months, to raise funds to *redeem* the property, meaning in essence to buy the property out of foreclosure by paying the foreclosed debt. In some states, foreclosure of the mortgage triggers the redemption period, ending with auction sale. In other states, sale triggers the redemption period, during which the buyer waits to see if the foreclosed mortgagor redeems. As indicated above, redemption rights are important because they protect homeowners from losing critical housing or losing home equity, or allow the foreclosed homeowner to accumulate savings and locate other housing, often while living in the premises without making mortgage payments.

Deed in lieu of foreclosure. The cost and delay of a foreclosure proceeding, the possibility that the borrower will raise defenses, and the difficulty, cost, and delay of collecting a deficiency judgment from the borrower, all encourage the lender to seek streamlined means of foreclosing. One such means is for the lender to simply take a **deed in lieu of foreclosure** from the borrower. If the borrower voluntarily grants the lender a deed, then the lender may be able to avoid judicial foreclosure entirely, particularly if the property has no subordinate mortgages or all mortgagees can reach terms of agreement as to the property's value and treatment. Borrowers typically demand that the lender *waive* any deficiency in exchange for the borrower's offer of a deed in lieu of foreclosure, evidenced by the lender executing an *estoppel affidavit*. Some states and some federally backed mortgages require deficiency waivers for deeds in lieu of foreclosure, to prevent lender overreaching. A deed in lieu of foreclosure allows the lender to promptly place the property on the private market for sale through a broker, a trusted and flexible process that may obtain a higher value than selling at auction. For similar reasons of efficiency and risk, the lender may alternatively agree to a **short sale** in which the borrower sells to a third party for less than the mortgage debt, the lender receives the sale proceeds, the borrower executes a deed to the buyer, and the lender discharges the mortgage and waives the deficiency.

Fluency Cards

Cover and uncover the response to each prompt until you fluently recall the exact response.

Security devices	**Mortgage**
Mortgages, deeds of trust, land contracts.	Security interest in land. Names grantor, property, and rights/duties.
Mortgage note	**Equitable mortgage**
Names borrower, amount, term, schedule, interest, and default.	When borrower executes and conveys deed to lender to hold as security.
Purchase-money mortgage	**Future-advance mortgage**
Used to buy the land. Has priority over prior liens.	Secures loans not yet made but have priority as of date recorded.
Land contract	**Absolute deed**
Finances land purchase without lender. Buyer has equitable title, seller legal.	Buyer gives to lender to record only on default. May be an equitable mortgage.

Security theories

Lien, title, or intermediate (title only on default).

Borrower duties

Maintain, pay taxes, insure, no illegal conduct, no waste.

Redemption right

Borrower may pay off obligation after default. No clogging this right.

Duty on transfer

New owner pays mortgage if *assuming* it but only faces lien right if taking *subject to*.

Novation

Rare case when lender relieves original borrower of paying note, looking only to buyer.

Subrogation

Lender or land-contract seller pay taxes and other charges, then recover from owner.

Surety

Co-signs borrower's note, owes same obligation but gets borrower exoneration.

Due on sale

Clause accelerating note on land's sale.

Holder in due course

Investor taking mortgage for value without notice. Takes free of personal defenses.

Discharge

Lender must record discharge on final payment or slanders title.

Foreclosure

Sale process to realize land value as security. Pays expenses first.

Foreclosure types

Judicial requiring court action or non-judicial with public auction.

Foreclosure defenses

Payment, inadequate disclosure, fraud, no notice, military service.

Omitted mortgagees

First recorded mortgage has priority over subsequent except purchase-money mortgage. May re-foreclose if omitted.

Sale proceeds

Surplus over note and costs goes to borrower. Deficiency results in judgment unless waived.

Deed in lieu

Lender takes deed, sells, and waives deficiency if short sale.

Definitions Worksheet

(Answers are on the reverse side.)

1. What is a *mortgage* and how do parties form one?

    _____

    _____

2. What is a *deed of trust* and how does it differ from a mortgage?

    _____

    _____

3. What is a *purchase-money mortgage* and how does it alter priority?

    _____

    _____

4. What is a *future-advance mortgage* and how does it alter priority?

    _____

    _____

5. What is a *land contract* and why do parties use it?

    _____

    _____

6. What are *lien, title,* and *intermediate* mortgage theories? What significance?

    _____

    _____

7. What are a borrower's duties to the lender during the mortgage term?

    _____

    _____

8. What is to *redeem* land? What does *clogging equity's redemption* mean?

    _____

    _____

9. How do taking *subject to* versus *assuming* a mortgage differ?

    _____

    _____

10. What is a *holder in due course* and why does it matter?

    _____

    _____

11. What is *foreclosure*? What are its two main types, and how do they differ?

    _____

    _____

12. What is a *deed in lieu of foreclosure*? How does it help borrower? Lender?

    _____

    _____

13. Who is a *surety*? What obligations does a *surety* owe?

    _____

    _____

Please do not review model answers until you have answered all questions fully and conferred with a seatmate to complete, correct, and supplement your answers.

Answers to Definitions Worksheet

1. A **mortgage** is a security interest in land securing the mortgage *loan* or *note*. The note is the borrower's contract obligation to the lender, including amount, term, payment schedule, interest, and default terms. The mortgage includes the grantor's identity, the property description, and the rights to assign, foreclose, or otherwise treat the mortgage, and obligations to discharge it on payment.

2. A **deed of trust** is a mortgage substitute in which the borrower executes a deed purporting to convey the land to the lender. The lender or escrow agent holds the deed, destroying or returning the deed if the borrower pays the full loan, or releasing and recording the deed if the borrower defaults. Courts may treat the deed of trust as an *equitable mortgage*.

3. A **purchase-money mortgage** is a security interest that the buyer grants to the lender whose loan pays the purchase price of the property. A purchase-money mortgage can also mean one that the buyer grants *back to the seller* to make up a financing shortfall. Purchase-money mortgages are generally treated with priority over other encumbrances such as mechanics' liens and judgment liens, even when the holders of those liens recorded them before the seller recorded the purchase-money mortgage.

4. An owner grants a **future-advance mortgage** without receiving loan proceeds or receiving only part of the funds that the loan anticipates. A future-advance mortgage enables the owner to draw future advances against the mortgage as the owner's needs arise. Many states give future draws priority as of the date of the mortgage's initial recording.

5. A **land contract** is both a means of conveying real property *and* financing the purchase. The contract specifies terms on which the buyer receives the deed, typically either payment of the full contract price after a long period or, more often, payments for a period of months or a few years until the buyer qualifies for a conventional mortgage.

6. A *lien* state treats a mortgage as a lien, a *title* state as passing title, and an *intermediate* state as a lien until default and then passing title. The distinction matters primarily for when a mortgage will sever the unity of title for a joint tenancy, converting it to a tenancy in common—only when the mortgage conveys title.

7. Standard mortgages require the borrower to maintain the mortgaged property in good repair, pay taxes, maintain insurance, and not conduct illegal activities on the premises such as would forfeit the land. The law of **waste** may permit a mortgagee to obtain court assistance in ensuring that the borrower does not destroy the property's value.

8. To **redeem** is the owner's statutory right to pay the full mortgage balance to take the land out of foreclosure. Law generally prohibits borrowers from waiving redemption rights in advance and lenders from demanding or contracting for that waiver, known as *clogging equity's redemption.*

9. When a buyer takes *subject to* a mortgage, the buyer does *not* become directly liable to the mortgage lender on the promissory note. The *seller* remains liable on the note, while the buyer's property remains subject to the mortgage. To *assume* an obligation means for the buyer to become *directly liable* to the mortgage lender for the indebtedness that the mortgage secures.

10. A **holder in due course**, meaning one who received the instrument in good faith, without knowing of defects, and having paid value. If the assignee is a holder in due course, then the assignee takes the borrower's obligation *free of personal defenses* from the note's formation like *fraud in the inducement, failure of consideration,* and *unconscionability*, but not *real defenses* like *legality* of formation like *forgery, infancy* or other *incapacity, illegality,* and *duress* or *coercion.*

11. **Foreclosure** is the process through which a lender secures and sells the land to satisfy the note balance on which the borrower defaulted. *Judicial foreclosure* requires a court proceeding in which the lender names the borrower as defendant and the court orders sale. *Non-judicial foreclosure* available in only some states involves private sale at auction after statutory notice and other procedures.

12. A lender takes a **deed in lieu of foreclosure** to avoid foreclosure costs. A borrower typically demands the lender's *deficiency waiver* for the deed, thus avoiding having to pay any deficiency. Borrowers and lenders may alternatively agree to a **short sale** to an already-identified buyer, in which lender waives the deficiency.

13. A surety signs the original contract along with the obligor to satisfy the lender's demand for better credit. The surety owes the obligation that the contract states, which is typically to pay when the primary obligor fails to do so. A surety may compel the primary obligor to perform, called *exoneration*, or to *reimburse* the surety for performing.

187

Application Exercises
(Answers are at the end.)

1. Distinguish the actions that refer to a *note* (N) from actions that refer to a **mortgage** (M):

____ The buyer signed to repay a $100,000 loan at 4% interest in monthly payments over 15 years.

____ The lender recorded an instrument reflecting the two acres as security for the business loan.

____ The homeowner granted the lender an interest to secure the $25,000 for kitchen improvements.

____ The lender sued for the loan deficiency after the home's sale left the owner underwater.

____ The bank foreclosed on the plant after the company ignored the notice, missing a sixth payment.

2. Distinguish the actions that refer to a deed (D) from those referring to a **trust deed (T)** as an equitable mortgage or mortgage alternative:

____ The seller conveyed a warranty deed to the buyer at closing in exchange for $250,000.

____ The buyer conveyed a quit-claim deed to the lender at closing in exchange for $300,000.

____ The homeowner conveyed a deed to the bank in exchange for $50,000 to add a sunroom.

____ The escrow agent accepted the buyer's warranty deed in seller's favor securing half the price.

____ The elderly homeowner conveyed a quit-claim deed to her son for the care that the son promised.

3. Distinguish the **purchase-money** (P), **construction-loan** (C), **home-equity** (H), and **future-advance** (F) mortgages:

____ The homeowners gave the bank a mortgage for $50,000 to pay for their child's college tuition.

____ The lot owner gave the bank a second mortgage for $200,000 to construct a lakefront cottage.

____ The buyer gave the credit union a first mortgage for the $400,000 price of the home.

____ The businessman gave the lender a mortgage for draws the owner expected to make for inventory.

____ The buyer gave the seller a mortgage to cover the last unpaid $50,000 of the sale price.

4. State whether the following draws made under a **future-advance mortgage** recorded when made before the other stated obligation, have priority (P) over that obligation or not (N):

____ $20,000 draw made after borrower grants a recorded mortgage for a $100,000 plant improvement.

____ $40,000 draw made after borrower grants a recorded mortgage for a new lot purchase.

____ $60,000 draw made after borrower gives lender cut-off notice to secure $500,000 improvement.

____ $80,000 draw made before borrower grants a recorded mortgage for $1,000,000 equipment buy.

5. Distinguish the **land contracts** (L) or *contracts for deed* from the other arrangements that are not (N) land contracts:

____ Buyer and seller sign agreement to close sale in ninety days contingent on financing.

____ Owner gives tenant possession for monthly payment with right of first refusal to buy.

____ Buyer can't get financing. Seller sells anyway, promising deed when buyer gets financing.

____ Owner gives tenant contract to buy for payments over five years ending in balloon payment.

6. State whether the joint tenant has destroyed unity of title (D) or not (N), converting the interest to a tenancy in common, in conveying a mortgage as follows:

____ In a *title-theory* state.

____ In a *lien-theory* state.

____ In an *intermediate-theory* state, before any default.

____ In an *intermediate-theory* state, after default.

7.   Identify whether the borrower has breached (B) standard **mortgagor duties** or not (N):

____ Borrower moves out after heat shut-off for failure to pay utilities, freezing and breaking pipes.

____ Borrower fails to improve home consistent with neighborhood improvements, reducing value.

____ Borrower fails to insure for fire and flood loss, although no damage has occurred yet.

____ Borrower fails to pay real-property taxes, although no tax sale has occurred yet.

____ Borrower grows marijuana crop on premises, violating state and federal law.

8.   Distinguish whether the owner has a **right to redeem** (R) or not (N), after defaulting on the mortgage and lender commences foreclosure proceeding:

____ Homeowner offers to resume monthly mortgage payments within statutory redemption period. N

____ Homeowner tenders full amount owed lender, within statutory redemption period. R

____ Commercial-property owner tenders full amount owed lender. N

____ Homeowner tenders full amount within statutory period but waived redemption rights at loan. R

____ Homeowner tenders full amount within statutory period, but lender holds absolute deed. R

9.   Identify whether the party is liable (L) on the mortgage note or not (N), on **land transfer**:

____ Buyer *assumes* seller's mortgage obligation. Bank sues buyer on buyer default.

____ Buyer takes *subject to* seller's mortgage obligation. Bank sues buyer on buyer default.

____ Buyer *assumes* seller's mortgage obligation. Bank sues seller on buyer default.

____ Buyer takes *subject to* seller's mortgage obligation. Bank sues seller on buyer default.

____ Buyer assumes mortgage note. Bank grants seller *novation*. Bank sues seller on buyer default.

10.   Identify whether the party is liable (L) or not (N) relating to **suretyship principles**:

____ Surety signs the borrower contract. Borrower fails to pay. Bank sures surety.

____ Guarantor signs separate guarantee on default. Borrower pays. Bank demands guarantor pay.

____ Surety orally agrees to stand for borrower's contract. Borrower fails to pay. Bank sues surety.

____ Bank sues surety for borrower default. Surety pays bank. Surety sues borrower in exoneration.

11.   Identify if a **holder in due course** (H) taking free of personal defenses or not (N):

____ Innocent investor takes mortgage note on assignment for 90% of face value, as investment.

____ National bank takes mortgage note on assignment for 20% of face value in bad-loans workout.

____ Hedge fund takes mortgage note in insider buyout of failed bank, for ten cents on the dollar.

____ Pension fund takes mortgage note in investment portfolio at market value.

12.   Distinguish the **personal defenses** (P) to which *holders in due course* are **not** subject from the **real defenses** (R) to which *holders in due course* remain subject:

____ Borrower claims lender or agent forged borrower's signature on loan documents.

____ Borrower claims lender gave no consideration when renewing mortgage note.

____ Borrower claims borrower was a minor lacking capacity to contract for mortgage.

____ Borrower claims lender defrauded borrower in failing to disclose adjustable interest rate.

____ Borrower claims lender's terms are unconscionable as an adhesion contract.

_____ Borrower claims lender coerced mortgage note by threatening credit report causing job loss.

13. Identify if **foreclosure** has *extinguished* (E) the italicized interest or not (N):

_____ Lender fails to follow state-mandated notice procedures as to *homeowner's interest*.

_____ *Foreclosed subordinate mortgage holder* wants payment after sale fails to satisfy superior lender.

_____ Sale proceeds are enough to pay mortgage but not costs and fees of sale owed to *professionals*.

_____ *Debtor* demands home equity after sale proceeds are enough to pay only two mortgage holders.

_____ Subordinate mortgage holder forecloses. *Superior mortgage holder* demands payment after sale.

_____ Superior mortgage holder neglects to foreclose *subordinate mortgage holder* before sale.

_____ Subordinate mortgage holder forecloses. *Superior mortgage holder* demands payment after sale.

_____ Mortgage holder conducts private sale without notice to *homeowner* in non-judicial state.

14. Identify whether the lender may pursue the sale **deficiency** (D) or not (N):

_____ Lender forecloses following judicial procedures. Auction nets less than mortgage amount.

_____ Lender agrees to private short sale at 90% of outstanding loan balance, for deficiency waiver.

_____ Lender takes deed in lieu of foreclosure from borrower who abandoned commercial structure.

_____ Lender takes deed in lieu of foreclosure offered by borrower contingent on deficiency waiver.

_____ Lender takes deed without deficiency waiver on federally backed low-income mortgage.

_____ Lender takes deed in lieu of foreclosure, executing an estoppel affidavit.

15. Identify if the lender has breached (B) its duty to **discharge** the mortgage or not (N):

_____ Borrower pays 90% of note balance with lottery winnings. Lender refuses mortgage discharge. N

_____ Lender cancels note, celebrating borrower successes. Lender later refuses mortgage discharge. B

_____ Borrower makes last note payment. Lender refuses mortgage discharge. B

_____ Borrower sells, conveying mortgage balance at closing. Lender refuses mortgage discharge. B

_____ Borrower sells to wealthy buyer on land contract. Lender refuses mortgage discharge. N

_____ Borrower refinances with another bank to prepay note. Lender refuses mortgage discharge. B

_____ Borrower prepays note. Lender promises discharge. Lender fails to record discharge. B

Answers: 1NMMNM 2DTTTD 3HCPFP 4PNNP 5NNLL 6DNND 7BNBBB 8NRNRR
9LNLLN 10LNNL 11HNNH 12RPRPPR 13NENENNNN 14DNDNNN

Drafting Exercise

Review the **land contract** on the following pages to answer these questions:

1. Who is the seller? _____ Who is the buyer? _____

2. What property is the seller selling? _____
Can you tell from the contract what kind of property (resident, commercial, urban, rural)
it might be? _____

3. What is the sales price? _____ How much of that price is the seller
financing (carrying)? _____ What is the interest rate? _____

4. How long does the land contract give the buyer to get bank financing? _____
What happens when the buyer gets bank financing? _____

5. What kind of deed must seller convey when the buyer gets financing? _____
Whom does that term favor, seller or buyer? _____

6. What does the contract anticipate if the buyer can't get financing within the allowed
period? _____

7. What remedies does the contract provide seller if buyer defaults? _____
_____

8. What, if anything, does the contract anticipate that the parties will record letting the
public know of the contract? _____

9. What terms might you negotiate to strike, alter, or add if you represented the seller?
_____
_____

10. What terms might you negotiate to strike, alter, or add if you represented the buyer?
_____
_____

11. The agreement anticipates one witness and no notarization. Is that sufficient, or
should the drafter have anticipated otherwise? _____
_____

12. If you were representing the *seller,* then would you advise entering into this land
contract? Why or why not? _____

13. If you were representing the *buyer,* then would you advise entering into this land
contract? Why or why not? _____

LAND CONTRACT

THIS LAND CONTRACT entered into on this _____ day of November, 2018, between, Smythe David ("Seller"), who resides at 318 Seldon Street, Muskegon, MI 49444, and Clark Beathune ("Buyer"), whose address is 424 Sunshine Avenue, Caldicott, FL 23123, upon the following terms and conditions:

1. DESCRIPTION OF PREMISES. Seller agrees to sell to Buyer land in the City of Muskegon, Muskegon County, and State of Michigan, commonly known as 234 Grange Street and legally described as:

Block 1005, Lots 4 and 5, except South 10 feet of Lot 5,

together with all improvements, hereditaments, and fixtures, if any, including, but not limited to: all mechanical equipment; all central heating, plumbing and electrical systems and equipment; hot water heaters; central cooling, humidifying and filtering equipment; fixed carpeting; built-in appliances, equipment and cabinets; water softener (except rental units); existing storm and screen windows and doors; attached shutters and shelving; roof or attic T.V. antenna; all planted vegetation; garage door openers and remote units. A pressure washer which creates its own hot water and steam is not a part of the sale but will be left by the seller for the buyer's use on the understanding and condition that buyer maintain it, for a six month period and such other period as seller and buyer may agree thereafter.

2. PRICE AND PAYMENT TERMS. Buyer agrees to purchase the Premises from Seller, and Seller agrees to sell, at a purchase price of $120,000, all payable as follows:

(a) Payment at Initial Closing: At the time of the initial closing, 15% of the total $120,000 purchase price, that being the sum of $18,000, plus or minus prorations and adjustments, if any, shall be paid;

(b) Contract Installments: Monthly payments in the amount of $984.32 commencing on the first day of each month, toward the $102,000 balance of the $120,000 purchase price, together with interest on the unpaid balance from the date of initial closing at the rate of 10% per annum, that monthly payment representing a 20 year term, until the lump sum/balloon payment described below is due, these Installment payments to be made per the attached amortization schedule, except that Buyer may prepay the land contract principal balance in part or in full at any time, with interest to be adjusted accordingly;

(c) Lump Sum/Balloon Payment: At the conclusion of the five years of monthly payments shown on the attached amortization schedule, Buyer shall pay Seller a lump sum/balloon payment in the principal amount then owing;

(d) Application of Payments: All payments received shall be applied as shown in the attached amortization schedule, based on the following order of priority: first, to interest accrued and owing upon the unpaid principal balance; second, to pay delinquent taxes and assessments which subsequent to the date of this Contract may become a lien on the Premises; third, to pay insurance premiums falling due after the date of this Contract; and fourth, to reduce said unpaid principal balance of the purchase price;

(e) Place of Payment: All payments shall be made to Seller at his street address 318 Seldon, Muskegon, MI 49444, or wherever otherwise directed by Seller.

3. DEED AND CONVEYANCE. If Buyer makes all payments and performs all the covenants and promises in this Contract, within the time and in the manner set forth, upon full performance of the covenants and agreements of Buyer, Seller shall at "final closing" convey title to the Premises to Buyer or the Buyer's legal representative, successors or assigns by Warranty Deed, subject only to: (a) easements for public utilities of record; (b) general real estate taxes not yet due and payable; (c) special assessments confirmed after the date of this Contract; (d) building, building line, and use and occupancy restrictions of record; (e) zoning laws and ordinances; (f) drainage ditches, feeders, laterals and drain tile, pipe or other conduit; and free from all other encumbrances except those, if any, expressly assumed by Buyer or those as shall have arisen through the acts or neglect of Buyer or Buyer's agents or assigns. Transfer tax due under 1966 P.A. 134, as amended, (MCLA 207.501 et seq) on the Warranty Deed upon completion of this Contract may be deducted by Buyer from the final installment payment due Seller under this Contract. Buyer shall pay the cost of recording such Warranty Deed and for all tax certification fees.

4. CLOSING. The "initial closing" shall occur on or before December 1, 2023, (or on the date, if any, to which said date is extended) at Seller's street address in Muskegon or other place agreed to between the parties. "Final closing" shall occur when all covenants and conditions to be performed by Buyer have been performed.

5. POSSESSION. The Buyer shall receive possession of the Premises at the time of the initial closing and shall be entitled to retain possession so long as there is no default by Buyer in carrying out the terms and conditions of this Contract.

6. PRORATIONS AND TAXES. Insurance premiums, general taxes, association assessments and, if final meter readings cannot be obtained, water and other utilities shall be adjusted ratably as of the date of initial closing. Real estate taxes levied in the year of possession shall be prorated as of the date of initial closing, subject to reproration upon receipt of the actual tax bill(s). Interest on principal balance of the purchase price from the initial closing until the date the first installment payment is due shall be prorated and credited to Seller at the initial closing.

7. WASTE. The Buyer shall maintain the Premises in the same condition it was in on the date of possession, reasonable wear and tear excepted. Buyer shall not, without the written consent of the Seller, remove, change or demolish the improvements on the Premises.

8. SURVEY. Prior to the initial closing, Buyer may obtain a survey of the Premises, certified by a licensed surveyor, showing all corners staked and showing all improvements, easements, building lines, and encroachments existing as of the initial closing date. Buyer shall pay the cost of such survey.

9. INSURANCE. Buyer shall obtain and keep in force fire, casualty, and extended coverage insurance covering the buildings and improvements now or hereafter placed on the Premises. Such policy shall contain a loss payable clause or other endorsement making the proceeds payable to the Seller and Buyer as their respective interest may appear, and be issued in an amount not less than the remaining balance of this contract. Buyer shall deliver a copy of the insurance policy(ies), or any renewals thereof, to the Seller reflecting all premiums paid.

10. TAXES AND CHARGES. Buyer shall pay when due, prior to the date when the same shall become delinquent, all general and special taxes, special assessments, water charges, sewer and/or water service charges, liens, homeowner association assessments, and any other charges levied, assessed, or charged against the Premises or on any improvements thereon, which accrue after the initial closing, furnishing Seller with the original or duplicate receipts for such payments.

11. INSURANCE AND/OR TAX DEFAULT. If Buyer fails to obtain, maintain, or deliver policy(ies) of insurance or to pay taxes or special assessments when due, Seller may: (a) pay the insurance premiums, taxes or special assessments and add them to the unpaid balance on the contract, or, (b) pay the insurance premiums, taxes or special assessments and treat Buyer's failure to pay them as a default, or, (c) not pay the insurance premiums, taxes or special assessments and treat Buyer's failure to pay them as a default.

12. SELLER'S RIGHT TO MORTGAGE. Seller shall give Buyer written notice of any existing mortgage or renewal, containing the name and address of the mortgagee, the amount and rate of interest on the mortgage, the due date of payments and maturity of the principal. Seller covenants to make all required payments as they mature on any existing or new mortgage and produce evidence of payment to Buyer on demand. If Seller defaults upon any mortgage obligation, Buyer shall have the right to do the acts or make the payments necessary to cure the default and shall be reimbursed by Seller directly or by receiving credit to apply on the payments due or to become due on this Contract.

13. ENFORCEMENT ON DEFAULT. If Buyer fails to timely perform any of the covenants or conditions contained in this Contract Seller may: (a) give Buyer a written notice specifying the default and informing Buyer that if the default continues for a period of fifteen (15) days after service of the notice that Seller will without further notice declare the entire balance due and payable, and proceed according to the common law or the statutes of the State of Michigan; and, (b) not declare the entire balance due and payable, and proceed according to the common law or the statutes of the State of Michigan including but not limited to the right of Seller to declare a forfeiture in consequence of the nonpayment of any money required to be paid under the contract or any other breach of the Contract, but in the event Seller elects to proceed under the sub-paragraph Seller shall give Buyer a written notice of forfeiture specifying the default which has occurred and shall give Buyer a period of fifteen (15) days after service of the notice of forfeiture to cure the default.

14. ASSIGNMENT. Neither party may assign, transfer or sell their interest in this contract or the Premises without the written consent of the other party, except that consent shall not be unreasonably withheld.

15. SELLER'S INSPECTIONS. Seller or Seller's authorized representative may enter the premises at reasonable times and upon reasonable notice for the purpose of inspecting same, provided Seller shall have no duty to make inspections and shall not incur any liability or obligation for making or not making any such inspections.

16. BUYER'S ACCEPTANCE OF TITLE AND PREMISES. Buyer acknowledges having been advised to request an attorney to examine title of the Premises. (a) At least one (1) business day prior to the initial closing, Seller shall furnish or cause to be furnished to Buyer, at Seller's expense, a commitment to issue a contract purchaser's/owner's title insurance policy in the current ATLA form of owner's policy (or equivalent policy) in the amount of the purchase price covering the date hereof, subject only to: (1) the general exceptions contained in the policy; (2) the "permitted exceptions" set forth in paragraph 3; (3) exceptions pertaining to liens or encumbrances of a definite or ascertainable amount, which may be removed by the payment of money and which shall be removed at or prior to the initial closing; and (4) acts done and/or suffered by, or judgments against the Buyer, or those claiming by, through, or under the Buyer; (b) If the title commitment discloses unpermitted exceptions, the Seller shall have thirty (30) days from the date of delivery to have the exceptions waived, or to have the title insurer commit to insure against loss or damage that may be caused by those exceptions and the initial closing shall be delayed, if necessary, during said thirty (30) day period to allow Seller time to have the exceptions waived. If Seller fails to have the unpermitted exceptions waived, or to obtain a commitment for title insurance over such exceptions, within the required time, Buyer may terminate this Contract, or may elect, upon notice to Seller within ten (10) days after the expiration of the thirty (30) day period, to take the title as it then is, with the right to deduct from the purchase price liens or encumbrances of a definite or ascertainable amount. If Buyer does not so elect, this Contract between the parties shall become null and void, without further action of the parties, and all monies paid by Buyer shall be refunded; (c) Every title commitment which conforms with subparagraph "a" shall be conclusive evidence of good

title as to all matters insured by the policy, subject only to special exceptions stated; (d) If a Special Tax Search, Lien Search, a Judgment Search or the title commitment disclose judgments against Buyer which may become liens, Seller may declare this Contract null and void and all earnest money shall be forfeited by Buyer; and, (e) Buyer's assumption of possession of the Premises shall be conclusive evidence that Buyer accepts and is satisfied with the physical condition of the Premises, all matters shown on the survey (if any), and the condition of title to the Premises on or before the initial closing. Upon delivery of possession, Seller shall have no further obligation with respect to the title or to furnish further title evidence, except that Seller shall remove any exception or defect not permitted under paragraph 16(b) resulting from acts done or suffered by, or judgments against the Seller between the initial closing and the final closing.

17. FIXTURES AND EQUIPMENT. Buyer shall also receive possession of the fixtures and equipment permanently attached to the improvements on the Premises, but until payment in full of the purchase price is made, no personal property, fixtures or equipment shall be removed from the Premises without written consent of Seller.

18. DISPOSITION OF INSURANCE PROCEEDS. In case of loss of damage as a result of which insurance proceeds are available in an amount sufficient to repair or rebuild the Premises, Buyer has the right to elect to use the insurance proceeds to repair or rebuild. To elect to exercise the right, Buyer shall give Seller written notice of the election within sixty (60) days of the loss or damage. If the election is made, the insurance proceeds shall be used for that purpose. If the insurance proceeds are not sufficient to repair or rebuild the Premises, Buyer may elect to use the proceeds to repair or rebuild by giving Seller written notice of the election within sixty (60) days of the loss or damage, and deposit with Seller an amount sufficient to provide for full payment of the repair and rebuilding. If the election and deposit, if required, are not timely made, the insurance proceeds shall be applied against the amounts owed Seller on this Contract. If the insurance proceeds exceed the amount required for repairing and rebuilding, the excess shall be applied first toward the satisfaction of any existing defaults under the terms of this Contract, and then as a prepayment upon the principal balance owing, without penalty, notwithstanding any other provision to the contrary. The prepayment shall not defer the time for payment of any remaining payments required under paragraph 2. Any surplus of proceeds in excess of the balance owing on this Contract, shall be paid to Buyer.

19. DEFAULT, FEES. (a) Buyer or Seller shall pay all reasonable attorney's fees and costs incurred by the other in enforcing this Contract, including forfeiture or specific performance, or in defending any legal proceedings to which Buyer or Seller is made a party as a result of the acts or omissions of the other party; (b) All rights and remedies given to Buyer or Seller shall be distinct, separate and cumulative, and the use of one or more thereof shall not exclude or waive any other right or remedy allowed by law, unless specifically waived in this Contract; and, (c) no waiver of any breach or default of either party hereunder shall be implied from any omission by the other party to take any action on account of any similar or different breach or default; the payment or acceptance of money after it falls due after knowledge of any breach of this Contract by Buyer or Seller, or after the termination of Buyer's right of possession hereunder, or after the service of any notice, or after commencement of any suit, or after final judgment for possession of the Premises shall not reinstate, continue or extend this Contract nor affect any such notice, demand or suit or any right hereunder not herein expressly waived.

20. FINAL CLOSING. Seller shall deliver to Buyer a Deed of conveyance and a Bill of Sale to all personal property to be transferred under this Contract upon full payment of all amounts due, in the form of cash, cashier's or certified check payable to Seller, without premium or penalty. Upon notice to Seller that Buyer is prepared to pay all remaining amounts due, Seller shall either produce and record at Seller's expense a release of Seller's mortgage(s), or obtain a loan repayment letter reflecting the amounts necessary to discharge and release such mortgage(s), and Seller may pay and discharge such prior mortgage in whole or in part from sums due from Buyer. Upon payment of the mortgage(s) Seller shall obtain and deliver release(s) to Buyer, giving Buyer credit against the balance of the purchase price for the cost of recording such release. If either party requests, the parties agree to complete the exchange at the offices of the holder of the note which is secured by the prior mortgage. At the time of delivery of the Deed, Buyer and Seller shall execute and furnish such real estate transfer declarations as may be required to comply with State, County or local law. Seller shall pay the amount of any transfer tax then imposed by State or County law and Buyer shall pay any transfer tax and meet other requirements as required by any local ordinance, unless otherwise provided in the local ordinance.

21. SERVICE AND NOTICES. All notices or demands shall be deemed given when served as follows: (a) by personal service on the party or to a member of the party's family of suitable age and discretion; or (b) by depositing the notice or demand in the United States Post Office with postage fully prepaid by first class mail, addressed to the party at the party's last known address.

22. TIME OF ESSENCE. Time shall be deemed of the essence of this Contract.

23. RESPONSIBILITY FOR ACCIDENTS. Buyer assumes all risk and responsibility for injury, damage, or liability to person(s) or property arising from Buyer's use, possession, and control of the Premises and improvements thereon, and Buyer shall indemnify Seller against and hold Seller harmless from.

24. PROHIBITION ON LIENS. (a) Buyer shall not suffer or permit any construction, mechanics' or judgment lien, or other lien(s) of any nature to attach to or be placed against title of the property; (b) Each and every contract for repairs or improvements on the Premises, or any part thereof, shall contain an express, full and complete waiver and release of any and all lien or claim of lien against the Premises, and no contract or agreement, oral or written,

shall be executed by the Buyer for repairs or improvements upon the Premises, except if the same shall contain such express waiver or release of lien upon the part of the party contracting, and a copy of each and every such contract shall be promptly delivered to Seller; and (c) If any lien(s) shall attach, Buyer shall cause the same to be discharged within thirty (30) days from the date of filing. Nothing in this Contract shall be deemed or construed to give Buyer the right or authority to contract for or to authorize or permit the performance of, any labor or services or the furnishing of any material that would permit the attaching of a construction lien to Seller's interest in the Premises.

25. RECORDING. The parties shall execute a memorandum of this contract which may be recorded at Buyer's expense.

26. BINDING EFFECT. The covenants and agreements of this Contract shall bind the heirs, assigns, and successors of the respective parties.

27. CAPTIONS AND PRONOUNS. The captions and headings of the various sections or paragraphs of this Contract are for convenience only, and are not to be construed as confining or limiting in any way the scope or intent of the provisions hereof. Whenever the context requires or permits, the singular shall include the plural, the plural shall include the singular and the masculine, feminine and neuter shall be freely interchangeable.

28. PROVISIONS SEVERABLE. The unenforceability or invalidity of any provision or provisions hereof shall not render any other provision or provisions herein contained unenforceable or invalid.

29. JOINT AND SEVERAL OBLIGATIONS. The obligations of two or more persons designated "Seller" or "Buyer" in this Contract shall be joint and several, and in such case each hereby authorizes the other or others of the same designation as his or her attorney-in-fact to do or perform any act or agreement with respect to this Contract or the Premises.

30. NOT BINDING UNTIL SIGNED. A duplicate original of this Contract duly executed by the Seller and spouse, if any, shall be delivered to the Buyer or his attorney on or before the date of the initial closing; otherwise at the Buyer's option this Contract shall become null and void and the earnest money, if any, shall be refunded to the Buyer.

31. REAL ESTATE BROKER. Seller and Buyer represent and warrant that no real estate brokers were involved in this transaction. Seller shall pay any brokerage commission at the time of initial closing.

SIGNATURE WITNESSED BY: SELLER: Smythe David

_____   _____
Printed name: Address: 318 Seldon Street, Muskegon, MI 49444
                                                Date: November _____, 2018

SIGNATURE WITNESSED BY: BUYER: Clark Beathune

_____   _____
Printed name: Address: 424 Sunshine Avenue, Caldicott, FL 23123
                                                Date: November _____, 2018

Prepared By:
Nelson P. Miller
41 Washington Street, Suite 280
Grand Haven, MI 49417
(616) 846-9875

Multiple-Choice Questions with Answer Explanations

619. A landowner entered into a future-advance mortgage with a bank, secured by a mortgage on land. The landowner subsequently drew $30,000 against the mortgage. The bank, though, mistakenly delayed in recording the mortgage. At the time of delayed recording, the bank discovered the landowner's recorded conveyance of the land to a buyer after the mortgage date but before the mortgage's recording. The buyer had no knowledge of the mortgage before paying the landowner $150,000 for the land and recording the conveyance after diligent title search. The jurisdiction, which follows the lien theory of mortgages, has a statute stating that "any conveyance of an interest in land is not valid against any subsequent purchaser for value without notice who first records." Will the bank prevail in an action seeking declaration that the buyer owns the land subject to the $30,000 mortgage?

A. Yes, because the bank acquired its interest for value before the buyer recorded.
B. Yes, because the mortgage was merely security for a loan rather than for purchase.
C. No, because the buyer purchased for value and recorded first without notice.
D. No, because the jurisdiction follows the lien theory of mortgages.

Answer explanation: Option C is correct because the first interest holder for value to record without notice prevails under a race-notice statute. Here, the buyer was a bona fide purchaser who recorded first without notice, under a race-notice statute. While the bank acquired its future-advance mortgage interest before the buyer, the buyer purchased the land for valuable consideration and without notice of the bank's interest. A future-advance mortgage is one that the parties enter into without money changing hands, and the mortgagor draws loan proceeds at a later date, like a line of credit secured by the mortgage. Option A is incorrect because to prevail, the bank must also have recorded before the buyer. Option B is incorrect because even though a mortgage interest is security for a loan, it is still an interest in land and under the statute still required recording. Option D is incorrect because whether the jurisdiction follows the lien theory or a title theory is irrelevant to the question. The outcome is the same under either theory.

642. A speculator mortgaged land that the speculator owned in order to borrow $150,000 to invest in other ventures. The lender recorded the mortgage. The speculator then sold the mortgaged land to a hunter who hoped to build a hunting cabin on the land. In completing the conveyance, the speculator signed a deed that clearly identified the mortgage and mortgage amount. The deed further recited that the hunter took the land subject to the mortgage and that the hunter expressly assumed and promised to pay the mortgage obligation. The deed did not require the hunter to also sign, but the hunter accepted the conveyance, recorded the deed, took possession of the property, and began paying the mortgage. Years later, the hunter grew tired of hunting, abandoned plans to build a cabin, and defaulted on the loan obligation. If the lender duly forecloses and sells the land leaving a $50,000 deficiency, then who has the primary liability on the deficiency?

A. The speculator who made the note and granted the mortgage, the hunter only a guarantor.
B. The speculator because the hunter did not sign the deed, the property having been sold.
C. The hunter for having made payments to the lender, thus being estopped from denial.
D. The hunter for having accepted the deed and thus its conditions and obligations.

Answer explanation: Option D is correct because a grantee who accepts a deed that expresses the terms of acceptance agrees to perform those terms including any promise that would protect the grantor, such as to pay a mortgage. Payment of a mortgage would include not just the value of the security but also the deficiency. Option A is incorrect because while the speculator would remain secondarily liable to the lender on the deficiency for having made the note, the court would enforce the hunter's promise by acceptance to pay the loan obligation. Option B is incorrect because a grantor may make a deed signed only by the grantor and not the grantee, and yet bind the grantee by the deed's express terms on the grantee's acceptance. The law calls this form of deed a *deed poll*. Option C is incorrect because making payments on an obligation would not alone make the payor liable on the remaining obligation. The payor must make a binding promise for the recipient of those payments to have an enforceable right against the payor.

652.   A homeowner used his $150,000 home on twin lots to finance a $50,000 business loan. The homeowner executed a mortgage that the bank making the loan duly recorded. The homeowner later determined to borrow another $25,000 as a home-equity loan to renovate the home's kitchen. The homeowner once again executed a mortgage that the home-equity lender duly recorded. After meeting both mortgage obligations for a year, the homeowner fell ill, lost a job, and defaulted on both mortgages. The bank promptly commenced foreclosure proceedings. The homeowner and home-equity lender filed a motion showing that the mortgaged home and twin lots had increased to $200,000 in value and that the severable lot alone had a value of $75,000, enough to secure the bank fully. What result if the motion requested the court to restrict the bank's foreclosure rights to the $75,000 severable lot, over the bank's objection?

A.   Motion granted because of marshalling's two-funds rule.
B.   Motion granted because pro-rata foreclosure fully secures the bank.
C.   Motion denied because the mortgage covered the entire property including the home.
D.   Motion denied because the bank holds a purchase-money mortgage.

Answer explanation: Option C is correct because senior lenders may foreclose on the entire interest despite that the owner and junior lenders have contrary interests. Option A is incorrect because marshalling's two-funds rule applies when a mortgage covers multiple parcels one of which is subject to a competing mortgage. In that case, the court could restrict foreclosure to the other property or properties if the foreclosing lender remained fully secured. Here, though, the junior lender only has a mortgage over the whole property just like the senior lender, and so the two-funds rule doesn't apply. The home-equity lender is subordinate to the bank. Option B is incorrect because only under the two-funds rule as just explained would full security under a portion of the mortgaged properties make a difference in the outcome. Here, the bank may foreclose on the entire mortgaged property. Option D is incorrect because the bank does not hold a purchase-money mortgage used to buy the home but instead loaned for business. Also, the type of mortgage, purchase-money or not, here makes no difference to foreclosure rights.

659.   The proprietor of a car-detailing service had for two years rented the building where he and his employees did the detailing work. The proprietor signed a land contract with the building's owner that gave the proprietor five years of making monthly land-contract payments at the old rent amount, before the proprietor would have to get bank financing to pay off the land contract in a balloon lump sum. The proprietor figured that he would be able to show a bank by then that he had the long-term business income and equity in the building to qualify for a commercial mortgage. Five years came and went quickly, with the proprietor making every monthly payment but still unable to qualify for a loan. What legal right and procedure, if any, does the owner have to realize the building's full value promptly?

A.   No right or procedure because the proprietor has made every monthly payment.
B.   Renegotiation of the contract to extend monthly payments until the proprietor qualifies.
C.   Forfeiture of the land contract to list and sell the building free of the proprietor's interest.

D.   Remove the proprietor through self-help to rent to a tenant who may buy with financing.

Answer explanation: Option C is correct because a land contract is a written agreement to sell real estate used for seller financing. Rather than borrowing money from a lender, the buyer makes payments to the seller under equitable title, until having paid in full or until a date when the agreement requires the buyer to obtain lender financing. When the buyer satisfies the terms, the seller conveys legal title by the form of deed that the land contract specified. Sellers treat buyer defaults by suit for land-contract forfeiture, while buyers enforce through suit for specific performance to convey deeded legal title. Option A is incorrect because the land contract called for a balloon payment of the full balance after five years, which the proprietor has not made and cannot make. The owner can proceed with forfeiture to extinguish the contract and sell the building to another, one hopes for cash or with bank financing. Option B is incorrect because extending the contract leaves the owner in no better situation than the owner is now, without having realized the full value of the building. The owner needs to forfeit the contract and find a buyer. Option D is incorrect because the law discourages self-help, self-help removal would not declare the land contract forfeited, and getting another tenant just starts the whole rental process over again when the owner wants to get the full value out of the building.

661.   A local bank made a large purchase-money mortgage loan to one of its own directors so that the director could buy a spectacular homestead property. The director and bank executed, exchanged, and recorded all of the appropriate documents to complete the transaction in the title-theory state in which both parties and the property were all located. The bank's board soon discovered that the director did not have the accounting degree and certification that the director had claimed when recruited to the board, and so terminated the director. In retaliation, the director refused to make any more payments on the loan and, shortly later, abandoned the homestead and fled out-of-state. What recourse is the bank most likely to have to extinguish the director's interest in the real property, sell the real property, and recover its loan?

A.   Judicial foreclosure of the mortgage lien followed by auction sale.
B.   Administrative proceeding for the director's fraud with restitution of the land.
C.   Civil lawsuit for breach of contract followed by execution on the land.
D.   Private, non-judicial foreclosure followed by listing and private sale.

Answer explanation: Option D is correct because the lien theory of mortgages, the majority rule, treats the borrower as retaining title but granting a lien on the property. By contrast, the title theory, recognized in a minority of jurisdictions, treats a mortgage as the borrower's conveyance of title to the lender. The intermediate theory treats the mortgage as a lien until default and as conveyance of title after default. The significance has to do with the procedures necessary for the lender foreclosing on the mortgage in the event of default, with the lender generally having the least procedure and greatest right in title-theory states where the lender may be able to follow a non-judicial, private foreclosure. Option A is incorrect because in a title-theory state, the lender holds title rather than having a lien, and may generally foreclose privately and sell in the usual course rather than follow judicial foreclosure and auction sale. Option B is incorrect because an administrative proceeding, even if available, would be an unnecessarily indirect and circuitous route to address the mortgage-loan obligation, where restitution of the land would be an improbable outcome. The bank would find it far better to simply privately foreclose on the mortgage in this title-theory state. Option C is incorrect because a civil lawsuit resulting in a judgment followed by execution on the homestead is an unnecessarily circuitous route when the homestead is already security for the obligation in a title-theory state where private foreclosure is most-likely possible.

663.   A newly licensed physician bought a nice home in an upscale subdivision, borrowing ninety percent of the cost from a local bank that had a private-lending program to professionals. The bank recorded a mortgage on the home in the lien-theory state in which the home, bank, and

professional were all located. The physician quickly discovered that she could not keep up with the complex demands of her new career, while also discovering that her income likely insufficient to pay her medical-school loans and the mortgage on her new home. The bank thus pressured her to give the bank a deed in lieu of foreclosure. If she declined, then what rights, if any, would the physician have before, during, and after foreclosure?

A.   A period in arrears before notice of foreclosure, continued possession and to bring arrears current during foreclosure, and to pay off the loan and redeem after foreclosure.
B.   Right to the effective assistance of counsel, due-process right to notice and opportunity to be heard, and right to a fair jury of her peers.
C.   Right to notice of claims, right to discovery, right to an alternative-dispute-resolution forum other than litigation, and right to trial.
D.   No rights because the bank may now deem itself insecure after which it may foreclose at its sole discretion.

Answer explanation: Option A is correct because the mortgagor's rights before foreclosure typically include a certain period (usually ninety days or more) in arrears, continued exclusive possession, to bring the loan current, to the lender's notice of intent to foreclose, to pay off the mortgage through sale, refinance, or other means, and to redeem within a certain period after foreclosure sale, although the mortgagor must also maintain the home while keeping it insured and paying taxes. Option B is incorrect because these rights approximate procedural rights of the criminally accused rather than the rights of a mortgagor during foreclosure. The physician may, for instance, hire counsel but would have no right to appointed counsel if indigent and no right to counsel's effective assistance. Option C is incorrect because these rights approximate procedural rights in any civil litigation rather than rights of a mortgagor during foreclosure. The physician would not, for instance, have a right to alternative dispute resolution, although voluntary alternative dispute resolution could help. Option D is incorrect because the law provides several significant rights. The bank, for instance, would not have a right to declare it insecure. The physician would instead have to miss several payments before the bank could institute foreclosure proceedings in this lien-theory state where judicial foreclosure is likely necessary.

666.   A large multinational corporation formed a joint venture with a small new limited-liability company for the company to develop a new set of business applications for the corporation and other customers. In order to carry out its part of the venture's work, the company needed to lease a small downtown office for its coding staff. When a commercial landlord rejected the company's credit for lack of earnings history, the corporation guaranteed the five-year lease for the company, giving the company the cash with which it paid the landlord for the first three years of the five-year lease. Within a year, the venture had failed because the company was unable to deliver the prototype applications timely. The company abandoned the leased premises with four years remaining on the five-year lease and two years still paid in advance. The landlord then sued the corporation as guarantor for the last two unpaid years of the lease. The corporation counterclaimed for reimbursement of the two remaining years paid in advance, claiming that the landlord could re-lease and mitigate. What are the legal theories that the landlord is advancing against the corporation and corporation against the landlord?

A.   The landlord pursues the corporation's breach of the lease while the corporation pursues the landlord's lease breach.
B.   The landlord pursues the corporation's suretyship while the corporation subrogates to the company's interest.
C.   The landlord pursues foreclosure of the lease while the corporation seeks an equity of redemption.

D.   The landlord pursues mitigation of the remaining lease obligation while the corporation seeks to show the corporation cannot mitigate.

Answer explanation: Option B is correct because one may subrogate to another's rights when paying a debt or other obligation that the other owes including on real property. Here, the corporation may subrogate to the company's right to have the landlord reimburse the prepaid years after mitigating by finding another tenant. One pursues suretyship principles when one party guarantees, or acts as a surety for, the obligations of another. The landlord would be suing the corporation on the corporation's suretyship for the company. Option A is incorrect because the corporation was a guarantor on the lease rather than the tenant, making lease breach an inapposite theory. Also, the corporation is subrogating to the company's claim against the landlord, not claiming that the landlord breached obligations owed the corporation. Option C is incorrect because foreclosures involve mortgages, not leases, and redemption involves recovering property after foreclosure, not recovering lease payments made in advance. Option D is incorrect because the landlord has the duty to mitigate by re-leasing rather than relying on a theory of mitigation against the corporation, while the corporation seeks to show that the landlord can mitigate, not that the corporation cannot mitigate.

668.   A welder at an auto plant bought a modest old home by borrowing $100,000 from a bank to which the welder gave a mortgage in that amount. The welder soon borrowed another $20,000 from a home-equity lender to renovate the old home's kitchen and bathroom. In a recession, the welder lost his job as the automaker downsized. Unable to make payments on the home, the welder cooperated with the bank's judicial foreclosure that resulted in a sale of the home to an investor who bid in and paid the bank's $100,000 outstanding obligation. The bank, however, failed to join the home-equity lender in the foreclosure proceeding. What are the relative rights, if any, of the investor and home-equity lender if the investor decides to re-foreclose to include the omitted home-equity lender?

A.   The investor holds title free and clear of the lender's $20,000 mortgage such that the lender has no rights and gets nothing in the re-foreclosure sale.
B.   The investor holds title free and clear of the lender's $20,000 mortgage but the lender may bid in the re-foreclosure sale to protect its interest.
C.   The investor holds title subject to the lender's $20,000 mortgage but in the bank's superior $100,000 position in the re-foreclosure sale.
D.   The investor holds title subject to the lender's $20,000 mortgage such that the lender gets the first $20,000 in the re-foreclosure sale.

Answer explanation: Option C is correct because when a foreclosure omits a mortgage holder, the proceeding fails to extinguish the omitted mortgagee's rights. The one taking fee title through foreclosure takes subject to the unextinguished mortgage although with the superior rights of any superior mortgage holder whose interest the proceeding foreclosed. The omitted mortgage holder retains its unextinguished mortgage but does not jump the queue into a position superior over superior mortgage holders whose interests the proceeding extinguished. Option A is incorrect because the first foreclosure omitted the lender, and the lender's $20,000 mortgage thus persists and would protect the lender in the re-foreclosure sale. Option B is incorrect because the lender's mortgage persists for not having been foreclosed in the first proceeding. Option D is incorrect because the investor stepped into the bank's superior purchase-money-mortgage position and so would find protection up to the $100,000 amount in the event of re-foreclosure.

682.   The owner of a rural home rented it out to a tenant who had bad credit. After a couple of years, the tenant convinced the owner to sell the home to the tenant on a land contract for a favorable price $50,000 below fair market value. Needing money to repair the home, the tenant

then borrowed $25,000 from a private lender who demanded and received an absolute deed from the tenant as security against the loan. The tenant soon defaulted on the loan. The private lender promptly foreclosed. Instead of selling the home, though, the private lender wanted to occupy and improve the home as his own. The tenant wanted instead to remain in the home or receive the equity in it after payoff of the loan. The original owner wanted return of the home. Which of the following accurately states relative rights?

A. The tenant likely has a right to redeem the home or recover the home's net equity.
B. The tenant's interest depends on whether the tenant recorded the land contract.
C. The private lender owns the home by absolute deed free of any interest in the tenant.
D. The original owner has no remaining interest given the deed in lieu of foreclosure.

Answer explanation: Option A is correct because foreclosed homeowners generally have rights to redeem, and the law discourages private actions that clog the equity of redemption. Here, the tenant has around $25,000 in equity in the home, and the private lender should not by absolute deed take that equity doubling the loan's amount. Trust deeds are for sale of the home at auction so that the borrower recovers any net equity. The lender should get the loan repaid out of the home's sale and then the tenant recovers the net equity. Option B is incorrect because although one may record a land contract or notice of the contract, the outcome here would not matter whether the tenant recorded the land contract but instead whether the tenant had a right to redeem or if not then to recover the home's equity net of the loan obligation. Option C is incorrect because of the tenant's redemption right and net-equity interest. As above, the law will construe an absolute deed taken as security as it would a mortgage or trust deed to preserve the equity of redemption or auction sale. Option D is incorrect because the tenant only supplied an absolute deed as security for the loan, not a deed in lieu of foreclosure, which would have been an offer and acceptance of a deed to the home after default on the loan, not as security for the loan before the loan. Moreover, the tenant had not completed the land contract and obtained a deed from the original owner, so that the tenant could not convey clear title by absolute deed as security or later by deed in lieu of foreclosure. The recording act won't help, either, because the private lender's search of the chain of title would not have shown any interest on the tenant's part unless the tenant recorded the land contract and then would have only shown the land contract obligation to the original owner. A check of title by property location would have shown that deeded title remained in the original owner.

685. A dentist owned a duplex residential property on which a bank had a recorded purchase-money mortgage securing a $100,000 loan balance that the dentist still owed from his original purchase. The dentist lived in one side of the duplex and a tenant in the other side. The dentist decided to move and so sold the duplex to the tenant on a written and signed land contract in which the tenant agreed that the tenant was subject to the dentist's mortgage on the duplex. The dentist and tenant did not notify the bank because the mortgage included a due-on-sale clause. The bank, knowing nothing of the sale, assigned its mortgage to a real-estate investment trust. What are the obligations if the tenant defaults on the purchase-money loan now held by the trust?

A. The bank may foreclose, sell, and collect any deficiency from the dentist.
B. The bank may foreclose and sell but may not collect any deficiency from the dentist.
C. The trust may foreclose, sell, and collect any deficiency from the dentist.
D. The trust may foreclose, sell, and collect any deficiency from the tenant.

Answer explanation: Option C is correct because while a mortgagor may sell the mortgaged property, the mortgagor remains personally liable unless the lender grants a novation. The buyer of the mortgaged property takes the property subject to the mortgage, but the buyer does not have personal liability for the mortgage loan unless expressly assuming the obligation. Here, the tenant only took subject to the mortgage rather than assuming the mortgage, which means that the tenant did not assume the mortgage obligation. Indeed, a transferee cannot assume a mortgage that includes a due-on-sale clause triggering the loan's acceleration with sale. Options A and B are incorrect because once a party assigns an interest such as a mortgage and loan receivable, the assignor loses the right to benefit from that interest. By taking assignment, the trust secured the right to foreclose. Option B is also incorrect because the dentist remains personally liable to the bank. The bank didn't know about the dentist's conveyance to the tenant and so could not have given a novation. Option D is incorrect because a person purchasing a mortgaged property does not become liable on the mortgage note unless expressly assuming the obligation.

687. An employer agreed to back a key employee's credit so that the employee could qualify for a high-value home loan. The employee completed the purchase, duly executing a purchase-money mortgage that the lender duly recorded. While the employee was the sole named obligor on the promissory note, the employer agreed in an attached writing to act as the employee's surety for the home-loan-note obligation. Over the next two years, the employee made regular payments on the home loan plus, when receiving a year-end bonus, a substantial lump-sum reduction of the loan's principal. The lender, though, improperly applied the lump-sum reduction to a credit-card balance that the employee also owed the lender. The employee then quit for another job in a foreign company and abandoned the home without making another payment. If the lender sues the employer to recover the outstanding home-loan obligation, then what theories should each side pursue in the litigation?

A. The employer subrogates as to the employee's rights while the lender pursues suretyship.
B. The employer assigns the employee's rights while the lender pursues subrogation.
C. The lender should foreclose while the employer relies on the equity of redemption.
D. The lender should assign while the employer seeks the employee's indemnification.

Answer explanation: Option A is correct because one may subrogate to another's rights when paying a debt or other obligation that the other owes. Here, the employer may subrogate to the employee's rights to have the lender account properly for the lump-sum reduction of the loan balance. Also, one pursues suretyship principles when one party guarantees, or acts as a surety for, the obligations of another. The lender would be suing the employer on the employer's suretyship for the employee. Option B is incorrect because the lender is not assigning (giving away) the employee's rights but instead seeking to exercise those rights. Also, the lender is not subrogating to any party's rights but instead seeking to pursue the employer's suretyship. Option C is incorrect because the lender has sued the employer to recover the loan balance rather than pursuing foreclosure and sale of the home to recover the loan balance. Also, the employer has no need for exercising the employee's right of redemption because the lender has not foreclosed. Option D is incorrect because the lender has nothing to gain by assignment, presumably meaning assigning the right of recovery. The lender is exercising that right and would not want to give it away. Also, while the employer might well seek the departed employee's indemnification, doing so may be fruitless with the employee out of the country and owing other debt, when the employer's first action should be to minimize the obligation owed the lender.

689. A mortgage broker obtained an appraisal on a new home that the broker knew was substantially more than the home's market value and then used that appraisal to loan an amount over the home's market value to an unsophisticated first-time homebuyer. The broker then sold the mortgage loan to a real-estate investment trust, which took an assignment. The homebuyer made several more payments on the loan to the broker, which had not notified the homebuyer of the broker's assignment to the trust. The homebuyer then refinanced with a bank for a lower interest rate but made no further payments because of job loss. How should the homebuyer defend if the broker sues on the loan and for foreclosure?

A. Plead novation, impossibility, and redemption.

B.   Plead misrepresentation, assignment, credit, and discharge.
C.   Plead poverty, immunity, release, and satisfaction.
D.   Demand that the refinance company defend and indemnify.

Answer explanation: Option B is correct because a lender that misrepresents material terms of the finance transaction causing loss is liable for misrepresentation, a lender who assigns to another loses the right to pursue the assigned obligation, a borrower who pays part of the obligation deserves a credit for those payments, and a borrower who refinances with a different lender paying off the prior obligation should have a discharge of the mortgage-loan obligation. Option A is incorrect because a novation would be a lender's agreement to release a borrower in favor of a new borrower assuming the obligation, impossibility would be if other events made a party unable to perform, and redemption regains a home after foreclosure. Option C is incorrect because poverty is not a defense, the facts suggest no immunity, the facts give no indication of the broker or trust having released the homebuyer, and while the refinance should have paid off the loan obligation, the defense would likely be payment and discharge rather than satisfaction, which refers to payment of a judgment rather than a loan obligation. Option D is incorrect because while the refinance company might owe defense and indemnity if it purposely, carelessly, or in breach of contract duties failed to pay and discharge the prior mortgage, right now the homebuyer needs to defend the pending action, and a demand on a non-party would not alone accomplish that defense, even if it might soon advance the homebuyer's interests.

694.   An elderly couple took out a mortgage on their home to pay the wife's medical bills. The wife passed away shortly later. The elderly man was unable to retire the loan obligation that the mortgage secured before his own demise. Shortly before his death, the man by valid will devised the home to the couple's eldest child, leaving the residuary of the estate to the couple's other, younger child. The will said nothing about how to treat the mortgage on the home. The home and residuary estate have approximately equal value, while the mortgage-loan balance is about half the value of the home. If the estate has no other assets or obligations, then what disposition of home, mortgage obligation, and residuary estate would the law provide, assuming that the couple's children make no agreed-upon adjustment?

A.   The younger child and eldest child will divide the estate equally after the estate pays the mortgage balance and treating the home as part of the estate.
B.   The younger child and eldest child will divide the estate equally, while the loan balance lapses and mortgage is discharged by the elderly husband's death.
C.   The eldest child receives the home encumbered by the mortgage, while the younger child receives the residuary estate free of the mortgage holder's claim.
D.   The eldest child receives the home free of the mortgage, while the younger child receives the residuary estate after reduction to pay the mortgage-loan balance.

Answer explanation: Option D is correct because exoneration entitles a devisee of an encumbered property to have the estate pay the encumbrance out of personalty in the estate, if any, rather than passing the encumbrance along with the property to the devisee, if as here the will makes no contrary provision. Option A is incorrect because the will devised the home to the eldest child, and treating it as part of the estate would frustrate that devise. Option B is incorrect because secured loans do not typically disappear with the debtor's death but remain attached to the security unless the loan agreement provides otherwise. The estate would owe the loan balance, which once satisfied would result in the mortgage's discharge. Option C is incorrect because exoneration would pay off the loan balance out of the residuary estate. Otherwise, the obligor's death would free the obligor to bequeath other assets (here, the residuary estate) without paying the mortgage-loan balance that the obligor owed before death, which would be contrary to the obligation and the policy supporting it.

697.   A tour operator owned a dock facility where he docked his tour boats. The operator had purchased the facility many years earlier using a mortgage-loan arrangement with the local bank on which the operator was still making payments. The operator had also used much of the equity that he had in the dock facility to finance his purchase of tour boats. The lender financing the tour boats had secured the loans with a second mortgage on the dock facility. The operator had also not fully paid a contractor who had repaired pilings supporting the dock, such that the contractor had recorded a workman's lien against the dock facility. The tour operator then sold the dock facility on a land contract to an entrepreneur for the entrepreneur to dock his yacht there, the contract reciting that the entrepreneur took subject to liens and mortgages. What, if any, are the entrepreneur's obligations to the bank, lender, and contractor?

A.   The entrepreneur owes nothing to any of them but must pay all of them out of any proceeds on any sale of the dock.
B.   The entrepreneur owes all of them their full obligation and must also pay them out of any proceeds on sale of the dock.
C.   The entrepreneur owes nothing to any of them and must pay only the bank out of any proceeds on sale of the dock.
D.   The entrepreneur owes only the bank but must pay all of them out of any proceeds on any sale of the dock.

Answer explanation: Option A is correct because one who takes *subject to* a mortgage or lien, rather than assuming the obligation, does not have direct liability to pay for that obligation, but the real property continues to serve as security for the obligation, which the new owner must pay before receiving any sale proceeds. Option B is incorrect because a buyer of land only owes mortgage and lien obligations if expressly assuming those obligations, which the entrepreneur did not do here. Option C is incorrect because the entrepreneur took subject to all three obligations and would owe all three out of any sale proceeds. Option D is incorrect because the entrepreneur does not owe even the bank for not having expressly assumed the bank obligation but indeed must pay both mortgages plus the lien out of any sale proceeds.

699.   A first-time home buyer with no assets and little earnings history joined a local lender's program to promote minority home ownership. Although the buyer did not qualify for a conventional loan, the lender's program granted the buyer a mortgage loan under special terms that enabled the lender to monitor the buyer's household budget closely. The program further required the buyer to execute a deed to the bank for the bank to hold in escrow while granting the bank full right to recover sole title to the home promptly, with the buyer waiving any further rights, if the buyer failed to make two consecutive payments. In the alternative, on default, the program gave the bank an option to buy the home back for one dollar if the bank canceled the buyer's loan obligation. If the buyer defaults, then may the bank lawfully pursue either alternative?

A.   Yes because the buyer did not qualify for conventional loan programs.
B.   Yes as to the deed in escrow but no as to the sham one-dollar option.
C.   No as to the sham deed in escrow but yes as to the one-dollar option.
D.   No because both alternatives clog the buyer's equity of redemption.

Answer explanation: Option D is correct because the equity of redemption refers to the foreclosed homeowner's right to redeem the real property by paying the outstanding obligation. Foreclosed homeowners generally have rights to redeem notwithstanding the efforts of lenders or others to discourage, or *clog,* redemption. Here, both of the bank's programs, the deed in escrow and the option, clog the buyer's equity of redemption. Option A is incorrect because both of the bank's programs, the deed in escrow and the option, clog the buyer's equity of redemption. The buyer would likely have the right to foreclosure procedures and to redeem after foreclosure according to state law. Option B is incorrect because the deed in escrow alternative would prevent the buyer from redeeming, as would be the buyer's right under state law, and from having the other protections of foreclosure proceedings. Option C is incorrect because the one-dollar option would prevent the buyer from redeeming and having the other protections of foreclosure proceedings.

700.   A clothier who owned his own store wanted to expand his inventory but could not find a commercial lender to help him do so. So instead, the clothier arranged with a local bank for a future-advance mortgage against his store. The clothier then made periodic draws totally $50,000 from the arrangement, except that the clothier spent the money renovating his seaside bungalow rather than buying clothing inventory for the store. On learning of the clothier's misuse of the funds, the bank accelerated the $50,000 loan obligation and demanded repayment in full under the terms of the loan agreement. If the clothier refuses, then what rights, if any, has the bank to collect the loan?

A.   File suit and foreclose the mortgage, seeking the store's sale at auction as loan security.
B.   File damages suit for breach of the loan agreement, but no right to foreclose the mortgage.
C.   Take the store's existing clothing inventory and equipment for auction as loan security.
D.   Seek foreclosure on the seaside bungalow into which the clothier put the loan proceeds.

Answer explanation: Option A is correct because a future-advance mortgage is one that the parties enter without money changing hands, and the mortgagor draws loan proceeds later, like a line of credit but secured by the mortgage. A future-advance mortgagee would then have the same right to foreclose the mortgage as would a conventional lender supplying a purchase-money mortgage. Option B is incorrect because the purpose of a future-advance mortgage is like that of a conventional mortgage, to make the real property stand as security subject to foreclosure in event of default. Option C is incorrect because the facts give no indication that the clothier offered inventory and equipment as security, although doing so might be common. The bank instead obtained a mortgage on the store, which may have been the more-valuable and more-secure security interest. Option D is incorrect because the bank has no mortgage on the seaside bungalow to foreclose. The only mortgage is against the store, not the bungalow.

Week 13

Title Assurance

Short Outline:

Title assurance systems assure that buyers receive title that sellers claim in the transaction to convey.

One title-assurance system involves state *recording act* and another involves *title insurance*.

Recording acts create systems for buyers, mortgagees, lienholders, and other claimants to **record** land interests.

Recording involves providing the deed or other instrument to the *register of deeds* for recording and indexing.

The register enters the instrument so that others can discover it on search relating to person or land.

Bona-fide purchasers take *for fair consideration* recording superior title *without knowledge or reason to know*.

Bona-fide purchases gain recording-act protection depending on recording-act form.

Notice acts hold bona-fide purchaser superior to earlier who did not record if bona-fide did not know of earlier.

Race acts look to who recorded first, without considering who had notice of earlier title.

Race/notice acts hold bona-fide purchaser superior only if not knowing of the earlier *and* recording first.

Indexes: key to effective title search is the **index** that the register maintains showing each instrument's recording.

Grantor/grantee index categorizes and indexes by grantor and grantee name, in alphabetical order.

Buyers examine *grantee* category, tracing sellers back to earliest recording ensuring buyer title.

Repeating the process in *grantor* index confirms no buyer sold to anyone other than the next buyer.

Tract index categorizes and indexes instruments by land, dividing by sections, blocks, and lots.

Buyers search land location to see what instruments the register of deeds has recorded as to that land.

Chain of title depends on establishing a sound chain from the earliest transaction to the most-recent transaction.

Marketable title shows chain without *gap*, *missing link*, *unaccounted-for interest*, or other defect.

Title searches through recording indexes determines whether chain of title has defects.

Buyer who discover defects from title search may refuse to close for failure of a material term of the contract.

Protected parties can depend on who buys first, whether one is a bona-fide purchaser, and who records first.

If neither purchaser records their deed, then the first purchaser has superior title under any recording act.

Sellers convey good title only once, to the first purchaser, unless recording act provides otherwise.

Also, bona-fide purchasers who record first always have superior title, no matter the recording act.

Also, if an earlier purchaser records before a later purchaser, then the earlier purchaser always has superior title.

The later purchaser cannot be bona fide because earlier recording establishes notice.

Priorities can differ depending on the form of recording act, whether **notice**, **race**, or **race/notice**

Notice recording acts protect **bona-fide purchasers** no matter who records *after* bona-fide purchaser takes.

Race recording acts protect parties who record first.

Race/notice acts protect only bona-fide purchasers who record first.

Thus one difference is when earlier purchaser records *after* later purchase but *before* later purchaser records.

Later purchaser would *not* have record notice at purchase, but earlier purchaser won *race* to record.

Notice acts favor later purchasers, while **race** acts favor earlier to record.

Race/notice act changes outcome only if later purchaser records *before* earlier, without notice.

Notice does not affect one who takes from a seller having superior title, superior title **sheltering** buyer.

Recording acts do not resolve how buyer discover owners taking by *adverse possession*.

Buyers must inspect for adverse possession because recording does not necessarily show adverse possession.

Recording shows adverse possession only if possessor received and recorded a judgment showing title.

Buyers failing to discover adverse possession may sue sellers under general warranty deed, not quit claim.

Title insurance protects buyers against undisclosed defects in title.

Sale contracts often include *title-insurance contingency* for buyer to inspect and approve insurer commitment.

Title-insurance commitment discloses encumbrances or other defects that title-insurer search discovered.

Insurer *title search* shows gaps in ownership, to which the buyer can then object before closing.

Title search also shows recorded covenants and easements.

Title insurance pays to resolve title defects that the insurer should have discovered and disclosed but did not.

If title insurer cannot cure title and buyer loses property or value, then title insurer indemnifies for the loss.

Special problems can arise relating to title.

After-acquired title involves grantor anticipating title purports to *transfer* title *before acquiring* title.

If grantor never acquires title, then transfer remains void. One cannot transfer title that one does not have.

Estoppel by deed holds that if grantor after-acquires title, then grantee *estops* grantor from denying transfer.

Grantee has good title except against a bona-fide purchaser for value without notice who records first.

Forged instruments are ones to which the signer signs someone else's name without that person's authority.

Witness and notary requirements discourage forgeries.

Deeds mistakenly recorded with facially apparent defects for recording do *not* give *constructive notice.*

Title search must reveal the defective instrument, giving actual notice.

If defects do *not* appear on the instrument's face, then recording satisfies constructive notice.

Undelivered deeds, grantor failing to deliver deed intending to complete grant, are generally ineffective.

Execution alone, without delivery, does not create an enforceable right of title.

When owner dies without having delivered, grant is incomplete and void.

Deed in escrow *to deliver at owner's death* remains an incomplete and ineffective gift.

Some states treat the escrow as an intended devise, subject to probate.

Purchase-money mortgages involving loans to buy the real property generally have priority over other liens.

Judgment and tax liens involve creditors recording against real property that the judgment debtor owns.

Judgment creditor and taxing authorities record liens and await the home's sale or foreclose the lien.

State laws provide *homestead exemptions* against execution on a judgment lien recorded on real property.

Homestead exemptions vary, some states offering unlimited or high amounts but others low amounts.

Long Outline:

Title assurance systems

Real-property law and practice offer two systems for assuring that a buyer of land receives the title that the seller should convey in the transaction. The first **title-assurance system** involves the state's *recording act*. As the next section addresses, a recording act establishes a practical system and legal mechanism in which owners of real property can record their deeds or other claims of title, interest, or right, with a local official, the effect of which is to give the recording claimant legal advantages over other claimants who have *not* recorded. The other title-assurance system that real-estate practice offers is *title insurance*. As a following section addresses, title insurers assume the obligation to a policy-holding property owner to litigate and indemnify in efforts secure the owner's title against adverse claims, while also compensating the owner when the owner loses a title challenge, possession, and ownership.

Recording acts. As just indicated, **recording acts** create systems in each state for real-property buyers, mortgagees, lienholders, and other claimants to interests in land to **record** their interests for the public to see. The act of *recording* involves providing to the local *register of deeds*, usually at the county level, the deed or other instrument that the person wishes to record so that the register can enter the instrument in the system in a manner that others can discover it on search for records relating to the real property. The system allows others, particularly potential buyers or mortgagees, to determine the state of title on the land including such things as who owns the land or has a security interest, easement, or other claim of an interest in it. Buyers of land record deeds promptly to ensure that others know that they are now the rightful titleholders. Once recorded, the register returns the original deed to the buyer, while keeping a copy.

Race, notice, and race-notice. Recording acts are significant not just for enabling buyers and lenders to determine who owns and what encumbrances the land's title. Recording acts can also determine which claimant prevails among multiple claimants, particularly when a devious owner purports to transfer title to multiple competing buyers. **Bona-fide purchasers**, referring to those who take *for fair consideration* and record superior title *without knowledge or reason to know* of superior claims, gain the recording act's protection. The conditions, though, under which a bona-fide purchaser gains superior title depend on the recording act's form, either **notice**, **race**, or **race/notice**. A *notice* jurisdiction holds a bona-fide purchaser's title superior to an earlier purchaser's title if the earlier purchaser did not record the deed and the subsequent purchaser did not know of the earlier transfer. By contrast, a *race* jurisdiction looks simply to who recorded first, without considering who had notice of other earlier title. And a *race/notice* jurisdiction grants the subsequent bona-fide purchaser superior title only if the subsequent purchaser did not know of the earlier transfer and records first.

Indexes. The key to an effective title search is the **index** that the register maintains showing each instrument's recording and that title searchers use to track recordings. Registers of deeds keep one of two different kinds of indices. A **grantor/grantee** index categorizes and indexes instruments by either grantor name or grantee name, in alphabetical order. Thus, if a buyer wanted to confirm that the seller had title, the title searcher would look up the seller in the *grantee* category because the seller would have previously gained title *as a buyer*. The searcher could then see who *sold* to the seller and look up *that* seller-to-the-seller in the grantee index, and on back to the earliest recording, ensuring a good chain of title *as to buyers*. The searcher must then repeat the process *in the grantor* index to see if any buyer sold to anyone other than the next buyer in the chain of title. By contrast, a **tract** index categories and indexes instruments by the land within the county. The tract index divides the county up first by cities, villages, townships, or like divisions, then by sections, then by blocks, and then by lots, or similar divisions. A title searcher can then search the index for any land location in the county, to see what instruments the register of deeds has recorded as to that land.

Chain of title. As the prior section suggests, good title depends on establishing a sound chain from the earliest transaction to the most-recent transaction in which the current owner took title. **Chain of title** refers to the continuity of transactions from owner to owner. Good, sound, or marketable title depends on showing that the chain of title leaves no *gaps, missing links, unaccounted-for interests*, or other defects. For example, if A sells to B who sells to C, then the chain of title suggests no defect. Yet if A_1 and A_2 first own as co-tenants, and then only A_1 conveys to B who conveys to C, the chain of title has not accounted for the interest of A_2, and the chain of title thus shows a defect. Similarly, if A conveys to B and then C conveys to D, the chain of title reflects a gap, meaning no conveyance, between B and C, showing a defect in D's title. The primary purpose of title searches through recording indexes is to determine whether the chain of title has defects. A buyer who discovers from a title search before close that the seller does not have sound, recorded title as the land sale contract required, may refuse to close for failure of a material term of the contract. A second significant purpose is to discover and disclose encumbrances.

Protected parties. As indicated above, *notice* recording acts **protect** bona-fide purchasers, meaning those who take for value and without notice, no matter who records *after* the bona-fide purchaser takes. By contrast, *race* recording acts protect parties who record first. And *race/notice* recording acts protect only bona-fide purchasers who record first, the bona-fide status of the purchaser satisfying the recording act's notice condition and the first-recording satisfying the recording act's race condition. The type of jurisdiction, whether *notice, race,* or *race/notice*, does not always affect the superiority of title in a dispute over title. Sometimes, the outcome is the same in all three types of jurisdiction. For instance, if neither purchaser records their deed, then the first purchaser has superior title. The seller can only convey good title once, to the first purchaser, unless the law provides otherwise. The recording acts can change the order, encouraging recording. Yet in *all* jurisdictions, a bona-fide purchaser has superior title to an earlier purchaser if the bona-fide purchaser, again meaning one who bought for value without notice of the earlier sale, records first. Similarly, in *all* jurisdictions, if the earlier purchaser records before a later purchase, then the earlier purchaser will have superior title because the later purchaser cannot be a bona-fide purchaser, which requires taking without notice. The earlier recording establishes notice.

Priorities. The above sections show that one purpose of recording acts is to establish reliable **priorities** for the purchaser who has superior title, so that buyers can follow reliable practices when buying. As shown above, the type of recording act can make a difference in the priority order. The clearest differences among *notice, race,* and *race/notice* jurisdictions arise when the earlier purchaser records *after* the later purchase but *before* the later purchaser records. The later purchaser would *not* then have record notice at the time of purchase, but the earlier purchaser would have won the *race* to record. **Notice** jurisdictions favor the later purchaser, if the later purchaser gave value and had no other notice (not having had record notice). **Race** jurisdictions favor the earlier purchaser who, after all, won the race to record. A **race/notice** jurisdiction would change the outcome only if the later purchaser managed to record *before* the earlier purchaser, assuming also that the later purchaser had no notice.

Notice. In a *notice* jurisdiction, transferees who take from any transferor who had superior title under the jurisdiction's recording act also have superior title, even if they have notice of a competing claim. The transferor's superior title **shelters** the transferee. Recording acts do not address every situation in which a buyer would have actual or constructive **notice** of a superior title. Specifically, recording acts do *not* resolve how a potential buyer would discover an owner taking by *adverse possession*. Only if the adverse possessor has already received and recorded a court judgment showing that the possessor has taken title from the owner, will the real-property records disclose the adverse possessor's interest to the potential buyer. If, instead, the adverse possessor has the right of adverse possession but has not yet reduced the title to a recorded judgment, then the potential buyer's title search will not disclose the possession. The potential buyer must inspect the property for the adverse possessor, whose possession must, after all, be open and notorious, meaning discoverable on inspection. If the buyer buys without discovering the adverse possessor and then loses title to the adverse possessor, the buyer's recourse is against the seller under the general warranty deed, unless the seller conveyed instead only by quit claim, in which case the buyer may have no recourse.

Title insurance. Buyers of land typically purchase **title insurance** to protect against undisclosed defects in title. Title companies insure title. Land sale contracts typically include *title-insurance contingencies*, enabling the buyer to inspect and approve the title insurer's commitment, which discloses encumbrances or defects that the title insurer's search discovered. Title defects can include not just adverse third-party claims to title but also *missing links* in the chain of title. Chain of title should show a continuous right of ownership, without unexplained gaps in the record of how the property passed from owner to owner. The title insurer's *title search* would show gaps in ownership, to which the buyer can then object when the title company shares its title-insurance commitment with the buyer before the closing. Title defects can also include encumbrances such as covenants and easements that burden or limit the property's use. The title search should also show recorded covenants and easements. Title insurance pays to resolve title defects that the insurer should have discovered and disclosed but did not do so. If the title insurance cannot cure title and the buyer loses the property, then the title insurer indemnifies the buyer for the loss.

Special problems. The following sections address a few remaining **special problems** relating to title to real property. The first section addresses *after-acquired title*, referring to instances when a transferor conveys before acquiring title but then acquires title after the transfer. The law addresses that issue following the doctrine of *estoppel by deed*. The next section addresses how the law deals with *forged instruments* and *undelivered deeds*. *Purchase-money mortgages* also get special treatment, as the following section addresses. Finally, the concluding section addresses *judgment and tax liens*.

After-acquired title (including estoppel by deed). One anomaly that can arise in real-property transactions is that a person who believes in having title or who anticipates soon acquiring title, purports to *transfer* title *before acquiring* title. If the person never acquires title, then of course the transfer remains void. One cannot transfer title that one does not have. Yet if the person who purported to transfer title that the person did not have *subsequently acquires* title, then fairness to the transferee would seem to dictate that the transferee somehow acquires the transferor's **after-acquired title**. Indeed, the law holds under the doctrine of **estoppel by deed** that the transferor who acquires title after having purported to transfer it, cannot deny the transferee's claim to title. The prior transfer of deed *estops* the transferor from denying transfer and refuting title. The transferee has good title as to the transferor's claim, under the estoppel-by-deed doctrine. However, a bona-fide purchaser taking for value and without notice from the same transferor, after the first transfer and after the transferor finally acquired title, may have the superior title over the first transferee, particularly if the bona-fide purchaser records first.

Forged instruments. Real-property law authorizes practices to discourage forging of deeds and other instruments. A **forged instrument** is one to which the signer has signed someone else's name without that person's authority. The purpose of forgeries is usually nefarious, such as to obtain the forgery victim's funds in purported purchase, although some forgeries, though wrong and damaging, are innocent and done with good intention. One way that states discourage forged real-estate instruments is to require witnesses and notary acknowledgment for recording. The signer must sign in front of witnesses who also sign, and a notary public who attests to the signer's identity and signature. These acknowledgment requirements reduce the incidence of forgeries, although not eliminating them. The law holds that deeds recorded with such facially apparent defects in the acknowledgment that the register should not have recorded them, do *not* give *constructive notice* of the recorded instrument, only notice if the title search reveals the instrument. On the other hand, if the only defects in the acknowledgment are not apparent from the instrument's face, such as that the notary's commission had expired or that a witness was underage, then the recording still satisfies to make the deed superior for a race or race/notice jurisdiction.

Undelivered deeds. As indicated in an above section, when the transferor has executed the deed, the transferor must **deliver** the deed to the transferee with the intent of completing the transaction for the transaction to be effective. Execution alone, without delivery, does not create an enforceable right of title. For example, if a seller executes a deed at the office of the seller's lawyer but instructs the lawyer to hold the deed awaiting some event or satisfaction of some condition, then the deed's execution does not transfer title. The problem of an **undelivered deed** becomes acute when the owner dies without having delivered. In such cases, the law holds the transfer incomplete. The real property does not pass by deed but instead through rights of survivorship, as the decedent's will directs, or as the laws of intestacy provide, depending on the circumstances. The owner's placing the deed in escrow *to deliver at the owner's death*, a tactic often intended to avoid taxes or probate, is equally problematic. The law in such cases tends to hold either that the deed remains an uncompleted and therefore ineffective gift or treat the escrow as an intended devise, subject to probate. An undelivered deed is generally ineffective in accomplishing anything that the owner may have intended, unless confusion and disappointment were the owner's intent.

Purchase-money mortgages. As indicated in an above section, property owners grant a **purchase-money mortgage** when they use the loan's proceeds to buy the real property on which the lender records the mortgage. Purchase-money mortgages are routinely *first* mortgages, lenders typically requiring that all parties, including any prior mortgagees, so agree, and law typically so providing. The law generally gives priority to purchase-money mortgages, particularly over mechanics' liens and judgment liens. Yet a purchase-money mortgage can also mean a mortgage that the buyer grants back *to the seller* to make up a shortfall in the buyer's other financing. The special problem that a seller taking back a mortgage from the buyer creates is that the seller only has a *complex, expensive,* and *time-consuming* remedy, which is foreclosure under the state's laws, generally protecting the mortgagor landowner, while granting that landowner a right of redemption. A mortgage back to the seller is a creative but disfavored device.

Judgment and tax liens. Judgment creditors may record a **judgment lien** against real property that the judgment debtor owns. A money judgment is a court order reducing the debtor's obligation to an obligation that the creditor may enforce against the debtor's non-exempt assets. State laws provide limited exemptions against execution on a judgment. Exemptions relating to real property are for *homesteads,* meaning the home in which the judgment debtor resides. The amount of the homestead exemption varies from state to state, with a few states offering unlimited or high dollar amounts but other states offering lower amounts a fraction of most home values. A judgment creditor may record a judgment lien and await the home's sale, when the debtor must pay the lien to be able to pass good title to the buyer. Alternatively, a judgment creditor may foreclose the lien, seeking the home's sale, although the debtor would realize the exemption amount before the creditor recovered anything. Federal and state tax liens operate similarly. Federal law authorizes the Internal Revenue Service to file a tax lien against the debtor's real property but requires or permits the Service to discharge the lien, subordinate the lien to other encumbrances, or withdraw the lien under some circumstances.

Fluency Cards
Cover and uncover the response to each prompt until you fluently recall the exact response.

Recording procedure

Register of deeds indexes instruments so bona fide purchasers for consideration get priority.

Recording acts

Notice (must record), race (must record first), and race/notice (must record first without notice).

Index

Grantor/grantee or tract search for chain of title.

Title search

Accounts for all interest and defects in chain of title.

Superior title

Earlier buyer if none record, or earlier buyer who records first, or bona fide buyer who records first.

Notice

Buyer must inspect for adverse possession.

Title insurance

Protects buyer from undisclosed title defects. Buyer inspects title-insurance commitment.

After-acquired title

Grant before title. Void if grantor never gains title but estop by deed if grantor gains title.

Forged instruments

Recording is still notice if defects do not appear on instrument's face.

Undelivered deeds

Grant is void without delivery, such as if grantor dies first.

Judgments and liens

Record against land, then await sale or foreclose.

Homestead exemption

State law protects homestead from judgment execution up to certain amount (some unlimited).

Definitions Worksheet
(Answers are on the next page.)

1. What is a *recording act*? What is the act's goal?

_____

_____

2. What are the three different *forms* of recording act? How does each operate?

_____

_____

3. What is an *index*? What are the two types, and how do they work?

_____

_____

4. Disregarding recording-act forms, who generally has *superior title*?

_____

_____

5. How does *adverse possession* relate to recording? What must buyers do?

_____

_____

6. What role does *title insurance* play in protecting title?

_____

_____

7. What is *after-acquired title*? How does law treat after-acquired title?

_____

_____

8. How does law discourage *forgeries* in title transfer?

_____

_____

9. What problems arise with *undelivered deeds*? How does law address them?

_____

_____

10. What is a *judgment lien*? How does law treat a judgment lien?

_____

_____

Please do not review model answers until you have answered all questions fully and conferred with a seatmate to complete, correct, and supplement your answers.

Answers to Definitions Worksheet

1. A **recording act** establishes a practical system for landowners to record their deeds or other claims of title, interest, or right, with a local official. The goal is to give the recording claimant legal advantages over other claimants who have *not* recorded, to increase the reliability of ownership and efficiency of land transactions.

2. The three forms of recording act are **race, notice,** and **race-notice.** A *notice* act holds a bona-fide purchaser's title superior to an earlier purchaser's title if the subsequent purchaser did not know of an earlier unrecorded transfer. A *race* act looks to who recorded first, without considering who had notice of earlier title. A *race/notice* act grants the subsequent bona-fide purchaser superior title only if not knowing of the earlier transfer and if recording first.

3. A register of deed's **index** shows each instrument's recording for title searchers to track recordings. A **grantor/grantee** index indexes by grantor name and grantee name, in alphabetical order. The title company searches back from buyer to seller and forward from seller to buyer. A **tract** index indexes by the land within the county. The title company examines the parcels for relevant transactions.

4. If neither purchaser records, then the first purchaser has superior title. Also, a bona-fide purchaser has superior title to an earlier purchaser if the bona-fide purchaser records first. Also, if the earlier purchaser records before a later purchase, then the earlier purchaser will have superior title.

5. Recording does *not* affect **adverse-possession** claims. Only if the adverse possessor has already received and recorded a court judgment showing that the possessor has taken title from the owner, will the real-property records disclose the adverse possessor's interest to the potential buyer. The potential buyer must inspect the property for the adverse possessor or, failing that, sue the seller for warranty breach.

6. Under **title insurance**, insurers assume the obligation to the policy-holding landowner to litigate and indemnify in efforts to secure the owner's title against adverse claims, while also compensating the owner when the owner loses a title challenge, possession, and ownership.

7. **After-acquired title** is when the grantor grants before acquiring title but then acquires title after the grant. If the grantor never acquires title, then the grant is void. If the grantor *subsequently acquires* title, then the doctrine of **estoppel by deed** holds that the grantor cannot deny the grantee's title. However, a bona-fide purchaser taking for value and without notice may have superior title if the bona-fide purchaser records first.

8. Law discourages forged real-estate instruments by requiring witnesses and notary acknowledgment for recording. Deeds recorded with apparent defects in the acknowledgment do *not* give *constructive notice* of the recorded instrument.

9. The problem of an **undelivered deed** becomes acute when the grantor dies without having delivered. In such cases, the law holds the grant incomplete. If the grantor places the deed in escrow *to deliver at the owner's death*, law tends to hold either that the grant remains incomplete or that the deed constitutes a devise subject to probate. An undelivered deed is generally ineffective in accomplishing anything that the grantor intended.

10. Judgment creditors may record a **judgment lien** against real property that the judgment debtor owns. State laws provide limited, or in a few states unlimited, exemptions against execution on a judgment against the debtor's *homestead*.

Application Exercises

1.   Identify if the bona-fide purchaser (B) or earlier purchaser (E) has **recording-act priority** for the real-property purchase:

____   Under *race* act, bona-fide purchaser records not knowing of earlier purchaser's unrecorded title.

____   Under *race* act, bona-fide purchaser buys not knowing of earlier purchaser's recorded title.

____   Under *race* act, bona-fide purchaser records knowing of earlier purchaser's unrecorded title.

____   Under *notice* act, bona-fide purchaser records not knowing of earlier purchaser's unrecorded title.

____   Under *notice* act, bona-fide purchaser buys not knowing of earlier purchaser's recorded title.

____   Under *notice* act, bona-fide purchaser buys not knowing of earlier purchaser's unrecorded title.

____   Under *notice* act, bona-fide purchaser buys knowing of earlier purchaser's unrecorded title.

____   Under *race/notice* act, bona-fide purchaser records not knowing of earlier unrecorded title.

____   Under *race/notice* act, bona-fide purchaser buys not knowing of earlier recorded title.

____   Under *race/notice* act, bona-fide purchaser buys knowing of earlier purchaser's unrecorded title.

2.   Identify if the bona-fide purchaser (B) or earlier purchaser (E) has **priority** for the real-property purchase without regard to recording-act forms:

____   Neither purchaser records.

____   Only the later bona-fide purchaser records.

____   Only the earlier purchaser records.

____   Both purchasers record, earlier purchaser before later bona-fide purchaser.

3.   Who prevails: **adverse possessor** (A), purchaser (B), or general-warranty seller (S)?

____   Bona-fide purchaser fails to inspect, buys without notice of possession, and sues possessor.

____   Bona-fide purchaser fails to inspect, buys without notice of possession, and sues seller.

____   Bona-fide purchaser inspects before close, discovers possession, and sues possessor.

____   Bona-fide purchaser inspects before close, discovers possession, and sues seller.

____   Possessor records judgment of title before bona-fide purchaser buys and sues possessor.

4.   State whether the **title insurer** must protect and indemnify (I) the buyer to remove or compensate for the burden, or not (N):

____   Insurer commits to policy without exceptions. Land has undisclosed easement.

____   Insurer commits to policy with standard exceptions. Land has necessary utility easement.

____   Insurer commits to policy with standard exceptions. Seller's ex-spouse claims dower rights.

____   Insurer commits to policy with standard exceptions. Co-owner of seller claims forged deed.

____   Insurer commits to policy excepting contractor liens. Buyer discovers drywaller-sub lien.

5.   Determine whether grantor (R), grantee (E), bona-fide purchaser (B), or none of them (N) have title, in these **after-acquired title** scenarios and under **estoppel by deed**:

____   Grantor acquires title after grant to grantee but then refuses to relinquish possession to grantee.

____   Grantor grants to grantee without having title and never subsequently acquires title.

____   Grantor acquires title after grant to grantee who records. Grantor conveys to bona-fide purchaser.

____   Same scenario but grantee doesn't record. Bona-fide purchaser records.

Answers: 1BEBBBEBEBEE 2EBEE 3ABABA 4INIIN 5ENEB

Drafting Exercise

Review the **land-contract memorandum** on the following page to answer these questions:

1. What is a land-contract *memorandum*? _____
_____

2. Why record a land-contract memorandum? _____
_____

3. Who are the sellers? _____ Who are buyers? _____

4. Who should record, buyers or sellers? _____

5. The memorandum notarizes only the sellers' signatures. Why only the sellers and not also the buyers? _____
_____

6. The memorandum has only one witness signing per buyer or seller. Is one witness sufficient? Why or why not? _____
_____

7. Whom, sellers or buyers, do you think the preparer represented? Why? _____
_____

8. Circle the legalese that you would clean up if you were the memorandum's drafter.

9. Referring to an attachment for the legal description will likely satisfy the recording statute if indeed the drafter attaches the legal description. Is that good form? Shouldn't the drafter just retype the legal description into the memorandum? Why or why not? ___
_____
_____

10. Why would the preparer include the so-called P-number, indicating the preparer's law licensure, after the preparer's name? May just anyone prepare an instrument for another to record? _____
_____

11. Why include both a legal description and a tax-identification number, and a street address, for the land? _____
_____

Liber   Page

MEMORANDUM OF LAND CONTRACT

The undersigned parties acknowledge that they have entered into a certain Land Contract ("AGREEMENT") wherein Duane A. Strassman and Kay L. Strassman ("SELLERS"), have agreed to sell to Donna James and Mark James ("BUYERS"), the following described property pursuant to the AGREEMENT executed on the ____ day of November, 2018, as to which the parties agree that this Memorandum shall be recorded in the Office of the Kent County Register of Deeds. The parties execute this Memorandum to give notice of the AGREEMENT between the parties.

LEGAL DESCRIPTION: See attached Exhibit A

said property being located in the City of Grand Rapids, Kent County, Michigan, and having the tax identification number PP # 41-31-36-334-012, and being commonly known as 901 Cauliflower S.W., Grand Rapids, Michigan. Upon recording, this memorandum shall constitute record notice to all persons of the existence of the underlying Land Contract and of Buyer's and Sellers' interest in and to the subject property.

IN WITNESS WHEREOF the parties have signed and executed this Memorandum of Land Contract on this   day of November, 2018.

WITNESSED BY: SELLERS:

_____   _____
Printed name: Duane A. Strassman

_____   _____
Printed name:_____   Kay L. Strassman

                                                       BUYERS:

_____   _____
Printed name:_____   Donna James

_____   _____
Printed name:_____   Mark James

STATE OF MICHIGAN   )
) ss
COUNTY OF KENT   )

On this   day of November, 2018, before me, a Notary Public in said County, personally appeared Duane A. Strassman and Kay L. Strassman, known to me as the same persons described in the foregoing Memorandum of Land Contract, and acknowledged that they executed this document as their free and voluntary act.

_____
Peter Patterson, Notary Public
Kent County, MI
Commission expires: 11/13/2020

Preparer:
Nelson P. Miller   (P40513)
Fajen and Miller, P.L.L.C.
1527 Pineridge Drive
Grand Haven, Michigan 49417

Multiple-Choice Questions with Answer Explanations

655. An elderly homeowner conveyed his home in fee simple to his caretaker. The homeowner's deed stated that the caretaker had paid $10 and other good consideration. The caretaker duly recorded the deed. A few days later, the homeowner executed and caretaker signed and accepted a trust instrument stating that the conveyance's purpose was that the caretaker hold the home in trust for the homeowner's granddaughter. No one recorded the trust. When the homeowner died shortly later, the caretaker rented out the home's main living quarters and paid the rent over to the granddaughter. A few years later, the caretaker sold the home to a young couple who had no knowledge of the trust. The young couple moved in while the caretaker moved with the market-value proceeds to warmer climates. No longer receiving rent payments, the granddaughter investigated and discovered the sale. What result if the granddaughter sues the young couple to perform the trust?

A. Young couple wins because the homeowner conveyed the home before creating the trust.
B. Young couple wins because they are bona fide purchasers who took free of the trust.
C. Granddaughter wins because parties need not record trusts creating equitable interests.
D. Granddaughter because a successor in title takes subject to the grantor's trust.

Answer explanation: Option B is correct because a recording act protects bona fide purchasers who take fee title without notice of the unrecorded encumbrance while paying valuable consideration. The young couple didn't know of the unrecorded trust. Option A is incorrect because the timing of the trust's creation doesn't matter when the recording act requires notice. Option C is incorrect because recording acts do require recording of trusts creating equitable interests just as they require recording of other instruments. Option D is incorrect because although successor ordinarily does take only the title that the grantor possesses, the recording act would require that the encumbrance on the title be of record in order to bind bona fide purchasers. The young couple were bona fide purchasers protected by the recording act.

657. A brother owned a rarely used resort vacation home on a golf course. His beloved sister visited the home often, calling it her own home. Facing financial difficulty, the sister secretly purported to convey the home to a buyer for valuable consideration. The buyer recorded the sister's warranty deed in which the sister reserved an estate in the home for three years. The brother died two years later leaving the home to his beloved sister a deed for which the personal representative of the brother's estate promptly executed and recorded. Six months later, the sister purported to convey the home again to an unsuspecting friend for valuable consideration. The friend recorded the sister's warranty deed and then took possession of the home, moving in. The friend and buyer were surprised to meet one another at the home a few months later when the sister's three-year estate would have ended. What would be the grounds if litigation between them to quiet title resulted in a win for the friend and loss for the buyer?

A. The buyer's deed was not in the friend's chain of title.
B. The friend was first in possession of the home.
C. The sister's deed to the buyer took effect after her deed to her friend.
D. The sister had nothing to convey to the buyer.

Answer explanation: Option A is correct because a bona fide purchaser for value without notice gains the protection of the recording act as to deeds not in the chain of title. The buyer's deed is not in the friend's chain of title because the buyer took from the sister before the sister had title, whereas the friend took from the sister after the sister had recorded title. The chain from brother to sister to friend gave the friend notice of only that chain and not the sister's deed to the buyer before the sister had become part of that chain of title. Option B is incorrect because possession does not bear under these circumstances on who has good title. Option C is incorrect because nothing delayed the buyer's deed taking effect. The buyer either had title or did not, the latter being the case because the sister then had nothing yet to convey. Estoppel by deed could give the buyer good title relating back to the date of the sister's conveyance, but the recording act gives the friend bona fide purchaser the valid title. Option D is incorrect because the doctrine of estoppel by deed would work in the buyer's favor to gain title from the sister once she came into possession of it but for the workings of the recording act in the friend's favor.

658.   A debtor owing $60,000 to a creditor inherited three contiguous vacant lots each having a $15,000 value for a total $45,000 total value. To pay down his debt, the debtor mortgaged all three lots to a bank in exchange for a $45,000 loan reflecting the mortgaged lots' full market value. The debtor used the $45,000 loan proceeds to pay the $60,000 debt down to $15,000. The debtor then forged and recorded the bank's mortgage release for one of the three lots to sell the released lot to an unsuspecting buyer. Relying on the forged release, the buyer paid the debtor the lot's full $15,000 value, recording the debtor's warranty deed under a recording act that protected bona fide purchasers without notice. The debtor used the $15,000 proceeds to pay off his debt, and then promptly skipped town. The bank and lot's buyer together soon discovered the debtor's forgery. What result if the bank and lot's buyer litigate whether the bank has a mortgage on the buyer's lot or the buyer owns the lot free of the bank's mortgage?

A.   Bank wins because the debtor's forgery was ineffective to remove the mortgage.
B.   Bank wins because the buyer should have discovered the forgery after reasonable inquiry.
C.   Buyer wins because the buyer relied on the recorded release under the recording act.
D.   Buyer wins because the bank should have discovered the recording of the forged release.

Answer explanation: Option A is correct because a forger cannot convey title that the forger never had, based on the forgery, and the forger's grantees get no advantage from the forgery. Recording acts protect against unrecorded interests but not against forgeries. Option B is incorrect because the law places no obligation on buyers who examine recorded title to discover forgeries, although they would certainly want to do so because they cannot gain title based on forgery. This option gives the right result for the wrong reason. Option C is incorrect because a buyer cannot gain interests purporting to arise based on the seller's forgery. Option D is incorrect because the law places no obligation on mortgagees or other holders of recorded interests to discover subsequent forgeries even if recorded. One has no duty to continue to examine recordings against an interest already acquired.

662.   A cabin owner had access to his land and cabin from a dirt road but wanted access instead to a paved road nearby, both for ease of use and to increase the cabin's value. The cabin owner negotiated with the neighbor for a driveway easement across the neighbor's land and out to the paved road. For valuable consideration, the neighbor signed and delivered to the cabin owner a written driveway easement, one that the cabin owner did not record. The cabin owner promptly completed the driveway. The neighbor then mortgaged his property to borrow money from a bank to construct his own cabin. The bank promptly recorded the neighbor's mortgage. Learning of the neighbor's plans, the cabin owner recorded the driveway easement. The neighbor decided not to build a cabin and instead defaulted on the loan and absconded with the loan money. The bank filed suit to foreclose on the mortgage to recover the defaulted loan from the sale of the neighbor's land, in doing so seeking to extinguish the cabin owner's easement. What would be the strongest grounds on which the court would preserve the easement?

A.   The bank had notice or constructive notice of the cabin owner's driveway use.

B.   The driveway easement was appurtenant and attached to the neighbor's land.
C.   The driveway easement was necessary for access to a paved public road.
D.   The cabin owner's recording before the foreclosure action protects the easement right.

Answer explanation: Option A is correct because a recording act ordinarily protects only bona fide purchasers who take and record without notice of superior rights. Purchasers who are or should be aware of the superior right, in this case the driveway easement, take subject to that right. Here, the cabin owner had a written easement but just hadn't recorded it. The bank knew or should have known of the easement because of the driveway's construction. Option B is incorrect because although an appurtenant easement, one pertaining to a particular benefitted parcel, ordinarily passes with the property, the question here is not whether the easement continues but which interest, mortgage or easement, is superior under the recording act. Because the bank took the mortgage with notice or constructive notice of the driveway, the bank does not get the protection of the recording act. Option C is incorrect because access to a paved road doesn't matter when the cabin owner already had access to a dirt road. Easements by necessity do not arise simply to improve access but rather to create access that doesn't exist. Option D is incorrect because recording before foreclosure would not matter. Recording before the bank recorded would matter, except that the bank had notice in any case.

667.   An uncle owned a vacant home at which his adult nephew often stayed with his uncle's permission. The uncle held the title to the home in fee simple, reflected in a deed duly recorded. Needing funds for drugs, the nephew purported to convey the home by warranty deed to a buyer. The buyer duly recorded the deed but allowed the nephew to remain in the home. The uncle then determined to aid his nephew by deeding the nephew the home in fee-simple title. The nephew duly recorded the deed. Needing yet more funds, the nephew then conveyed the home by warranty deed to a second buyer who duly recorded the deed and took possession. When the first buyer from the nephew discovered the nephew's second buyer in the home, suit ensued to determine which of the two buyers had title. Who prevails?

A.   The first buyer because of the recorded deed senior to the second buyer's deed.
B.   The second buyer because recording without notice of the first buyer's claim.
C.   Depending whether the first buyer's deed was in the second buyer's chain of title.
D.   Depending whether the court imposes an equitable division of title.

Answer explanation: Option C is correct because how the register of deeds indexes the titles can determine whether a deed from a grantor who only later obtains title appears in a later grantee's chain of title. A recording act protects a bona fide purchaser for value without notice of superior claims. If the second buyer's chain of title did not reflect the first buyer's deed because the indexing system only supported tracing chain from those who hold title when conveying, then the second buyer would win. But if the indexing would have revealed the first buyer to the second buyer, then the second buyer would lose the recording act's protection. Option A is incorrect because the grantor nephew did not have title when conveying to the first buyer, and so the first buyer's deed might not appear in the second buyer's chain of title, giving the second buyer the recording act's protection. Option B is incorrect because the second buyer could have had notice depending on the indexing system. Option D is incorrect because courts have no authority to impose equitable divisions when the deeds and law will determine title.

678.   A first-time home buyer found a home for sale by owner that the buyer wished to purchase. The owner showed the buyer the home including a new kitchen that a contractor was just finishing. The buyer and owner negotiated and signed a purchase agreement calling for the sale to close in ninety days and for the buyer to take possession one week after the closing. The buyer's bank required that the buyer purchase title insurance on the home effective on the closing date that covered both the bank and buyer. The title-insurance commitment disclosed

just before the closing showed no special exceptions to coverage but included standard exemptions. One week after the closing, when the buyer tried to move in, the buyer discovered that the owner had leased the home to a tenant for six months. The buyer soon also discovered that the owner had not paid the kitchen contractor who had just recorded a contractor's lien against the home the day after the closing. What right, if any, has the buyer to the title insurance's coverage for the loss and expense associated with the lease and lien?

A.   Full coverage as to the lease and lien as existing after the policy's effective date.
B.   Full coverage as to the lease but none as to the lien not of record at effective date.
C.   None as to the lease but full coverage as to the lien arising after effective date.
D.   None as to the lease or lien as not of record at the time of effective date.

Answer explanation: Option D is correct because title insurance protects a homeowner from claims made against the property's insured title (ownership history) but has standard exemptions from coverage. A policy would not cover interests that are not of record, such as an unrecorded lease, or that enter the record after the insurer issued the policy. Option A is incorrect because title insurance does not cover what arises after the effective date but instead defects in title that it should have discovered and disclosed that existed before the commitment and effective date. Here, the lease was not of record and so would not have appeared in the title search. The lien arose only after the title search, commitment, and effective date. So neither lease nor lien is part of the coverage. The buyer's only recourse would be against the seller, not the insurer. Option B is incorrect because the insurer would not have found the lease because it was not of record. The buyer's inspections should have discovered the lease, so the buyer takes that not-of-record risk. Option C is incorrect because a policy only insures for title defects that would have been of record at the commitment (effective) date. The insurer has no opportunity to discover and disclose liens that arise later, which the buyer must thus address with the seller rather than the insurer.

683.   The longtime owner of an aging residence received an online solicitation from an unknown new home-equity lender for a very low-interest home-equity loan. Intrigued at the possibility of renovating parts of the home, the owner completed the lender's online application, disclosing confidential details of the owner's identification and credit history. The lender approved the application, but the owner decided not to borrow. One year later, a national company well known as a mortgage collector contacted the owner demanding that the owner pay the online lender's mortgage then in default. The owner replied truthfully that the owner had never executed the forged mortgage and loan documents that the online lender had conveyed to the collector for the collector's purchase payment and without the collector's knowledge of the forgery. What result if the collector sues the owner anyway?

A.   Collector wins because the owner should not have disclosed confidential information.
B.   Collector wins as a holder in due course having taken for value without knowledge.
C.   Owner wins because the collector is not a holder in due course having taken a forgery.
D.   Owner wins because forgery is a real defense to which the collector remains subject.

Answer explanation: Option D is correct because while holders in due course who pay valuable consideration and take without knowledge avoid defenses *personal* to the mortgagee such as that the mortgagee did not pay the mortgagor the loan when receiving the mortgage, holders in due course instead take subject to *real* defenses including the mortgagee's forgery or duress, mortgagor's incapacity, and mortgage's illegality. Option A is incorrect because the collector loses on the owner's real defense of forgery and because a party's willingness to disclose confidential information does not make the person responsible for subsequent forgeries using the information. That is, the owner does not lose the real defense simply because of an argument that the owner should not have disclosed the information on which the forger based the forgeries. Option B is incorrect because although the collector is a holder in due course, the owner has the real defense that the documents were all forgeries. Option C is incorrect because the collector is a holder in due course for having taken for value without knowledge. The forgery goes to a real defense, not to the collector's status as a holder in due course.

684. An aunt who wanted to see her niece do well after college graduation agreed to help the niece buy a home by loaning the niece the home's down payment. The niece and aunt signed a loan agreement that required the niece to repay the loan on a specific schedule and that stated that the home would be the aunt's loan security. The niece told her commercial mortgage lender about the aunt's loan and even offered the lender a copy of the unrecorded loan agreement, but the lender declined. The lender made the loan and then duly recorded the niece's properly executed mortgage, which said nothing about the aunt's loan of the down payment. The niece subsequently moved out of the home and defaulted on both loans after she failed to pay utilities and the utility company shut off the heat and lights to the home in the freezing winter. Which of the following would be most pertinent to which creditor, the aunt or the commercial mortgage lender, has priority in foreclosure proceedings?

A.   The jurisdiction follows the title theory for mortgages.
B.   The jurisdiction follows the lien theory for mortgages.
C.   The jurisdiction follows the intermediate theory for mortgages
D.   The jurisdiction's recording act follows race rather than notice.

Answer explanation: Option D is correct because a race recording act gives priority to the first to record. Because the lender loaned to help the niece buy the home, the lender held a purchase-money mortgage. When the lender recorded, it was the first and only to record, because the aunt did not record her loan agreement with the niece. The facts are not even clear that the aunt has a mortgage because the facts only refer to a loan agreement including a statement that the home would be security. A mortgage is the recordable document in which the borrower formally grants the lender a security interest in the real property, and the aunt and niece may not have prepared such a document. Options A, B, and C are incorrect because the jurisdiction's mortgage theory likely wouldn't matter. The title theory, recognized in a minority of jurisdictions, treats a mortgage as the borrower's conveyance of title to the lender. The lien theory, the majority rule, treats the borrower as retaining title but granting a lien on the property. The intermediate theory treats the mortgage as a lien until default and as conveyance of title after default. Whether the aunt's security was a lien or conveyance of title would be less significant than whether the lender had the advantage of a race recording act. Note that the niece may have not only defaulted but breached her other duties before foreclosure by not maintaining heat to the home in the freezing winter. The lender would have the right to inspect and take action to ensure that freezing pipes or other conditions diminish the home's value.

686. To acquire financing necessary for a major commercial development, a developer promised a bank in a signed writing to that the bank had a mortgage not only in the development lands but also in any other real property that the developer subsequently acquired. The development proceeded with the bank's financing. The developer later acquired vacant lands for the developer's next development, granting an investor a mortgage the proceeds from which paid for those vacant lands. When the developer's major commercial development ran into trouble, the bank foreclosed not only on the development lands but also on the after-acquired vacant lands. Who has priority, the bank or the investor, on the bank's foreclosure on the after-acquired vacant lands?

A.   The investor because the investor was a purchase-money mortgage lender.
B.   The investor because the investor didn't know about the other development.

C.   The bank because the bank had the earlier mortgage than the investor.

D.   The bank because the investor should have known of the bank's interest.

Answer explanation: Option A is correct because while the general priority rule in foreclosure is that the earlier mortgagee comes before later mortgages, purchase-money mortgages, those the funds from which went to buy the property, have priority even over earlier mortgages of after-acquired real property. Option B is incorrect because the facts do not disclose whether the investor knew of the other development or not, and the investor's knowledge would not matter to the investor's priority based on purchase-money-mortgage status. Option C is incorrect because although the bank had the developer's earlier grant of mortgages in subsequent real-property purchases, a purchase-money mortgage has priority over such earlier promises of security. Option D is incorrect because the priority of a purchase-money mortgage does not depend on whether the mortgagee knew or should have known of earlier promises by the borrower to grant mortgages on after-acquired real property. Also, the facts give no indication of whether the investor should have known or not. The investor would not, for instance, have discovered the earlier promise from a title search of the purchased vacant land because the bank wouldn't have been able to record a mortgage until after the developer purchased the vacant lands.

688.   The young owner of a small home fell into arrears on real-estate taxes on the home when the owner developed a serious drug addiction costing the owner most of her income. After taxes went unpaid for three years, the local taxing authority foreclosed and sold the home to a speculator buyer at auction whose purchase price satisfied the tax obligation. What are the relative rights of the owner and buyer?

A.   The owner has the right to continued ownership and occupancy, but the buyer gets a mortgage that the owner must satisfy to avoid foreclosure.

B.   The owner has a period within which repay the buyer with interest, but the buyer gets title to the home if the owner doesn't timely redeem.

C.   The owner has a period within which to pay the taxing authority the taxes and remain in the home as a renter, but the buyer owns the home.

D.   The owner has no remaining rights, while the buyer has the right to immediate occupancy and title clear of the tax lien and owner's interest.

Answer explanation: Option B is correct because a tax lien, whether for unpaid real-property taxes or unpaid federal income taxes, allows the tax collector to satisfy unpaid taxes through the real property's foreclosure and sale. Owners generally have an extended period during which to redeem the property by paying the taxes plus interest to the winning bidder on the amount bid. The winning bidder gets clear title if the owner doesn't timely redeem. Option A is incorrect because the buyer gets title to the home, not a mortgage, if the owner doesn't pay to redeem. Option C is incorrect because the buyer has already paid the taxes. If the owner did pay the buyer for the taxes plus interest on the bid amount in redemption, then the owner would keep the home's title, not become a renter. The buyer would then no longer have any interest. Option D is incorrect because the owner retains the right to redeem and would have occupancy during the redemption period.

691.   The owner of a print shop suffered a $100,000 civil judgment to a syndicate in a case involving the owner's investment in the syndicate's resort project. The syndicate recorded the $100,000 judgment lien against the owner's print-shop building. Over the ensuing years three years, the owner paid the interest on the judgment but nothing else. The owner then decided to sell the print-shop business and building. What effect will the $100,000 judgment lien have on the building's sale?

A.	No effect because the owner's obligation to the syndicate bore no relationship to the print-shop business or building.

B.	No effect because three years passed without the judgment's enforcement, relieving the owner of the judgment lien.

C.	The owner must pay the $100,000 judgment out of the sale proceeds before receiving anything from sale.

D.	The owner will first recover the owner's adjusted basis in the building before the syndicate gets up to its $100,000.

Answer explanation: Option C is correct because a judgment lien against real property can arise either by law or recording after entry of a civil judgment on a personal obligation, out of which the judgment creditor will receive sale proceeds after any higher-priority mortgages or liens but before the judgment debtor's recovery of anything. Option A is incorrect because the judgment obligation need not relate to the property but only to the property's owner. Option B is incorrect because while judgment liens do expire, the periods tend to be longer such as seven or ten years and often include rights to renew for equal periods. Option D is incorrect because the owner gets no higher-priority recovery even of amounts put into the real property. The judgment creditor has the higher priority over the owner unless statutory exemptions modify that priority, which they tend not to do for commercial properties.

Multistate Bar Exam Topics Table
Keyed to Multiple-Choice Questions

Real Property

I. **Ownership**
    A. Present estates
        1. Fees simple[601,660]
        2. Defeasible fees simple[601,603,672]
        3. Life estates[601,606,615,633]
    B. Future interests
        1. Reversions[603,606,633,672]
        2. Remainders,[608,633,672,674] vested[601,608,674] and contingent[608,672]
        3. Executory interests[611,617,672]
        4. Possibilities of reverter,[608,672] powers of termination[674]
        5. Rules affecting these interests[611,672]
    C. Co-tenancy
        1. Types
            a. Tenancy in common[613,616,643,669]
            b. Joint tenancy[616,640,673]
        2. Severance[616,640]
        3. Partition[618,670]
        4. Relations among cotenants[613,618,643,669,670,673]
        5. Alienability,[613,616,669] descendibility,[613,616,669] devisability[616,640]
    D. The law of landlord and tenant
        1. Types of holdings[621,623,632]: creation[621,623,677] and termination[621,623,635]
            a. Terms for years[621,623,677]
            b. Tenancies at will[621,677]
            c. Holdovers[621,623,635] and other tenancies at sufferance[621,623,677]
            d. Periodic tenancies[621,623,677]
        2. Possession[621,635] and rent[623,677]
        3. Assignment[607] and subletting[607,625]
        4. Termination (surrender,[635,677] mitigation of damages,[679] and anticipatory breach[679])
        5. Habitability[628,679] and suitability[628,679]
    E. Special problems
        1. Rule Against Perpetuities[608,611,617,620,672]: common law[611,617,620] and as modified[672]
        2. Alienability,[676] descendibility,[660] and devisability[660]
        3. Fair housing/discrimination[631,681]

II. **Rights in land[626]**
    A. Covenants at law[636,665] and in equity[638,647]
        1. Nature[636,665] and type[636,638,647]
        2. Creation[636,638,647]
        3. Scope[612,665]
        4. Termination[636,638,647]
    B. Easements,[609,639,662] profits,[644,698] and licenses[605,641]
        1. Nature and type[639,644]
        2. Methods of creation[634,639,644]
            a. Express[614,644]
            b. Implied[639,662,664]

226

    i. Quasi-use[639,696]
    ii. Necessity[662,696]
    iii. Plat[638,664]
   c. Prescription[609,614]
  3. Scope[609,644]
  4. Termination[605,644]
 C. Fixtures[604,646] (including relevant application of Article 9, UCC[604])
 D. Zoning (fundamentals other than regulatory taking)[602,664]

III. Contracts
 A. Real estate brokerage[648,681]
 B. Creation and construction
  1. Statute of frauds[647,649] and exceptions[610,651]
  2. Essential terms[649,680]
  3. Time for performance[637,654]
  4. Remedies for breach[637]
 C. Marketability of title[624,653]
 D. Equitable conversion (including risk of loss)[654]
 E. Options[676] and rights of first refusal[656,676]
 F. Fitness[679] and suitability[628,679]
 G. Merger[647,653]

IV. Mortgages/security devices
 A. Types of security devices
  1. Mortgages[619,642,694] (including deeds of trust[609])
   a. In general[619,642,652]
   b. Purchase-money mortgages[652,684]
   c. Future-advance mortgages[619,700]
  2. Land contracts[613,659,682,685]
  3. Absolute deeds as security[682,699]
 B. Some security relationships
  1. Necessity[694] and nature of obligation[661,684]
  2. Theories: title,[661,684] lien,[661,663,684] and intermediate[661,684]
  3. Rights and duties prior to foreclosure[663,684]
  4. Right to redeem[663,682,689] and clogging equity of redemption[682,699]
 C. Transfers by mortgagor[642,685,694]
  1. Distinguishing "subject to"[685,697] and "assuming"[642,685,697]
  2. Rights and obligations of transferor[685,694]
  3. Application of subrogation[666,687] and suretyship principles[666,687]
  4. Due-on-sale clauses[685]
 D. Transfers by mortgagee[685,689]
 E. Payment,[687] discharges,[689,694] and defenses[689]
 F. Foreclosure[642,652,663]
  1. Types[652,663]
  2. Rights of omitted parties[652,668]
  3. Deficiency[642] and surplus[652,682]
  4. Redemption after foreclosure[663,682,689]
  5. Deed in lieu of foreclosure[663,682]

V. Titles
 A. Adverse possession[614,626,630,670]
 B. Transfer by deed[622,647]
  1. Warranty[650,693] and non-warranty[624,650,653] deeds (including covenants for title[650,693])
  2. Necessity for a grantee[645] and other deed requirements[647,695]

3. Delivery[645,671] (including escrows[645])

C. Transfer by operation of law[673] and by will[620,640,674]

    1. In general[645,673]

    2. Ademption[675,690]

    3. Exoneration[690,694]

    4. Lapse[690,692]

    5. Abatement[675,690]

D. Title assurance systems

    1. Recording acts[655,658] (race,[684] notice,[655,684] and race-notice[619])

       a. Indexes[667]

       b. Chain of title[655,667]

       c. Protected parties[655,658]

       d. Priorities[655,667]

       e. Notice[655,658,662,667]

    2. Title insurance[650,678]

E. Special problems

    1. After-acquired title[637,657] (including estoppel by deed[637,657])

    2. Forged instruments[658,683] and undelivered deeds[645,671]

    3. Purchase-money mortgages[652,686]

    4. Judgment[640,691] and tax[688] liens

Complete Short Outline

WEEK 1: Acquisition by Discovery or Capture
Most U.S. landowners trace their land's title back to **government grants**.
The U.S. government traces its title to *discovery* or *conquest,* and *treaty* or *purchase.*
Discovery meant first right to negotiate with aboriginal populations for ownership.
Only government had the right to negotiate or to conquer and acquire by treaty.
Discovery, treaty, and conquest are no longer common local means of acquiring title.
This origin of title highlights that property rights depend on government power to defend them.
Related principles of **possession, first in time**, and **labor expended** remain important to ownership.
The law of **capture** requires that the claimant have appropriated the property, not merely pursued it.
For example, *accession* law involves ownership or compensation claims based on added-value labor.
Oil and gas, severed from the land, becomes the capturer's property even if reinjected for storage.
The English rule for water gave the landowner unlimited right to withdraw from a reservoir.
The American rule limits withdrawal to *reasonable use* so as not to affect neighbors.
Western states allocate surface waters to the first-in-time user, called *prior appropriation.*
Eastern states recognize *riparian rights* of landowners to use adjacent waters.
The claimant must also have been the first in time to capture.
Taking from a capturer may be the tort of conversion and crime of theft.
Maliciously interfering with pursuit may also give rise to remedies against the interferer.
A landowner may have *constructive possession* of wild animals on the land until they leave.
Trespassers may have to relinquish wild animals to the landowner under that theory.
But government may confiscate wild animals landowners capture in regulatory violation.
Custom and usage may influence the decision whether a claimant captured the property.
Rules of capture can exacerbate the *tragedy of the commons*, promoting destructive over-pursuit.
Law must account for *externalities*, internalizing costs to the acquiring actor.
But rules should also not exacerbate the tragedy of the *anticommons*, where vetos frustrate good.
Under the *Coase Theorem*, rules do not increase efficiency, just creating winners and losers.
Courts generally reject equitable divisions (Solomonic compromises), except in rare cases.

WEEK 2: Acquisition by Find
Finders generally hold title to **lost** *personal property* against everyone other than the true owner.
The finder keeps the personal property in dispute with anyone other than the original owner.
Owners recover the personal property in *replevin* or its value in *trover.*
Finders must possess lawfully. Thieves have no right to recover from anyone.
Landowners may generally recover personal property that a trespasser finds on the premises.
Landowners may or may not recover lost items that a person lawfully on the premises finds.
May depend if the finder uncovers it by labor unrelated to the reason for being on the land.
Finders generally acquire no right to **mislaid** property left behind, only *lost* property out of place.
Finders have superior title to **abandoned** property, as against everyone *including the true owner.*
Employees may have to relinquish to their employer property found during employment.
Depends on factors including the nature of their work and item's relationship to it.
American law rejects *treasure trove* in which the government recovers hidden money.
States instead apply the *mislaid-lost-abandoned* distinctions, sometimes under complex statute.
Shipwrecks may remain the property of the ship's owner unless abandoned.
Common law gives abandoned shipwrecks to government with salvage award to finder.
Federal law grants title to shipwrecks in territorial waters to states making their own rules.

WEEK 3: Adverse Possession
Adverse possession is lawful means by which one who occupies land acquires title without dealing with the owner.
Possessor must use in *exclusive, open and notorious*, and *continuous* manner under *claim of right* for the period.
Possessor satisfying all conditions may file suit for clear title or defend owner's ejectment action.
The court issues a recordable judgment granting marketable title to the person adversely possessing.
The former owner then no longer has any right or title to, or interest in, the land.
Possessor must be on the property **exclusively** as an owner would exclude, in residence or by exclusive use.
Possessor need not use all to adversely possess the whole, if limited use excludes others from the whole.
Possessor who occupies part *without* excluding others from other parts adversely possesses only the part.
Two or more can adversely possess land, as when a married couple or family continuously use the land.

Possession must be **open and notorious** in that the owner would likely discover in inspection's ordinary course.

Open and notorious is *visible* to others, especially the owner. Possessors may need to notify absent owners.

Owner knowledge of possessor's use establishes that the use was open and notorious.

Occupier who leave when owner visits, by owner request or to avoid detection, are not open and notorious.

Possession must be adverse, hostile, or otherwise under a **claim of right**, without owner consent.

Possession is adverse and under a claim of right when possessor intends and appears to stay permanently.

Claim of right does *not* mean a *legal* claim but appearing as if to exclude the owner.

Tenants cannot adversely possess landlord land, and co-tenants cannot possess co-tenants' rights.

Owner permission destroys claim of right. Conceding owner right fails to satisfy hostility.

Possessor need *not* have malicious intent or, in most states, even *know* possession is against owner's title.

Possession must be **continuous**, meaning *uninterrupted* for longer than the statutory period on ejectment.

Periods vary between five and twenty-one years, with ten or fifteen years being common lengths.

Continuous does not mean every hour of every day but use typical of one owning the land.

Abandonment of the property interrupts continuous possession.

Voluntary transfer from possessor to another supports **tacking** periods of possession.

Possession runs against all successive owners, no matter how many own the land during statutory period.

WEEK 4: Acquisition by Gift

A **gift** is a definite voluntary transfer of a present property interest.

A personal-property **gift** requires *intent* to make present title transfer, *delivery* (possession transfer), and *acceptance*.

For a gift of non-movable personal property, *constructive delivery* of a token of access (key) should suffice.

Symbolic delivery of a writing declaring the gift is traditionally enough only for items *too large to deliver*.

Some state statutes permit symbolic delivery of small items, reversing the common-law delivery rule.

For a gift of land, delivery involves a deed.

Law may *presume acceptance* of a gift of value. Gift acknowledgments are direct acceptance evidence.

Generally, a donee cannot enforce a *promise to make a gift* because the promise lacks consideration.

Traditionally, the donor of an engagement ring recovers it on a breakup only if the donor is without fault.

Gift of a check may require the donee to deposit it and the drawee bank to pay it before the donor dies or revokes.

Gifts *causa mortis* (anticipating death) are effective with intent and delivery. The donor may revoke if recovering.

Gifts causa mortis are *present* gifts anticipating death. *Future* gifts *after* death generally require a will.

The donor may have to redeliver if the donee already had the property before the donor expressed the gift intent.

Courts tend to construe the constructive-delivery and symbolic-delivery limits strictly for gifts causa mortis.

WEEK 5: Possessory Estates

Ownership of land involves *duration* of interest and *relative rights* of holding, known as **estates**.

The deeded language by which an owner transfers land ordinarily determines the estate that the transfer creates.

Present estates mean an owner may take *immediate possession*, the type of present estate depending on duration.

Fee simple, a *freehold estate*, has *infinite* duration but when a **defeasible fee** can terminate earlier.

Fee tail, a *freehold estate*, lasts until the grantee's bloodline terminates.

Life estates, another *freehold estate*, last only for the grantee's life.

A **term of years**, a *non-freehold estate* or *tenancy*, lasts for a period of any duration, not necessarily in years.

Fee simple, shorthand for **fee simple absolute**, is the theoretical right to hold the property *in perpetuity*.

An owner of a fee simple *absolute*, rather than *defeasible* fee, holds unaffected by future events.

Fee-simple estates are **alienable**, the owner may transfer to another, and **inheritable**, the owner may pass by will.

A fee simple arises in a transfer *to A and A's heirs*, or in modern law's fee-simple presumption, simply *to A*.

Modern law presumes fee-simple transactions unless the parties use other words of limitation.

Defeasible fee-simple estates are fees simple that *end on the stated future condition or event*.

A grantor creates a defeasible fee to control the property's future use and ownership.

Defeasible fees simple are *determinable, subject to condition subsequent*, or *subject to executory limitation*.

Fee simple **determinable** attaches a *condition subsequent* that terminates the land's continued ownership.

If the condition occurs, the property automatically reverts by law to the grantor who created the interest.

The grantor's potential future interest is a **possibility of reverter**.

A transfer creates a fee-simple determinable with *durational* words like *so long as, unless*, and *until*.

Fee simple **subject to condition subsequent** attaches a condition *not* automatically terminating title.

Grantor retains a **right of entry** with the *option* to take back the land or ignore the condition's occurrence.

Typical **words of limitation** are *but if..., then O may reenter and retake the property*.

The limitation must be expressly conditional *and discretionary*, as in *may* reenter.

Fee simple **subject to executory limitation** transfers *to a third party* when the condition subsequent occurs.

Typical words of limitation are *to A, but if..., then to C*.

The third party holding the **executory interest** receives the land automatically when the condition occurs.

WEEK 6: Future Interests

Life-estate owners hold the interest for the *duration of the owner's lifetime*, whether one day or fifty years.

  A life estate is *not* inheritable or descendible, the owner having nothing left to give on demise.

  Life estates are *alienable*, meaning that the owner can sell or transfer a life estate.

    The law measures the transferred life estate's term by the original life tenant's life.

  Typical transfers creating a life estate are *to A for life* or *to A for A's natural life*.

  All life estates include a future interest because the property must go somewhere after the life tenant dies.

  A life estate's future interest can either be a *reversion* or *remainder*.

Future interests are *reversions*, vested or contingent *remainders, executory interests*, or *possibilities of reverter*.

  Future interests arise when a person must wait to take possession until the present estate ends.

  Future interests belonging to the original grantor include *reversions, possibilities of reverter*, and *rights of entry*.

  Future interests granted a third party include *vested or contingent remainders*, and *executory interests*.

Reversions are future interests that grantors retain when transferring a present interest less than the grantor owns.

  Conveyance from grantor *to A for life* creates a life estate in A with a *reversion in fee simple* in the grantor.

  Grantors who don't convey the entire interest and don't say to whom the land then goes, retain a reversion.

    The land reverts to grantor or grantor's heirs or devisees if grantor has died, when possession ends.

  Possibilities of reverter arise when the possessory estate is determinable, ending automatically on the condition.

  Right of entry arises when the possessory estate is subject to condition subsequent, giving grantor the option.

Remainders, vested and contingent, are future interests in a third party after the possessory estate ends.

  A **vested remainder** is one that an *ascertained person* holds *and* that is not subject to a condition precedent.

    An *ascertained person* is someone then named or identifiable, thus not including unborn children.

    A condition precedent is an event that must occur before the person obtains the future interest.

    A grant *to A for life, then to B*, creates a vest remainder because B takes without condition precedent.

  A **contingent remainder** is one that *either* an *unascertained person* holds *or* is subject to a *condition precedent*.

    A grant *to A for life, then to B if B attains the age of 21*, creates a contingent remainder because B must be 21.

    A grant *to A for life, then to B's children*, when B has no children, creates a contingent remainder.

  Contingent remainders vest when the condition precedent occurs or unascertained person is ascertained.

    When events could vest others, then vested remainders are **subject to open**.

    When nothing can further dilute the future interest, the holders have **indefeasibly vested remainders**.

  Owners of vested remainders have equal interests as tenants in common.

  Grantors form **alternative contingent remainders** when creating two options for what will happen, such as

    grant *to A for life, then to B if B reaches 21, but if B does not reach 21, then to C*.

Executory interests grant to *a third party* taking effect *when a condition subsequent divests the prior interest*.

  Executory interests vest when someone else loses a vested interest *subject to divestment*.

    Grant *to A for life, then to B, but if B does not reach the age of 21, then to C*, gives C an executory interest.

    B's interest is *subject to divestment* if B dies before 21, that possibility creating C's executory interest.

Possibility of reverter is the future interest that remains after a fee-simple determinable.

  A **fee-simple determinable** attaches a **condition subsequent** the occurrence of which terminates ownership.

  Fee simple determinable arises whenever the grantor has a future interest, called a **possibility of reverter**.

  A **right of entry**, a/k/a **power of termination**, arises with a fee simple **subject to condition subsequent**.

    The grantor retains the **right of entry**, or **power of termination**, at the grantor's option.

WEEK 7: Special Future-Interest Rules

Rules affecting these interests limit *dead-hand control* of land, seeking reasonable *alienability* and *marketability*.

  A few states follow **destructibility of contingent remainders**, eliminating unvested remainders after life estates.

  Merger creates one fee simple when a person acquires both vested life estate and future interest.

  A few states follow the **rule in Shelley's Case** giving fee simple to a life tenant whose heirs hold the remainder.

  A few states follow the **doctrine of worthier title** giving a reversion to a grantor whose heirs hold the remainder.

The common-law rule against perpetuities requires *executory interests* and *contingent remainders* to vest timely.

  These future interests must vest, if at all, within 21 years of a *life in being* when the grant creates the interest.

    The rule does *not* limit interests that the grantor *keeps*, like reversions or rights of re-entry.

    Some states address the rule's absurdities by presuming that women older than 55 will not bear children.

  First, determine whether a grant creates either a **contingent remainder** or **executory interest**.

    If not, and the grant only creates *vested* remainders, then the rule does not apply, and the conveyance is valid.

    If a grant *does* create a contingent remainder or executory interest, then see if a condition *may never occur*.

      If so, as grant *to A so long as A does not use for a landfill, then to B*, then the rule voids the grant.

    If an interest vests when *living persons* die, see if vesting can occur more than 21 years after the last death.

      If so, as grant *to A, then to A's oldest living child at age thirty*, then the rule voids the grant.

The rule against perpetuities as modified has an exception for **class gifts** as *to A's children or grandchildren*.

  The common-law rule is *all-or-nothing*, invalidating the grant if invalid for even one class member.

The modified *rule of convenience* closes the class to new members when at least one member's interest vests.

The common-law rule voids grant *to A's children when they reach age 25* even if a child is 25 at grant.

The modified rule vests the over-25 child's interest at grant, closing the class, allowing in after-born children.

The *Uniform Statutory Rule Against Perpetuities* in over 20 states has a 90-year waiting period for vesting.

If no vesting occurs, then the court may modify the interest.

Other states adopt a similar *wait-and-see approach* to see if circumstances resolve the vesting problem.

WEEK 8: Co-Ownership

Co-tenancies divide ownership interests among two or more persons, *tenant* here *not* referring to leaseholds.

Types of co-tenancies include **tenancies in common** and **joint tenancies**, *grantor language* determining type.

Tenancy in common is a shared fee-simple title that does *not* grant *survivorship rights* in the co-tenants.

Each of two or more tenants in common owns an *alienable* and *inheritable* share of the property.

Tenants in common may own *unequal shares* that they may transfer to other owners during life or at death.

A co-tenant's interest passes at death as the tenant directs in a will or law directs by intestacy.

Tenants in common, equal or unequal in share, hold **undivided** interests, using all or any part of the property.

Tenants in common may sell their share so that the remaining co-tenant shares with a new co-tenant.

Grant *to A and B* creates a tenancy in common, as does *to A and B as tenants in common*.

Tenants in common may receive interests separately, an owner conveying to a tenant in common with the owner.

Joint tenancy is a co-tenancy of *equal* undivided interests with *rights of survivorship*. Joint tenants own equally.

If a joint tenant dies, the other joint tenant or joint tenants receive the decedent's interest automatically by law.

Grant *to A and B as joint tenants* or *to A and B with full rights of survivorship* creates a joint tenancy.

Grant not indicating intent to create a joint tenancy or survivorship right creates a tenancy in common.

Joint tenants must have *unity of time, title, interest,* and *possession*, taking at once under the same document.

A joint tenant may alienate the interest, but doing so severs the joint tenancy, creating a tenancy in common.

A **tenancy by the entireties** is a joint tenancy between married individuals.

Grant *to A and B as tenants by the entireties* or *to A and B as husband and wife* creates an entireties tenancy.

Most states presume tenancy by the entireties from grant *to A and B as joint tenants* if A and B are married.

Divorcing tenants by entireties become tenants in common.

A creditor of only one spouse cannot reach the spouse's tenancy-by-the-entirety interest.

Married owners hold entireties property free of claims of creditors of either spouse, but not both spouses.

Tenants by the entireties cannot transfer their individual interests.

Severance refers to the process, intentional or inadvertent, of converting a joint tenancy into a tenancy in common.

Severance *destroys the right of survivorship* that accompanies a joint tenancy.

Joint tenants may agree to sever their joint tenancy, for instance by selling the land and dividing proceeds.

A conveying joint tenant severs the joint tenancy, the grantee then a tenant in common with the other co-tenants.

Lease of a joint tenancy does *not*, in most states, sever the joint tenancy in favor of a tenancy in common.

Conveying to a trustee for one's own benefit, or in some states to one's self, severs the joint tenancy.

Partition involves equitable division of the land to represent each co-tenant's individual interest.

A court may at the request of any co-tenant impose and enforce partition, if the co-tenants cannot agree.

Partition may be **in-kind**, physical division, or **by sale** if division is impossible, impractical, or not best interest.

Co-tenants must divide sale proceeds equitably to represent their individual interests.

Relations among cotenants, whether in-common or joint tenants, involve sharing possession, rent, and duty.

One co-tenant may not **oust** another, pays rent if the tenant does, but need not o/w pay rent for sole possession.

Co-tenants share in **rents** received from the premises and may enforce their right to a fair share.

Co-tenants generally *share expenses*, each having a right to make the other contribute as necessary.

Alienability, descendibility, devisability differ among types of co-tenancy.

Tenants in common and joint tenants may **alienate** their co-tenancy interest, meaning *transfer* it away.

Tenants by the entireties cannot transfer their co-tenant interest.

Tenants in common convey whatever fractional interest they own. Joint tenants convey their equal interest.

A tenant in common's interest is **descendible**, heirs inheriting, and **devisable**, passed by will.

A joint tenancy is *not* descendible or devisable because of the right of survivorship in the other co-tenants.

When a joint tenant dies, the tenancy interest passes by law to the surviving joint tenant or joint tenants.

WEEK 9: Marital Estates

Most states have common-law marital property, but ten states have community property systems.

In theory, common-law marital property means separate marital estates, while community means one estate.

The difference is much less significant today. Most states treat property acquired during the marriage as marital.

Before-marriage property commingled during marriage can also become marital property.

Degrees earned or licenses obtained during marriage are likely not marital property but may warrant support.

Property received as gift or by inheritance during the marriage remains separate property.

Common-law marital property distinguishes rights during marriage, on divorce, and at death.

Sole creditors of one spouse cannot reach property two spouses hold together as tenants by the entireties.

Most states recognize tenancies by the entirety as to personal property, too, not just real property.

Divorce converts a tenancy by the entirety into a tenancy in common.

Federal tax liens attach to one spouse's interest in entireties property.

Federal forfeiture law permits attachment only as to the criminally responsible spouse's survivorship interest.

The criminally responsible spouse may have had to use the property for the criminal activity.

Nearly all states have abolished dower rights of a wife and curtesy for a husband after death of the other spouse.

Where dower survives, the wife obtains a life estate of a portion of the deceased husband's lands.

The key, though, is to simply have both husband and wife sign deeds no matter who holds formal title.

States also have elective-share or forced-share statutes.

A surviving spouse may take a statutory portion of the deceased spouse's estate no matter what the will said.

Community marital property treats property acquired and accumulated during marriage as owned equally.

Neither spouse may sell community property without the other's consent, like entireties property.

But either spouse *may* dispose of their half of community property by will at death, *unlike* entireties property.

Either spouse may manage community marital property but only to benefit both spouses.

Creditors of only one spouse may reach only the portion that spouse manages and controls.

For spouses moving between common-law/community-property states, property remains as initially characterized.

Unmarried couples depend on contract rights, not community-property theories.

WEEK 10: Land-Sale Contracts

Contracts for the sale of land follow contract law but also address unique or unusual issues.

Real estate brokerage involves a **broker** or *agent* representing seller, buyer, or both, under **listing agreement**.

The listing agent assumes the duty to list, show, and sell the land, the seller paying a percentage *commission*.

Listing agents earn the commission if sale occurs during the agreement's term, split with buyer's agent.

Seller and buyer may consult lawyers for a land sale contract or use a standard form broker prepares.

Some listing agreements require commission if a contract forms, others only when the sale closes.

If seller refuses to perform the sale contract with a willing buyer, then the seller owes the commission.

Creation and construction: seller & buyer form a *purchase contract, purchase agreement,* or *land sale contract.*

Statute of frauds requires that contracts transferring interests in land be *in a writing signed* by the charged party.

A *purchase agreement* anticipates a later closing weeks or months following the agreement's execution.

Buyer prepares and presents a signed purchase agreement, constituting the buyer's offer.

If seller accepts, then seller countersigns the offer and delivers the completed agreement to the buyer.

Seller countersigning but not delivering, and not notifying buyer, would not complete the agreement.

If seller counteroffers presenting countersigned but modified agreement, then buyer must sign and deliver.

Part performance can take a contract out of the statute of frauds: possession with part payment acknowledged.

Where buyer makes no payment, some states may accept buyer *improving* the land as *detrimental reliance.*

Possession alone is not enough to take the transaction out of the statute of frauds.

Essential terms must be in the land sale contract or it will ordinarily be unenforceable.

Essential terms *identify seller and buyer*. Identifying buyer's agent for *unidentified principal* is sufficient.

Essential terms provide *description*, ordinarily metes and bounds, but address is enough if no ambiguity.

Metes-and-bounds description controls over reference to different number of acres.

Essential terms include **price** or objective means of calculating price, agreement to agree *not* sufficient.

Other essential terms arise only if intended, like *financing, inspection,* and *attorney-review contingency.*

Parties benefitting from contingencies must exercise them in **good faith**, not to alter or avoid the agreement.

Time for performance involves setting a *closing date* when seller exchanges deed for payment.

Buyer needs time to complete contingencies, while seller needs to pack and move.

When contingencies reveal defects, the parties may adjust the sale price.

The **closing date** requires both sides to perform as *time of the essence*, failure voiding the contract at election.

Remedies for breach of land sale contracts follow remedies for breach of other contracts.

Parties may *rescind* and seek *damages* when the other party fails to close or may seek *specific performance.*

Specific performance requires seller to convey deed and possession or buyer to pay the purchase price.

Specific performance may require seller to vacate, provide keys or other access, and remove equipment.

If seller refuses to execute a deed, then buyer may obtain the court's recordable order conveying title.

When a party breaches some other term or condition of transfer, the non-breaching party may sue for damages.

Damages include additional expense or consequential and foreseeable losses.

Land sale contracts may provide for liquidated damages, such as seller overstaying, charged at $100 per day.

Closing agreements, releases, and merger may not prevent the buyer from later claiming the seller's fraud.

Marketability of title: land sale contracts routinely require that the seller convey **marketable title**.

Law *implies* a *promise* or *warranty* of marketable title in the absence of an express term.

Marketable title is title that reasonable persons would not doubt validity and third parties would not challenge.

Sellers conveying title that reasonable persons would reject due to impending challenges breach the warranty.

Buyers may pursue one of the above remedies including rescission and damages, or specific performance.
Specific performance may include that the seller act to clear title, including paying just claims.
Sellers convey marketable title showing good **chain of title** reflecting seller's clear ownership.
Real-property records enable seller, buyer, lawyer, or title company to complete a **title search**.
A seller may instead prove good title by adverse possession, requiring *court judgment* as recordable order.
Common law does not require sellers to disclose other defects and conditions beyond marketable title.
The rule of *buyer beware* requires buyers to exercise the inspection contingency with *due diligence*.
Many states today require residential sellers to disclose certain defects, using *statutory disclosure forms*.
Law today may also require seller to disclose defects seller knew but not apparent to buyer on inspection.
Law also prohibits seller from *actively concealing* defects to frustrate the buyer's discovery.
Breaches of these duties may give rise to fraud remedies including rescission and damages for lost bargain.
Equitable conversion holds equitable interest to transfer to buyer *on land-sale-contract execution*.
The traditional doctrine passes the risk of interim loss or gain *to the buyer* who holds equitable ownership.
Equitable conversion enables court to adjust rights and duties to reflect changes between contract and close.
Some states alter equitable conversions' *risk-of-loss* rule so that the seller retains the risk until the closing date.
If either party is *responsible* through deliberate act or carelessness for the loss, then that party bears the loss.
Fire, flood, or other loss insurance adjusts rights and responsibilities for the best and fairest outcome.
Options: seller and buyer may form an **option contract** for the sale of land to keep an offer open for a period.
An *option contract* must ordinarily have consideration, although nominal consideration is traditionally enough.
An option contract must be in a writing signed by the charged party, to satisfy the *statute of frauds*.
Buyer may exercise the option at any time during the period, while seller *cannot revoke the offer* until expiration.
Option contracts must state the *sale price* or a reliable way of calculating a certain price, as an essential term.
Option-contract breach gives the buyer alternative remedies of specific performance or damages.
Rights of first refusal, instead of stating an option sale price, require seller to present to buyer third-party offers.
The buyer may match the offer, requiring seller to sell under the right of first refusal.
When seller presents third party's good-faith offer, buyer must buy or lose the property and right of first refusal.
One typically finds rights of first refusal in leases or other relationships closer than an arm's length.
Fitness and suitability: law implies a **fitness** warranty for residential sales / **suitability** warranty for commercial.
The warranties arise for *new construction* on lands, breach of which creates damages or rescission remedy.
Law generally rejects implied warranties of fitness and suitability in the purchase of *established* construction.
Parties then treat conditions through any statutory disclosure requirements and inspection rights.
Most states allow initial *and* subsequent buyers to enforce implied warranties but a minority only initial buyers.
Claimants must trace the defect to the construction rather than subsequent conditions and events.
Buyers must enforce within a reasonable time from discovery of the defect.
Merger doctrine holds that guarantees either party makes in the land sale contract *merge* into the deed at closing.
Merger eliminates buyer's right to rely on sale-contract terms once the buyer accepts seller's deed at closing.
Merger bars post-closing claims over quality of title, as the deed reflects, and defects in the premises.
Merger also bars disputes over unpaid taxes and other charges against the property.
Some states treat merger more like a rebuttable presumption against claims than an absolute bar.
States are more likely to apply the doctrine and bar the claim when having to do with the property's *title*.
Courts also look to the parties' intent as to what rights and claims they meant to merge into the deed.
Claims for misrepresentation fall outside the doctrine's bar.

WEEK 11: Deeds
Transfer by deed: land transfers usually involve seller executing a **deed** in buyer's favor, meeting requirements.
Sellers offer and buyers accept *warranty* or *non-warranty* deed, including *covenants for title*.
Warranty: the land sale contract specifies the *type* of deed that the seller promises to convey at the closing.
Deed type determines **warranties** that the transferor makes in the transfer, not the actual title buyer receives.
Seller has whatever title seller has, notwithstanding warranties, which only create breach causes of action.
General warranty deed is a standard term in the common form of land sale contract.
Sellers covenant *owning* with *right to convey* without *encumbering* mortgages, liens, or easements.
Sellers must also *defend* buyer's *superior title* and *right to enjoy* the land, *curing title defects*.
Special warranty deed assures only that no defects or encumbrances arose *during the seller's ownership*.
Special warranty deed makes no assurances about title of prior owners.
Non-warranty deeds, common form **quit-claim deed**, make *no* warrants, even what seller knows.
Quit-claim deeds transfer only what the seller in fact owns without assurances or rights of action to enforce.
Covenants for title involve assurances limited to whatever deed recitals expressly state.
Buyer only has recourse if seller's title does not match the special covenants seller's deed makes.
Necessity for a grantee and other deed requirements: a deed must meet two precise requirements.
A deed must include a **granting clause** identifying grantor and grantee while indicating transfer of title.
Deed usually *name* grantor and grantee but need not do so if identification leaves no ambiguity.

A deed must also **describe the property** in a way that clearly and precisely identifies what the deed conveys.

Metes-and-bounds description is custom, but references to survey, features, markers, or monuments does.

Street address, city, and state will also do if description leaves no ambiguity as to property contours.

Courts allow external evidence to resolve ambiguities.

A deed need *not* mention consideration, although some do to show *bona fide purchaser* taking for value.

Deeds should state what warrants of title, but if not, then law presumes a *general warranty deed*.

State law determines requirements for deed execution, beginning with grantor signature intending execution.

Two adult and competent witnesses may need to sign acknowledging grantor identity and signature.

Most grantees record with the county register of deeds, recording acts adding other deed requirements.

Notary public signature indicating that the grantor signed under oath creates presumed validity.

Recording acts may also require name and address of deed preparer.

Delivery with intent to complete transfer must ordinarily take place after grantor executes the deed.

Execution without delivery and delivery without intent to transfer do not create enforceable right of title.

Escrow involves execution and delivery of deed to an *agent* awaiting conditions to satisfy escrow terms.

Escrow agreements determine conditions on which the agent may release deed, payment, and other items.

Escrow facilitates transactions by eliminating the need for contemporaneous exchange.

Escrow agents bear liability for breaching escrow terms, insuring exchange against mistake or wrongdoing.

WEEK 12: Mortgages

Mortgages/security devices: parties use *mortgages*, *deeds of trust*, and *land contracts*, as forms of security.

Mortgages: a **mortgage** is a security interest in land that secures the mortgage *loan*, written for statute of frauds.

In general: mortgage transactions involve borrower signing a *note* and *mortgage* instrument lender records.

The note is borrower's contract with lender including amount, term, schedule, interest, and default terms.

The mortgage is the lender's security interest including grantor, property description, and rights and duties.

Rights include to assign or foreclose, and obligations to discharge on payment.

Absent writing, courts may find an **equitable mortgage** if borrower conveys a **deed in trust** to lender.

Some states expressly recognize a **deed of trust** as a mortgage alternative.

Borrower executes a deed purporting to convey to lender, which lender or escrow agent hold.

Lender destroys or returns the deed if borrower pays the full loan, but records deed if borrower defaults.

Lender can then readily execute on the real property, typically without judicial foreclosure.

Lenders may record a deed-of-trust instrument just as lenders do with mortgages, to show superior rights.

Purchase-money mortgages are security interests that buyers grant to purchase the real property.

Purchase-money mortgage can also mean one that the buyer grants *back to the seller* to meet financing shortfall.

Purchase-money mortgages have priority over other encumbrances such as mechanics' liens and judgment liens.

Property owners also grant mortgages for *construction loans* and *home-equity loans* as a general line of credit.

The associated mortgages are often second or subsequent mortgages behind purchase-money mortgages.

Mortgage priority is critical in sale of *underwater* properties secure against debt greater than land value.

Future-advance mortgages secure loans not yet made, enabling the owner to draw future advances on need.

Future-advance lenders have priority as of recording date even if only later advancing funds.

Some states only give retroactive priority to *obligatory* future advances rather than optional future advances.

Other states permit borrowers to give lenders *cut-off notice* so that borrower can give priority to new lenders.

Land contracts are means of purchasing *and* financing real-property purchase without lenders.

A contract conveying land creates a security device in the seller because only deeds convey title.

A land contract specifies the terms on which the buyer will receive a deed.

Land contracts are also known as *installment sales contracts*, *contracts for deed*, or *contracts for sale*.

Distinguish a land contract from the *purchase contract* that seller and buyer execute anticipating closing.

Even though buyer does not receive a deed, buyer holds **equitable title**, while **legal title** remains with seller.

Buyers under land contract often record a **memorandum of land contract** to show their interest in title chain.

They then have priority of equitable title over later interests, memorandum acting in place of deed.

Absolute deeds as security: lenders may take an **absolute deed** from borrowers, granting lender fee-simple title.

Absolute deed appears as if lender owns, which is the legal effect, but lender holds awaiting borrower default.

On default, lender records the absolute deed to sell the property as defaulted-loan security.

In disputes, borrowers may prove by parol evidence that absolute deed was instead an *equitable mortgage*.

Absolute deeds as security may violate truth-in-lending and other laws, exposing lender to fines and penalties.

Security relationships arise around mortgages, land contracts, deeds in trust, and absolute deeds.

Necessity and nature of obligation: borrower and lender must agree in writing satisfying **statute of frauds**.

Theories of security include **title**, **lien**, and **intermediate**, rights and duties varying accordingly.

In a *lien-theory* state, a mortgage is simply a lien against the property, *not* conveyance of title in the property.

Joint tenants granting a mortgage do *not* destroy unity of title for joint tenancy, retaining survivorship.

In a *title-theory* state, a mortgage conveys title to the property, joint tenants destroying unity of title.

The mortgage severs the joint tenancy, creating a tenancy in common and ending rights of survivorship.

In an *intermediate-theory* state, a mortgage is a lien until borrower defaults when the mortgage conveys title.

Rights and duties prior to foreclosure: standard mortgage forms require borrowers to maintain the property.

Borrowers must also pay taxes, maintain insurance, and not conduct illegal activity on the premises.

Lenders may sue for breach of these contract promises, obtaining specific performance and damages.

Lenders may pay taxes, insurance, and other charges to preserve land value and get reimbursement.

The law of **waste** also permits lenders to get court help to ensure borrowers do not destroy property value.

Mortgage default may include a significant change in the use of the premises including its abandonment.

Lenders must grant borrowers free use of the mortgaged property if borrower is not in default.

Lenders may **enter for inspection** against waste, but borrowers retain full owner rights to use and enjoy.

Lenders interfering with borrower rights may be liable in trespass or contract breach, or by statute.

Borrowers have rights that lenders not place clouds on borrower's title such as by refusing due discharge.

Right to redeem: borrowers may have statutory rights to **redeem** mortgaged residential property out of foreclosure.

Redemption requires paying the mortgage obligation within a statutory period, before or after foreclosure sale.

Lenders may not demand that borrowers waive redemption rights.

Clogging the equity of redemption: law prohibits alternative arrangements skirting redemption rights.

Law holds invalid *clogs on the equity of redemption*, protecting owners' critical housing or home equity.

Transfers by mortgagor: mortgages do not bar borrowers from conveying mortgaged property.

Lenders *record* mortgages to ensure borrower conveyance does not affect lender security, protecting lenders.

Lenders *discharge* mortgages when borrowers pay off the mortgage using sale proceeds.

Distinguishing "subject to" and "assuming" becomes important when transfer does *not* pay off the mortgage.

Buyers taking *subject to* mortgages do *not* become directly liable to the lender on the mortgage note.

Seller remains liable on the note, while buyer's property remains subject to the mortgage.

Buyer expressly agreeing to **assume** an existing mortgage obligation is *directly liable* to lender on the note.

Rights and obligations of transferor: borrowers *remain obligated* on the note when conveying the property.

The note remains a contract between borrower and lender even after borrower sells the land.

If buyer does not make mortgage payments, then lender may look to seller/borrower to make note payments.

Lenders may agree to accept buyer *assuming* the note debt and to relieve seller/borrower from obligations.

Law calls a **novation** this rare action of lender relieving the original borrower.

If buyer defaults on mortgage payments, seller's agreement with buyer likely grants seller buyer recourse.

Recourse may include damages from buyer to pay note or seller recovery of land under right of re-entry.

Unless lender granted seller a novation, seller owes lender, but seller looks to buyer for help in paying.

Subrogation: sellers may pay taxes, insurance, or other charges buyer owes, and **subrogate** to recover from buyer.

To *subrogate* is to take the place or *stand in the shoes* of another to exercise that other's rights.

Seller's contract with buyer provides for subrogation, absent which law implies **equitable subrogation**.

Lender may also subrogate to pay taxes and charges and then obtain reimbursement from seller or buyer.

The mortgage provides contractually for subrogation, absent which law implies *equitable subrogation*.

Suretyship principles involve a *surety* guaranteeing borrower's mortgage obligation to borrower and lender.

A **surety** signs the original contract along with the borrower, while a **guarantor** signs a separate guarantee.

A surety or guarantor owes what the contract or guarantee states, typically to pay when borrower fails to pay.

Suretyships and guarantees require a *signed writing* satisfying the **statute of frauds**.

A surety or guarantor may compel borrower to perform, called **exoneration** or to *reimburse* for performance.

A surety may obtain *contribution* from other sureties and has the primary obligor's defenses against the lender.

Due-on-sale clauses: many mortgages include a **due-on-sale** clause permitting lender to *accelerate* on sale.

Under a typical clause, lender have the *option* to call the entire principal balance due if the buyer sells the land.

Due-on-sale clauses often include a trigger for *land-contract* sales, which are efforts at private financing.

Federal law limits the ability of states to frustrate due-on-sale clauses.

Transfers by mortgagee: lenders may transfer notes and mortgages to assignees such as investors.

Rights on assignment depend on whether assignee is a **holder in due course**.

A holder in due course is one who receive in good faith, without knowing defects, and having paid value.

Assignees who are *not* holders in due course take *subject to borrower defenses* against the lender.

Assignees who *are* holders in due course take *free of borrower personal defenses*.

Personal defenses address loan formation and include *fraud*, *lack of consideration*, and *unconscionability*.

Holders in due course or not take *subject to real defenses* on loan *illegality* like *forgery*, *incapacity*, or *coercion*.

Payment: borrowers owe lenders **payment** on mortgage-note obligations, the note stating the obligation.

Note terms include amount, interest rate, payment schedule, payment amount, and note term.

Notes may amortize principal and interest over the full term or lower payments and require balloon payment.

Payment is borrower's primary obligation but also to maintain the property and not cause destruction or waste.

Mortgage and note require borrower to pay property taxes and assessments, and keep buildings insured.

Mortgage permits lender to make borrower payments and subrogate to recover payments from borrower.

Discharge: lender has contractual obligation to *discharge* the mortgage when borrower pays the note.

Note cancellation relieves borrower of further obligation. Mortgage discharge ends lender's security interest.

Discharge occurs at end of note term when borrower pays final installment or earlier when borrower sells.

Notes also typically permit borrower to prepay the note without sale including in a refinancing.

Discharge is a signed instrument borrower records in chain of title to reflect title clear of mortgage.

Lender who fail to promptly discharge may be liable for **slander of title** when borrower loses a sale.

Defenses: borrowers may have *defenses* to mortgage and note obligations in a judicial foreclosure.

If the state permits foreclosure outside of a judicial proceeding, then borrower raise defenses in a civil action.

Lender may have *misapplied payments* or made other *mistakes* in calculating amounts due.

Lender may not have followed default *notice procedures* in the mortgage or mandated by state or federal law.

Lender may have *misrepresented* terms, inducing borrower to deal, or imposed *unconscionable* terms.

Lender may not have complied with federal and state truth-in-lending *disclosure requirements*.

Federal law grants a *servicemember on active duty* a stay against foreclosure.

Defenses may lead to rescission of mortgage and note obligations, reform, damages, and correcting credit.

Foreclosure is the process through which the lender executes on the land as security.

Lenders must follow state-mandated procedures and mortgage terms, to *accelerate* debt and foreclose on land.

Foreclosure results in the mortgaged property's sale in satisfaction of the debt.

Sale proceeds first go to sale expenses including costs and attorney's fees as statute or mortgage provide.

Proceeds then pay the foreclosed debt, then subordinate mortgage holders, and only then debtor equity.

Any mortgagee may foreclose, naming subordinate mortgagees whose interests foreclosure extinguishes.

Foreclosure does *not* extinguish *superior* mortgages, whose holders need not participate.

Types: most states require **judicial foreclosure**, but some **non-judicial foreclosure** if mortgage so provides.

Non-judicial states require *public auction* rather than private sale and strict mortgagor and owner notice.

Law discourages self-help and closely regulates foreclosure to avoid overreach and breach of the peace.

Law may require or seller desire judicial rather than private **land-contract forfeiture**.

Land contracts typically provide that on forfeiture, buyer loses or *forfeits* payments already made to seller.

A recordable forfeiture judgment confirms seller has extinguished buyer's equitable and legal title.

Rights of omitted parties: a **first mortgagee** has priority over subsequent mortgagees, using *recording* dates.

Purchase-money mortgages are an exception, giving priority to lenders or sellers financing purchase.

Purchase-money mortgages also have priority over mechanics' liens, judgment liens, and other encumbrances.

Subordinate mortgage holders are *necessary parties* to foreclosure, which *extinguishes* their subordinate rights.

If foreclosure proceeds without a subordinate mortgage holder, the action does *not* extinguish the right.

Winning bidders take subject to superior mortgages and un-foreclosed subordinate mortgages.

Winning bidders may *re-foreclose* in a second proceeding naming the subordinate mortgagee.

Deficiency and surplus: *judgment of foreclosure* provides for debt acceleration, sale, and proceeds application.

Judgment includes *deficiency* award for total indebtedness less sale amount net of costs if sale not satisfy.

Lender may enforce deficiency by other means such as wage or account garnishment.

If sale produces **surplus** over lender's costs, fees, and loan, surplus pays subordinate debt and then to borrower.

Redemption after foreclosure: states allow borrowers to **redeem** property by paying mortgage indebtedness.

Common law treats the right as **equity of redemption**, but many states provide for greater *statutory* rights.

Redemption gives the mortgagor additional time, often six months, to pay the foreclosed debt.

Foreclosure triggers the redemption period in some states, ending with auction sale.

In other states, sale triggers the redemption period, during which buyer waits to see if mortgagor redeems.

Deed in lieu of foreclosure: lenders may try to take a **deed in lieu of foreclosure** from the borrower.

If borrower voluntarily grants lender a deed in lieu of foreclosure, lender may avoid foreclosure.

Borrowers typically demand lender *waive* deficiency, lender then executing an *estoppel affidavit*.

Some states and federally backed mortgages require deficiency waivers for deeds in lieu of foreclosure.

Lenders may instead agree to a **short sale** in which the borrower sells to a third party for less than the debt.

Lender gets proceeds, borrower gives deed to buyer, and lender discharges mortgage, waiving deficiency.

WEEK 13: Title-Assurance Systems

Title assurance systems assure that buyers receive title that sellers claim in the transaction to convey.

One title-assurance system involves state *recording act* and another involves *title insurance*.

Recording acts create systems for buyers, mortgagees, lienholders, and other claimants to **record** land interests.

Recording involves providing the deed or other instrument to the *register of deeds* for recording and indexing.

The register enters the instrument so that others can discover it on search relating to person or land.

Bona-fide purchasers take *for fair consideration* recording superior title *without knowledge or reason to know*.

Bona-fide purchases gain recording-act protection depending on recording-act form.

Notice acts hold bona-fide purchaser superior to earlier who did not record if bona-fide did not know of earlier.

Race acts look to who recorded first, without considering who had notice of earlier title.

Race/notice acts hold bona-fide purchaser superior only if not knowing of the earlier *and* recording first.

Indexes: key to effective title search is the **index** that the register maintains showing each instrument's recording.

Grantor/grantee index categorizes and indexes by grantor and grantee name, in alphabetical order.

Buyers examine *grantee* category, tracing sellers back to earliest recording ensuring buyer title.

Repeating the process in *grantor* index confirms no buyer sold to anyone other than the next buyer.

Tract index categorizes and indexes instruments by land, dividing by sections, blocks, and lots.

Buyers search land location to see what instruments the register of deeds has recorded as to that land.

Chain of title depends on establishing a sound chain from the earliest transaction to the most-recent transaction.

Marketable title shows chain without *gap, missing link, unaccounted-for interest*, or other defect.

Title searches through recording indexes determines whether chain of title has defects.

Buyer who discover defects from title search may refuse to close for failure of a material term of the contract.

Protected parties can depend on who buys first, whether one is a bona-fide purchaser, and who records first.

If neither purchaser records their deed, then the first purchaser has superior title under any recording act.

Sellers convey good title only once, to the first purchaser, unless recording act provides otherwise.

Also, bona-fide purchasers who record first always have superior title, no matter the recording act.

Also, if an earlier purchaser records before a later purchaser, then the earlier purchaser always has superior title.

The later purchaser cannot be bona fide because earlier recording establishes notice.

Priorities can differ depending on the form of recording act, whether **notice**, **race**, or **race/notice**

Notice recording acts protect **bona-fide purchasers** no matter who records *after* bona-fide purchaser takes.

Race recording acts protect parties who record first.

Race/notice acts protect only bona-fide purchasers who record first.

Thus one difference is when earlier purchaser records *after* later purchase but *before* later purchaser records.

Later purchaser would *not* have record notice at purchase, but earlier purchaser won *race* to record.

Notice acts favor later purchasers, while **race** acts favor earlier to record.

Race/notice act changes outcome only if later purchaser records *before* earlier, without notice.

Notice does not affect one who takes from a seller having superior title, superior title **sheltering** buyer.

Recording acts do not resolve how buyer discover owners taking by *adverse possession*.

Buyers must inspect for adverse possession because recording does not necessarily show adverse possession.

Recording shows adverse possession only if possessor received and recorded a judgment showing title.

Buyers failing to discover adverse possession may sue sellers under general warranty deed, not quit claim.

Title insurance protects buyers against undisclosed defects in title.

Sale contracts often include *title-insurance contingency* for buyer to inspect and approve insurer commitment.

Title-insurance commitment discloses encumbrances or other defects that title-insurer search discovered.

Insurer *title search* shows gaps in ownership, to which the buyer can then object before closing.

Title search also shows recorded covenants and easements.

Title insurance pays to resolve title defects that the insurer should have discovered and disclosed but did not.

If title insurer cannot cure title and buyer loses property or value, then title insurer indemnifies for the loss.

Special problems can arise relating to title.

After-acquired title involves grantor anticipating title purports to *transfer* title *before acquiring* title.

If grantor never acquires title, then transfer remains void. One cannot transfer title that one does not have.

Estoppel by deed holds that if grantor after-acquires title, then grantee *estops* grantor from denying transfer.

Grantee has good title except against a bona-fide purchaser for value without notice who records first.

Forged instruments are ones to which the signer signs someone else's name without that person's authority.

Witness and notary requirements discourage forgeries.

Deeds mistakenly recorded with facially apparent defects for recording do *not* give *constructive notice*.

Title search must reveal the defective instrument, giving actual notice.

If defects do *not* appear on the instrument's face, then recording satisfies constructive notice.

Undelivered deeds, grantor failing to deliver deed intending to complete grant, are generally ineffective.

Execution alone, without delivery, does not create an enforceable right of title.

When owner dies without having delivered, grant is incomplete and void.

Deed in escrow *to deliver at owner's death* remains an incomplete and ineffective gift.

Some states treat the escrow as an intended devise, subject to probate.

Purchase-money mortgages involving loans to buy the real property generally have priority over other liens.

Judgment and tax liens involve creditors recording against real property that the judgment debtor owns.

Judgment creditor and taxing authorities record liens and await the home's sale or foreclose the lien.

State laws provide *homestead exemptions* against execution on a judgment lien recorded on real property.

Homestead exemptions vary, some states offering unlimited or high amounts but others low amounts.

Complete Long Outline

WEEK 1: Acquisition by Discovery or Capture

Most U.S. landowners trace their land's title back to **government grants**. The U.S. government traces its title to *discovery* or *conquest,* and *treaty* or *purchase*. Discovery does not necessarily mean that one instantly owns what one first possesses before any other possesses. Discovery in the context of the European settlement of the United States meant the first right to negotiate with aboriginal populations for ownership. Importantly, only government had the right to negotiate or to conquer and acquire by treaty. Individuals could not alone do so. Law rejected their claims of title, instead requiring federal acquisition, even if the federal government often transferred its right to states to grant private ownership. With settlement of the continental United States and other territories, discovery, treaty, and conquest are no longer common local means of acquiring title. This origin of title simply highlights that property rights depend on government power to defend them. And related principles of **possession, first in time**, and **labor expended** remain important to ownership.

The law of **capture** requires that the claimant have *appropriated* the property, not merely pursued it. For example, the law of *accession* involves ownership or compensation claims based on the claimant's value-added labor. Thus, oil and gas becomes the capturer's property once *severed from the land*, even, as many cases hold, if reinjected into the land for storage. The English rule for ownership of water gave the landowner unlimited right to withdraw from a reservoir. Water isn't so scarce in England. The American rule limits withdrawal to *reasonable use* so as not to affect neighbors who also draw from the same reservoir. Western states allocate surface waters to the first-in-time user, called *prior appropriation*, relating to the scarcity of Western waters. By contrast, Eastern states recognize *riparian rights* of landowners to use adjacent waters (passing rivers and streams, or stable lakes) without limit.

The claimant must also have been the **first in time** to capture to have rightful ownership. Taking from someone who has already captured the thing may be the tort of conversion and crime of theft. Another theory involving *malicious interference* with pursuit may also give rise to remedies against the interferer. A landowner may have *constructive possession* of wild animals on the land until they leave. Thus, trespassers may have to relinquish to the landowner any wild animals that they capture on the trespassed land, under that constructive-possession theory. But government may confiscate wild animals that landowners capture in regulatory violation. Constructive possession and landowner rights do not overcome regulations.

Custom and usage may influence the decision whether a claimant captured the property such as to acquire ownership. Look to what others usually do in that activity. Rules of capture can exacerbate the *tragedy of the commons*, promoting destructive over-pursuit of common resources. Law must in that sense account for *externalities*, internalizing costs to the acquiring actor. Don't let one profit unduly at the expense of others, when harvesting from the commons. But rules should also not exacerbate the tragedy of the *anticommons*, where veto by anyone may frustrate good by some. Under the *Coase Theorem*, rules do not increase efficiency, just creating winners and losers. Finally, courts generally reject equitable divisions (Solomonic compromises, dividing the discovered or captured resource among equal claimants), except in rare cases.

WEEK 2: Acquisition by find

A finder's *title*, the legal right to possess the property, is good against everyone other than the true owner. The finder may keep the personal property in dispute with anyone other than the original owner. Property is thus not a relationship between the person and thing as much as a relationship between persons relative to the thing. Title is often relative, qualified, rather than absolute. Owners may recover the personal property in an action traditionally called *replevin*. Alternatively, owners may recover the personal property's value in an action traditionally called *trover*. To have superior title over subsequent finders, the one who possesses property must do so lawfully. A thief who steals and then loses an item has no right of action against a finder for the item or its value. Similarly, a landowner or homeowner may generally recover personal property that a trespasser finds on the premises but not necessarily lost items that a person lawfully on the premises finds, especially if the finder uncovers it by labor unrelated to the reason for being on the land. Finders generally acquire no rights in *mislaid* property accidentally left behind. Finders have superior title to *lost* property out of place, as against anyone other than the true owner. Finders have superior title to *abandoned* property, as against everyone including the true owner.

Employees may or may not have to relinquish to their employer property found during employment, depending on factors including the nature of their work and the relationship of the property to it. American law tends to reject the traditional law of *treasure trove* in which the government recovers buried or otherwise hidden money. American states may instead apply the *mislaid-lost-abandoned* distinctions. Many states have complex statutes addressing those distinctions. Shipwrecks may remain the property of the ship's owner unless abandoned. Traditional common law treated abandoned shipwrecks as government property, perhaps with a salvage award up to half for the finder. Federal act grants title to shipwrecks in territorial waters to the state, the states making their own rules.

WEEK 3: Adverse possession

Adverse possession is a lawful means by which one who occupies or uses land can acquire title to the land without dealing with the land's owner. To acquire title by adverse possession, a person must possess the property in an *exclusive*, *open and notorious*, and *continuous* manner for longer the statutory limitations period for ejectment actions, under a *claim of right*. In this context, **possession** means the satisfaction of each of those conditions. If a person can establish each of those conditions either in an action that the person files to gain clear title to the land, or in defense of the owner's ejectment action, then the court may enter a recordable judgment that has the purpose and effect of granting title to the person adversely possessing. The former owner then no longer has any right or title to, or interest in, the land. The adverse possessor's title will be marketable title if the adverse possessor should wish to sell the land.

For adverse possession, the person must first be on the property **exclusively** as an owner would be able to exclude. The person may move onto the property as in residence or may simply use the property exclusively, as an owner would. The person need not use the entire land to gain the entire land by adverse possession, if the limited use of the land that the person makes succeeds in excluding others from the entire land. Conversely, an adverse possessor who occupies only part of the land *without* excluding others from other parts adversely possesses only the used part. *Exclusive* use does not necessarily mean *sole* use. Two or more can simultaneously adversely possess land, as when a married couple or family move onto or continuously use the land, the couple or family then taking title together as adverse possessors when they satisfy the conditions.

240

The person's possession must then **open and notorious**, meaning that the property's true owner would likely discover the person's possession in inspection's ordinary course. Open and notorious means *visible* to others, particularly the owner. If the owner does not ordinarily visit the property or the occupied part of it for inspection, then the occupier's use of the property may not be sufficiently open and notorious, unless the occupier takes special steps to ensure that the owner knows. The owner's knowledge of the use is sufficient to establish that the use was open and notorious. If the occupier leaves the land each time the owner visits, whether by the owner's request or to avoid detection, then the possession is not open and notorious.

The possession must then be adverse, hostile, or otherwise under a **claim of right**, meaning that the possession is without the owner's consent in conflict with owner interests. Possession is adverse and under a claim of right when the possessor remains on the property intending and appearing to remain so permanently. A *claim of right* in this context does *not* mean a legal claim but instead appearing as if having the right to exclude the owner. Thus, tenants cannot adversely possess their landlord's land, and co-tenants cannot adversely possess their co-tenants' rights, because tenants do not occupy with the intent and appearance of ownership rights. The owner's permission destroys the person's claim of right. The person who concedes the owner's right fails to satisfy the hostility condition. Yet to establish adverse possession, the person need *not* have malicious intent or, in most states, even *know* that the possession was unlawful or against the owner's claim of title.

Finally, the possession must be **continuous**, meaning *uninterrupted*, for longer than the statutory limitations period on ejectment actions, varying from state to state between five and twenty-one years, with ten or fifteen years being particularly common lengths. Continuous does not necessarily mean every hour of every day but instead the use typical of one owning the land, depending on its type. Thus, a person would have to remain in a residence more often and consistently than on vacant lands, to adversely possess the residence. By contrast, even occasional use of a guest house or other property that an owner would only use sporadically may suffice. Abandonment of the property, though, interrupts continuous possession.

Claims of adverse possession sometimes raise the question of **tacking** successive periods of possession by different persons, each of whose possession is shorter than the statutory period. Generally, *voluntary transfer* from one possessor to another supports tacking their periods of possession. Claims of adverse possession also might raise the question of whether changes in ownership of the land interrupts the occupier's adverse possession, except that the rule simply holds that once adverse possession begins, it runs against all successive owners, no matter how many own the land during the statutory period.

WEEK 4: Acquisition by Gift

A **gift** is a definite voluntary transfer of a present property interest. Completing a **gift** of personal property requires the donor and donee to meet three conditions: (1) donor *intent* to make a present transfer of ownership; (2) *delivery* of the personal property, typically by transferring possession of the personal property, or an equivalent to delivery that law recognizes; and (3) donee *acceptance* of the gift, typically presumed if the gift has value but with acknowledgment as direct evidence.

Donor intent is typically by an oral or written statement of gift. Look closely, though, at the words used to ensure that they communicate a present intent to convey a present interest in the gift property. Delivery typically involves the donor moving the personal property into the donee's possession. Where no one disputes donor intent, and the donor believed the gift complete, *constructive delivery* of a token, such as a key for access or operation, suffices in some courts. By contrast, *symbolic delivery* of a writing declaring the gift is traditionally enough only for items *too large to deliver*, for example, difficult-to-move personal property such as heavy equipment. Symbolic delivery of a writing declaring the gift would not be enough for a movable item, although some state statutes permit symbolic delivery of small items, reversing the common-law delivery rule. A gift of land requires delivery of a deed.

Generally, a donee cannot enforce a *promise to make a gift* because the promise lacks consideration. Traditionally, the donor of an engagement ring recovers it on a breakup only if the donor is without fault. Gift of a check may require the donee to deposit it and the drawee bank to pay it before the donor dies or revokes.

A gift *causa mortis* is one that the donor makes anticipating the donor's death. Gifts causa mortis are *present* gifts anticipating death, not *future* gifts on (after) death. A *future* gift *on* death generally requires a will (a writing satisfying the law of wills). Gifts causa mortis are effective with donor intent and delivery. The donor may revoke a gift causa mortis if the donor recovers rather than dies. Some states require the donor to make an explicit revocation of the gift if and when the donor recovers, otherwise presuming that the donor intends the gift to remain. Also, as to gifts causa mortis, the donor may have to redeliver at the time of the gift if the donee already had the property before the donor expressed the gift intent because the courts tend to construe gift-causa-mortis requirements strictly. Courts also tend to construe strictly the constructive-delivery and symbolic-delivery limits, for gifts causa mortis. The donor would have to make undisputed intent especially clear to allow constructive delivery, and the item would have to be non-movable to accept symbolic delivery through a note.

WEEK 5: Fees simple

The term **fee simple** is shorthand for the **fee simple absolute**. When a person owns property in fee simple absolute, the person has the theoretical right to hold the property in perpetuity. Fee-simple estates are **alienable**, which means that the owner may sell or transfer the land to another, and **inheritable**, which means that the owner may devise the land by will to another, who would then own the property in perpetuity. The vast majority of land sales today transfer fee simple absolute.

The way that the parties write a land transaction determines the estate that they transfer. The language needed to create a fee simple absolute is *to A and A's heirs*, where *A* refers to the buyer's full legal name that would appear in the transfer documents. This language includes **words of purchase** and **words of limitation**. The words of purchase in this transaction are *to A*. The words of limitation in the transaction are *and A's heirs*. Traditionally, the law required the words *and A's heirs* to show that the seller intended to deliver fee-simple estate to the purchaser. Today, however, a transaction *to A* suffices to transfer fee simple. Modern law presumes fee-simple transactions unless the parties use other words of limitation.

Defeasible fee-simple estates are estates in fee simple that *end on a stated future event*. By *defeasible*, the law means terminable on the occurrence of the stated condition or event. By contrast, the owner of a fee simple *absolute*, rather than a *defeasible* fee, holds the property in perpetuity unaffected by future events. A grantor creates a defeasible fee estate when wanting to control the property's use and ownership. The law recognizes **three types of defeasible fee estates**, a fee simple *determinable*, a fee simple *subject to condition subsequent*, and a fee simple *subject to executory limitation*. The type of defeasible fee depends on the words of limitation used in the transfer that creates the interest.

A fee simple **determinable** is an estate that would be a fee simple absolute but for the language of the conveyance that attaches a condition to the property's ownership. The law calls the **condition subsequent** the event that would terminate the fee-simple interest. For example, a conveyance from grantor *to A so long as A never commits a felony on the property* includes the condition subsequent that A not commit a felony on the property. Thus, A owns the property in fee simple, but if A commits a felony on the property, A's fee simple terminates, and the property automatically reverts to the grantor who created A's interest. When a grantor creates a fee-simple determinable, the law calls the grantor's future interest a **possibility of reverter**. Reverter happens automatically by law when the condition subsequent occurs. To create a fee-simple determinable, the conveyance must include *durational* words of limitation indicating the intent that the possessory estate will end automatically on the happening of the stated condition. Typical words of limitation that suggest a fee-simple determinable include *so long as*, *during*, *while*, *unless*, and *until*. When one of these words addresses a condition subsequent, then the purchaser acquires a present possessory fee-simple determinable, while the grantor retains a possibility of reverter.

A fee simple **subject to condition subsequent** relates closely to the fee-simple determinable. Here, though, with a fee simple subject to condition subsequent, while the owner holds in fee simple, the grantor has attached a condition subsequent that will *not* automatically terminate the owner's fee-simple title. Instead, the grantor retains a future interest called a **right of entry** that gives the grantor the *option* to take the property back *or* let the owner keep the property. The conveyance's **words of limitation** determine whether the fee simple is determinable or, instead, subject to condition subsequent. Typical words of limitation for a fee simple subject to condition subsequent include *but if*, *provided that*, *on condition that*, *if, however*, and *provided, however*. For example, a fee simple subject to condition subsequent arises in a conveyance *from O to A, but if A commits a felony on the property, then O may reenter and retake the property*. These words of limitation are expressly conditional *and discretionary*, reflected here in the operative word *may*, rather than purely durational. The grantor may invoke *or ignore* the condition's occurrence.

The final form of fee simple, a fee simple **subject to executory limitation**, is easier to distinguish. Like a fee simple determinable and fee simple subject to condition subsequent, the owner possesses the property in fee simple but subject to a condition subsequent that may terminate the interest. Yet for a fee simple *subject to executory limitation*, the person who takes the property when the condition subsequent occurs is a third party rather than the original grantor or grantor's heirs or assigns. If the interest doesn't revert to the original grantor, then the purchaser has a fee simple subject to executory limitation. For example, a fee simple subject to executory limitation arises in a conveyance from grantor *to A, but if A ever commits a felony on the property, then to C*. The fact that a third party, C in this case, would get the property if A committed a felony on the property indicates the executory limitation. The law calls the third party's interest the **executory interest**, discussed in the future interest section below. If the condition subsequent occurs, then the property automatically goes to the third party.

WEEK 6: Life estates

A **life estate** is a third type of freehold estate. As the estate's name implies, the owner of a life estate owns the property for the *duration of the owner's lifetime*, whether that lifetime lasts one day or fifty years. Because of a life estate's limited and uncertain duration, a life estate is *not* inheritable or descendible. A life estate's owner has nothing left to give on demise. On the other hand, life estates are *alienable*, meaning that the owner can sell or transfer a life estate, although the law continues to measure the transferred life estate's term by the original life tenant's life, not the life of the person who received the life estate. The most common way that transfer documents create a life estate are with the language *to A for life* or *to A for A's natural life*. All life estates include a future interest because the property must go somewhere after the life tenant dies. The future interest can either be a reversion or remainder as following sections discuss in more detail.

Future interests. A second ownership area to address after present estates involves **future interests**. Future interests include *reversions*, both vested and contingent *remainders, executory interests*, and finally *possibilities of reverter* including powers of termination. A following section also addresses special rules affecting these interests. Generally, a **future interest** arises when a person must wait until some future time in order to take possession of the property. Estates involve the property's timeline of ownership. The present interest owner possesses the property for some duration, then the **future interest holder** may come into possession of the property after the present estate ends. Future interests belong to two categories, those retained by the original grantor and those held by a third party. Interests retained by the grantor include *reversions, possibilities of reverter*, and *rights of entry*. Interests granted a third party include *vested remainders, contingent remainders*, and *executory interests*, all addressed in the following sections.

Reversions. A **reversion** is a future interest that the grantor retains when transferring a present interest less than the grantor owns. For example, a conveyance from grantor *to A for life* creates a life estate in A with a *reversion in fee simple* in the grantor. When the grantor both doesn't convey the grantor's entire interest in the property and doesn't say to whom the property passes after the lesser estate ends, then the law construes a reversion in the original grantor or grantor's heirs or devisees if the grantor has already died when the present possessory estate ends. Thus, reversion is an interest that returns to the grantor. The law also recognizes a **possibility of reverter** and **right of entry**, each arising only in limited circumstances when the present possessory estate ends. As stated above as to defeasible fees, **possibilities of reverter** arise only when the present possessory estate is a fee simple determinable, that is, when the determinable fee ends automatically on the condition's occurrence. A **right of entry** arises only when the present possessory estate is a fee simple subject to condition subsequent, that is, when the grantor has the option of retaking the land after the condition occurs. A following section addresses these latter interests.

Remainders, vested and contingent. A **remainder** is a future interest granted to a third party after the present possessory estate ends naturally. Two conditions define remainders. First, the future interest must go to a third party, not revert to the grantor or the grantor's heirs or assigns. Second, the remainder holder must wait until the natural end of the prior possessory estate to take possession. This last point is critical to determining whether the future interest left over is an executory interest or some type of remainder, which the next section addresses.

Remainders can be either **vested remainders** or **contingent remainders**. A vested remainder is one that an *ascertained person* holds, meaning someone named, *and* that is not subject to a condition precedent. A condition precedent is an event that must occur before the person obtains the future interest. For example, the transaction from grantor *to A for life, then to B if B attains the age of 21*, includes a condition precedent to B obtaining the estate that B must attain the age of 21. Thus, B's interest is *not* a vested remainder but instead a **contingent remainder** because of the condition precedent. Similarly, a grant *to A for life, then to B's children*, when B has no children, would be a grant to unascertained persons and thus create only a contingent rather than vested remainder. Again, a contingent remainder involves either an unascertained owner or one who receives the interest subject to a condition precedent. A vested remainder cannot be contingent.

Contingent remainders can vest either when the condition precedent occurs or the unascertained person is ascertained. Thus, in the prior example, if the grantor had granted *to A for life, then to B's children*, and B then had a child, that child would take a *vested* rather than contingent remainder as an ascertained person within the grant. Because B could have other children, the child already born would have a vested remainder **subject to open** to account for the interests of any other children subsequently born to B. Thus, if when B died, B had three children, then those three children would have **indefeasibly vested remainders** because no further births could dilute their interests. Each child would have a one-third interest in the property as tenants in common.

Grantors can form **alternative contingent remainders** when the grantor creates two options for what will happen to the property. For example, the grantor creates alternative contingent remainders in the conveyance from grantor *to A for life, then to B if B reaches 21, but if B does not reach 21, then to C*. In this conveyance, B has a contingent remainder conditioned on B's reaching age 21. Here, though, the grant holds that if B doesn't reach age 21, then the property goes to C. The grantor retains no reversion here because of the stated alternatives.

Executory interests. **Executory interests** are a third type of future interest, one that the grantor creates *in a third party*. Executory interests relate closely to vested and contingent remainders. Yet an executory interest is a future interest in a third party that takes effect only *when a condition subsequent divests, or terminates, the interest that precedes the executory interest*. Executory interests vest when someone else loses a vested interest. For example, in the conveyance from grantor *to A for life, then to B, but if B does not reach the age of 21, then to C*, we have already seen that B has a vested remainder that B could lose if B dies before 21. The ability of B to lose the interest means that B's interest is *subject to divestment*. The possibility of divestment creates C's executory interest, which would vest only if B died before reaching age 21. An executory interest also arises in C in the conveyance from grantor *to A for life, then to B, but if B joins a biker gang, then to C*. Here, if B receives the property on A's death but then joins a biker gang, the condition subsequent occurring would divest B's defeasible fee simple, vesting C's executory interest.

Possibilities of reverter, powers of termination. As the defeasible-fee section addresses, a **possibility of reverter** is the future interest that remains after a fee-simple determinable. A **fee-simple determinable** is an estate that would be a fee-simple absolute but for the conveyance's language of the conveyance attaching a **condition subsequent** to ownership. For example, a conveyance from grantor *to A so long as A never commits a felony on the property* means that A takes the property in fee simple, but if the condition subsequent occurs, A committing a felony on the property, A loses the property, which automatically reverts to the grantor. A fee simple determinable arises whenever the grantor has a future interest, called a **possibility of reverter**. Reverter happens automatically by operation of law on the condition's occurrence.

Also as the defeasible-fee section states, a **right of entry**, also known as a **power of termination**, is the future interest that arises from a fee simple **subject to condition subsequent**. Recall that a fee simple subject to condition subsequent relates closely to the **fee simple determinable**. For any defeasible fee, the owner holds in fee simple, but the grantor attached a **condition subsequent** that could cause the person to lose their present possessory interest. Yet unlike the fee simple determinable, the owner does *not* lose the fee-simple interest automatically on the condition's occurrence. Rather, the grantor retains the **right of entry**, or **power of termination**, to take the property back *or not* at the grantor's option. The **words of limitation** in the conveyance determine the interest. A fee simple subject to condition subsequent arises under words of limitation like *but if, provided that, on condition that, if, however*, or *provided, however*. For example, a fee simple subject to condition subsequent arises in a conveyance *from O to A, but if A commits a felony on the property, then O may reenter and retake the property*.

WEEK 7: Special rules affecting future interests

The law recognizes several rules that limit *dead-hand control* over real property, meaning how long and how much a person can control what happens to the person's property after the person's death. The rules seek to ensure reasonable *alienability* and *marketability* of property. Some of these rules no longer apply in most jurisdictions. For example, a few states still follow a rule for the **destructibility of contingent remainders**. In those few jurisdictions, the rule eliminates any contingent remainder that has not vested by the time that all preceding life estates have terminated. The rule for destructibility of contingent remainders ensures that the law can ascertain the person who would have the discretion to exercise a possibility of reverter.

The law continues to recognize a **merger rule** holding that when a person who owns a vested life estate acquires the vested future interest behind the life estate, the two vested estates merge into one fee-simple title. For example, in the conveyance *from O to A for life, remainder to B*, if B then sells B's future interest to the life-estate holder A, then A would own both the present vested life estate *and* B's vested remainder, the two interests of which would merge into fee-simple title in A.

The **rule in Shelley's Case**, in the few states that still recognize it, applies where a life tenant's heirs hold the remainder to the life tenant's present interest, to merge the interests into the life tenant in fee simple absolute. Thus, in a conveyance *from O to A for life, remainder to A's heirs*, the rule in Shelly's Case would give A the fee-simple title to the property. Having a grant of a life estate that also gives that person's heirs the remainder merge into fee-simple title in the life estate holder gives the grantee the ability to convey the property in fee-simple absolute, promoting the land's marketability. Buyers need not wait for the life-estate holder to die to ensure that they properly ascertain, and gain conveyance from, the persons who hold the remainder interests. Only one person, the grantee of the life estate, need sign the deed conveying fee-simple title.

The **doctrine of worthier title**, again in the few states that continue to recognize it, works like the rule in Shelley's Case to simplify future interests, except that the rule applies to future-interest conveyances back to the grantor's own heirs. Thus, the doctrine of worthier title would treat a conveyance *from O to A for life, remainder to O's heirs* as simply leaving the grantor a reversion, as if the conveyance were just *from O to A for life*. The doctrine of worthier title destroys remainders to the grantor's own heirs in favor of leaving the grantor a reversion. Again, the rule promotes the land's marketability because otherwise, buyers could not ascertain a grantor's heirs until the grantor died. The doctrine of worthier title allows the grantor and life tenant to convey the property while both are still alive.

The **rule against perpetuities** provides that *executory interests* and *contingent remainders* must vest, if at all, within twenty-one years of a *life in being* at the time that the grant created the future interest. The rule's purpose is to preserve property's alienability and marketability, while preventing the wishes of persons long dead from controlling the disposition of lands. The rule against perpetuities does *not* limit interests that the grantor *keeps*, like reversions to the grantor or rights of re-entry in the grantor, because a grantor should be able to control the grantor's own property. The rule against perpetuities makes sense to promote alienability and marketability but can produce absurd results, for instance by voiding a conveyance on assumption like a ninety-year-old woman having a child. Some jurisdictions address that absurdity by presuming that women will not bear children after age fifty-five.

Policy aside, to apply the rule against perpetuities, simply determine whether a grant creates either a **contingent remainder** or **executory interest**. If not, and instead the grant only creates *vested* remainders, then the rule does not apply, and the conveyance is valid. Thus, a conveyance *to A for life, then to B*, does not violate the rule against perpetuities because the only remainder interest, B's interest, is a *vested* rather than contingent remainder. The interest does not depend on a condition that may not ever occur or that will vest more than twenty-one years after a currently living person dies. For another example, a conveyance *to A as long as A does not use the land for a landfill* also reserves only a *vested* rather than contingent remainder, in the form of a possibility of reverter in the grantor. Thus, the conveyance does not implicate the rule against perpetuities, and the conveyance is valid even if A's grandchild or a later descendant misuses the land as a landfill and the land reverts to the grantor or grantor's heirs.

If instead a conveyance *does* create a contingent remainder or executory interest, then determine whether the grant limits the interest's vesting by a condition that *may not ever occur*,

246

in which case the grant violates the rule. For example, a conveyance *to A as long as A does not use the land for a landfill, and then to B*, creates an executory interest in B that may not ever occur, if A and A's heirs never use the land for a landfill. Thus, the rule against perpetuities applies to void the interest. If instead the interest will vest when *currently living persons* die, then determine whether the grant allows vesting more than twenty-one years after the last such person dies. For example, a conveyance *to A, then to A's oldest living male child*, does not violate the rule, even though the remainder is contingent, because the remainder vests or not immediately on the measuring life A's death, rather than more than twenty-one years later. If, on the other hand, the prior conveyance was *to A, then to A's oldest living male child when that child reaches age thirty*, then the contingent remainder would violate the rule against perpetuities because it could vest more than twenty-one years after the measuring life A's death. A could die leaving an oldest male child who was under age nine and whose interest would therefore not vest for more than twenty-one years after A's death.

As modified. The modern form of the rule against perpetuities recognizes an exception for **class gifts**. Class gifts are to a group as in *to A's children or grandchildren*. The common-law rule against perpetuities operates under an *all-or-nothing* rule that invalidates the entire conveyance if invalid for even one member of the potential class. Courts, though, have created an exception to the all-or-nothing rule called the *rule of convenience*, closing the class to new members (typically, children born after the conveyance) when at least one member of the class takes possession of the property. For example, in the conveyance *O to A's children when they reach age 25*, the rule against perpetuities may invalidate this interest if A is still alive at the time of the conveyance because A could have after-born children. However, if at the time of the conveyance, A has at least one child who is over twenty-five, that child's interest would vest. The *rule of convenience* would then close the class gift, so that after-born children would not share in the gift.

Because of the harshness of the common-law rule against perpetuities, many states have further modified it for results consistent with the grantor's intent. The *Uniform Statutory Rule Against Perpetuities*, adopted in over twenty jurisdictions, provides a waiting period of ninety years to see if the future interest vests. If it does not, then the court may modify the interest. Other states have adopted a similar *wait-and-see approach* that, instead of invalidating all potential future interests that could remain unresolved, waits to see if the circumstances do resolve before invalidating the interest.

WEEK 8: Co-tenancy

Another area to address on ownership, after treating present estates and future interests above, involves **co-tenancies** between or among owners. Grantors may divide ownership interests among two or more persons, creating co-tenancies. Co-tenancies come in two different *types*, treated in the following sections. Co-tenancies also involve the *severance* of co-tenancies or their *partition*, each addressed in following sections. Another following section addresses the *relations* of co-tenants in their common use of the property. This part on co-tenancies then ends with rules on *alienability*, *descendibility*, and *devisability*.

Types. The following two sections address **tenancies in common** and **joint tenancies**, as the two types of co-tenancy. As the sections illustrate, one significant distinction between the two types of co-tenancy has to do with *rights of survivorship*, addressing the question of whether a co-tenant's heirs or devisees receive the co-tenant's interest on the co-tenant's death or, instead, the other co-tenant or co-tenants receive the interest. Tenancies in common differ from joint tenancies in other ways, too, such as the ability to form and hold unequal shares, and rights of use and conveyance. As to each type of co-tenancy, the *grantor's language* determines the type of co-tenancy formed. Ensure that you recognize the language that forms each type, while being able to distinguish the survivorship, use, and other rights afforded as to each type.

Tenancy in common. A **tenancy in common** is a type of co-tenancy that does *not* grant *survivorship rights* in the co-tenants. *Tenant*, in this context, does *not* mean one taking under a lease but instead means a co-owner in fee-simple title. Each of two or more tenants in common owns an alienable and inheritable share of the property. In contrast to a joint tenancy, tenants in common may own *unequal shares* that they can freely transfer to other owners either during life or at death by inheritance or will. Because death does not terminate the tenant in common's interest, the interest passes as the tenant directs in a will or law directs by intestacy. Whether tenants in common own equal or unequal shares, all tenants in common have the right to occupy and use all or any part of the property. A tenant in common's ownership interest is an **undivided** interest. Thus, if tenants in common own a home, then each may use any part of the home, even if one tenant owns a one-quarter share and the other tenant owns three quarters.

Either tenant in common may sell their share so that the remaining co-tenant would share with a new tenant in common. Language *from grantor to A and B* creates a tenancy in common, as would more-specific language *to A and B as tenants in common*. Tenants in common may also receive their interests from separate conveyance documents. Thus, a grantor may convey fee-simple title to an owner who then conveys a tenancy in common to a co-tenant with the owner. Either co-tenant may then convey to other co-tenants whose interests arise out of those other conveyance documents. A tenancy in common differs from a joint tenancy in this additional respect, insofar as only a single conveyance document can create a joint tenancy.

Joint tenancy. A **joint tenancy** is a co-tenancy in which two or more co-tenants have equal undivided interests in the property with *rights of survivorship*. Thus, if a joint tenant dies, the other joint tenant or joint tenants receive the deceased joint tenant's interest automatically by operation of law. Joint tenants all have equal rights of the property's use. Unlike in a tenancy in common, joint tenants cannot own unequal shares. Language *from grantor to A and B as joint tenants* or *to A and B with full rights of survivorship* creates a joint tenancy, if the co-tenants have *unity of time, title, interest,* and *possession*, meaning that they take at precisely the same time, under the same document, with the same interest, and the same right of possession. The conveyance language must indicate the grantor's intent to create rights of survivorship either by saying so or by indicating that the grantees take as joint tenants. A conveyance that does not indicate the intent to create a joint tenancy or rights of survivorship instead creates a tenancy in common. As indicated in the prior section, only a single conveyance document can create a joint tenancy. A joint tenant may alienate, meaning transfer, the joint tenant's interest, but in doing so the joint tenant severs the joint tenancy and creates a tenancy in common.

A **tenancy by the entireties** is a joint tenancy between married individuals. Language *from grantor to A and B as tenants by the entireties*, or *to A and B as husband and wife*, creates a tenancy by the entireties, if A and B are in fact married. Most states also presume a tenancy by the entirety from a grant *to A and B as joint tenants* if A and B are then married. If grantees are not married but receive property in a grant indicating rights of survivorship, then they can be at most joint tenants. If they divorce, then they become tenants in common. An advantage of a tenancy by the entireties over a joint tenancy or tenancy in common is that a creditor of only one spouse cannot in execution reach the spouse's tenancy-by-the-entirety interest. Married couples hold entireties property free from the claims of creditors of either spouse, if the creditor has a claim only against one of the spouses. Creditors whose claims are against both spouses can reach entireties property. Unlike both tenancies in common and joint tenancies, tenants by the entireties cannot convey away their individual interests.

Severance. **Severance** refers to the process, whether intentional or inadvertent, of converting a joint tenancy into a tenancy in common. Severance is significant because it *destroys the right of survivorship* that accompanies a joint tenancy. Joint tenants may agree to sever their joint tenancy, as for instance by agreeing to sell the land and divide the proceeds.

Also, one joint tenant may convey away the interest, in doing so severing the joint tenancy and leaving the grantee in a tenancy in common with the other co-tenants who remain joint tenants as to one another. Lease of a joint tenancy does not, in most states, sever the joint tenancy in favor of a tenancy in common. Yet a joint tenant can by other action indicate the intent to sever and in doing so accomplish it, for instance by conveying to a trustee for the co-tenant's own benefit, or in some states, to the co-tenant's self, thus destroying the unity of time and title. Indeed, a conveyance to a trust, trustee, conservator, or other individual would inadvertently destroy the unity of time and title, and sever the joint tenancy, even if the co-tenant had not so intended.

Partition. Tenants in common and joint tenants may at any time seek **partition** of the land. Partition involves equitable division of the land to represent each co-tenant's individual interest. A court may at the request of any co-tenant impose and enforce partition, if the co-tenants cannot agree. Some real property co-tenants can easily divide, while other real property they cannot. Partition may thus be **in-kind**, accomplishing a physical division of the property, or partition may be **by sale** if the court cannot divide the property, division is impractical, or division is not in the co-tenants' best interests. Co-tenants must divide sale proceeds equitably to represent their individual interests.

Relations among cotenants. Co-tenants, whether tenants in common or joint tenants, share the rights of possession and rent, and share in responsibility. One co-tenant may not **oust** another co-tenant from possession. Most jurisdictions do *not* require one co-tenant to pay another co-tenant rent even if the co-tenant has the property's only use *unless* the co-tenant ousts the other co-tenant, in which case the tenant in possession may owe for the other's lost use. Co-tenants share in **rents** received from the premises. Thus, if one co-tenant collects rents but refuses to share, other co-tenants may enforce their right to a fair share. Co-tenants generally *share expenses*, each having a right to make the other contribute as necessary. Thus, if one co-tenant pays real-property taxes, mortgage payments, and reasonably necessary insurance, upkeep, or repair expenses to which other co-tenants refuse to contribute, then the paying co-tenant may enforce a right of contribution.

Alienability, descendibility, devisability. Both tenants in common and joint tenants may **alienate** their co-tenancy interest, meaning sell or otherwise *transfer* it away. By contrast, tenants by the entireties cannot transfer their co-tenant interest. Tenants in common convey whatever fractional interest they hold, whereas joint tenants convey their equal interest. The interest of a tenant in common is also **descendible**, meaning that an heir can inherit the interest, and **devisable**, meaning that the tenant in common can pass the interest to another by will, on the co-tenant's death. By contrast, a joint tenancy is *not* descendible or devisable because of the right of survivorship attendant on a joint tenancy. When a joint tenant dies, the tenancy interest passes by operation of law to the surviving joint tenant or joint tenants.

WEEK 9: Marital Estates

How law treats the personal and real property of married couples depends on whether the state is a **common-law marital property** state or a **community marital property** state. Forty states including Michigan and New York have common-law marital property, but ten states including California and Texas have community property. In grand theory, common-law marital property means separate marital estates, husband and wife each owning that which they earn or acquire and hold in their own name. In grand theory, community property means one estate, husband and wife owning together everything that either earns or acquires during the marriage, no matter how they title the property. The difference, though, is much less significant today, at least in the event of divorce, which is one of the main events where the forms once made a bigger difference.

Common-law marital property distinguishes rights during marriage, on divorce, and at death. During marriage, sole creditors of one spouse cannot reach real property that two spouses hold together as tenants by the entireties. Most states recognize tenancies by the entirety as to personal property, too, not just real property. During marriage, federal tax liens do attach to one spouse's interest in entireties property but not to the interest of the other spouse who did not owe the tax obligation. The IRS typically waits until the property's sale or until divorce to foreclose the lien on the owing spouse's interest. Federal forfeiture law permits attachment only as to the criminally responsible spouse's survivorship interest. Indeed, the criminally responsible spouse may have had to use the property for the criminal activity for the attachment to work at all.

Divorce, though, severs the tenancy by the entireties, which can only exist between spouses. Divorce converts a tenancy by the entirety into a tenancy in common. Today, in divorce cases, most common-law states treat property acquired during the marriage as *marital property*—in effect, like a community-property state would treat the property. Law in most states presumes that *each spouse gets half* of property earned or acquired during marriage. Indeed, property that either spouse brings into the marriage may also become marital property if *commingled* with other marital property rather than held separately. Degrees earned or licenses obtained during marriage are not marital property in most states but may warrant additional spousal support for the other spouse lacking equal earning power. Property received as gift or by inheritance during the marriage remains separate property.

Nearly all states have abolished dower rights of a wife and curtesy rights of a husband after death of the other spouse. Where they exist, dower and curtesy rights protect the surviving spouse's interest on the other spouse's death. Where dower survives, the wife obtains a life estate of a portion of the deceased husband's lands. Dower and curtesy rights can also protect a spouse from the other spouse conveying away property on which the non-conveying spouse may depend. Spouses may, though, relinquish their dower and curtesy rights. The key, then, to avoiding dower and curtesy problems in the chain of title is to have both husband and wife sign deeds as either of them conveys away property, no matter who holds formal title to the property.

States also have elective-share or forced-share statutes that protect a surviving spouse when the deceased spouse has willed away to others, property that the surviving spouse deems necessary for that spouse's continuing support. Under an elective-share statute, the surviving spouse may take a statutory portion of the deceased spouse's estate, often one third or one half, no matter what the decedent's will provided. Some states require the electing spouse to relinquish anything that the will would otherwise have provided to them, but other states let the spouse keep willed property and add to it the elective share.

Community marital property treats property acquired and accumulated during marriage as owned equally in undivided shares. Property that either spouse owned separately before the marriage remains separate property. During the marriage, neither spouse may sell community property without the other's consent, like entireties property. But either spouse *may* dispose of their half of community property by will at death, *unlike* entireties property. Either spouse may manage and control community marital property but only to benefit both spouses, in effect acting as a fiduciary for the other spouse. Creditors of only one spouse may reach only the portion of community property that spouse manages and controls. For spouses moving between common-law and community-property states, property remains as initially characterized when either spouse acquired it. If it was originally separate property under that state's law, then it remains separate property even if the state to which the spouses move would have characterized it as marital property. Unmarried couples depend on contract rights, not community-property theories.

WEEK 10: Land-Sale Contracts

The law treats **contracts** for the sale of land as it treats other contracts. However, unique practices having to do with the sale of land, such as **real estate brokerage**, implicate other principles, rules, and concerns outside of the ordinary concerns surrounding contracts. Real-estate transactions also follow certain *customs* in the **creation** and **construction** of contracts. Also, unique questions over the **marketability of title** to land arise, given land's permanence and significant value, and the complex relationships and transactions of persons taking interests in the land. The following sections also treat **equitable conversion**, **options** and **rights of first refusal**, **fitness** and **suitability**, and the doctrine of **merger**, all unique issues relating to contracts for the sale of land.

Real estate brokerage. Because of land's high value and the complexity of a real-estate transaction, land sales often occur through a **broker**. A broker is the agent who either represents the seller in preparing, listing, and selling the land, or the agent who represents the buyer in locating, evaluating, and buying the land. Agents sometimes act as both the *listing agent* or *seller's agent* and *buyer's agent*. The seller of land forms a **listing agreement** with the listing agent under which the agent assumes the duty to list, show, and sell the land. The seller promises to pay a *commission* reflecting a sale-price percentage, often around six percent, whether the listing agent finds the buyer or not, if the sale occurs during the listing agreement's term. Listing agreements typically have a term of around three months to give the buyer the opportunity to list with a more-effective agent if the land doesn't sell. When a seller and buyer agree to terms, the seller and buyer may consult lawyers to prepare, review, and negotiate the land sale contract, although often the broker prepares a standard contract form that includes an attorney-review contingency.

When the land sells, the listing agent typically *divides* the commission with the buyer's agent, unless of course the listing agent has also attracted the buyer. States and listing agreements may follow different rules as to when a commission is due. A traditional rule required the seller to pay the broker a commission if the broker brought a buyer who signed a contract to purchase the land, even if the buyer subsequently refused to perform the contract. While some states and listing agreements still follow this rule, many other states and listing agreements now provide instead that the seller owes the commission only when the sale closes with the buyer's payment of the purchase price. Uniformly, though, if the seller fails or refuses to perform the land sale contract with a willing buyer, then the seller owes the commission for which the listing agreement calls.

Creation and construction. Because of their complexity and unique issues around financing and inspections, real-estate transactions follow two steps. The first step involves the seller and buyer forming a contract for the sale of the land, variously called a *purchase contract*, *purchase agreement*, or *land sale contract*, as just mentioned above. A signed purchase contract is necessary to complete or compel the sale of land, which is subject to the **statute of frauds**, as the next section addresses. As is true for other contracts, land sale contracts must include the **essential terms**, treated in a following section. Another following section addresses the **time for performance** of land sale contracts. The second step in the two-step procedure involves a *closing* at which the seller conveys the *deed* and the buyer conveys the sale price. The seller may also execute a *bill of sale* for any personal property transferred in the transaction such as appliances or furnishings. Closings in which the buyer finances the purchase through a mortgage lender involve executing many other documents including the mortgage, promissory note, and statutory disclosure forms. A last following section addresses **remedies for breach** of land sale contracts.

Statute of frauds and exceptions. The **statute of frauds** requires that contracts transferring an interest in real estate be *in a writing* and *signed* by the party against whom another seeks to enforce the contract. As indicated in the prior section, the enforceable writing that seller and buyer typically prepare is the *purchase agreement* anticipating a later closing, usually thirty, sixty, or ninety days following the purchase agreement's execution. Usually, the buyer will prepare and present a signed purchase agreement, constituting the buyer's offer. If the seller accepts, then the seller countersigns the offer and delivers the completed agreement to the buyer so that the agreement is formed and enforceable. The seller's simply countersigning but not delivering the completed agreement and not notifying the buyer of its countersigning with the intent to deliver would not ordinarily complete the agreement. Delivery completes the agreement. If the seller counteroffers by presenting the countersigned but modified agreement, then the buyer must sign and deliver the seller's counteroffer.

As is true for other contracts, parties may in certain circumstances enforce an agreement for the sale of real estate without a writing signed by the charged party. **Part performance** can take a land sale contract out of the statute of frauds, just as part performance can in other statute-of-frauds restricted transactions. Part performance in land sales typically involves the buyer taking possession of the land while also making part payment that the seller accepts in acknowledgment of the transfer. Where the buyer has not yet made any payment, jurisdictions may instead accept that the buyer *improve* the land, such as by commencing renovations, or otherwise change position in *detrimental reliance* on the sale. Possession alone is not enough to take the transaction out of the statute of frauds.

Essential terms. As is true for other contracts, a land sale contract must include the **essential terms** for either party to enforce the contract. A contract missing one or more essential terms is ordinarily unenforceable. Because land sale contracts fall within the statute of frauds, their essential terms must be in a *writing* that the charged party has signed. The essential terms in a land sale contract begin with *identifying the seller and buyer*. A contract may identify a buyer's agent acting for an *unidentified principal*, even a principal unknown to the seller, if the contract adequately identifies the agent and agency role. The next essential term involves a *property description*. Ordinarily, land sale contracts will include the land's metes-and-bounds description, often by reference to an attachment already stating that description. A metes-and-bounds description, though, is not always necessary if identifying the street address, city, and state, or other manner in which others commonly know the property, adequately remove ambiguity as to the parties' intent. If the contract refers to the number of acres sold but includes a metes-and-bounds description that contradicts the acres number, then the metes-and-bounds description controls.

Other essential terms include land's **price**. If the contract does *not* include the price, then it *must* include an objective means of calculating the certain price. Agreements to negotiate a price are *not* sufficient to satisfy the essential price term but are instead merely unenforceable commitments to continue negotiating, sometimes called *agreements to agree*. Again, because of the statute of frauds, a land sale contract must include any other terms and conditions on which either party intends to rely in completing the transaction. Common terms, none of which would necessarily be essential to a complete agreement but any of which may be essential to the party's interests, include a *financing contingency* that the contract is not enforceable unless the buyer qualifies for financing, *inspection contingency* that the buildings pass inspection to the buyer's satisfaction including as to environmental contamination, and *attorney-review contingency* that the seller and buyer may consult counsel about the agreement's legal sufficiency. Parties benefitting from contingencies must exercise them in **good faith** rather than manipulate them to change contract terms or avoid the agreement.

Time for performance. As briefly indicated above, land sale contracts typically include **time for performance** by setting a *closing date* when the seller will exchange a deed for the buyer's payment of the purchase price. The closing date, constituting time for performance, is ordinarily long enough after the land sale contract's execution, typically thirty, sixty, or even ninety days, for the buyer to accomplish several important tasks. One of those tasks is to confirm that the buyer has the necessary *financing* to complete the purchase. An appraisal satisfactory to the mortgage lender is routinely part of the financing process. The buyer may thus need some weeks to have the buyer's mortgage lender approve the purchase agreement and appraisal, and even confirm or re-confirm the buyer's creditworthiness. Another common buyer task between the land sale contract and time of performance at closing involves exercising the common *inspection* contingency in which the buyer reserves the right to retain a builder or other expert to examine the premises for defects. Scheduling, completing, and reviewing the results of inspections requires some time before closing. Commercial lands in particular may also require *environmental* testing before the closing date.

When contingencies reveal defects, the parties may require additional time to negotiate and accept adjustments to the land sale contract, including adjustments to the sale price. The seller may also require time for performance between the land sale contract and closing date, particularly if the seller must pack and move either residential furnishings and personal property, or business equipment. The **closing date**, though, sets a time limit within which both sides must be ready to perform. Land sale contracts often make the closing date *time of the essence*, where a party's failure to close by the required date voids the contract at the other party's election. In a hot market with land values increasing, the seller may have other buyers ready to perform and thus may hold the buyer to the closing date. In a soft market, the seller may accept extensions of the closing date to ensure a sale to a buyer who may have overpaid. The time for performance, in the form of a hard closing date, gives the parties grounds on which to enforce, modify, renegotiate, or void the contract. A party who fails to perform within the time for performance may also owe the other party contract-breach damages.

Remedies for breach. Remedies for **breach** of land sale contracts follow remedies for breach of other contracts. Buyers may *rescind* and seek *damages*. For example, a buyer whose contract calls for the seller to convey title to a commercial premises for $500,000, when the buyer can prove that the premises have a $750,000 value, may obtain the $250,000 difference in damages on rescission. A buyer may alternatively seek *specific performance*, disfavored in other contracts unless involving a unique subject but common as a remedy in land sales because land is routinely unique. **Specific performance**, the equitable remedy requiring the parties to perform their contract obligations, involves the reluctant seller conveying a deed to the land and possession of the land, or the reluctant buyer to pay the purchase price. Orders for specific performance may require that the seller vacate, unlock locks or provide keys or other access, and remove equipment. If the seller fails or refuses to execute a deed as ordered, then a buyer due specific performance may obtain the court's recordable order conveying title.

Occasions also arise where seller and buyer are willing to transfer the land for the agreed sale price but one party breaches some other term or condition of the transfer. In those cases, the non-breaching party may sue for damages that the other party's breach caused, notwithstanding that the parties followed through with the land transfer. For example, a buyer may not close by the required date, causing the seller to incur additional expense or consequential and foreseeable losses, in which case the buyer could recover those damages in a breach-of-contract action. Likewise, a seller may convey the premises in an unclean or unsafe condition that the sale contract prohibited. Parties often use a closing agreement to attempt to address, resolve, and require release of contract-breach claims, so that litigation does not follow the closing. The land sale contract itself may provide for liquidated damages, particularly as to the seller overstaying, often treated at a charge of $100 per day or a like figure approximating damages. A concluding section below also addresses the doctrine of **merger**, barring certain claims over defects in the transaction predating deed transfer at closing. Closing agreements, releases, and the doctrine of merger may not prevent the buyer from later claiming the seller's fraud in inducing the sale, when the seller has actively concealed and misrepresented the premise's true condition.

Marketability of title. Land sale contracts routinely require that the seller convey **marketable title**. Indeed, in the absence of a contrary term, the law *implies* a *promise* or *warranty* of marketable title. *Marketable* title is title that reasonable persons would not doubt as to validity and that third parties would not likely challenge with claims or ownership or encumbrances like mortgages or easements limiting the buyer's rights in the property. When a seller fails to convey marketable title, and instead conveys title that reasonable persons would reject due to impending or actual third-party challenges, then the seller breaches the contract, and the buyer may pursue one of the above remedies including rescission and damages, or specific performance. Specific performance may include that the seller act to clear the title, including by paying the just claims of competitors to the marketable title or otherwise obtaining their release.

Sellers typically convey marketable title by showing the property's good **chain of title** reflecting a history of the property's sale that shows the seller's clear ownership. Real-property records enable either seller or buyer, or a lawyer or title company employed by either seller or buyer, to complete a **title search** revealing and confirming the condition of title. A seller may alternatively prove good title by adverse possession, although doing so would likely require a *court judgment* including a recordable order of title, to constitute marketable title. Buyers are otherwise understandably reluctant to accept the seller's proof of adverse possession, which would not be recordable. Unmarketable title reflects a defect likely to cause a buyer to reject the purchase or to suffer injury in the future from accepting purchase. The buyer having to defend a third party's lawsuit over title may constitute injury due to unmarketable title, even if the proceeding proves that the seller had good title. A later section addresses a land sale contract's common contingency for **title insurance** and the title insurer's obligation to defend and indemnify as to title challenges, and cure title defects.

While sellers have a duty to convey *marketable title*, traditional common law does not require sellers to disclose other defects and conditions. The rule of *buyer beware* would instead require the buyer to exercise the inspection contingency with *due diligence* to discover those conditions. Yet many states today require that the seller disclose certain defects, using *statutory disclosure forms*, particularly in residential sales. Even absent a statutory disclosure requirement, the law today would tend to require that the seller disclose defects about which the seller knew but that would not be apparent to the buyer on reasonable inspection. The law also prohibits the seller from *actively concealing* defects to frustrate the buyer's discovery. Breaches of these duties may give rise to fraud remedies in the buyer's favor, including rescission and damages for lost benefit of the bargain.

Equitable conversion (including risk of loss). Issues can arise when events occur changing the property's condition between the time that the seller and buyer execute the land sale contract and the closing date. In that interim period, the buyer has the right to own the land, but the seller still has possession and legal title. The doctrine of **equitable conversion** holds in its majority form that equitable interest in the property transfers to the buyer *on land-sale-contract execution* rather than later at the closing date. The traditional form of the doctrine passes the risk of interim loss or gain *to the buyer* who, after all, has the equitable ownership. Equity does what is fair and just. Equitable-conversion doctrine enables the court to adjust the rights and responsibilities of the parties to reflect changes occurring between contract execution and closing. For example, if the buyer dies after contract execution but before closing, then the buyer's estate remains the equitable owner. Likewise, if fire or flood destroys buildings on the property in interim, then the buyer must still go through with the closing. On the other hand, if the parties discover oil, gas, or minerals on the property in the interim, the seller must still go through with the closing.

Some states alter equitable conversions' *risk-of-loss* rule so that the seller retains the risk until the closing date. In those states, if natural disaster destroys or diminishes the property's value, then the law reduces the land's sale price to reflect the loss, forcing the loss on the seller. If, though, either party was *responsible* through deliberate act or carelessness for the loss, then the law in all jurisdictions places the loss on that party rather than the other. Fire, flood, or other loss insurance may also affect the rights and responsibilities of the parties. If, for instance, the buyer bears the loss risk under the traditional rule, but the seller has insurance that would pay for a structure's damage or other reduction in land value, then the court acting in equity would adjust the parties' rights and responsibilities accordingly for the fairest outcome.

Options. A seller and buyer may form an **option contract** for the sale of land, just as parties may form option contracts for personal property or other goods or services, the same rules applying. An *option contract* is a contract promise, ordinarily supported by consideration, to keep an offer open for a specific period. In land-sale option contracts, the buyer may exercise the option at any time during the option period, while the seller *cannot revoke the offer* during the option period. Land option contracts can be especially beneficial to buyers who need time to obtain financing, sell other property, or, if already a tenant on the land, investigate and confirm the land's suitability for business or other purposes. For example, a tenant intending to lease, improve the premises, and operate a business for the five-year lease term may also negotiate a *purchase option* at the end of the five years or any other time during the lease, at a specific purchase price.

Option contracts relating to land sales must be in a writing signed by the charged party, to satisfy the *statute of frauds*. Like option contracts addressing other subjects, land-sale option contracts also require *consideration*, although the law traditionally accepts nominal consideration to support an option contract. Option contracts must state the *sale price*, or a certain way of establishing the sale price, as an essential term to make the option complete and enforceable. The seller's option-contract breach gives the buyer alternative remedies of specific performance or damages.

Rights of first refusal. Option contracts within a land *lease* often take the alternative form of a **right of first refusal**. Instead of stating an option sale price, a right-of-first-refusal clause in a lease requires the landlord to present to the tenant any third-party offers to buy the land during the term of the lease. If the tenant chooses to match the offer, then the landlord must sell the premises to the tenant rather than to the third-party offeror. Rights of first refusal solve the option-contract problem of setting a sale price for the land in advance of the date on which the tenant decides to exercise the option. Rights of first refusal also solve the landlord's option-contract problem that an option contract prevents sale of the land. Whenever a landlord presents a third party's good-faith offer under the right of first refusal, the tenant must either buy the land or give up the option. Seller and buyer may contract for a right of first refusal outside of a lease, too, although one typically finds them in leases or other relationships closer than an arm's length sale between unrelated seller and buyer.

Fitness and suitability. The law implies a warranty of **fitness** in favor of residential buyers, and warranty of **suitability** in favor of commercial buyers, in the purchase of *new construction* on lands. Thus, if a buyer of a new residence finds defects in the home that make the home unfit for habitation, then the buyer may have warranty-breach remedies including damages or rescission. Settling soil, foundation cracks, significant materials defects exposing occupants to hazards, and defects in the home's plumbing, electrical, and heating/cooling systems are examples of possible warranty breaches. Similarly, if a buyer of a commercial premises finds roof leaks, nonworking electrical, plumbing, or heating/cooling systems, and structural defects that make the premises unsuitable for commercial use, then the buyer will warranty-breach remedies. In most jurisdictions, both the initial purchaser and subsequent purchasers may enforce the implied warranties relating to new construction, if they can trace the defect to the construction rather than subsequent conditions and events, while a minority of jurisdiction limit the rights to the initial purchaser. Buyers, though, must act to enforce the right within a reasonable time from discovery of the defect. The law is generally unwilling to imply warranties of fitness and suitability in the purchase of *established* construction. The parties instead treat the condition of the premises through any statutory disclosure requirements and through inspection contingencies.

Merger. The doctrine of **merger** holds that guarantees that either party make, although particularly the seller, in the land sale contract *merge* into the deed at closing. The effect of merger is to eliminate or limit the buyer's right to rely on sale-contract terms once the buyer accepts the seller's deed at closing. In effect, the merger doctrine encourages or requires that all negotiations to resolve disputes over the condition of the premises, the condition of title, and other terms and conditions of the sale, take place before or at the closing, so that the parties can leave the closing without any continuing dispute or subsequent litigation over pre-closing rights. If the deed does not reflect the right that the buyer wishes to claim based on the sale contract, then the buyer has no such right.

Where recognized and enforced, the merger doctrine can bar post-closing claims not only over the quality of the title that the seller conveys to the buyer, as the deed reflects, and defects in the condition of the premises, but also disputes over unpaid taxes and other charges against the property. The doctrine, though, has fallen into some disfavor so that it many jurisdictions it operate more like a rebuttable presumption against claims than an absolute bar. Decisions are more likely to apply the doctrine and bar the claim when it has to do with the property's *title,* which is at the core of what the deed conveys, but less likely to apply the doctrine when the claims are only incidental to the title that the deed reflects. Courts will also look to the parties' intent as to what rights and claims they may have meant to merge into the deed versus which claims they did not intend to merge. Claims for misrepresentation, in particular, tend to fall outside the doctrine's bar. Indeed, exceptions to the merger doctrine may today be as numerous as applications of its rule.

WEEK 11: Transfer by Deed

The usual way of transferring land involves the seller executing a **deed** in the buyer's favor. The first section below on *transfers by deed* shows that sellers may offer, and buyers may accept, either *warranty* deed or *non-warranty* deed, including *covenants for title*. The quality of the deed thus varies, some transferors warranting, in the deed itself, more than others. The next section summarizes *deed requirements*, referring to what a transferor must include in a deed for the deed to accomplish the transfer in the manner that transferor and transferee intend, followed by a section on the necessary *delivery* of deeds including the treatment of deeds *in escrow*.

Warranty. The land sale contract usually refers to the *type* of deed that the seller promises to convey at the coming closing. The type of deed determines the **warranties** that the transferor makes in the transfer. Just because the seller or other transferor executes and delivers a certain type of deed, with greater or fewer warranties, does *not* mean that the transferee in fact receives that quality of title that the deed warrants. The transferor has whatever title the transferor has, whether the deed is accurate in its warrants or not. Thus, the effect of transferring a certain type of deed is to give the transferee a breach-of-warranty cause of action if the transferor's title does not match the deed's warrants. Even though deeds in general *merge* the land sale contract's obligations into the deed's warrants, deeds thus serve in their own way, somewhat like the land sale contract, of creating or continuing assurances on which the transferee may rely and that the transferee may enforce.

The standard form of land sale contract provides for a **general warranty deed**. When sellers convey under general warranty deed, they covenant that they *own the land* with the *right to convey,* that the land has no *encumbrances* such as mortgages, liens, easements, of covenants, that the seller will *defend* the buyer's *superior title* and *right to enjoy* the land, and that the seller will *cure title defects.* So, if a seller transfers the property to a buyer by executing and delivering a general warranty deed, but the seller instead has defects in the title including mortgages, liens, or easements, then the buyer may look to the seller to cure those defects when the buyer discovers them. If the seller does not cure, then the buyer may sue to enforce those warrants, often joining the title insurer in the suit to have the insurer's resources to cure the defect and indemnity in the event of its failure. Title defects can include the seller's co-tenant, including a spouse or ex-spouse, who failed to sign the deed transferring the co-tenant's interest, predecessor co-tenants who failed to sign a deed transferring to the seller, a lien for unpaid improvements to the property, or other undisclosed defects or encumbrances.

While the general warranty deed offers the transferee the greatest assurance, other deeds offer less. A **special warranty deed** is one in which the transferor warrants and assures only that no defects or encumbrances arose *during the transferor's ownership*. The special warranty deed makes no assurances about the knowledge, experience, or title of prior owners. The only enforcement action that the transferee can thus take is as to defects that arose during the transferor's ownership, a limited remedy that leaves the transferee with the risk that the transferor held that the transferor's own title had defects or was subject to mortgages, liens, easements, covenants, or other encumbrances.

Non-warranty deeds. If a transferor wishes to make *no* warrants at all, not even as to what the transferor knows or doesn't know, then the transferor executes and delivers only a **quit-claim deed**, transferring only what the transferor in fact owns without making any assurances. If the transferor owns nothing, then the transferee gets nothing. Quit-claim deeds purport to give no right of recourse to the transferee at all. In theory, the transferee must accept whatever defects the title includes, although given trends away from the *merger doctrine*, especially around misrepresentations inducing the transaction or defects not going to the core of title, quit-claim deeds do not effectively bar all litigation. Yet in an arm's length sale on an open market in which the seller seeks full market value, the seller would typically need to offer a general warranty deed because offering anything less transfers to the buyer greater risk of owning land having title defects and unmarketable title.

Covenants for title. A similar type of deed to a special warranty deed, in that it provides only limited assurances, is one that makes specific **covenants for title**. Covenants for title warrant only what the deed's recitals state, rather than making the general warrant of fee-simple title against all challengers or special warrant of no defects arising during the transferor's ownership. The specific assurances may include that the transferor has *no knowledge* of title defects, owns the property without *known* co-tenants, or *knows of* no easements or covenants, leaving open whether the title has defects, the owners include co-tenants, or the property has easements and covenants *about which the transferor does not know*. Specific covenants may also include affirmative assurances such as that the transferor received, holds, and transfers the full former rights of a certain co-tenant or predecessor in title. If the transferor's title does not match the special covenants, then the transferee has special recourse as to those defects.

Necessity for a grantee and other deed requirements. The transferor's deed must meet two precise **requirements**. The deed must include a **granting clause** that identifies the transferor and transferee together with a statement that the transferor is transferring title to the transferee. The deed usually identifies the transferor and transferee *by name* but need not do so if the deed's identification leaves no ambiguity as to the parties, such as that the transferor is a named person's eldest son or only daughter. The other requirement beyond the granting clause is that the deed must **describe the property** in a way that clearly and precisely identifies what the transferor conveys. The usual means will be by *metes-and-bounds* description, although references to survey maps, natural features, artificial markers or monuments, common name, or a street address, city, and state can do if that description leaves no ambiguity as to the property's contours. Courts will allow external evidence to resolve ambiguities.

A deed need not mention consideration, although some deeds do so to promote that the transferee is a *bona fide purchaser*, having taken for value. Deeds should state what warrants of title the transferor makes. Indeed, deeds typically bear a title *General Warranty Deed*, *Special Warranty Deed*, or *Quit Claim Deed*, indicating the warrants that they include. Yet the text of the deed itself should then refer specifically to the warrants that the transferor makes, such as that *grantor warrants generally that grantor has and transfers fee-simple title free of all defects and encumbrances*, or, conversely for a quit-claim deed, that *grantor transfers in quit claim only that title that grantor holds, making no warrants*. If the deed does not state its type, then the law presumes that the deed is a general warranty deed.

State law determines the requirements for a deed's execution. The transferor must sign the deed, not mistakenly but with the intent of its execution. State law typically requires two adult and competent witnesses to sign, acknowledging the transferor's identity and signature. Most transferees record the deeds that they receive, with the county register of deeds. Recording acts may add other requirements as to the deed's form and execution for recording, such as that a notary public also sign indicating that the transferor signed under oath. The addition of a notary's attestation and signature creates a presumption of the execution's validity. Recording acts may also require the name and address of the deed's preparer, often a lawyer for the transferor, transferee, or title company.

Delivery. As is true to make other contracts and commitments enforceable, when the transferor has executed the deed, the transferor must **deliver** the deed to the transferee with the intent of completing the transaction. Execution alone, without delivery, does not create an enforceable right of title. Nor does delivery without the intent of transferring title. For example, if a seller executes a deed at the office of the seller's lawyer but instructs the lawyer to hold the deed awaiting the buyer's payment or other action, then the deed's execution does not transfer title. Likewise, if the seller executes the deed and then delivers it to the buyer instructing the buyer to hold it until the buyer supplies the payment or satisfies some other condition, then the seller will also not yet have transferred title. The action would still lack the seller's intent to transfer title. But if the seller executes the deed and delivers it to the buyer with acknowledgment of transfer, or in silence without condition, then the actions would complete delivery and effect transfer.

Escrows. As just mentioned, some transfers involve the transferor's execution of a deed and delivery of the deed to a person acting as an **escrow** agent. *Escrow* involves an agent holding an instrument, funds, or other items anticipating exchange, while awaiting satisfaction of the conditions of escrow. Escrow agreements, often in writing but also oral, determine the conditions on which the agent may release the items. An agent, often a title company or one of the parties' lawyers, typically holds the seller's deed awaiting the buyer's funds from the lender financing the transaction. The agent only releases the items out of escrow, directing them to the appropriate party, when the agent can meet all conditions of the escrow. The agent would direct the deed to the buyer for the buyer's recording, the funds to the seller for the seller's deposit, the buyer's executed promissory note and mortgage to the lender, among other items. Escrow facilitates transactions by eliminating the need for contemporaneous exchange. An escrow agent can also bear liability for breaching the escrow agreement, thus insuring the exchange against mistake or wrongdoing.

WEEK 12: Mortgages

Buyers and owners of land use several forms of security, including *mortgages*, *deeds of trust*, and *land contracts*, to draw on and benefit from the value of the secured land. While lenders make unsecured loans, lenders gain advantages when securing the loan against the borrower's assets. Real property makes peculiarly valuable security because of its permanence, immobility, and value. Thus, mortgages and other forms of security in real property are critical not only to the sale, purchase, and improvement of real property but also to personal and business economics in general. The following sections address the above *types* of security devices in land, security *relationships*, *transfers* by either the mortgagor or mortgagee, the effect of *payment* of the loan, and *foreclosure* of the security interest.

Types of security devices. As just indicated, landowners and lenders to landowners use several types of security device both for the purchase and development of the land, and for other economic interests of the borrower. **Mortgages**, as the next section addresses, are the primary real-property security device, enabling the lender to record a document against the property reflecting the lender's security interest. States also recognize, and convention sometimes prefers, a **deed of trust** operating much like a mortgage but in which the borrower grants the lender a deed to the real property to hold in trust contingent on payment. Sellers of land also sometimes offer a **land contract** as an alternative, particularly when the buyer cannot qualify for a mortgage but also for other purposes. Less common is the **absolute deed**, as the last section on types of security device addresses.

Mortgages (including deeds of trust). A **mortgage** is a security interest in land that secures the mortgage *loan*. The word *mortgage* at times refers to the entire transaction involving borrower and lender but also has a strict meaning as to the *specific document* that the lender records against the real property. While the lender's purpose in obtaining a mortgage is to have a security interest to protect the loan, the lender's purpose in *recording* the mortgage is ensure that the lender's security interest has *priority* over the interests of others who may obtain second or subsequent mortgages on the land or record liens arising out of other obligations. A later section on foreclosure addresses the relative priority of mortgages. Borrowers use mortgages for different purposes, and mortgages come in different types, as the next sections address.

In general. A mortgage transaction typically involves the borrower signing both a *note*, also referred to as a *promissory note*, reflecting the loan *and* signing a *mortgage* instrument that the lender records to show the world that the lender has perfected a priority security interest. The note is the borrower's contract obligation to the lender, including amount, term, payment schedule, interest, and default terms. The mortgage is the lender's security interest against the land, typically referring to the note but not including the note's detailed terms. The mortgage instead includes the grantor's identity, the property description, and the rights to assign, foreclose, or otherwise treat the mortgage, and obligations to discharge it on payment. Recording statutes may require other mortgage terms. Because mortgages are interests in real property, they must ordinarily be in writing signed by the mortgagor (the borrower) to satisfy the **statute of frauds**.

Where the borrower signs no written mortgage, courts may recognize an **equitable mortgage** if, for instance, the borrower conveys a **deed** in trust to the lender. Some jurisdictions expressly recognize a **deed of trust** as a mortgage alternative. With a deed of trust, the borrower executes a deed to the property purporting to convey the land to the lender. The lender, or a trustee agent, then holds the deed according to the terms of the trust, which provide for destroying or returning the deed if the borrower pays the full loan, or releasing and recording the deed if the borrower defaults, so that the lender can then readily execute on the real property, typically without judicial foreclosure. Lenders can typically record a deed-of-trust instrument in the real-property records and transfer a deed of trust by assignment, just as lenders can do with mortgages.

Purchase-money mortgages. A **purchase-money** mortgage can mean one of two things. In the conventional sense, a purchase-money mortgage is a security interest that the buyer grants to the lender whose loan pays the purchase price of the property. Yet in the special sense, a purchase-money mortgage can also mean one that the buyer grants *back to the seller*, usually to make up a shortfall in the financing that the buyer can get from other sources. Purchase-money mortgages are generally treated with priority over other encumbrances such as mechanics' liens and judgment liens, even when the holders of those liens recorded them before the seller recorded the purchase-money mortgage. The rationale is that a purchase-money mortgage does not further encumber the property in the way that mortgages taken out of the land's equity for other purposes would encumber the property. Yet no matter the rationale, purchase-money mortgages gain higher priority than other mortgages.

Beyond a purchase-money mortgage, a property owner may also grant a mortgage for a *construction loan* for improvement of the real property or *home-equity loan* or other line of credit for any other purpose. In such cases, particularly as to home-equity loans, the associated mortgages are often second, third, or subsequent mortgages behind the purchase-money mortgage. Mortgage priority can become critical in attempted sales of an *underwater* property, referring to property mortgaged to secure greater debt than the land's value. Mortgage priority can become even more critical in foreclosure, as a later section addresses.

Future-advance mortgages. A property owner may alternatively grant a lender a **future-advance mortgage**. An owner grants a future-advance mortgage without yet receiving a loan in return or when receiving only part of the funds that the loan anticipates. A future-advance mortgage enables the owner to draw future advances against the mortgage as the owner's needs arise, operating in effect like a line of credit. The owner's advantages can include to arrange for funds before the owner needs them, for greater speed and flexibility in financing, and to secure interest rates and other mortgage terms when advantageous. The lender's advantage can include to have priority for the security interest as of the date of the mortgage's recording, even if the lender only later advances funds, as law typically provides. State laws vary, though, on the treatment of future advances, some

259

giving retroactive priority only to *obligatory* future advances rather than optional future advances, while others give retroactive priority to *all* future advances but permit the borrower to give the lender a *cut-off notice* so that the borrower can give other new mortgages priority over subsequent advances.

Land contracts. A **land contract** is both a means of purchasing real property *and* a means of financing the real-property purchase. Deeds formally convey title to real property, not contracts. By declining to grant a deed to a buyer, and simply signing a contract conveying the land instead, a seller in effect creates a security device. The contract specifies the terms on which the buyer will receive a deed, typically either payment of the full contract price after a long period or, more often, payments for a period of months or a few years until the buyer qualifies for a conventional mortgage, at which time the mortgage proceeds will pay off the land contract. Sellers who offer a land contract expand the market for the property to buyers who cannot obtain mortgage financing. Land contracts are also known as *installment sales contracts*, *contracts for deed*, or *contracts for sale*.

Distinguish a land contract from the *purchase contract* that seller and buyer execute in anticipation of a closing where they would exchange the deed. Even though the buyer does not receive a deed until paying off the land contract, the law considers the buyer to hold **equitable title**, while the **legal title** remains with the seller. Buyers under land contract often record a **memorandum of land contract** to show their land-contract interest in the chain of title, ensure the priority of their equitable title over later-recorded interests, and prevent a devious seller from selling the property again to an unwitting buyer. The memorandum acts in the place of recording a deed, which of course the land-contract buyer does not yet have.

Absolute deeds as security. Lenders desire the most-efficient manner of executing on their security. Mortgages are not especially efficient, particularly when the state's law requires judicial foreclosure of mortgage and a lengthy redemption period in the mortgagor delaying the finality of sale for as much as up to a year. Lenders thus sometimes demand an **absolute deed** from the borrower, granting fee-simple title to the lender, as an attempt to avoid restrictions on foreclosure, particularly the right of redemption. The absolute deed appears as if the lender owns the real property, which is the deed's legal effect, although in practice the lender will hold it escrow awaiting the borrower's default. On default, the lender may record the absolute deed to list and sell the real property as security for the defaulted loan. Disputes, though, sometimes arise when the lender records the absolute deed without default or under terms with which the borrower does not agree. The borrower may then prove by parol evidence that the absolute deed was instead an *equitable mortgage*, invalidating the deed so that the court can treat it as a mortgage. The law disfavors absolute deeds as security, which may violate truth-in-lending laws and other restrictions and expose the lender to fines or other penalties.

Some security relationships. While the above sections describe *types* of security used in real-property transactions, the following sections address certain **security relationships**. The first section addresses the *necessity* and *nature* of a security obligation. The next section addresses three alternate *theories* of security in land, used in different jurisdictions. Other following sections address rights and duties *before* foreclosure (later sections addressing foreclosure), and the right to *redeem* along with efforts at *clogging the equity of redemption*.

Necessity and nature of obligation. Security interests in land do not arise by implication. Borrower and lender must instead express their agreement, as previously indicated, in a signed writing satisfying the **statute of frauds**. On the other hand, also as previously indicated, mortgages are frankly necessary to transactions in real property, including not only land purchasers but also construction and improvement of buildings, because of the high relative cost of real property. A home is the most-expensive asset that most individuals buy, just as a business premises is the most-expensive business asset that most businesses buy. The value of a home or business real property also serves as capital on which to draw for other personal or commercial economic activity. Thus, mortgages are ubiquitous. Without mortgages or equivalent security devices for land, the economy would not function as it does. Debt financing through real-estate mortgages is critical to many individuals and businesses.

Theories: title, lien, and intermediate. States vary in whether they treat a mortgage as a **lien** against the land or instead as passing a special form of **title** to the land. The distinction matters primarily when a *joint tenant* grants a mortgage. In a lien-theory state, the joint tenant granting a mortgage does *not* destroy the unity of title on which a joint tenancy depends. By contrast, in a title-theory state, a joint tenant who conveys a mortgage destroys the unity of title with other joint tenants, thus severing the joint tenancy as to the mortgaging co-tenant, and creating a tenancy in common between that mortgaging co-tenant and other joint tenants. Some states, though, follow an **intermediate** theory that applies the lien theory unless the borrower defaults, giving the parties the relative convenience of dealing only with a lien rather than transfer of title. On default, though, the law applies the title theory, giving the lender greater enforcement rights as a title-holder in the land.

Rights and duties prior to foreclosure. Standard forms of mortgages require the borrower to maintain the mortgaged property in good repair, pay taxes, maintain insurance, not conduct illegal activities on the premises such as would forfeit the land, and otherwise protect the mortgagee's security interest. These obligations are contractual, and the mortgagee who identifies their breach can sue for specific performance. The mortgage will also likely grant the mortgagee the right to pay taxes, insurance, and other charges or costs to preserve the value of the land, and then have the borrower's reimbursement, as further described in a section below on subrogation. While contract terms impose the borrower's primary obligations, the law of **waste** may permit a mortgagee to obtain court assistance in ensuring that the borrower does not destroy the property's value. A building without heat in the winter or with a leaky roof can quickly depreciate because of natural conditions, as can a building with inadequate lighting, locks, and other security against vandalism.

The borrower's principal right, on the other hand, and the corollary mortgagee restriction, is for the borrower's free use of the mortgaged property if the borrower is not in default. A mortgage may grant the mortgagee a right to **enter for inspection** against waste, but generally, the borrower retains full rights of an owner to use and enjoy the premises, including to exclude others. Mortgagees interfere with those borrower rights at their peril of trespass, breach of contract, or statutory actions for breach of the peace with respect to security interests. A mortgage may, on the other hand, define the terms of default to include a significant change in the use of the premises including its abandonment. Once again, these terms are contract obligations, enforceable in specific performance or damages, like other contracts. While mortgagees properly record a mortgage, borrowers would also have rights not to have a mortgagee place other clouds on the borrower's title.

Right to redeem and clogging equity of redemption. The law of mortgages and other security interests in land grants the borrower rights to **redeem** the mortgaged property out of a foreclosure proceeding, meaning to pay off the mortgage obligation either before or a certain statutory period, such as six months, after foreclosure sale. A section below summarizes those redemption rights after foreclosure. Here, though, recognize that the law generally prohibits borrowers from waiving redemption rights in advance and prohibits lenders from demanding or contracting for that waiver. The law also prohibits borrower and lender from fashioning alternative loan arrangements, such as a deed in escrow or an option to purchase on default, treating default in ways intended to skirt redemption rights. The law holds that *clogs on equity are invalid*. Redemption rights can protect homeowners from losing critical housing or losing home equity, if the homeowner is able to redeem, although prospects for doing so are usually poor because the mortgagor could not even meet the original mortgage. Alternatively, the statutory period of redemption simply allows the foreclosed homeowner to accumulate savings and locate other housing, often while living in the premises without making mortgage payments. Public policy judges these redemption rights and their advantages sufficiently important to deny parties the opportunity to alter them in advance.

Transfers by mortgagor. Mortgages do not prohibit the borrower from selling or otherwise conveying away the mortgaged land, although seller and buyer must deal with the mortgage. Lenders taking mortgages as security for their loans routinely *record* those mortgages to ensure that the borrower's conveyance of the mortgaged land does not adversely affect the lender's security interest. A recorded mortgage protects the mortgagee's interest on transfer. If, as happens in the typical case, the borrower sells the mortgaged land while realizing sufficient funds to pay off the mortgage lender, then the lender *discharges* the mortgage. A mortgage securing indebtedness greater than the property's value, though, can make transfer difficult as a practical matter. If a sale does not bring sufficient funds to satisfy the mortgage, then the mortgagee will not discharge the mortgage, and the buyer will not buy, unless the buyer is willing to take **subject to** the mortgage or even to **assume** the mortgage as the following section addresses. Other following sections address related issues of the seller's rights and obligations on transfer, and application of **subrogation** and **suretyship** principles, and **due-on-sale** clauses.

Distinguishing "subject to" and "assuming." In some situations, the seller and buyer of land find it either necessary or advantageous *not* to pay and discharge a mortgage on the land. For example, the buyer may not be able to obtain financing or locate financing on the same advantageous terms as the existing mortgage. In such instances, and if the mortgage permits it, the buyer may agree to take the property's title **subject to** the mortgage. The buyer pays a reduced sale price that reflects the mortgage obligation and then makes the mortgage payments to the lender. When a buyer takes *subject to* a mortgage, the buyer does *not* become directly liable to the mortgage lender on the promissory note. Rather, the *seller* remains liable on the note, while the buyer's property remains subject to the mortgage, giving the buyer incentive to make the seller's note payments.

In other instances, a buyer may expressly agree to **assume** an existing mortgage obligation. To *assume* an obligation here means for the buyer to become *directly liable* to the mortgage lender for the indebtedness that the mortgage secures. Direct liability means that the buyer then has personal liability on the seller's promissory note with the mortgage lender, rather than merely having the buyer's property at risk as mortgage security. Ordinarily, buyers would prefer not to accept such direct, personal liability. On the other hand, sellers *would* prefer that buyers assume mortgage indebtedness rather than merely take subject to the mortgage, for the increased incentive that assumption of debt creates. In other words, a seller may in negotiations require a buyer to assume. If, as a following section on *due-on-sale* clauses addresses, the mortgage lender also has a say in the transaction, then the lender may also require the buyer to assume.

Rights and obligations of transferor. Just because a borrower manages to sell the mortgaged land subject to the mortgage, or even with the borrower assuming the mortgage obligation, does not mean that the borrower has no further obligations. To the contrary, the borrower *remains obligated* on the promissory note that accompanied the mortgage. The note remains a contract between borrower and lender even after the borrower sells the land. The terms of that contract determine the borrower's obligation, which is routinely that the borrower remains liable notwithstanding the borrower's conveyance of the note's security. If the buyer does not make the mortgage payments reflecting the note obligation, then the lender may look to the borrower to make those payments. In some cases, the mortgage lender may expressly agree to accept the buyer's new commitment to pay the mortgage, including the buyer's *assuming* the note debt, to relieve the borrower from the note's contractual liability. The law calls this action of lender relief of the original borrower a **novation**.

The seller does not necessarily lose all rights when selling to a buyer who takes subject to the mortgage or agrees to assume the mortgage note. If the buyer defaults on payments, leaving the seller exposed to the unpaid mortgage note, then the seller's agreement with the buyer will likely provide the seller with recourse against the buyer. That recourse may include money from the buyer so that the seller can pay the note, in the nature of specific performance, or the seller may recover the property under a right of re-entry on default, extinguishing the buyer's interest. Unless the mortgage lender granted the seller a novation releasing the seller from liability, the seller owes the lender, but the seller has the buyer to whom to look for help in meeting the mortgage-note obligation.

Application of subrogation. The prior section shows that a borrower/mortgagor who sells the real property subject to the mortgage, or with the buyer even assuming the mortgage, retains the risk that the buyer does not pay make the mortgage payments, unless in the unlikely instance the mortgage lender grants the borrower a novation and release from the mortgage-note obligation. The prior section also shows that when the buyer fails to make a mortgage payment, the seller has contract rights against the buyer to make the buyer perform. Yet in those instances, the buyer may also have failed to pay real estate taxes, insurance, or other charges associated with maintaining the property. Because the seller retains an interest, the seller may make those payments for the buyer and then **subrogate** to the rights of the assessor, insurer, or other creditor to recover the payments from the buyer.

To *subrogate* is to take the place or, proverbially, *stand in the shoes* of another to exercise that other's rights. A seller has sound economic reasons to preserve the property's title and value against the destruction or the claims of others. The seller's sale contract with the buyer may provide for subrogation rights, or the law may imply *equitable subrogation*. Even more commonly, the mortgage lender, the financial resources of which are seldom in question and whose economic interest is often greatest, will exercise similar rights to pay taxes and charges related to the property to preserve its value and then *subrogate* to those creditors' rights to obtain reimbursement from the seller or buyer. The mortgage instrument will ordinarily provide contractually for those subrogation rights, while in their absence, the law would likely imply them through *equitable subrogation*.

Suretyship principles. Mortgages can also involve the law of **suretyships**, referring generally to the relationship of a *surety* or *guarantor* for the borrower's mortgage obligation to both the borrower and the lender. A surety signs the original contract along with the obligor, while a guarantor signs a separate guarantee, although the distinction is unimportant here. Lenders do sometimes require a surety or guarantor, also loosely referred to as a *co-signer*, for a mortgage note when the borrower's credit is insufficient. The surety or guarantor owes the obligation that the contract or guarantee states, which is typically to pay when the primary obligor fails to do so. Suretyships and guarantees require a *signed writing* satisfying the **statute of frauds**. The surety or guarantor has rights, too, though, including to compel the primary obligor to perform, called *exoneration*, or to *reimburse* the surety or guarantor for performing, in the nature of *subrogation* as the prior section discussed. If the suretyship involves more than one surety, then the paying surety may also obtain *contribution* from other sureties. A surety also has the primary obligor's defenses, if any, when the lender pursues the surety.

Due-on-sale clauses. The above sections treat the lender as acquiescing in the borrower's transfer of the land subject to the lender's mortgage, or with the buyer assuming the mortgage. Yet many mortgages include a **due-on-sale** clause. The clauses typically permit the mortgage lender to accelerate the mortgage note and call its entire principal balance due if the buyer sells the land. Due-on-sale clauses typically give the lender the *option* of declaring the note due, enabling the lender to determine which action to choose, whether approval of the sale subject to the mortgage, approval of the sale only with the buyer assuming the debt, or simply acceleration of the debt. Federal law limits the ability of states to frustrate due-on-sale clauses. Due-on-sale clauses typically include a trigger for *land-contract* sales, in other words for efforts at private financing, giving the lender the greatest leverage.

Transfers by mortgagee. For their part, lenders may either hold the note and mortgage pending the borrower's payments or, as is commonly the case with residential mortgages, transfer the note and mortgage to an assignee such as an investor or mortgage-servicing company representing investors. Issues can arise, though, when the borrower defaults but raises defenses, such as fraud, against the lender about which the assignee may not have been aware. The rights of a person taking a note and mortgage on assignment can depend on whether the person is a **holder in due course**, meaning one who received the instrument in good faith, without knowing of defects, and having paid value. If the assignee is *not* a holder in due course, then the borrower can raise any defenses against the assignee that the borrower could have raised against the lender.

If the assignee is a holder in due course, then the assignee takes the borrower's obligation *free of personal defenses*. Personal defenses, addressing conduct surrounding the obligation's formation, include *fraud in the inducement, failure of consideration*, and *unconscionability*. Thus, if the lender misrepresented the loan's terms in order to induce the note and mortgage, but the assignee took the assignment as a holder in due course, in good faith for consideration without knowing of the misrepresentation, then the borrower owes the assignee the full obligation. Holders in due course, though, take *subject to real defenses*. Real defenses, addressing the *legality* of the obligation's formation rather than surrounding conduct, include *forgery, infancy* or other *incapacity, illegality*, and *duress* or *coercion*. Thus, if the lender forged the instruments, or the transaction violated state or federal statutes regulating mortgage loans, then the borrower could raise those defenses to defeat an assignee, even one who was a holder in due course.

Payment. The borrower owes the lender **payment** on the mortgage-note obligation. The note states the total obligation, interest rate, periodic payment amount, and note term over which the borrower pays. A note may amortize the full amount of principal and interest over the full term, or the note may lower payments and require a balloon payment at the end of the note's term. Mortgage notes are often for ten, fifteen, twenty, or even thirty years, although notes with balloon payments may be for terms as short as five, three, or two years, or even one year. Payment is the borrower's primary obligation, although the borrower will have other duties to maintain the property and not to cause its destruction or waste. The mortgage and note will also require the borrower to pay property taxes and assessments, and keep buildings insured, often through an escrow that the lender maintains out of the payments. As indicated in another section, the mortgage instruments will permit the lender to make those payments for the borrower if the borrower fails to do so and to recover the payments from the borrower on foreclosure.

Discharges. The lender has the contractual and legal obligation to **discharge** the mortgage when the borrower satisfies the note's payment obligations. Cancellation of the note relieves the borrower of further note obligation, while discharge of the mortgage ends the lender's security interest in the land. Discharge may occur at the end of the note's term when the borrower makes the final payment or at an earlier date when the borrower sells the property and pays off the note out of the sale proceeds at close. Notes also typically permit the borrower to prepay the note without sale. Borrowers may do so out of other funds or may do so in a refinancing of the mortgage. The lender's discharge is a signed instrument that the borrower records in the property's chain of title to reflect that the title is clear of the prior mortgage. The lender who fails to promptly discharge a mortgage when payment of the note requires the lender to do so may be liable not only for breach of contract but also for **slander of title**, particularly when the borrower loses an opportunity to sell, mortgage, or otherwise benefit from clear title to the land.

Defenses. The borrower may have **defenses** to a mortgage and its note obligation. In a judicial foreclosure, the borrower will plead and argue defenses in response to the lender's foreclosure action. If the state permits foreclosure outside of a judicial proceeding, then the borrower may have to bring a civil action to raise mortgage and note defenses. For example, the lender may have *misapplied payments* or made other *mistakes* in calculating amounts due. Alternatively, a lender may not have followed default *notice procedures* in the mortgage or mandated by state or federal law. The lender may have *misrepresented* mortgage terms, fraudulently inducing the borrower into the mortgage transaction without disclosing such things as adjustable interest rates or balloon payments. The lender may not have complied with federal and state truth-in-lending *disclosure requirements* on terms like the annual percentage rate, finance charges, and total interest over the loan term. Also, federal law grants a *servicemember on active duty* a stay against foreclosure. A borrower may also object to *unconscionable* mortgage terms. Defenses may lead to rescission of the mortgage and note obligation, reform of terms, damages, and equitable remedies such as specific performance of terms or correcting credit records.

Foreclosure. **Foreclosure** is the process through which the lender or other mortgage holder executes on the land as security. For a lender to *foreclose* a mortgage requires following the state's mandated procedures and procedures spelled out in the mortgage, to *accelerate* the total mortgage debt beyond overdue payments and then to secure and sell the mortgaged property in satisfaction of the debt. Sale proceeds first go to sale expenses including costs and attorney's fees as provided by statute or mortgage, then to pay the foreclosed debt, then to subordinate mortgage holders, and only then to the debtor if proceeds are sufficient. Any mortgagee may bring a foreclosure action, although who brings the action is of no consequence to priority. A foreclosing mortgagee names subordinate mortgagees whose interests the foreclosure would extinguish. Because the foreclosure does *not* extinguish *superior* mortgages, superior mortgage holders need not participate, although in practice many would simultaneously foreclose, treating the subordinate foreclosure and sale as an event of default.

Types. Most states require a court proceeding, known as **judicial foreclosure**, to foreclose on a mortgage in most instances, particularly with residential mortgages where concerns for overreaching are greater than in commercial mortgages. Some jurisdictions alternatively allow for **non-judicial**

foreclosure in some circumstances, *if* the mortgage or deed of trust expressly permits non-judicial foreclosure. Because of concerns about lender overreach, particularly as to residential mortgages, and to protect the borrower's equity, those states tend to require *public auction* of the foreclosed property rather than private sale through a broker and strict advance personal notice to the mortgagor and other recorded owners. As indicated above, a few jurisdictions also allow borrower to grant and lender or trustee to hold a *deed of trust* as a mortgage substitute, although the law will likely regulate that alternative form closely and may require specific foreclosure procedures as just indicated. The law strongly discourages lender self-help and closely regulates foreclosures to avoid lender overreaching including breaches of the peace.

When seller and buyer form a land contract instead of the buyer obtaining lender financing and granting the lender a mortgage, and the buyer defaults on the land contract, the law may require or seller may desire to pursue a judicial **land-contract forfeiture**. Land contracts typically provide that the buyer *forfeits* payments made to the seller in the forfeiture proceeding. The forfeiture proceeding confirms that the seller has extinguished the buyer's equitable title. After the forfeiture judgment enters, the seller will once again have legal title, which the seller never relinquished under the land contract, and equitable title, restored to the seller from the buyer. The seller can also record the judgment of forfeiture so that the chain of title reflects the extinguishment of the land-contract interest reflected by the recorded memorandum of land contract.

Rights of omitted parties. As a prior section suggests, the **first mortgagee** generally has priority over subsequent and thus subordinate mortgagees as to sale proceeds, using *recording* dates and times to establish that priority. The law ordinarily grants an exception for *purchase-money* mortgages, meaning a mortgage that the buyer grants to the lender who finances the purchase *or* back to the seller as seller financing, usually to make up a shortfall in the financing that the buyer can get from other sources. Purchase-money mortgages generally take priority over prior encumbrances. States are especially likely to recognize the exception when the competing security interests are mechanics' liens, judgment liens, and other similar interests. Also as indicated above, a foreclosing mortgage holder need not add superior mortgage holders because the foreclosure would not extinguish those superior mortgages, only *subordinate* mortgages. Superior mortgage holders may, on the other hand, join in a subordinate mortgage holder's action, treating the subordinate foreclosure as a default if the mortgage so permits.

A problem arises when a foreclosing mortgage holder fails to join a subordinate mortgage holder. Subordinate mortgage holders are *necessary parties* to the action because the action affects, indeed *extinguishes*, their subordinate rights. A court will require that subordinate parties join when learning about their non-joinder. Yet if the foreclosure proceeds without a subordinate mortgage holder participating, the law does *not* extinguish the subordinate mortgage. The winning bidder at foreclosure auction takes subject not only to any superior mortgages who did not seek foreclosure but also as to the subordinate mortgages that the foreclosing mortgagee did not name. The winning bidder, though, may *re-foreclose* the foreclosed mortgage in a second proceeding that names the subordinate mortgagee, either extinguishing the subordinate mortgage by bidding in the superior mortgage's value or, if the sale realizes more, then paying off the subordinate mortgage.

Deficiency and surplus. Foreclosure of the mortgage, execution on the real property, and the real property's sale are not the lender's only rights. The borrower will also have executed the promissory note, constituting a contract for the breach of which the lender may also sue. Thus, judicial foreclosure proceedings typically include a contract-breach count in addition to the foreclosure count. The *judgment of foreclosure* will provide for acceleration of indebtedness, execution on and sale of the real property, and application of proceeds to reduce the debt. Yet the judgment may also include a money judgment against the debtor for the total indebtedness, reduced by the sale amount net of costs. If the sale does not satisfy the judgment debt, then the lender may treat the remaining money obligation as a **deficiency** enforceable by other means such as wage or account garnishment, depending on the borrower's collectability.

If, on the other hand, the sale proceeds produce a **surplus** above the foreclosing mortgagee's costs, attorney's fees, and loan indebtedness, then as previously indicated, the law provides that the proceeds go first to extinguish debt owed to subordinate mortgagees. If the land has no subordinate mortgages, or if any proceeds remain after their payment, then the borrower landowner receives the remaining surplus representing the borrower's equity. Borrowers rarely receive any equity because if the land had any equity value, then the borrower would have sold the land to avoid foreclosure or would have refinanced either with the lender threatening foreclosure or with another lender.

Redemption after foreclosure. As introduced well above, foreclosure does not entirely terminate the mortgagor's rights. All states allow the borrower to **redeem** the mortgaged property before foreclosure sale, by paying the mortgage indebtedness. The common law treats the right as the **equity of redemption**, although many states provide for greater *statutory* rights of redemption, especially for residential mortgages. A right of redemption gives the mortgagor additional time, defined differently from state to state but often six months, to raise funds to *redeem* the property, meaning in essence to buy the property out of foreclosure by paying the foreclosed debt. In some states, foreclosure of the mortgage triggers the redemption period, ending with auction sale. In other states, sale triggers the redemption period, during which the buyer waits to see if the foreclosed mortgagor redeems. As indicated above, redemption rights are important because they protect homeowners from losing critical housing or losing home equity, or allow the foreclosed homeowner to accumulate savings and locate other housing, often while living in the premises without making mortgage payments.

Deed in lieu of foreclosure. The cost and delay of a foreclosure proceeding, the possibility that the borrower will raise defenses, and the difficulty, cost, and delay of collecting a deficiency judgment from the borrower, all encourage the lender to seek streamlined means of foreclosing. One such means is for the lender to simply take a **deed in lieu of foreclosure** from the borrower. If the borrower voluntarily grants the lender a deed, then the lender may be able to avoid judicial foreclosure entirely, particularly if the property has no subordinate mortgages or all mortgagees can reach terms of agreement as to the property's value and treatment. Borrowers typically demand that the lender *waive* any deficiency in exchange for the borrower's offer of a deed in lieu of foreclosure, evidenced by the lender executing an *estoppel affidavit*. Some states and some federally backed mortgages require deficiency waivers for deeds in lieu of foreclosure, to prevent lender overreaching. A deed in lieu of foreclosure allows the lender to promptly place the property on the private market for sale through a broker, a trusted and flexible process that may obtain a higher value than selling at auction. For similar reasons of efficiency and risk, the lender may alternatively agree to a **short sale** in which the borrower sells to a third party for less than the mortgage debt, the lender receives the sale proceeds, the borrower executes a deed to the buyer, and the lender discharges the mortgage and waives the deficiency.

WEEK 13: Title assurance systems

Real-property law and practice offer two systems for assuring that a buyer of land receives the title that the seller should convey in the transaction. The first **title-assurance system** involves the state's *recording act*. As the next section addresses, a recording act establishes a practical system and legal mechanism in which owners of real property can record their deeds or other claims of title, interest, or right, with a local official, the effect of which is to give the recording claimant legal advantages over other claimants who have *not* recorded. The other title-assurance system that real-estate practice offers is *title insurance*. As a following section addresses, title insurers assume the obligation to a policy-holding property owner to litigate and indemnify in efforts secure the owner's title against adverse claims, while also compensating the owner when the owner loses a title challenge, possession, and ownership.

Recording acts. As just indicated, **recording acts** create systems in each state for real-property buyers, mortgagees, lienholders, and other claimants to interests in land to **record** their interests for the public to see. The act of *recording* involves providing to the local *register of deeds*, usually at the county level, the deed or other instrument that the person wishes to record so that the register can enter the instrument in the system in a manner that others can discover it on search for records relating to the real property. The system allows others, particularly potential buyers or mortgagees, to determine the state of title on the land including such things as who owns the land or has a security interest, easement, or other claim of an interest in it. Buyers of land record deeds promptly to ensure that others know that they are now the rightful titleholders. Once recorded, the register returns the original deed to the buyer, while keeping a copy.

Race, notice, and race-notice. Recording acts are significant not just for enabling buyers and lenders to determine who owns and what encumbrances the land's title. Recording acts can also determine which claimant prevails among multiple claimants, particularly when a devious owner purports to transfer title to multiple competing buyers. **Bona-fide purchasers**, referring to those who take *for fair consideration* and record superior title *without knowledge or reason to know* of superior claims, gain the recording act's protection. The conditions, though, under which a bona-fide purchaser gains superior title depend on the recording act's form, either **notice**, **race**, or **race/notice**. A *notice* jurisdiction holds a bona-fide purchaser's title superior to an earlier purchaser's title if the earlier purchaser did not record the deed and the subsequent purchaser did not know of the earlier transfer. By contrast, a *race* jurisdiction looks simply to who recorded first, without considering who had notice of other earlier title. And a *race/notice* jurisdiction grants the subsequent bona-fide purchaser superior title only if the subsequent purchaser did not know of the earlier transfer and records first.

Indexes. The key to an effective title search is the **index** that the register maintains showing each instrument's recording and that title searchers use to track recordings. Registers of deeds keep one of two different kinds of indices. A **grantor/grantee** index categorizes and indexes instruments by either grantor name or grantee name, in alphabetical order. Thus, if a buyer wanted to confirm that the seller had title, the title searcher would look up the seller in the *grantee* category because the seller would have previously gained title *as a buyer*. The searcher could then see who *sold* to the seller and look up *that* seller-to-the-seller in the grantee index, and on back to the earliest recording, ensuring a good chain of title *as to buyers*. The searcher must then repeat the process *in the grantor* index to see if any buyer sold to anyone other than the next buyer in the chain of title. By contrast, a **tract** index categories and indexes instruments by the land within the county. The tract index divides the county up first by cities, villages, townships, or like divisions, then by sections, then by blocks, and then by lots, or similar divisions. A title searcher can then search the index for any land location in the county, to see what instruments the register of deeds has recorded as to that land.

Chain of title. As the prior section suggests, good title depends on establishing a sound chain from the earliest transaction to the most-recent transaction in which the current owner took title. **Chain of title** refers to the continuity of transactions from owner to owner. Good, sound, or marketable title depends on showing that the chain of title leaves no *gaps, missing links, unaccounted-for interests*, or other defects. For example, if A sells to B who sells to C, then the chain of title suggests no defect. Yet if A_1 and A_2 first own as co-tenants, and then only A_1 conveys to B who conveys to C, the chain of title has not accounted for the interest of A_2, and the chain of title thus shows a defect. Similarly, if A conveys to B and then C conveys to D, the chain of title reflects a gap, meaning no conveyance, between B and C, showing a defect in D's title. The primary purpose of title searches through recording indexes is to determine whether the chain of title has defects. A buyer who discovers from a title search before close that the seller does not have sound, recorded title as the land sale contract required, may refuse to close for failure of a material term of the contract. A second significant purpose is to discover and disclose encumbrances.

Protected parties. As indicated above, *notice* recording acts **protect** bona-fide purchasers, meaning those who take for value and without notice, no matter who records *after* the bona-fide purchaser takes. By contrast, *race* recording acts protect parties who record first. And *race/notice* recording acts protect only bona-fide purchasers who record first, the bona-fide status of the purchaser satisfying the recording act's notice condition and the first-recording satisfying the recording act's race condition. The type of jurisdiction, whether *notice*, *race*, or *race/notice*, does not always affect the superiority of title in a dispute over title. Sometimes, the outcome is the same in all three types of jurisdiction. For instance, if neither purchaser records their deed, then the first purchaser has superior title. The seller can only convey good title once, to the first purchaser, unless the law provides otherwise. The recording acts can change the order, encouraging recording. Yet in *all* jurisdictions, a bona-fide purchaser has superior title to an earlier purchaser if the bona-fide purchaser, again meaning one who bought for value without notice of the earlier sale, records first. Similarly, in *all* jurisdictions, if the earlier purchaser records before a later purchase, then the earlier purchaser will have superior title because the later purchaser cannot be a bona-fide purchaser, which requires taking without notice. The earlier recording establishes notice.

Priorities. The above sections show that one purpose of recording acts is to establish reliable **priorities** for the purchaser who has superior title, so that buyers can follow reliable practices when buying. As shown above, the type of recording act can make a difference in the priority order. The clearest differences among *notice*, *race*, and *race/notice* jurisdictions arise when the earlier purchaser records *after* the later purchase but *before* the later purchaser records. The later purchaser would *not* then have record notice at the time of purchase, but the earlier purchaser would have won the *race* to record. **Notice** jurisdictions favor the later purchaser, if the later purchaser gave value and had no other notice (not having had record notice). **Race** jurisdictions favor the earlier purchaser who, after all, won the race to record. A **race/notice** jurisdiction would change the outcome only if the later purchaser managed to record *before* the earlier purchaser, assuming also that the later purchaser had no notice.

Notice. In a *notice* jurisdiction, transferees who take from any transferor who had superior title under the jurisdiction's recording act also have superior title, even if they have notice of a competing claim. The transferor's superior title **shelters** the transferee. Recording acts do not address every situation in which a buyer would have actual or constructive **notice** of a superior title. Specifically, recording acts do *not* resolve how a potential buyer would discover an owner taking by *adverse possession*. Only if the adverse possessor has already received and recorded a court judgment showing that the possessor has taken title from the owner, will the real-property records disclose the adverse possessor's interest to the potential buyer. If, instead, the adverse possessor has the right of adverse possession but has not yet reduced the title to a recorded judgment, then the potential buyer's title search will not disclose the possession. The potential buyer must inspect the property for the adverse possessor, whose possession must, after all, be open and notorious, meaning discoverable on inspection. If the buyer buys without discovering the adverse possessor and then loses title to the adverse possessor, the buyer's recourse is against the seller under the general warranty deed, unless the seller conveyed instead only by quit claim, in which case the buyer may have no recourse.

Title insurance. Buyers of land typically purchase **title insurance** to protect against undisclosed defects in title. Title companies insure title. Land sale contracts typically include *title-insurance contingencies*, enabling the buyer to inspect and approve the title insurer's commitment, which discloses encumbrances or defects that the title insurer's search discovered. Title defects can include not just adverse third-party claims to title but also *missing links* in the chain of title. Chain of title should show a continuous right of ownership, without unexplained gaps in the record of how the property passed from owner to owner. The title insurer's *title search* would show gaps in ownership, to which the buyer can then object when the title company shares its title-insurance commitment with the buyer before the closing. Title defects can also include encumbrances such as covenants and easements that burden or limit the property's use. The title search should also show recorded covenants and easements. Title insurance pays to resolve title defects that the insurer should have discovered and disclosed but did not do so. If the title insurance cannot cure title and the buyer loses the property, then the title insurer indemnifies the buyer for the loss.

Special problems. The following sections address a few remaining **special problems** relating to title to real property. The first section addresses *after-acquired title*, referring to instances when a transferor conveys before acquiring title but then acquires title after the transfer. The law addresses that issue following the doctrine of *estoppel by deed*. The next section addresses how the law deals with *forged instruments* and *undelivered deeds*. *Purchase-money mortgages* also get special treatment, as the following section addresses. Finally, the concluding section addresses *judgment and tax liens*.

After-acquired title (including estoppel by deed). One anomaly that can arise in real-property transactions is that a person who believes in having title or who anticipates soon acquiring title, purports to *transfer* title *before acquiring* title. If the person never acquires title, then of course the transfer remains void. One cannot transfer title that one does not have. Yet if the person who purported to transfer title that the person did not have *subsequently acquires* title, then fairness to the transferee would seem to dictate that the transferee somehow acquires the transferor's **after-acquired title**. Indeed, the law holds under the doctrine of **estoppel by deed** that the transferor who acquires title after having purported to transfer it, cannot deny the transferee's claim to title. The prior transfer of deed *estops* the transferor from denying transfer and refuting title. The transferee has good title as to the transferor's claim, under the estoppel-by-deed doctrine. However, a bona-fide purchaser taking for value and without notice from the same transferor, after the first transfer and after the transferor finally acquired title, may have the superior title over the first transferee, particularly if the bona-fide purchaser records first.

Forged instruments. Real-property law authorizes practices to discourage forging of deeds and other instruments. A **forged instrument** is one to which the signer has signed someone else's name without that person's authority. The purpose of forgeries is usually nefarious, such as to obtain the forgery victim's funds in purported purchase, although some forgeries, though wrong and damaging, are innocent and done with good intention. One way that states discourage forged real-estate instruments is to require witnesses and notary acknowledgment for recording. The signer must sign in front of witnesses who also sign, and a notary public who attests to the signer's identity and signature. These acknowledgment requirements reduce the incidence of forgeries, although not eliminating them. The law holds that deeds recorded with such facially apparent defects in the acknowledgment that the register should not have recorded them, do *not* give *constructive notice* of the recorded instrument, only notice if the title search reveals the instrument. On the other hand, if the only defects in the acknowledgment are not apparent from the instrument's face, such as that the notary's commission had expired or that a witness was underage, then the recording still satisfies to make the deed superior for a race or race/notice jurisdiction.

Undelivered deeds. As indicated in an above section, when the transferor has executed the deed, the transferor must **deliver** the deed to the transferee with the intent of completing the transaction for the transaction to be effective. Execution alone, without delivery, does not create an enforceable right of title. For example, if a seller executes a deed at the office of the seller's lawyer but instructs the lawyer to hold the deed awaiting some event or satisfaction of some condition, then the deed's execution does not transfer title. The problem of an **undelivered deed** becomes acute when the owner dies without having delivered. In such cases, the law holds the transfer incomplete. The real property does not pass by deed but instead through rights of survivorship, as the decedent's will directs, or as the laws of intestacy provide, depending on the circumstances. The owner's placing the deed in escrow *to deliver at the owner's death*, a tactic often intended to avoid taxes or probate, is equally problematic. The law in such cases tends to hold either that the deed remains an uncompleted and therefore ineffective gift or treat the escrow as an intended devise, subject to probate. An undelivered deed is generally ineffective in